Geo. S. Morris.
March. 1865.

GERMAN RATIONALISM,

IN ITS RISE, PROGRESS, AND DECLINE.

GERMAN RATIONALISM,

IN ITS RISE, PROGRESS, AND DECLINE,

IN RELATION TO THEOLOGIANS, SCHOLARS, POETS, PHILOSOPHERS, AND THE PEOPLE:

A CONTRIBUTION TO THE CHURCH HISTORY OF THE EIGHTEENTH AND NINETEENTH CENTURIES.

BY

DR. K. R. HAGENBACH,

PROFESSOR OF THEOLOGY IN THE UNIVERSITY OF BASEL.

EDITED AND TRANSLATED BY

REV. WM. LEONHARD GAGE,

AND

REV. J. H. W. STUCKENBERG.

NEW YORK: CHARLES SCRIBNER.

MDCCCLXV.

CONTENTS.

[*Chapters I. to XIII. inclusive, and Chapter XXIV. are translated by Mr. Gage: Chapters XIV. to XXIII. inclusive, by Mr. Stuckenberg.*]

V.

THE PIONEERS OF RATIONALISM.

VI.

VII.

THEOLOGICAL SCIENCE, INCLUDING BIBLICAL CRITICISM IN THE FIRST HALF OF THE EIGHTEENTH CENTURY.

VIII.

LESSING.

IX.

INFIDELITY CARRIED TO ITS FARTHEST ISSUES.

X.

THOROUGH-GOING PROTESTS AGAINST INFIDELITY.

XI.

HALF-WAY RATIONALISM.

XII.

ZINZENDORF THE FOUNDER OF THE MORAVIANS.

XIII.

XIV.

JOHN GODFREY HERDER.

XV.

IMMANUEL KANT.

XVI.

SCHILLER.

XVII.

SALZMANN, CAMPE, PESTALOZZI, HAMANN, AND CLAUDIUS.

XVIII.

FREDERIC WILLIAM JOSEPH SCHELLING.

XIX.

FREDERIC HENRY JACOBI.

XX.

JOHN GOTTLIEB FICHTE.

XXI.

RICHTER, GOETHE, AND NOVALIS.

XXII.

SCHLEIERMACHER.

XXIII.

HEGEL AND HIS SUCCESSORS.

XXIV.

THE RISE OF THE PROTESTANT SPIRIT IN THE ROMAN CATHOLIC CHURCH DURING THE PAST AND PRESENT CENTURIES.

ERRATA.

Page 256, line 1, *for* Schripfeuthal, *read* Schnepfenthal.
„ 280, „ 30, *for* characteristic, *read* characterization.
„ 333, „ 5 in poetry, delete comma after freudigen.
„ 333, „ 20 do. *for* Gift-ward, *read* Giftward.
„ 336, „ 6, *for* "Wanderjahren," *read* "Wanderjahre."

INTRODUCTION.

PROF. HAGENBACH of Basle is so well known to the theologians of Great Britain and America, through his widely circulated History of Doctrines, that the editors of this volume do not need to speak at any length of his learning, his candour, his piety, his soundness in doctrine, his thoroughness, and his graceful style. In Germany he is even more widely known than abroad. Though a professor in a Swiss University, his lectures are delivered in the German language, and are issued from the publishing houses of Leipsig. All his works have passed through repeated editions, and in introducing this one, we are but putting the reader of English in possession of a volume which has long been a standard in Switzerland and Germany. The first book which Prof. Tholuck of Halle puts into the hand of a young man who wishes to become acquainted with the history, present condition, and future hopes of the cause of Christ in its relation to the philosophy, scholarship, and poetry of Germany is this work of Hagenbach.

With the advice of Prof. Tholuck, and under the sanction of the author, the editors have abridged this work, omitting matter which was of comparatively little interest in Great Britain and the United States. And we would take occasion to deprecate in behalf of the abridged translation, a charge of one-sidedness, as though the development of Rationalism in Germany had been made much more prominent in this than in the original edition. Though the title of the work has been literally retained, still it is to be honestly confessed that the Church History of both of Dr. Hagenbach's volumes is largely and almost exclusively confined to Germany and Switzerland. France has but a little corner assigned to it:

Great Britain still less; the United States none at all. We have excluded the Swiss portions almost entirely; they were of unquestioned interest to the students of that Swiss University, before whom these Lectures were read; they have less interest to readers in Germany, and almost none to the outside world, engrossed with affairs on a much larger scale. We have retained the names of all those men in the departments of theology, philosophy, literature, and poetry, who made the eighteenth century the Augustan age of Germany, and who ushered in and accompanied a good way on its course this nineteenth century, whose results have been less in Germany than in Great Britain and France, in relation to the eighteenth. The entire progress of the Rationalistic movement in Germany, from the importation by way of France of the light, frivolous and blasphemous scepticism of Bolingbroke, to the closing of the sad procession in the discords and utter confusion which followed the death of Hegel, resulting in the re-enthronement of the old "faith once delivered to the saints" in the leading pulpits and universities of that land, has been fully portrayed. The work of combining scattered passages, of omitting, of condensing, has been so responsible and so difficult, that it is a great satisfaction to see before us as we write, this line from the author's pen, "I am entirely satisfied with the condensed work, the plan of which you have laid before me."

The period embraced in these sketches is one of stirring literary, theological and philosophical activity, full of strife and revolutions in all departments of learning. In the sixteenth and seventeenth centuries the Protestant church had spent most of its energies in fixing its doctrines, and defending itself against the attacks of Catholicism. In the eighteenth century, when its doctrines were established, when the persecutions of the Catholics nearly ceased, and when the Evangelical Church had acquired strength of number, the peace it enjoyed gave it an opportunity of reflecting on itself, of criticising and developing its dogmas. It is not at all surprising that the mind which had been fettered should go too far when it regained its freedom. It is always very difficult to keep the right proportion between reflection and faith, and almost impossible when the one has been cultivated in a one-sided manner, while the other has been almost entirely neglected.

The questions that have occupied the minds of evangelical Christians since the commencement of last century are mostly such as have arisen in the Protestant Church itself. During this period the beautiful tree of Protestantism has been little disturbed by storms from without, but many poisonous branches have been grafted on it which have borne much pernicious fruit, and poisonous vines have twined around it, sometimes being so luxuriant and numerous as almost entirely to hide the tree itself, with its foliage and fruit. A hasty glance will satisfy us that in this period the most various elements have been thrown together. In these the mind has been working, attempting to remove those that would not mingle with the rest, and exerting all its energies to form a system, complete, united, and harmonious. The most prominent of these elements, all of which have more or less asserted their claims to predominance, were—an Orthodoxy clinging tenaciously to the dogma, but dead in its idolatrous worship of the letter and buried in the stony sepulchre of cold forms; a Pietism full of life and zeal, but caring less for confessions and the cultivation of sound learning; the so-called enlightenment, imported about the middle of last century from the English Deists and French Encyclopedists, with its cultivation of the understanding, but neglect of the heart, accepting the clear, but rejecting the symbolical, the mystical and divine; a Rationalism, making morality the centre of religion, and searching chiefly for it in the Bible, but losing sight of the deeper truths of the Gospel; a Mysticism lost in the depth of its feeling, and hearkening only to the divine voice, whose whispers it thought might be heard in the inmost recesses of the soul, and a Pantheism uniting into one stupendous whole Spirit and matter, God and nature, and finding in its One and All the acme of its speculation. In these tendencies, as in history in general, there are certain individuals elevated above the rest, who may be regarded as the leaders of their respective parties and the mirrors in which the systems and ages are reflected. To study these representative men is to study the systems in their practical workings and the ages in their greatest significance.

The title of this work indicates, that the Church History of the Eighteenth and Nineteenth Centuries is regarded from the side of Evangelical Protestantism. It is so important that the significance of the last two words be perceived, that we are constrained to dwell on them at more length than would be required, were there not a greatly perverted use of the word Protestantism largely prevalent in our current literature.

When Luther and the Reformers inaugurated Protestantism, their mission was to lay again for all time the foundation-stone of Christianity, to reaffirm its fundamental doctrine, viz., that the WORD OF GOD is the ultimate object of appeal in all religious questions, the umpire in all ecclesiastical contentions. The Romish Church had drifted to the placing of the decisions of popes and councils above the simple meaning of the Bible, as received and interpreted by the private judgment of every man. Protestantism protested against this, and demanded with all urgency and importunity that the Bible alone, without note or comment, should be placed at the command of every child of God. And this was all: here its demand stopped. Protestantism as a positive force, as not a merely negativing movement, but a living truth, finds its limit at the Word of God. That is its rock-bound barrier. It comes to its legitimate goal when it touches this Bible. This Luther made a first principle: this remains a first principle of Protestantism: and this it must remain.

This we affirm in denial of the statement made in some quarters, that Protestantism finds its final and legitimate issue in the most remote pushing of the human mind, unchecked even by the limits of the Divine Word. The right of private judgment, according to this statement, is independent of the limitations of Scripture. Protestantism, according to this, begins at the point where it begins in its protest against Romanism, but it runs on and on, claiming as its divine right the unqualified power of the mind to discern all truth. Among many who have no ecclesiastical relations, and who belong in every strict use of language to the "world," this opinion is prevalent, vague indeed and unexpressed, yet subtle and destructive, and which when formed and uttered will bring danger to church and world alike. Our current literature is largely tinctured with this novel and untrue usage of speech, and Protestantism has been allowed to protest and protest, to annul this and disallow that, to strike out point after point, doctrine after doctrine, article after article, till it has been lost in the fathomless abysses of blank, inconsolable infidelity. The pillar which Luther and the Reformers set has been subtly undermined, the pedestal has been riven, and year by year corners have been taken away, till at last we need to come back to see how great the loss has been. And here is where the author of this work takes his stand, with Luther and the Reformers, that Protestantism has certain definite and assigned limits, and that the Bible, the old honoured, everlasting Word of God, is one of those limits, bidding the reason of man come thus far but no farther; giving scope indeed for the highest powers in studying it, in opening its obscurities, blending its harmonies, making its discords accordant, and developing its infinite resources.

If any one were to ask what is the great advantage of going to Germany to study theology? what can one gain there that he cannot gain at home? we should answer that it is the power of seeing the closed issue of problems now working out with us. The sceptical spirit arose in England, passed thence to France and thence to Germany: the more reverential deists of England, Morgan and Tyndal, and the brilliant but earnest Hobbes gave place to the light and trifling school of Bolingbroke and his dissipated compeers. To England comes just then, to complete his education and to travel, the young and witty Francois Arouet, whom we best know by the self-imposed name which he assumed in manhood, a name so dreaded and feared when he lived, and for years after, but which has lost its power now. To England comes this witty, sarcastic, trifling, keen, and handsome young man, and sits at the feet of the wild, reckless, profligate, superficial and accomplished Bolingbroke, the representative of English deism. The Frenchman returns to his own land, takes the name so well known, publishes his imported English deism, and his nation kindle at once, and France was filled with infidelity. There sprang up like flame the school of Rousseau, d'Holbach, and the Encyclopedists, their rank, poisonous blasphemy brought from England by that brilliant Voltaire. But not content with sowing the seeds of unbelief among his own countrymen, not content with the thrifty crop that sprang into fruitage under his own eye, he carries it to a new field, becomes the daily companion of the King of Prussia, and the admired head of the culture of Germany. The king set the fashion of infidelity, and thousands followed in it, and there began the unbelief of that land, carried by this subtle man from England from London, by way of Paris to Berlin. Never did the devil employ an ambassador more potent, effective, and destroying than this brilliant, watchful, untiring Voltaire.

Thus in France all rotten, and waiting for any change which should not be death, and in Germany where the great Frederick gave eclat to unbelief by the very brilliance of his military genius, the advance of a superficial deism was as rapid as the course of light. In England it was not so: Bolingbroke was too profligate, too light, too trifling, too evidently a mere brilliant writer, too clearly devoid of scholarship or earnest love of truth, to gain much influence over the solid English mind. Hence it accomplished little there; and it is only in our day that England has gone to Germany again to borrow what has there run through its course and been discarded, giving not only to its uneducated millions but to its educated thousands and to hundreds of the ministers of its own establishment those ideas, which this book will shew have all had their day in Germany. And in America scepticism did not begin till Thomas Jefferson brought it in from France, taking the virus which Voltaire carried thither from England, innoculating the veins of the American national life, even shutting the name of God out of the constitution of the United States, and leaving no trace in the great Organic Law of the nation, that it is even nominally a Christian people.

Hence a cycle has been traversed in Germany, while in Great Britain and America it is incomplete. Hence what is tendency here has become fulfilment there. We are now where they were in the past century. It is thrillingly interesting to discover while exploring the history of religion and irreligion in Germany during the eighteenth century, that we are following in lines which there came to their issue, utterly without profit, excepting to warn us. Changing the names of men, it would seem to be but history renewing itself. There we can see the gradual growth of evil, seductively blandishing the world, enlisting the sympathy of all who were not resolutely good, and at last startling the world as a full grown monster of wickedness. Movements which we think entirely safe, and which we deprecate in the mildest language, there became the gravest perils resulting in a very gospel of lewdness. The sure growth of great evils from little ones, the certainty that where wrong is, there is death, ultimate death, is nowhere more clearly pictured than in the history of the rise of the infidel spirit in Germany during the last century. The end of all was that in the very land of Luther, Protestantism, beginning where he placed it, the right of private judgment to interpret the Bible was lost sight of, and the word was forced at last to mean the right of private judgment to decide absolutely on the ways and will of God. Protestantism protested the Bible out of sight and hearing. When Dr. Tholuck was appointed Professor in the great University of Halle, where there were hundreds of students preparing to enter the ministry, he could find but one who ever read the Bible for devotional purposes, and his own house was attacked, his windows broken, and he himself rudely treated in the streets, because he believed in the Scriptures as the word of God. In the beginning of this century the work of infidelity had been so thorough going, that the Bible and evangelical religion, represented by a handful of true souls, had arrayed against them the three great worlds, of literature, education and art. Most unnatural divorce! Those divine gifts which ought to illumine and illustrate each other, were rudely sundered; the "faith once delivered to the saints" was compacted in a little isolated body, while poetry, philosophy, scholarship, educational science, music, and all art either ignored it or ridiculed it, or assailed it. The Bible had been protested out of all knowledge of men, out of all the domain of culture or breeding, or forceful thought.

Great minds then tried to deal single-handed with religion. Without the Bible as their chart, they ventured out into the dim void, and felt their own way. With their own unaided eyes, they tried to "find out the Almighty to perfection." It does not seem an overstatement of language to say that all that the human mind can do to explore the domain of God, was done by them. There was a race of intellectual giants; men of the loftiest powers. They followed each other, each taking the work which had been bequeathed him by him who went before. Beginning at Kant, and ending at Hegel, was a succession of philosophers, whose superiors the world never saw. Aristotle rose, lived and laboured alone; Plato rose, lived, and laboured alone, building not on Aristotle but on an entirely different foundation. Bacon was alone, separated by centuries from his master Aristotle. Newton and Leibnitz lived and laboured alone. But Kant surrendered his work to Fichte, Fichte to Schelling, Schelling to Hegel, and there it reached the end. In concentration, abstraction, grasp and force, those men were singly of the mightiest. But they were linked: they make a chain: each took up the task dropped by the one before him and forwarded the work. The conditions for solving the problems of religion without the Bible could not conceivably be finer. Whatever men could do, they could do. But what was the end of their work? Nothing but miserable doubt, uncertainty, blank, unmitigated hopelessness. A "born Hegelian" is the most compact term to define a man who, in relation to religion, is always seeking but never finding. At the end of this long search Germany had gained not a single step: it was

"Blinded with doubt, in wildering mazes lost,"

But not even Newton's one pearl on the shores of the ocean of infinite truth had it attained. The nation had been cut loose from its moorings. As were the leaders so were the followers. F. A. Bahrdt, the extreme product of the infidel reaction in the last century, ended his days in an ale-house, the clergy were the most unbelieving of all classes; the gospel idea of regeneration was utterly lost sight of, and the process of raising the world by self-culture, by educating the inner life to a perfection attainable of itself, was the only moral specific. The failure was utter, final, irremediable.

At the end of this long career of "protesting," the simple way was to leave the generation to die in its infidelity, while a few who had all along preserved the hidden truth—who had carried the ark—began to work again with the simple elements of divine power as revealed in the old and yet new, the imperishable Bible.

This work supplied another great want in our literature, in defining distinctly and yet with a generous candour the relation of the great German poets to Christianity. For living in an age when theological questions were of the first importance, they entered into those questions more deeply, perhaps, than any other class of men, though their poems may not display this to the superficial glance. But, to take a single example, no one can understandingly read Schiller who is not acquainted with Kant's philosophy, and does not see that Schiller made it the burden of his life, not to entertain, nor æsthetically charm his countrymen, but to interpret to them in symbolic language, and in the clinging phrase of poetry, the philosophy of Kant. Schiller is as much Kant versified, as Pope's Essay on Man is Bolingbroke in verse. Schiller was as devoted to this task in the selection of subjects, as Carlyle is to the canonization of single-handed might, in our days. And so with the other great German poets: their lives and their writings cannot be divorced from the philosophy and theology of their age. And the author of this work has rendered an inestimable service in showing how the writers on education, the essayists, and the poets as well as the philosophers and preachers, stood in relation to the central cause of Christianity.

With these introductory remarks, we commit this volume to the readers of Great Britain and the United States, confident that it is one of the choicest gifts which Germany has yet bestowed upon the world, and trusting that the favour which has been abundantly shown to it in the country of its birth may be continued in the countries of its adoption.

WM. LEONHARD GAGE.
J. H. W. STUCKENBERG.

I.

CHARACTERISTICS OF THE EIGHTEENTH CENTURY.—TOLERATION AND RELIGIOUS INDIFFERENCE.—THE DECADENCE OF THE ECCLESIASTICAL SPIRIT.—THE REFORMATION THE COMMON PROPERTY OF CHRISTIANS, AND SPECULATIVE RADICALISTS.—THE TRUE STANDARD OF APPEAL IN ALL RELIGIOUS MEASUREMENTS.

S with the traveller, approaching his home after a long journey, what is strange disappears with every step, and what is familiar comes more into view, until at last he stands at his own door and sits at his own hearth, so is it with him who passes from the history of the past to the history of the present. The forms and the circumstances which he associates with times gone by, recede more and more from sight, and the men and the things which are nearer to him come clearer before him, men and things not cotemporaneous, indeed, but removed from him by only a few years, and so seemingly related to the present. It is with us, then, as if our fathers were telling us of their own fathers or grandfathers, as if our mothers were telling us of their own mothers and grandmothers; or as if we were introduced into a great family hall, where hung the coats-of-arms and the portraits of governors, of judges, of preachers, and professors, among whom we could recognise the faces of some ancestors of our own, of our relatives, and friends. How many traces of a family resemblance we seek to find, and how many points of likeness between those of the present and those of the past we discover in the expression, in the bearing, and even in the raiment itself!

And thus it is with us when we enter upon the history of the eighteenth century, considered first in its religious, and then in its general aspect.

Looking then at the period before us, it is evident at a glance that it differs widely from the sixteenth and seventeenth centuries. As those composed the epoch of religious persecutions and religious wars, so the eighteenth century was the epoch of rationalism and of universal toleration. This is still truer of the second than of the first half of the century. At its opening the old warlike spirit had not ceased; but was becoming, from new motives, to be political rather than ecclesiastical. We shall therefore rarely have occasion to allude to civil strife, from that of the Spanish succession to the Seven Years' war. And not only were the great struggles with arms mostly over, but those tremendous conflicts of faiths, of Protestantism and Catholicism, of Lutherans and Calvinists, were withdrawing to the background, and when they continued to be waged, it was by the schools mostly, which still keep the old ideas alive, and go on spinning the tough threads when the people have lost all their interest. The people in the eighteenth century turned their thoughts with increased interest to political, economical, and industrial affairs: ecclesiastical matters were of less import. And here is the dark side of the picture which we are to study. With a tolerant spirit comes also a spirit of indifference to religious things; with persecution for faith's sake, dies away active spiritual life; with an increase of light rises also scepticism; unbelief contends with superstition for the mastery, and the tyranny of the former is not less baleful than that of the latter. And it is the history of ecclesiastical decay, its causes and consequences, that we are to study. It may doubtless be less pleasant to trace this decay than to transport ourselves back to the times when men's faith was undisturbed, but it may not be less profitable for the spiritual life.

And, indeed, it is well that we investigate the history of ecclesiastical decadence, and study it on all sides, in order that we may be enabled to judge what has been rightfully outgrown, and therefore abandoned, as incapable of resurrection, and what it is the mission of our time to re-establish, and to preserve as a sacred inheritance, even though it be now in the dust. And therefore we have to trace not only the process and progress of decadence, but also observe that which has still continued to exist, and which, either in large measure or in small, has increased in life and power; and it is not right to overlook that, which, although in partial and constrained manner, has served the useful purpose of aiding in the germination of every good and productive thing. It is especially necessary that we study the spirit of the age, of which so much is said; to hold it clearly in sight and not mistake which way it leads; that we carefully discriminate from it our special opinion, modified by our own humours as it is; so that on the one hand we be not hardened against correct judgments although they may be new, and on the other that we be not at the mercy of every novelty; and that we may not be of the number of those who contend against God, but of those who boldly declare war upon all which is not of God.

The task which we thus impose upon ourselves is not a light one. The more deeply rooted our age is in the age just gone by, the more closely the views and opinions now held, link in with the subjects of our historical study, the more danger we run of falling into partial judgments. The time of the Reformation, to which we must go back to find the springs which feed the channels of the present, is the common property of all Protestants; every one claims to find his own therein, whatever may be his belief now. The strict evangelical Christian sees in the reformers the primitive champions of the faith, the pillars of the church, the authorities beyond which it is folly to go. The man of so called liberal ideas, of progress, appeals to the same reformers as the friends of light and the enemies of darkness; he sees in them the prophets of liberalism, who did not themselves go far enough, but who opened a way for us to go in the same direction, but farther on. The former lament bitterly when they compare the present times with those when the reformers lived; "we have lost the old purity of doctrine, we are on the way to error:" the latter exclaim in triumph, "we have attained to what our fathers promised, we have mounted on their shoulders, and are permitted to look away into the bright dawn of a better day." So two parties, entirely distinct and opposed to each other, build on the same foundation, look back to the same events as precedents, and to the same men as leaders. Both are one sided, and therefore wrong; for he alone has grasped the true idea of Protestantism who sees in it the capacity of progressive development, as well as the power of conserving what is fixed in the nature of things and has a positive existence: true Protestantism opens a way into the future, and at the same time animates with new life the real truths which are the inheritance of the present from the past. But in the eighteenth century the two extremes to which we have alluded, do not lie side by side in embryo existence, as mere possibilities, they exist as facts, as great powers, manifestly widely apart, and separated by a deep abysm. On the one side are the freethinkers as they love to call themselves; spirits entirely emancipated from the past, the enemies of all authority in thought, of all traditional faith, of all that has been believed before; religious radicals who construct all theology out of the pure nature of man as they would cut anything out of clean bright wood; who do not accept any truth unless it commends itself to that human reason from which it springs: on the other side are the old fashioned Christians who will not depart a finger's breadth from the faith of their fathers, and who deem it a religious duty and trust, to meet with all zeal and boldness the unbelief and coldness of their age before the judgments of heaven are upon them. Both of these claim to represent the Protestant spirit; and between them arises a great and generally undecided mass of men, both scholarly and unlearned, who would gladly enjoy what was good in the older times, and yet would like to taste of the fruits of a newer age. And so there is an endless chaos of opinions in which we live, in which little seems to be settled; and therefore it is an imperative duty for him who feels that he has reconciled any antagonisms, or found any solid and substantial basis of truth, to reach the hand and rescue, if may be, any who are tossed to and fro in this surging ocean of doubts and fears.

The peculiar difficulty with which I have to contend is the granting its measure of truth to every movement, one sided and injurious as it may have been, and to point out also whatever is false, and partial, and hostile to the best interests of men. Grotius has well said that no sect is in possession of all religious truth, but every one has more or less of it; and his remark we shall find confirmed on every page of modern ecclesiastical history. But who shall deliver a measuring rod to us? Shall our judgments be based on our own preconceived prejudices or predilections, or the accidental whim of the moment? Assuredly not. We must discover some common standard of measurement. And this standard is nothing less than evangelical Protestantism. It is impossible for us to decide what is and is not absolute truth; all that we can do is to appeal to the spirit of the Reformation. Only in this way can we attain to any uniformity of judgment: but here is a standard to which we can appeal with good hope of rectifying all individual opinions, of eliminating all personal conceits and humours, and of establishing what will be satisfactory to all.

II.

A BRIEF SURVEY OF THE RISE OF RATIONALISM IN GERMANY.

We have already remarked, that although the great religious wars had terminated at the opening of the eighteenth century, yet that there was visible for some time a kind of mechanical continuation of the old strifes; for the epochs of history are not sharply sundered from each other, but fade away gradually into one another, the older characteristics being supplanted step by step by those of the new age. And so at the beginning of the eighteenth century we discover the existence of the earlier type of orthodoxy, and the protracted struggle between the Lutherans and the Calvinists; but we also discern the rise of two new adversaries, opposed to each other, no less than to the older forms of faith,—these were pietism and philosophy. The result of all this clashing was such a revolution of ideas as had not been witnessed since the great Reformation.

In order to understand this great and complex movement, it will be necessary to hold in our grasp, as distinctly as possible, the various directions of thought, and to study the men who have led the human mind into these new channels.

On the very confines of the seventeenth and eighteenth centuries, we find, as has already been remarked, an old element which was passing away and a new one which was coming in with great strength. By the former we mean that stiff, hard, literal orthodoxy, which had transformed the fresh and life-giving doctrines of the Reformation into stone. This theology had done its work, had fulfilled its mission, it had trained a former generation to those strict and patient habits of thought, whose fruits even the scholars of our own age are now reaping, and it had given a sharply defined system of faith to the Church, an inestimable gift. But such a theology could not always satisfy the needs of men, and, least of all, when it had degenerated into strife and a bitter intolerance. Yet to this theology we are indebted for the deep but dark mysticism of Jacob Böhme and Weigel, and at a later day for the more practical Christianity of Arndt and Scriver, and at last for the simple yet vigorous and useful faith and devoted lives of the pietists, with the names of whose leaders, Spener and Francke, most readers are already familiar.

This mystic and pietistical movement was the resolute opponent of the older and harder orthodoxy which just survived the seventeenth century, and whose momentum rather than its organic life, carried it into the eighteenth. This movement will therefore be our first subject of study,—its development, its varied manifestations, its partial divisions. It has become the source of that powerful and beneficent Christian life, which has produced so great a change in the organization of the moral world, and has been such a blessing to the entire Church.

But it was not the pietist movement alone which went out from Halle over the whole of Germany and Switzerland, that was the destroyer of the earlier orthodoxy. There arose other antagonists on every side. Reason itself turned against its own advocates and defenders, for it lies in the very nature of reason, that in religious matters it divides against itself, and in the very workshop, where its sharp weapons gain their edge and temper, the doubts are made equally keen which are to be used against it. The right of free inquiry which Protestantism grants, was turned against the Protestant church itself, and at last against the Bible. There had indeed been, before the eighteenth century began, some, who with a cool manner and an indifferent heart, had begun to undermine the mysteries of faith held by all orthodox believers. These were the Arminians and the Socinians. Several followed their guidance, some secretly, others openly. Their writings were read in the desire to disprove them; but much that was read with this motive left its sting in the mind, and led to deeper doubts, and so, many of the orthodox were induced to abandon their former rigidness in doctrine. Thus there was gradually formed a moderate school of theologians, which, without wandering very widely from a sound faith, yet began to compromise with the enemy, or at least to ignore him. But this state of things could not remain long without a change. The spirit of inquiry now evoked, did not turn back to the old mysteries of religion, such as the Trinity and Election, but began to inquire into the very foundation of Christianity, its historical development and its summaries of doctrine; and then almost immediately questions began to press in as to its beginning, its evidence, the possibility, reality, and necessity of a divine revelation, the truth and authenticity of the Gospels: the reality of miracles, and the confirmation of prophecies. These bold inquiries had already been started by the English deists during the seventeenth century: in the eighteenth they were pushed still further, not only in England, but also in France and Germany. Voltaire and Frederick the Great are representatives of that epoch.

Yet the frivolous spirit of French scepticism touched only the surface of the German mind, while a deeper current of ideas penetrated to its heart. The Germans are an earnest, thoughtful people. They have been charged with too great a love of pure, abstract, unpractical speculation, and it is true that in business affairs they are slower and less skilful than some of their more facile neighbours. But in the realm of the spirit, the domain of science, of faith, and of deep thought, the palm rightfully belongs to them. For even the highly praised understanding of the English is rather political, mathematical, and practical, than metaphysical and transcendental.

Slowly, step by step, and almost entirely independently of foreign influences, the German thinkers, with Leibnitz and Wolf at their head, began to evolve a philosophical theology out of the clouds, as a sculptor would fashion a statue out of rough marble. Filled with an earnest love of truth, this philosophy did not seek to build a portly card house in the place of the stately temple which the church had once erected, or to give to a godless easy life, the charm of a deceitful gilding of fanciful speculation, as the French have done, some at least among them, and have taught a young school in Germany to do. On the contrary, Leibnitz and Wolf had no other aim than to compel their philosophy to give strong support to morality and religion. They supposed that the force of that reason which the Creator has given to man would be able to lift the human mind from the seen world to the world unseen, and establish new grounds for faith and the practical ethics of life. Their philosophy never was designed, with all its commendation of reason, to encroach upon the sphere of a divine revelation. They supposed, on the contrary, that natural theology, which the human reason could compose, and which revealed the existence of God and the immortality of the soul, was the best preparation for revealed religion. They thought that by means of the mathematical method they could convince unbelievers of the credibility of the truths which Christianity announces. Leibnitz, himself, went so far as to try to demonstrate the Trinity and the significance of the Lord's Supper mathematically. But soon it was suspected by able thinkers that the bringing of religion into the circle of the exact sciences would do as much harm as good. The establishing of a natural theology, claiming existence side by side with revealed religion, and yet having an existence separate from it, and independent of it, seemed to them a matter of serious import. What would become of Christianity if a belief in God and immortality and the ethics which lead to a moral life, could exist without it? Would not many be content with this religion of nature, recommended by the deists, and think of revealed religion as of little more worth than an imposing heap of ruins? Therefore the so-called pietists, the decided advocates of a living, strictly biblical faith, grounded on experience, set themselves in as decisive antagonism to the demonstrative method of Leibnitz and Wolf, as they had before to a cold and dead orthodoxy. Their relative place in the battle-field was thus changed. Before they had seemed, in contrast to the orthodox, as the radicals, the innovators, the enemies of the older traditional faith. Now, in contrast with the new philosophy, they appeared to be orthodox, the opponents of the modern ideas, the conservatives who felt it their duty to re-affirm the doctrines, not of the schools, but of the church and the Bible, in the face of philosophical pride and the arrogance of scepticism. The intentions of the pietists were noble and high, but even Spener and Francke sometimes made mistakes, and allowed their zeal to outrun their discretion. After seeking in vain to oppose the spirit of their age, they withdrew into quiet circles, and there uttered bitter words of complaint that they could no longer exert a controlling influence upon their times. Yet the abstract philosophy which they feared would never have attained to a large popularity, the mathematical method would never have inaugurated a new order of things, if another set of opinions had not come in and offered itself to the people rather than to the deep thinkers. Deep speculation is not what commends itself to the great mass of men. These demand results, convictions, quick dashes of thought, not long and patient and profound investigation. So partly out of the propositions which Wolf had propounded, and partly out of the teachings of the English deists, there arose a popular philosophy, readily apprehensible, a system which laid great stress on its practical utility, and which promised the best enjoyments of this life and of the life to come, as the reward of virtue, meaning by this honourable dealing, industry and regularity, considering it of little profit to trouble oneself with the difficulties and mysteries of faith. Many of the clergy took up these ideas and acted upon them. They confined their pulpit instructions to a dry morality; they combated what they called superstition, and recommended whatever they thought was serviceable to the use of the body with little regard to the soul.

Yet there were many changes in theological science in that epoch which may be regarded as improvements. The study of the Bible had made great progress. Scholars had penetrated deeply into the languages in which it was written, the manners of action and the modes of thought of the people of whom it speaks, and much which had hitherto baffled our Western minds, and had been passed over as strange and inexplainable, became clear by a more intimate acquaintance with the general habits of the East. A distinction began to be made between what is conditioned by time and space, and what is eternal and immutable: and the peculiarly picturesque style of the ancients became more intelligible. It is true, the scholars of that time were not always careful, not to say honest. Under the broad plea of the usage of language they used in some cases to cast away that which constitutes the very peculiarity of Christianity, and discriminates it from other religions: and while meaning to tear away but the outward husk, they sometimes stripped off large pieces of the kernel, so that the very meat itself disappeared under their hands. Thus arose gradually an empty narrow theology, shrunk all away to the poorest common places of religious truth, and calling itself by the name Neology. Yet we must be on our guard against confounding all the neological movement of that day in one class. There were superficial thinkers who could not reach any thing deep, and so took up these new notions; and there were also those who heartily wished to rescue what they believed to be really the pith of Christian doctrine; to remove the obstacles which stood in the way of many, and to adjust Christianity to the taste of the time. They gave up the outworks to hold the citadel. Nor ought we to forget that during the process of excision in which so much was cut off from the expression of Christian faith, much good was done: much was removed which was a real injury to it, and it was left more free to awake to an increased activity and power. God had his hand in all these things, though when they took place they seemed so hostile to the interests of a true faith. Since the Seven Years' war the German nation has risen to an intellectual vigour never attained before. Its literature and poetry have taken a new start; and the virtues of the older epoch have been grafted in the newer, while its faults have been cast aside. We need refer only to Lessing, whose powerful mind effected an almost complete revolution in theology and in esthetics. In education, too, men left the old paths, and the work which was done in France by Rousseau was continued in Germany by Basedow, Solzmann, and Campe, not, indeed, without vehement opposition on all sides from men who had grown old in the service of the church—not without many mistakes, and yet not without many good fruits, as the result of the contest.

It was, therefore, an idle task to attempt to impose limits to this genius of innovation. The Prussian edict aimed to suppress it, and issued in 1788, was a complete failure. There had to be a re-action, and that re-action had to follow its own laws. The old orthodoxy had blunted its weapons in its contest with pietism, and the latter had been so much weakened as to need new elements to awaken it to power again, that it might not fall into a merely passive existence, and sigh itself away. The more the church fell into decay, and found its impotence to quicken itself into a new and vigorous life, the more did the vital power of Christianity display itself in individuals, and in large or smaller groups of true hearts. In some it appeared in the form of devout and consecrated but thorough and philosophical thought, in others rather as practical piety, but in all more or less tinged with personal traits and peculiarities. Many of the deepest thinkers of their age did not hesitate to declare their adherence to a rigid interpretation of the Scriptures, even on the peril of being the sport of the high priests of rationalism. Others put themselves at the head of societies, of sects, and of brotherhoods, or established minor churches within the great State Church. We may mention here two organizations which had a very wide influence upon the eighteenth century, and which continue to exert great power over our own age: the Moravian brotherhood, founded by Zinzendorf, and the English Methodist Church, founded by Wesley. Other eminent men, such as Bengel, Swedenborg, Oetinger, and later Lavater and Stilling, have been the rallying points of no inconsiderable sects; and while their successors have perpetuated the follies and extravagancies of their predecessors rather than their good qualities, yet they have done good service in opposing the superficial and cold spirit of unbelief. It has been a theme of remark, that the great development in German literature, under the conduct of Wieland, Klopstock and Lessing, and later of Herder, Schiller, and Goethe, has run in parallel course to the political Revolution in France; and that in the former country the old intellectual ideas were as much shattered as in the latter were the old political ones. It is now our task to trace this whole upheaval of old opinions, and see how in all the conflicts which followed, the flame of Christian life never was lost wholly from sight, and was preserved of God to continue to bless the world: to show how the deep foundation of Protestantism was never touched, but remains sure and strong, and lasting as truth.

III.

LIFE AND MANNERS IN GERMANY, DURING THE FIRST HALF OF THE EIGHTEENTH CENTURY, AS PICTURED IN THE REIGN OF FREDERICK WILLIAM THE FIRST OF PRUSSIA.

"To divide history according to centuries is a difficult task. Great events do not cease with one and begin with the next; they dovetail into each other, and are lost gradually from sight, when absorbed in the one paramount spirit of the age. We can see the leading characteristics of successive centuries, without knowing their sources or their results."

We are reminded of this expression of Goethe, when we look for a point to which we can link the interior history of Protestantism at our point of departure. We stand on the frontier, as it were, with our glance thrown backward into the seventeenth, and forwards into the eighteenth, and yet discover no stone to indicate the boundary line. The period of transition which connected these two centuries is not especially interesting. The reader finds himself at home nowhere there. He comes into contact with the stiff figures of the time of Louis XIV., and yet is dreaming of a newer and better day to come. Great personages like Leibnitz, Newton, Spencer, Thomasius, stand like the Colossus of Rhodes, with a foot on either shore, while a race of pigmies sail beneath, spreading their merry pennons to every passing breeze.

Turning to Germany, with which country we shall have mainly to do in our inquiries, we miss the old and truly German life which prevailed at the Reformation, and which was characteristic of the seventeenth century. French modes and customs had crept into the German courts during the reign of Louis XIV., and had even affected the manner of life among the more wealthy citizens; and a French tone of thought had also begun to be current. We can but picture that epoch by quoting the words of a very strict and yet candid critic of his own times. "If we look at the present condition of Germany we see that it has undergone a great change. It is too well known that during the sway of the French devil that rules us, our natural life, our modes and our usages have altered; and that if we be not called naturalised Frenchmen, we ought to take some new name as a people, for Germans we are no longer. Formerly the French were not held in the highest estimation amongst us, now-a-days we cannot live without them, and everything must be French—our language French, our clothes French, our food French, French housekeeping, French dances, and French music. This Gallomania has caressed us and flattered us as skilfully as the serpent did our first parents in Eden, in order to rob us of all our old German freedom. The most of our German princes have their palaces furnished with French upholstery; and whoever will find favour at their courts must know French, and have been in Paris, which has become a kind of university of gentility; if he has not had his training there, he need have no hope of success. From the courts this false and foreign style has descended even to the great mass of the people. If the children have begun to talk a little, and have passed their fourth or fifth year, they are ready to be offered to the French Moloch, and the parents bethink themselves at once of a French teacher of the language or of dancing. In France no one speaks German, unless it be the Germans in their intercourse with each other; but with us the French tongue has become so common, that in many places already, cobblers, tailors, children, and servants, speak in it. If a young man wishes to pay his addresses now-a-days to a young woman, he must wear a French hat, a French vest, and French hose, and if he has only the condition of a bat in his head, he is Monsieur, even before he can "parlez vous" half-a-dozen sentences."

It may be said that these things are slight and immaterial; that the speech and the clothing have nothing in common with religion; and there will be some readers who will wonder that we have alluded to things so unimportant and irrelevant in this place, and in connection with our subject. But these things have an appositeness, although it may not appear at the first glance. A man can worship God in the French language as well as in the German, but that is not the point, it is the spirit of the worship of which we speak. If this has become light, and trivial, and fickle, there is no longer that true depth to the soul which will enable it to receive and retain strong impressions. The clothes do not make the man, but they are often an exponent of what is in the man. And so manners are the expression, the physiognomy of an age, of a people, and where this is not the case, and speech, and modes, and customs, stand in contrast with national character, we find a partly ludicrous and partly pitiable contradiction. And this contradiction between French and German elements we discover prominently at the opening of the eighteenth century. In many hearts still lived the old German churchly spirit, as the catechism of the age before taught it the primitive sincere ways of life; but the German faith, and the German manners, had no longer their old expression. Everywhere could be read, the former things are passed away, all things shall become new; there is another spirit abroad, only not yet fully disclosed. There was an evident struggle between the past and the present, but the combatants showed a want of skill. Instead of accepting the good which the new age offered to them, they grasped at the shadows, at empty show; and instead of holding on to what the older time had proved and established, they held on to what was effete and valueless, and fought for life or death, yet letting the prize slip out of their reach during the contest. Such has been the case in all the course of history, but more especially at the times of great revolution in thoughts and opinions. And it was repeated at the opening of the eighteenth century. And now that we are seeking to gain a clear view of this transition period, and not to let it escape us in a too general portraiture, we will set in the foreground a vigorous and sharply defined personality, a man who struck with energy into the ecclesiastical movements of his day, a king who united wonderfully the virtues and the faults of the older time, and who yet was compelled, against his will, to open the way for the newer epoch, even if it were only by the power of contrast—I mean the figure of Frederick William I., King of Prussia. And we place him the more readily at the outset of our inquiries into the historical development of the Protestant spirit, because in his son Frederick the Great, we shall find at a later stage of our progress the finest exponent of the characteristics of the age to which his father will introduce us.

The Great Elector had left to his son a country in a high degree of prosperity. The latter, a prince devoted to pomp and show, an imitator of the French style, as it had been under the reign of Louis XIV., had tried to give a more imposing effect to his authority by assuming the title of king, and of opening the eighteenth century with his coronation ceremonies. His wife Sophia Charlotte, of the house of Brunswick, was one of the most gifted women of her time. To a French education, from childhood she united a love for German thoroughness, which had been fostered by Leibnitz himself. She mingled in the discussions both of Free-thinkers and of Jesuits, and shewed equal ability in either case. The son of these parents was King Frederick William I., who was born in August 1688. His primary education was committed to a Calvinistic lady from France, but as soon as he began to display elements of independent character, he was placed in the hands of Count Dohval, a rigid disciplinarian. In the instructions given to the count by the king, regarding the training of the young prince, we find the following:—"The true fear of God shall betimes be impressed upon his young heart, that it may take root and bring forth fruit through his whole life, and more especially when he is beyond the care of parents and teachers. Besides, the Crown Prince must be thoroughly instructed regarding the majesty and the omnipotence of God, that there may be awakened in him a holy fear and veneration of God and his commandments, for this is the only means to hold a sovereign freed from the penalties of human law within the bounds of duty; and just as other men are induced by the hope of reward and the fear of punishment to obey the commands of their rulers, so must the reverence of God awaken the same salutary fear in those who have no occasion to dread the decisions of human tribunals." In another place it is further ordered,—"That the Crown Prince, with all his attendants, shall, every morning, offer prayer to God, on bended knees; after the exercise he shall read a chapter in the Bible, and afterwards repeat a summary of it; and shall also commit to memory appropriate passages from the Psalms, and verses which will be useful for him to know; that he must be thoroughly versed in the principles of religion, in the Creed, and in the leading Calvinistic works, and be subject to a frequent catechising; that he be a regular attendant at church, and be required to give an account of the sermons; that no one shall associate with the Crown Prince, who shall teach him to swear, or to use blasphemous and filthy language." His mother undertook one part of his education; she read some hours to him daily from Fénélon's Telemachus, and made it the text of many running comments and observations. The gifted queen had one great defect, she was over-indulgent, and her son used afterwards to speak of her in these very severe terms, "She was a talented woman but a sorry Christian." When the young prince grew into a youth, he manifested a very simple and marked German taste in contrast with the French style, and the very ceremonious display of his father's court. He showed a great predilection for military affairs, and a singular and whimsical fondness for men of huge size. In his eighteenth year, not long after the early death of his mother, he was married to the Crown Princess of Hanover, Sophia Dorothea. After seeing something of actual field service with Marlborough and Prince Eugene, and being present at the battle of Malplaquet, he turned back to Berlin, and in 1713 ascended the throne. The year before his coronation, the son who became his successor, the renowned Frederick the Great, was born. Frederick William I. had reached his twenty-fifth year when he inherited the crown. We do not purpose to recount the story of his reign, but to paint his character and to indicate what he had in common with the Protestant German princes of his time, and what he evidently owed to the age in which it was his fortune to live.

As we have already remarked, the king loved the greatest simplicity. He commanded his court fools to dress in the French style, so as to bring it into the greatest derision. Everything French was his abhorrence, and he tried to strip off the thin mask of gentility which had been worn during his father's time, which he thought covered the face of true sincerity. He himself regarded with primitive rigidness his marriage vow, and ruled his family with a firm hand, and rebuked the prevalent laxness with stern words. The virtue of his private life shamed many of the princes of his time, for he shunned every appearance of evil. When the queen was too late home one night from one of her receptions in Monbijou, this rigid husband went to the house of his chaplain, and left a letter instructing him to chide the delinquent wife for her late hours. With a single stroke of his pen he swept away the lavish appropriations which his father had made for the royal expenses, and out of what he saved he paid his father's debts. He himself had a duty for every hour of the day, and he adhered strictly to his arrangements unless sudden emergencies disturbed his plans. As he had been taught to do when Crown Prince, he continued to do as king, commencing the day with a religious exercise; then he received communications from his counsellors, and passed his decisions upon them, often expressing himself very laconically in the margin. At ten was parade, and then he visited the stables. While at both of these places he received petitions, sometimes certainly more graciously than at other times, according to his humour, which it must be confessed was a very changeable one, and which he never learned to master. At eleven he met his privy conncil; at twelve dinner was served, much more simply than during his father's reign, yet he did not spare the Rhine wine, and used to laugh at those who did not join him in deep glasses. He loved merriment at table, yet was scrupulous about the language used, never permitting anything which was unworthy for his family to hear.

After dinner the king was accustomed to ride out; or, when he was at Potsdam or Wüstershausen, he went frequently on foot. When on such excursions, he used to stop those who met him and ask them many questions; and if he caught them idling, or engaged in an employment which he did not approve, it went hard with them: he either made them feel his heavy walking-stick, or sent them to prison at Spandau. But they had the hardest lot to bear who were discovered oppressing the poor. He made every one who talked with him look him directly in the eye, for he believed he could read men at a glance. Of course most, especially women and children, could not meet this test, but the king did not let them off; and if they ran away he had them pursued, and they had to stand and tell their story. An anecdote is preserved which is very characteristic. A Jew having fallen in his way, and concealed himself so as not to be seen, the king had him brought from his hiding-place and set before him. "Rascal, why did you run away?" "For fear, your Majesty." The king gave him a sound caning, and then bade him go away, and thenceforth not to fear him, but to love him.

In summer at seven o'clock, and in winter at five, the king went in to join his usual social evening circle, generally known under the name of the Tobacco Parliament. This Parliament, so called, which met regularly at Berlin, or at Potsdam and Wüstershausen if the king was there, was composed of seven or eight persons, mostly generals and cabinet officers, but distinguished strangers who were in the city were sometimes invited. Every guest was furnished with a common Dutch pipe, and if he did not smoke, he must at least hold the pipe in his mouth: a white jug filled with beer was set before every one, and early in the evening bread and butter were served. It was rare that a more expensive entertainment was provided. At these meetings the king and his friends talked over the news of the day, and sometimes played chess: cards were not allowed. The king was generally in a merry mood on these occasions, but in consequence of his extreme sensitiveness, his humour could not be reckoned on, and sometimes he was thoroughly disagreeable. The most indispensable companions at these evening entertainments were the court jesters and weak learned men, or his jolly counsellors, as the king loved to call them. Among the latter the most eminent was Gundling, a man of extensive historical research, and of reputation as an author, but who had sunk so far below the rank of a scholar, and who had so far forgotten the dignity of his profession, that he had hired himself to a tavern keeper, making fun for the guests, and having the free run of the bar as his pay. General Grumkow had discovered him and recommended him to the king, who conceived a great liking for him, and made him the subject of constant practical jokes, which Gundling took in the best of spirits. The king made him a Baron, and called him Your Excellency, and to show his contempt of scholars, raised him to the chair of

President of the Royal Academy of Arts and Sciences, which the great Leibnitz had just left vacant. But what pleased the king most of all was, to set Gundling and Fossmann the royal biographer against each other in some petty controversy, and then urge them on till they came to blows, as they not seldom did. We need nothing more than this to learn the attitude of Frederick-William towards scholarship and literature. He despised men of letters as thoroughly useless: he classed them with comedians, mountebanks, rope dancers, and the like, and wished to drive them all out of the kingdom at once. He himself was very ignorant, and wrote in the most incorrect manner, mistaking alike in orthography and syntax. We can excuse in part his contempt for scholars, for in truth they were at that time mostly a foolish and pedantic class. The king was simply a practical man, and wanted none round him but men of quick and sure judgment. He cared nothing for philosophers and poets. Schelling, Tieck, and Rückert would have had a very quiet career in his day. He was a special foe of the Latin language, as well as of all dead tongues and ancient history. All such lore he held as useless, and once, when he discovered the tutor of his son, Frederick the Great, teaching him the Aurea Bulla, he broke in upon him with his formidable cane, and used it effectually over his shoulders, throwing in his rough, "Wait, you rascal; I'll Aurea Bulla you to your hearts' content." And yet, with all this, he was a truly pious man; he was devotedly attached to his religion. How this could have been, with all his strange humours and his passionate nature, has been considered a psychological riddle; but to solve it, we must take into account the times in which he lived, the education which he had received, and his strongly marked individuality. We should judge very hastily if we should say, that to the rough and barbarous manners of the king there was joined nothing but a dead, heartless, or even a hypocritical piety. From hypocrisy he was far removed, and we have no reason to doubt that he was a man of the most serious and settled religious convictions. Dead and heartless, it would be wrong to call him. Wherever he heard a complaint of ecclesiastical despotism in the Palatinate, in Poland or in Austria, he espoused the Protestant side with his whole heart, and took a deep interest till the wrong was retrieved. His piety took other practical directions, as the magnificent Hospital *de la Charitè* in Berlin, and the Orphan House in Potsdam, bear witness. From many of his expressions we see that he was a man profoundly convinced of the truth of Christianity; and yet his piety appears to be rather that proceeding from law than from love; to be rather the effect of fear than of the Gospel; although there are times when the radiant spirit of Christ seems to break through his life. As we have already mentioned, it was laid down in the instructions given by his royal father, that he should be trained in the fear of God, which should teach him to bridle his spirit. But this fear of God, which did not comprise the great idea of Christian liberty, was very inadequate to give him self-control, and to preserve him from the strong sway of his passionate caprices. An example may show this. The preacher, Freylinghausen, son-in-law of the celebrated Francke, of Halle, was once invited to dine with the king at his hunting-lodge at Wüstershausen; and he thought it his duty to give Frederick-William a lecture on the wickedness of the chase. "Hunting is a sin," said the good man, "a disallowed pleasure, because no man can do right to torment and kill a poor beast after it has been run down and lies panting and exhausted: that panting is the sighing of the creature to its Creator, and you must give an account to God for what you do then." The king was much affected by this plain dealing, but the next day he went out hunting again.

Nor was hunting the worst. The cruel means with which he got possession of men of great stature to make them members of his body-guard, the cool giving to death of offenders, and particularly of deserters, his unfatherly treatment of his son Frederick,—how have these anything to do with the fear of God, which he considered, in other things, the basis of all royal virtues? If any man's life is a running commentary on the Apostle's words of the double law working within us, of the flesh and of the spirit, that man is King Frederick William; but he never came, as the apostle did, to a consciousness of this warfare within himself. Dogmatical with the understanding, he yet ascribed to the Gospel a power which could re-mould life and make it capable of its highest possibilities. But as with so many others, who have understood that this is indeed so, he did not wholly feel it with the heart. The atonement and faith in Christ became a kind of cushion which should give his conscience repose, and on which he could securely rest; even when on the death-bed, he lacked that sincere repentance, without which the atonement is of no avail. But when he lay at the door of death, his chaplain Roloff dealt very plainly with him, and tried to waken him out of this deceitful sleep. "I have often told your majesty," said Roloff, in presence of the whole court, "that Christ is the hope of our salvation, on the two conditions that we accept Him with the heart, and follow His example and precepts. So long as we fail in either of these conditions, so long can we not enter into His rest. And if your majesty were to be saved by a miracle, of which, however, we have no reason for expectation, you would not enjoy heaven, in the condition of mind in which you now are. Your army, your treasures, your lands must remain here—no courtiers can follow you there, no servants on whom you can wreak your anger. In heaven a man must have a heavenly mind." Those were words worthy of a Nathan. The king remained silent, and yet he looked round with an appealing, supplicating eye, as if to say, Will no one come to my relief? But when the attendants retired and the monarch began to recount his sins one by one, Roloff refused to listen to so unprotestant a confession, and only demanded that the king should acknowledge the need of a change of heart, and this Frederick William would not grant. He thought that in this kings had the advantage of other men, and he insisted on justifying himself by his good works. And when some one who stood by sided with the dying man, Roloff charged upon the poor monarch the blows which he had inflicted upon his subjects, the tyranny he had exercised over them, and the unjust sentences of death which he had passed.

A rigid orthodoxy in externals, joined to a common and unspiritual frame of mind, and a want of appreciating true culture, worked most unfavourably on the education of his son Frederick, and doubtless produced that reaction which we know was experienced in the life of that son when he passed out of his father's hands. The instruction which the father ordered to be imparted to the crown prince, was to a hair the same which he had received when a boy. "In special," he says, "must my son have a righteous love and fear of God, as the corner-stone and the only pillar to sustain our earthly well-being, and he must shun all those baleful and seductive sects, such as the atheistical Arians and Socinians, who work on young spirits like poison. Let them not be spoken of in his presence, and let him be taught to abhor the Catholic religion, which must be classed in the same ranks, and be instructed to despise the absurdity of its pretensions; but let him be carefully trained in the true Christian religion, which teaches that Christ died for all men, and that He is our only confidence and trust. Let him also be so carefully shown the proofs of God's omnipotence, that he shall always retain "a holy fear and veneration of God and His commandments; for this is the only means of holding a sovereign, freed from the penalties of human law, within the bounds of duty." The last are the very same words which his own father had written years before. All very good. But where the living spirit was wanting, what could the dead letter do? Would not the holiest thing have a touch of the ridiculous in it, if it were conjoined with that stiff military style of expression: as for example, that a prayer should take just twenty minutes' time? At any rate it awakens peculiar feelings to read the well-meant and, in many respects, excellent orders for the Crown Prince's observance of the Sabbath. "On Sunday my son Fritz (Frederick the Great later) shall rise at seven. As soon as he shall have put on his trousers, he shall fall on his knees before the bed and pray to God, and loud, too, so that all in the chamber can hear him. The prayer shall be this, and shall be learned by heart: Lord God, holy Father, I thank thee heartily that thou hast graciously preserved me this night; make me to do thy holy will, and suffer me to do nought this day nor all the days of my life which can separate me from thee, for Jesus, my Saviour's sake. Amen." Certainly a fine, simple, and appropriate prayer, such as would be well for every monarch's son in Christendom to repeat every morning. But what a check to our enjoyment of it is the continuation of the same document, with its stiff business air: "So soon as this is over, he shall dress himself nimbly, wash himself well, comb, tie up and powder his hair, and must accomplish all, the prayer included, in fifteen minutes' time, at quarter past seven. Then he shall breakfast in five minutes. When this is through, all the domestics shall come in, Duhon shall read a chapter from the Bible, lead in a good hymn, and pray, till it shall be quarter of eight; the domestics shall then withdraw. Duhon shall then go on explaining from the Bible, instructing the prince in the principles of Christianity," &c.

This military exactness the king also carried into the public worship of God. He laid on all preachers the injunction not to allow their sermons to be more than an hour long, under penalty of two rix thalers.

Yet Frederick William took the greatest care to procure able ministers for his people. He regarded himself as the head of the National Church, and charged himself with its whole interests and affairs. He himself issued an order that candidates for the ministry should be instructed in a clear, sensible, and edifying method of sermonizing. They shall have no high flights, shall use no allegorical and flowery words, which might be well enough from the professor's chair, but which are worse than useless, yes, even injurious to the interests of Christianity, when uttered from the pulpit. To further this, Reinbeck's sermons were particularly recommended. The court chaplains, Reinbeck and Roloff, were most excellent men, to whom the king gave his full confidence, and who could say many things to him which he would not bear from others. Reinbeck belonged to the men who were able to look with clear and rare discrimination into the theology of his times: he was (perhaps too strongly), an advocate of the new philosophy of Wolf, which the king disliked extremely at first, but was afterwards reconciled to. Reinbeck's name will always be mentioned in the history of pulpit eloquence among those who, even before the days of Mosheim, introduced a more tasteful style of preaching, and one more satisfying to thoughtful minds. Roloff is not known as a writer, so far as I have been able to learn; but the words which he spoke at the king's deathbed, are worth volumes of printed sermons. Reinbeck, too, did not hesitate to speak plainly to Frederick William when occasion required. When the latter once put on airs, and said that he knew already what was right and what was wrong, Reinbeck answered him with the words of Christ, "The servant who knoweth his Lord's will and doeth it not, shall be beaten with many stripes." The king was sensitive, but he usually regarded these faithful dealings. To those two, the king, near the end of his life, added the pious and learned Sack. We quote the account which the son of the latter gives of the invitation to his father.

"Early in the year 1740, Noltenius, one of the preachers to the court, died suddenly at Berlin. A few days after that event my father received the following letter:—

'WORTHY, VERY DEAR AND TRUSTED!—Because on Sunday next you are to preach to me, I will that you take extra post, so as to arrive in Berlin on Saturday.—I am your very affectionate king, FREDERICK WILLIAM.'

"My father started the same day, and arrived at Berlin the next evening. Early on Saturday the king sent a page to him, who repeated the order to preach to the court the next day, and soon after another, who brought a little Testament from which Frederick William would have him preach. He officiated the next day as ordered. After service the king gave him to understand that he was much pleased with the sermon, and commanded him to dine with the queen the same day. The king, who was very sick, was rolled in to table in an easy chair, talked in an extremely easy and familiar manner with my father, and directed him to preach the next day, with the remark that he might be deceived by *one* sermon, and wished to be surer that he was the man he sought. The second service only strengthened the good opinion already formed, and my father was called at once to the vacant pulpit. My father had an interview subsequently with the king during his sickness, and he has often repeated a remark which the monarch dropped: 'Stick to the New Testament; I will tell you what is the chief thing in religion, to fear God, to love Jesus Christ, and to do right; the rest is nothing.'"

This military roughness, joined to an unmistakeable love of religion, together with a certain geniality, showed itself in the manner in which the king attempted to reform public worship. In the rites of the Lutheran Church, which together with the reformed or Calvinist Church were sanctioned by the State, there were many relics of the older Catholic ceremonies, lights, choristers, vestments, priestly gowns, Latin songs, the sign of of the cross, &c. All this the king wanted to put away, as a remnant of Popery, and proscribed them by an order issued in 1733. Some preachers gave up readily to the king's reformatory spirit, others held these changes as inconsistent with their consciences, and as injurious to the old Lutheranism; others still believed that the people would be led astray by the abandonment of what had been established so long; for, said they, if we are to abolish every relic of Popery, we must destroy the churches too, for they were mostly built by the Papists. One preacher came with the announcement that the first time the simplified service was held, the people looked on in wonder; others reported the sighs and sorrowful expressions which they had heard in their congregations. They alluded especially to the deep symbolic significance of the lighting of candles, by which were typified the burning love of the Saviour and shining of the Christian's light before men. But the king remained fixed in his decision, and renewed the order in 1737, with this additional announcement, that if any minister found any trouble to his conscience in conforming to it, his resignation would be accepted. And in fact one preacher, who had stoutly opposed the king's order, was deposed from office. Not much of the spirit of Protestantism in that act. Yet in some matters Frederick William was even tolerant. Orthodox and pedantic as he was, so far as concerned the externals of religion, he was very much opposed to theological polemics, or "parsons' quarrels," as he called them. He himself was Calvinistic, the queen Lutheran, but he often sought out Lutheran preachers, and in consequence of their heartiness and popular way, he gave them the preference over the Calvinists, whose sermons, framed on the models of Tillotson and Saurin, were more elaborate and learned. "It is a shame," said the king, "that the Lutherans have all the excellent theologians, and that their sermons are so much more edifying than our Calvinists' are." Therefore he selected mostly from the Lutherans for army chaplains, because he believed that their hearty style would make more impression upon the soldiers than the more stately manner of the Calvinistic preachers.

Frederick William I. died May 31, 1740. We have already

alluded to his last hours. The particularity with which he specified the arrangements for his funeral is remarkable. He ordered where each battalion should assemble, where it should mount, and in what order it should fire over the grave. Amid all this military preparation he did not overlook spiritual matters. This blending of warlike with religious discipline clung to him to the last, for it was the very nature of the man. He himself chose the funeral text: "I have fought a good fight," and ordered the hymn, "Who suffers only God to rule." "Of my life and career, of my actions and what is personal to me, let not one word be spoken, but let the people be told that I have expressly ordered it so, with this in addition, that I died a great and poor sinner, but hoped for grace from God for the Saviour's sake. The clergy shall neither blame nor praise me in their sermons after my obsequies."

The king himself anticipated the verdict of the historian. He cannot be praised without qualification, for there was much that was unpraiseworthy mingled with what was good and worthy, especially when we apply that *Christian* measuring line which the king was the first to apply to himself. But who, measured by that standard, does not come short? And so Frederick William's character is not to be despised, and in despising him, historians have committed a great mistake, and done him a great wrong. He has been commonly measured by his son, and those who have regarded Frederick the Great as the type of all greatness, have naturally had no eye for what was excellent in his father and in his father's time. So Voltaire has collected everything that was ridiculous and hateful in Frederick William, and even the daughter of the king, the Princess of Baireuth, has tried to depreciate him, while Frederick the Great always extolled his father, and gave him credit for real abilities.

On the one side of his nature Frederick William I. was a thoroughly Protestant character, who well deserved to be enrolled as one of the guardians of Protestantism. And this not only on account of his true fatherly care for the Lutheran and Reformed Church, but also from his decided love of truth, the earnestness with which he treated all religious things, and his rigid discipline, so far as externals were concerned. But he had only this one side of Protestantism. He initiated that course, which has from his day to ours been followed by some,—the blending of a genuine piety with an unconquerable roughness of manners, the union of religion with ignorance. Religion does not consist, indeed, in knowledge, nor in an elegant address, nor in a cultivated mind; for there can be piety among men who are not the most highly educated. But the want of learning must be carefully discriminated from purposed ignorance, from that coarseness which prides itself on its little knowledge and narrowness, and which assumes moral worth from such an ignoble possession. What we should not criticise in a shepherd or in a peasant, would pain us in a king. The scorn which Frederick William showed to science was a sin, although not regarded by him as such. How much does this Protestant king stand below those rulers which, at the time of the Reformation and since, have laboured for the advance of Protestantism by labouring for the advance of science, below Frederick the Wise, below Elizabeth, below William of Orange, below Gustavus Adolphus, below his own model, the great Elector! Frederick William was not only opposed to all science, but to all knowledge the practical worth of which he did not see, and so to all the dead languages and ancient history. Here was the rough nature of the man. The old reformers and the princes who adhered to them, even the age in which they lived, prized knowledge for itself alone, as the light of the mind, which is just as solacing to the inner eye as the greenness of the meadows is to the external eye which enjoys it. The appreciation of ancient literature and the appreciation of the Bible, awakened at the time of the reformation, were allied most closely, and one served the other. It was now no longer so. Learning had sunk into pedantry, and a living piety into dead orthodoxy.

Honourable to the king was his faithful observance of private religious services; but, where no high spiritual life is awakened by this, even these must lead to a mechanical religion, which has no connection with a sound faith. A prayer, such as he prescribed for his son, to be repeated at just such an hour and in just such words, is not the best means to lead a young soul to contemplate its own deepest wants and to guide it to God. The history of Frederick II. will show us how much this satiety of religious teaching and worship, without any true spiritual instruction, estranged him from all religion. And how many examples of this will be found in all history, ancient and modern! What we blame in Frederick William in this respect, concerns more or less the "good old times," which is praised so much, or rather those who so foolishly praise it. How often the past is brought into contrast with the present, as though its piety was wholly without defects! But how often was that piety only the outer form, "the letter that killeth," and not "the spirit that maketh alive." Where it was both we will not withhold our praise of piety, even though it may have been joined to some old and stiff forms. But it is not a matter of entire regret that the old forms have passed away, if we have, as I think we have, the spirit of religion put forth in other shapes. That spirit is happily not dependent upon forms, and it is a matter of congratulation that it is now less fettered by them, and is more free to put forth its power than it was in those older times, when the external husk was prized above the inner kernel.

Taken as a whole we cannot say that Frederick William resisted the best tendencies of his age. On the contrary, he himself helped to open the way to a better time, and amid all that was rough and thorny in him, we recognize the buds of a more advanced and a regenerated epoch. His very disinclination to empty and pedantic learning led to learning more stable and sincere, and the desire to see religious sects live in harmony was only a glimpse into what will one day be realized, when theological strifes will be ended and the Spirit of Christ shall reign.

IV.

PIETISM AND ITS OPPONENTS.

STRIFE BETWEEN THE LUTHERANS AND THE CALVINISTS.—THE PHILOSOPHER WOLF, A SKETCH OF HIS CAREER, HIS BANISHMENT FROM HALLE AND HIS RECAL.—HIS SYSTEM IN ITS REAL THEOLOGICAL RELATIONS.—LATER DEVELOPMENT OF PIETISM, ITS EXCELLENT INFLUENCES DURING THE WARS OF FREDERICK THE GREAT, AND ITS SUBSEQUENT DECLINE.

PASSING from the royal personage who has just engaged our attention, and who, more than any other, was the representative man of his time, we come to a nearer view of the great ecclesiastical controversies which occupied the first half of the eighteenth century. There were three of these—the protracted contest between the Lutheran and the Reformed or Calvinistic Churches; the contest between the orthodox and the pietists; and the contest between the pietist and the new philosophy of Wolf. The first, with however much zeal it is now prosecuted, had then sunk into a passive state, and had to be reckoned among the things gone by, and to make way for a more tolerant spirit; the second, too, which had begun in the seventeenth century, had gradually lost its importance; while the third, the contest between pietism and philosophy, then in its beginning, was destined to absorb all attention, and to continue on, even to the days in which we live.

Beginning with the first, there were not wanting at that time hard rubs between the Lutherans and the Calvinists, which sometimes were very hateful in their spirit. Up to the middle of the eighteenth century, these controversies were not merely about matters of doctrine, the Calvinists denied that the Lutherans had the right of using the churches, even in Lutheran cities, such as Frankfort, Worms, and Hamburg. In the last named place a controversy had long existed between Lessing and Gotze, a pastor there, who in his foolish zeal called the doctrine of the Calvinists, "the devil's theology," and considered it as very dangerous to extend any privileges to them. For half a century Pastor Neumeister had used the same language. He had tried to prove, with a sad and yet ludicrous acuteness, that the Calvinists did not hold to any one of the twelve articles of the apostles' creed, nor to any of the petitions of the Lord's prayer; that with their doctrine, they sinned against the ten commandments, that they had no religion at all, that their theology was a beggar's cloak, composed of bits of heresy sewed together, and that he would rather be an irrational creature, or a poor worm, than the most celebrated Calvinistic theologian; for the latter will certainly go straight to hell. That Christ and Belial will strike hands together sooner than Luther and Calvin. Yet to the honour of the century, let it be said, that this was only the talk of a few senseless men, that the spirit of the age was against them, and that the books were in far greater demand which spoke out freely and boldly of a union between these two churches, before distant and widely apart.

By PIETISM we do not mean all that malice and ignorance has saddled upon the word, but that decisive movement in the Protestant Church of Germany, which had been begun by Spener and Francke, and which, making Halle its starting point at the opening of the eighteenth century, had extended over the whole land: a movement in antagonism to the theology of the schools, and aiming to restore a practical kind of piety, and a simple primitive order of things in the Church: laying great stress upon a profound conviction of sin, the depravity of human nature, and a change of heart, and exercising a severity of judgment as to externals, so as sometimes to fall into a one-sided and morbid conscientiousness. This movement, from the very fact that it awakened many out of their slumber, aroused many opponents, and these long remained in a hostile attitude.

Up to the call of the philosopher Wolf to Halle, an event of great importance in those times, and commented upon largely by all historians, that city had been the centre of pure and strong religious influences. Philosophy had modestly given way to theology. The independent spirit with which the former now stepped forward in the person of Christian Wolf, the boldness of his system, so much misunderstood, awoke in pious minds an anxiety which we need not be surprised at, without ascribing to ambition and jealousy the opposition which the pietistic leaders manifested towards him. We cannot avoid speaking quite fully of this great man, since he gave direction to so much that was characteristic of the age.

Christian Wolf, born at Breslau, January 24, 1679, was the son of a tanner, and, as he tells us in the account of his own life, received a rigidly religious education; when a child he went to Church, without regard to weather, read the Bible, was familiar with the best hymns, and, in fact, was dedicated by his parents even then to a clergyman's life. At the gymnasium of his native place he had become so conversant with theology, that on entering the University at Jena, he says that he found little new to learn. The lectures on physics and mathematics attracted him rather than those on theology; yet it remained his constant determination to "serve God by preaching," and the more so, since he had been consecrated to such a career by a vow of his parents.

Wolf tells us in his autobiography, that even while he lived at Breslau, where there were many Catholics, who were always in controversy with the Lutherans, the thought occurred to him, "Whether it is not possible to make the truth of religion appear so plainly, that no chance for doubt can exist." As he heard that mathematics is a science so exact that every one has to grant what it proves, he studied mathematics assiduously, in order to transfer to theology the same certainty. This was a preparation for preaching which few made, and the young candidates were left by him to their study of language and history, while he went on with the prosecution of the exact sciences. He preached a number of times, and as he tells us with great applause. "My method of sermonizing was praised, because I sought to convey the most clear and exact idea of my subject, and to let one thing be deduced from another. It has often been said to me, that when it was asked how I always held the attention of all who came to hear me, the answer was that they could always understand me but they could not others." This eminent talent for instructing was apparent in his sermons, as it was ever after in the professorial chair. As mathematics had been auxiliary with him to theology, it begun to lend its aid to philosophy, and the latter, thus supported, gradually became the study of his life. In original power, as a philosopher, Wolf was second to Leibnitz, in whose steps he walked; but he had a happy and comprehensive grasp of philosophical truths, and entered successfully on the vocation of making philosophy, which had till then been inaccessible to men of average talents, an interesting study—in other words, to be the mediator between the highest thinker and the educated mind of his age.

In 1707 he was called to the Chair of Mathematics and Physics at the University of Halle, but subsequently to 1709 he delivered lectures on Metaphysics, Logic, and Morals. His reputation grew commensurately with the hearty zeal with which he gave himself to his work. His style was remarkable for its transparent clearness; but in proportion as he won applause on one side, he incurred the suspicion of the other, that his method of dealing with philosophical and theological themes, would bring peril to the religious belief of men and the soundness of their doctrine. This peril seemed to be grounded on the double reason of form and of substance. Unquestionably the stern mathematical, the purely intellectual expression, a mode of address destitute of all imagination and picturesque language, must excite opposition on the theological field, in an age when men were accustomed to keep the dogmas of the church obscured in a twilight gloom. Yet in the effort to make everything clear and intelligible to all, there lay the danger of reducing the exalted truths of Christianity to trivialities, especially as there were not lacking blind imitators who could not have enough of a good thing. So the story is told that once one of the Wolf school of preachers, who wanted to explain his text as fully as possible, chose the verse from eighth chapter of Matthew, "When Jesus was come down from the mountain, great multitudes followed him," and began to expound as follows:—A mountain is a high elevation of land, a multitude is a large concourse of people, &c. In this way preaching became more like an exercise in logic than a means of edification; breadth was taken for depth, a tedious style was taken as an exhaustive style, and so it was inevitable that those who sought in preaching not only what instructs but also what edifies and cheers, were entirely opposed to this pedantry.

But it was not merely the demonstrative form which was criticised in Wolf's philosophy, and which, when transferred to the pulpit, was a true source of offence, but which should never have been charged upon the great founder of the system himself; the substance of his doctrine also, gave rise to much misunderstanding. It is always difficult to cull single expressions from a rigid philosophical system, and then to judge of them from the stand-point of common sense, or from that of practical piety. It is the mark of an uneducated mind, one unused to high processes of thought, to wish to detach each link from such a chain as is a strict philosophical system, and to examine it by itself. There are many sentences which derive all their significance from their context, and that which, in the mouth of a wise man, and in connection with his mode of thought, has an evident intelligibility, can become in the mouth of the people a mere jumble of nonsense. It is, therefore, always easy to turn philosophers into ridicule, and just as easy to bring them under suspicion. When that which philosophy establishes as a matter of pure thought, is transformed into an article of faith, or a clause in the catechism, it serves neither philosophy nor religion, it only confuses both. Not that philosophical and religious truths are in contradiction to each other; but there is in philosophy and in religion a method of thought, and a method of speech, appropriate to each; the one is for man's knowledge, the other for man's faith; the one is within the province of the understanding, and the other is within the province of feeling, and can only be attained with a large experience of life. And the confounding of these two so widely different subjects together, produces the confusion, so often witnessed, and which has been, and still is, the source of so many controversies. We cannot find anything more analogous to the relation between philosophy and faith, than that between physical science and the daily facts of life. It would not be greater folly to be unwilling to see, before the theory of light is explained, than it would be to cease all investigations into the nature of light, because we can enjoy it amply, without those investigations. Since God said, Let there be light, and there was light, theories have made no difference in the recurrence of night and morning; and so it will be with the inward light which Jesus has kindled. Faith clings to this light, rejoices in it, seeks by it; but science explores its nature and laws. We may argue the sun out of the heavens, but it will keep on shining still. But the theories of physical light might possibly insist upon some point, which to the uneducated mind might seem like denying the very existence of that light. A representation of God, an unused style of expression regarding His nature and existence, seem to the mind unaccustomed to it, to be a denial of His being. Therefore there ought always to be caution on both sides. If faith is true faith, not a mere acceptance of truths on authority, but life and experimental piety, scientific theology may go on in its work, and will place no impediments in the way. Faith must come first, science afterwards, but they are both in harmony; and when the mind has advanced far enough, it will see that they are so; but if there be not time for prolonged inquiries, yet faith abides sure, and stands on its own secure foundation. And in the days of which we write, the pietists ought to have been content to judge from their own stand-point. But they were not. The pietists were shocked at Wolf's philosophical propositions, they saw in them only dangerous heresies, and the result was natural that Wolf and his adherents should see in the pietists opposers of science, stupid ignoramuses, even if not hypocrites, afraid of the light. The reader who goes through the whole history of that foolish quarrel, will find that passions were roused on both sides, and that not much that was edifying arose on either side, unless we except the lesson so useful for us, to be on our guard in like circumstances.

It was the doctrine of the so called pre-established harmony which first roused the opposition of the pietists,—the doctrine which Leibnitz had framed and Wolf had expanded, of an eternal attraction of monads to one another, in accordance with which the world was formed. The Biblical account of a creation seemed to be put in peril by this theory, and so did that of human freedom, although as a mere hypothesis of the schools it did not have that danger to the Church which was suspected to lie in it. Francke himself confesses that in the stillness of his chamber he prayed to God to stand in the way of this false doctrine, and to ward off the darkness of atheism. And who can blame the pious man for this? He and his colleague Joachim Lange, held it to be their duty to warn the students of Wolf's errors; and they cannot be chided for their conscientious opposition, but rather praised for it. This was their error, that out of short sightedness they undertook to check what they feared, by meeting it with statutes and the restraints of law.

The contest between Wolf and the pietists broke out openly at the celebration of the laying aside of the Protectorate of the University of Halle. Lange had been appointed his successor. Wolf's address on retiring was on the ethical teachings of Confucius, which he set very high. The rigid theologians inferred that he tacitly implied a depreciation of the Christian ethics, and an unseemly exalting of heathen ideas, and called Wolf to an account. This he did not care to give, or rather he did not wish to acknowledge any dependence upon the theological department, and contended for the privilege of perfect freedom of speech on his own field. Meanwhile one of the theological faculty had carried the matter into the pulpit, and had begun to rouse the popular mind. This did not bring Wolf into any better frame of mind. The larger number of students sided with him, many out of their vanity, for students generally rank themselves under the banner of those who introduce startling novelties. And so pietism came very much into ridicule among the students; controversies arose and a great deal of hard feeling. The new rector was received in the most insulting manner, and he had to bear much contumely from the philosophical students, and most unjustly too, for Joachim Lange, with all his one sidedness, was a learned scholar, and a devoted servant of the gospel. Meanwhile the contest went on, and was at last carried so far that Wolf received his dismission. The manner in which Frederick William, whose feeling towards men of learning we have already seen, was set against him, is not a pleasant tale to tell. The very wrong, to which we have so recently alluded, of culling from any philosophical system, special detached sentences or propositions, and making them irreconcilable to common sense, or absolutely ridiculous, was done to Wolf in this affair. It was said to the king, whose weakness for huge soldiers is well known, that if Wolf's doctrine of pre-established harmony were to become popularly received, his grenadiers would desert on account of its being predestinated that they should do so. This moved the king more than any other argument could, and he issued in 1723 the following order :—" Whereas we have been informed that Professor Wolf has been engaged through lectures and publications in diffusing objections to the Christian religion, and whereas we are not inclined to bear longer with the same, but are firmly resolved that he shall be dismissed from his office and be not permitted to teach ; we do hereby order that within forty-eight hours from the receipt of this, he leave the city of Halle and all our dominions, under PENALTY OF DEATH."

Such a result even Wolf's most bitter enemies had not expected. Lange felt deeply grieved at it. He himself tells us that for three days after hearing the tidings, he could neither eat nor sleep. And we can readily imagine how his conscience must have wavered between theological zeal and natural feeling, a struggle which goes hard with every sound nature. Nor did all cease with the banishment of Wolf, King Frederick William forbade the reading of atheistical writings, Wolf's included, under a heavy penalty, and disallowed, under a penalty heavier yet, the delivering of any lectures on the new philosophical system. It is singular that the Jesuits, who were the first to take up Kepler when he was proscribed by the Protestants, were the first to side with Wolf; and they not only allowed his writings to pass uncondemned, but it was a Jesuit who first proposed that he be made a baron.

After the great uproar that was made, one would suppose that Wolf's doctrine was either really atheistical or at least highly sceptical; but whoever will take the pains to run through his writings will find in them a degree of religious soundness which would be creditable to many an orthodox man of our own times. The orthodox theologians became in fact the most firm adherents to Wolf's doctrine. We must admit, indeed, that his system was not specially adapted to Christian edification ; it was too hard, meagre, dry, and stiff for that ; but that is not the question ; it was neither atheistical nor unchristian. And had it been this, still it was not for true Protestants to try to keep off its evil, by resorting to the discipline of prison walls or banishment.

After his banishment from Halle, Wolf found an honourable position as professor at Marburg; and later Frederick William regretted the act which drove him from his dominions. It was the pious, mild Reinbeck in particular, of whose high Christian character we spoke in connection with the king, who espoused Wolf's side, and was mainly instrumental in procuring a change in the monarch's mind regarding the great philosopher. Reinbeck had studied his system, and gradually approached Frederick William, till at last he entirely won him over, and incited to great efforts to induce Wolf to return to Halle. But all in vain. Large pecuniary offers did not move him. The memory of threatened hanging was too fresh. When Frederick II. ascended the throne and the epoch of toleration had arrived, Wolf consented to return, and entered Halle in triumph. This event occurred in December 1740. Wolf himself has given us an account of his reception. "A great number of the students had rode out to welcome me and to escort me, with six postillions all heralding my approach. In the villages nearest to Halle there were crowds of the people who had gone outside the gates to meet me. The streets were full as I entered the city, and I advanced through shouts on every side. On the street where my house was there were trumpeters and cymbal players, who greeted me noisily on my approach, and there was such a concourse before my door that I could hardly alight and make my way to a private room. The next day I received calls from the magistrates of the city and the professors, among whom was Dr. Lange who treated me with marked courtesy, and whom I received in an entirely friendly spirit."

Glittering as was this reception, the day of Wolf's glory was over. But the best period of the Halle pietism was also over. And yet this pietistic direction, incomplete as it looks in this early period, and running counter as it does to many good movements, is worthy of our study. It is now more than a century since Wolf returned to Halle, and he and his opponent Lange shook hands together (though rather coldly) and yet we see the same hostility between philosophy and faith. Indeed the contest between a *certain* kind of philosophy and a *certain* kind of faith, is even sharper than it was then. But there is a philosophy and there is a faith which can go well together, and which can not only go together, but which can mutually help and further each other, and are supplementary to each other. While the one kind of philosophy and the one kind of faith draw apart from one another, and only leave a choice between a cold, cheerless, and unspiritual worldly wisdom and confused and light-avoiding piety, the more gifted minds of the age are striving after a reconciliation of faith and philosophy, which shall raise the former to the plane of a clear and intelligent belief, and which shall find the roots of the latter down in the subsoil of a living religious life. And therefore we bid welcome to every honest effort to join those two in friendly amity and in a beneficent co-operation. We see in every such effort an advance of true Protestantism, which embraces an increasing clearness in our religious knowledge and an increasing depth in our faith.

The philosophy of Wolf, which caused so great excitement then, has wholly passed away, and no longer reckons adherents among theologians nor philosophers; but the Germans have not ceased to philosophize since the days of Christian Wolf. One system has been crowded out of sight by another, and with every change the demand for philosophy has continued unabated. It would be very foolish to be unwilling to look into the history of these successive systems, to hold it as the idle story of human error, as a series of new and even grosser deviations from Christianity. With such a hasty decision, the labour of investigation would be much abridged, but one incurs a great responsibility who judges of things, or condemns them without understanding them.

One-sided as it would be to view the history of modern philosophy as a mere impediment in the way of Christianity, it would be just as one-sided to view the history of Christianity and of Protestantism independently of the rise of that philosophy. We have to avoid two extremes, into both of which people fall,—the undervaluing of philosophy and the overvaluing of it. If the uneducated, little versed in habits of difficult thought, fall into the first; those who pride themselves on their philosophical training fall into the second, underrating all that has developed itself in life, independently of the help of a scholastic system, and blind to the richness of that blessing which true religion has conferred on both the educated and uneducated, on philosophers and common people. Systems have changed, like clothing and manners, but Christianity has remained the same, awakening, enlightening, and blessing all men.

Had it been from the beginning onward the self-imposed task of pietism to make a practical Christianity a matter of the heart and the life, it could not have failed to serve the most valuable results, provided it continued true to its work. On the field of *practical* religion was its true home, and there it fulfilled its mission in a time which was stormy and most unfavourable to it.

Although the affair with Wolf gave a severe blow to Halle pietism, it did not destroy it. Halle remained, as before, the university which, more than any other in Germany, gave the stamp to most of the theologians of the land. During twenty-nine years it had sent out six thousand clergymen, besides the thousands who had been educated in the Orphan Institute of Francke. This great establishment was in the very meridian of its usefulness, and was the prolific parent of many others of a similar character. And of more power still were the agencies which tended in the same direction, and enlarged the sphere of ministerial labour, the books of devotion, the spiritual songs now so largely known as the "Lyra Germanica," very many of them composed by the pietists of that epoch,—in one word, the daily, spiritual food which nourished Christian families and gave them constant strength. These all combined, a living ministry and a widely diffused literature, formed a weighty counterpoise to the sceptical tendencies of the times, and gave to the pietists a great power, which increased all the more as the new infidelity gained in its control of leading and influential minds.

And, indeed, when we look back at those days, and picture them forth as we did the reign of Frederick William First, when we see the growing effeminacy and worldliness, the change of manners as the new French spirit struck to the very heart of the old German nationality, when we realize the war-like epoch that followed the period of the Silesian war, and see the calamities which came in with that sorrowful strife, the trouble, the sorrow, the rudeness of manners which grew universal, and ask what it was that kept men's minds from sinking, and their hearts in good cheer, that preserved the old domestic purity and discipline, and cherished the old spark of the fear of God in the breast of many a rough warrior, as the light which, though but glimmering, yet gave some comfort, we find that it was not the philosophy of Wolf or of any other man, it was not the theological system of any school, it was not a finished literature or any fine arts, from which the common man drew his religious life in those dark days, but it was simply the high moral power of Christianity; and this power the pietism of that age supplied. As certain medicines have their true time of usefulness, when and when alone they can do good, so it seems to have been with this new development of Christian faith. And therefore the singular fact, that the first recognition of the value of pietism came from those who had ridiculed and despised it before. Men who were not approachable on any side by the new rationalizing theology, who could not listen to any learned reflections on God and divine things without wearisomeness, as if such things lay beyond their circle of thought, were quickly stirred and moved to the depths by that earnest life which was displayed in such gifted spirits as the poets Tersteegen and Bogatsky. The spiritual history of that time is rich in the narratives of the conversions of noblemen and baronesses, of courtiers and warriors, of citizens and students, of huntsmen, shepherds, and peasants; and although the military history of Frederick the Great's reign does not dwell on what the power of Christ was doing, amid all the tumult of the camp, yet painstaking hands were not wanting, to give to us faithful records of the Christian life and its fruits. Professor Arndt of Bonn, published in 1834, the life of an evangelical clergyman, Christian Gottfreid Aszmann, a pastor in Hither Pomerania, from which we could almost reconstruct a full view of pietism in the first half of the eighteenth century. Such a life, says the author rightly, is a practical commentary on the results of Francke's and Spener's teachings and lives. "In my childhood," says Aszmann himself, "I have heard old men of Francke's and Spener's school preaching in houses and pulpits; and the joy of a fixed, assured faith, the cheerful and serene kindliness of a life undisturbed by any of the storms which swept through that bleak and wintry age, still lingers like the fragrance of a flower, and drives me, although now old myself, to look deeper and with more steady gaze upon the great realities which meet me in my advancing pilgrimage."

And yet it must be confessed that there was a dark side to pietism. It is plain that from the first it contained within itself the germs of onesidedness, which developed more and more, and which were brought to their largest degree of ripeness among the imitators of pietism. Phrases which, when introduced, were full of tenderness and feeling, became by much repetition, formal and jejune. Controversies arose, which instead of feeding the religious life, only distracted and troubled it. Men arose, willing to take the part of hypocrites, in order either to gain popular repute and further their own base ends by an assumption of holiness, or to gratify a love for a kind of sensual delight in the earnest and kindling outpourings of the pietists. Unfortunately, the adversaries of the latter did not care to discriminate hypocrites from consistent believers, and rather favoured the blending of good with bad in one mixed mass. Semler, who, though accused of a want of fairness, is yet a good reporter of facts, tells us that the directors of the pietistic churches carried their discipline to the tyrannical height of making a weekly register of the frames of mind which all true Christians ought to experience each week, and to inquire rigidly, whether the sequence of emotions had been felt by every one. This offered a direct premium to hypocrisy, and gave a truly unprotestant power into the hands of the pietistic clergy, over simple-minded and honest believers. Semler narrates the case of a brother, who, under a constant remorse for sin, was thoroughly unmanned and unfitted for any kind of duty, spent his nights in agony and self-reproaches, and was only temporarily solaced by what was said to him. A kind of democratic frenzy prevailed: a duke carried a number of cobbler wives to some kind of a camp meeting, and drove the carriage himself; meetings were held in the moonlight; pilgrimages were made; a morbid, isolated, rank religious experience became the object of universal striving, and, at last, by the confusion of all, what began as a healthy, useful movement, and was eminently blessed of God, became, in its decay, and in the second generation of its adherents, a source of evil and a reproach to the cause of Christ.

V.

THE PIONEERS OF RATIONALISM.

RATIONALISM DEFINED.—DEISM AND NATURALISM.—BOLINGBROKE.—VOLTAIRE.—DIDEROT.—D'ALEMBERT.—MATERIALISM.—HELVETIUS—BARON VON HOLBECK.—SENTIMENTALISM.—J. J. ROUSSEAU.—MARIA HUBER.—DEISM IN FRENCH AND ENGLISH LITERATURE.

FROM the history of pietism we turn to that movement which gave a distinctive name to the eighteenth century, often known, as it is, as the century of rationalism and philosophy. Rationalism, philosophy, toleration, those were the catchwords of the age.

It is singular how certain names, which, taken etymologically, only express what is good, easily assume a secondary meaning, which gives them an evil sound, or a double signification. If by rationalism be meant a *rational* system of religious doctrine, Protestantism, and Christianity itself demand it. An enemy of a reasonable faith, must necessarily be an enemy of the light, a friend of darkness. Christ calls his own, children of the light. He bids us to keep the inner eye of the spirit clear and open; he bids us to let our light shine before men, and not to hide it under a bushel. Yet it cannot escape us that the representations of light are very different from one another, that one calls light what another calls darkness, and *vice versa*. The mystic glories in his inner light, and believes that he walks in it, while the rationalist reproaches him with groping in the darkness of mere feeling, and praises his own system as the only bringer of light. And so two words sometimes arise which have both of them a good meaning at the outset, and the same etymological significance in fact, yet one acquires at last a bad sound, while the other does not lose its worth.

And so it always is. Men constantly separate what God joined together, so that the divine and human, instead of being reconciled and made one in Christ, fall farther and farther apart, and the spiritual and worldly, faith and knowledge, mind and soul, seriousness and sport, strength and mildness, are always appearing as antagonists, and the medium between them is a lost paradise, the entrance to which a cherub guards with flaming sword. Those who assume the one have no sensibility for the other, if indeed they are not set directly against it. The pietist, solely engrossed with keeping his spiritual life untroubled and undisturbed, looks with dismay upon the advance of doubt-awaking science, and holds himself carefully aloof from the joy and the cheer which the world offers to him. The rationalist, on the other hand, sees in every expression of living piety a timid pietism or Jesuitism; in every decisive espousal of faith he detects fanaticism, and often busies himself with attacking, like Don Quixote, imaginary windmills, in order to defend his strong posts of Reason and Liberty.

At the opening of the eighteenth century we see these contrasts more sharply drawn than at any other period. In the seventeenth century pietism and scepticism joined hands in opposition to the old orthodoxy, but now the orthodox and the pietists had met in close alliance to meet the common enemy, who, as it seemed, was now about to ravage the church. We have already seen what a movement Wolf's philosophy occasioned. And yet the system of Wolf was innocence itself in comparison with that which, under the name of deism and naturalism, came in from England and France, and appeared either openly or in more covert manner, and sought to recommend itself to those whose wish was to defend what was permanent in religion, and to let only the transitory go.

In the eighteenth century William Tindal, Thomas Morgan, and Lord Bolingbroke, inaugurated this infidel movement. We confine ourselves to the last named, because he formed as it were the step of transition to the French deists, who worked more directly upon the Germans than the English did. Bolingbroke is the real precursor of Voltaire. The earlier school of sceptics in England gave themselves to scientific discussions and investigations, but Bolingbroke appears a personified frivolity, which, under the name of culture and reason, sought to mount higher and higher in public estimation. In his attacks on the Christian religion, he assumed a light and witty rather than an earnest tone. Ridicule was the weapon with which he fought. Henry St John, his name before he entered the peerage, was born in 1672, of a noble family, and received his education at Eton and at Oxford. A fine figure, handsome manners, combining equally grace and ease, a vivacious mind, a lively imagination, a charming gift in conversation, made his fortune in the great world. By nature without self-control, he gave way to his passions, and at eight-and-thirty was an exhausted rake. In the place of sensuality came ambition. As a member of the House of Commons he espoused the tory side. Queen Anne made him a peer, Viscount Bolingbroke, yet he made his politics serve his ambition, and changed his colours as circumstances demanded. After George I. ascended the throne, Bolingbroke's career came to an end; after losing title and estate he fled to France, to escape trial for high treason. This was in 1715. The Pretender appointed him his keeper of the seal, but later Bolingbroke renounced his allegiance, became a whig, and received the royal pardon. Still after his return to England he was met with so much suspicion, that he held himself aloof from public gatherings, and confined himself to authorship. He died in 1751, nearly eighty years of age. He regarded religion, as Hobbes had done before him, as merely a part of the machinery of the state. Christianity and the church are only for governmental purposes. In consequence of his taking this low stand-point, he arrayed himself *against* the freethinkers, but only for this reason, because, by the destruction of Christianity, they took out of the people's mouth the bit which their coarse nature craved. All the religions of history he held to be the fabrication of priests, made for the uses of government, or the foolish and empty speculations of philosophers. Man can only know what his senses teach him, and that is what is reasonable; for the great crowd it is a good thing to have a divine revelation, or something called by that name. Sometimes Bolingbroke speaks as if he believed in the divine origin of primitive Christianity, and only rejected the theology which, in the course of time, had been spun out of the simple truth; but at other times he throws the mask wholly away, and Jesus is to him at the best but a Jewish reformer, who adapted himself to the Jewish prejudices when he did not himself share them. A rigid system is nowhere to be found in Bolingbroke. How could this be expected from a man who despised science as heartily as he did religion? Philosophy, which the other deists set so high, was to him a ridiculous thing, a web of vanity. Almost everything which a pure love of knowledge rescued from the past, he called mere useless antiquities; the whole east, with its rich poetry, and the whole of the Middle Ages, that mirror of the Orient in European history, was to the meagre understanding of the Englishman a long time of darkness and of barbarism. The darkness and the barbarism were rather in his own soul, and yet such wisdom as his was ravenously drunk up by his age. The approbation of the so-called good society, as it had been since the days of Louis XIV., was Bolingbroke's highest authority. What was ridiculed there he ridiculed, and what he, the accomplished man of the world, ridiculed, thousands laughed at in imitation. The applause which Bolingbroke received can be the more readily understood, when it is remembered that philosophy and history had become merely the property of the learned, and considered as having no connection with life. Science took a leap from stiff pompous pedantry to a light and attractive superficiality. Once taken thousands followed.

We have called Bolingbroke the precursor of Voltaire, and with Voltaire we begin to trace the great rationalistic movement which became the characteristic of the century. We cannot give here the history of Voltaire, nor offer a criticism of his works. He was in one word the representative of deism at the beginning of the eighteenth century. In our history of Protestantism we have to look rather at the influence of Voltaire over the Protestantism of Germany than to study him and his character. To him personally Protestantism and Catholicism were of equal worth; they were only various manifestations of the same superstitious spirit, which it was his mission to overthrow and annihilate. He was tired, he said, of hearing that it took twelve men to carry Christianity throughout the world, he would show that it takes but one to destroy it.

The first piece in which Voltaire assaulted Christianity was his poetical "Epître à Uranie," published in 1728, after his return from England. In this production he ridiculed the doctrines of the fall of man, original sin, the atonement of

Christ, eternal punishment—as ideas which he could not make harmonize with a sound reason and with a belief in a good God. He declares thus early his hostility to Christianity, and his belief that he can believe in God and yet not be a Christian, and in this we see his deism in contradistinction to atheism. "Only a madman," says Voltaire, "will blaspheme against God. I pray to Him. I am not a Christian, but only because I can worship God better as I am." Just as, still later, Schiller tells us that "out of sheer religion he belongs to no positive religion."

There was a time when Christian men wished to bind Voltaire's ideas with chains and put them behind stone walls, as it were, that they might be beyond the reach of those who would only draw poison from them into their own veins. I think, however, that I may say with confidence that the writings of Voltaire do not make the same impression as formerly upon a moral and thoroughly cultivated man. Even aside from all that relates to religion and Christianity, there is in the views of Voltaire on history, on literature, on poetry, with many spirited and witty remarks, a levity, there is a superficiality of judgment, which only repels the true thinker and the thorough inquirer, so that when any antagonist of Christianity arises, he only sharpens his arrow in Voltaire's sarcasm without borrowing any weapons from him. Nevertheless Voltaire's opinions have been diffused among a large class of men, without their reading a single word of his seventy volumes, or having much desire to go through such a mass. They drink his spirit in from a thousand sources, and so come just as speedily to his goal as if they were conversant with his own works. But where is this adoption of Voltaire's opinions the most general? Not among the thoroughly educated, not among the representatives of science, not among scholars and philosophers, but among that great class of the half-educated, those people who are not in a position to give any valuable judgment of their own on religious things, and who, while they are ashamed to believe in the simple Bible, have no misgivings about swearing allegiance to any infidel newspaper, or putting themselves under the guidance of any party leader. And I am convincd that a great part of what is called Straussism is less the expression of an intelligent appreciation of Strauss or any critical school, than it is a mere echo of Voltaire, whose outgrown philosophy, only lightly covered with a thin gloss of German thought, now exerts the same influence in lower circles that it once did in the higher.

If, for example, it belongs to a true scientific training, to be able to transfer oneself away from the limitations of his own mind, his own age, his own prejudices, and to live in other times and in the manners of thinking among past races of men, to seize upon the point of view adopted among other people, and to pass with readiness out of the common world of daily prose to the purer atmosphere of an ideal, poetical view, as the opponents of Christianity to-day are so able to do, we find no traces of such a power in Voltaire. We see him putting forth his flashing witticisms and gathering together random notes on nature and history, making himself merry over the Bible as a boy amuses himself with a starling or a floweret, making a melange of colours with his rough hand, and taking away all the beauty; or as he excites the cheap laughter of his schoolmates by painting a moustache on some fine antique. Just such the skill with which Voltaire treats the Bible, nor does he spare the Son of Man himself. Everything must be food for his merriment, and the grinning jaws devour all that comes in their way.

We will not deny to Voltaire a certain acuteness and a skill in discovering incoherences and mistakes, which others had unwittingly overlooked. He has called attention to many such in the Scriptures, to many chronological, historical, and dogmatic difficulties, which are hard to set aside. He has even brought to light many contradictions which commentators have been perplexed about, although the most of these he has not himself discovered, but has copied them from Celsus, Porphyry, and the English deists. But what the last named expressed with serious earnestness, he, at best an echo of Bolingbroke, has lightly thrown out into the public street, to be trampled under foot of all. Take for instance his manner of dealing with the Scriptural account of the creation. To him it is a matter of great difficulty that there was light four days before there was a sun! That man was made in the image of God is an idea which, more than any other, raises us out of the dust and gives us our glory, and yet to him it is a proof that Moses must have regarded God as a being in human form, and he is not ashamed to add this vile commentary on the whole, that "probably cats conceive of gods in the feline shape." In reference to the tree of knowledge of good and evil, he writes, "it is well known that *wine* makes men eloquent, but it is not known that it makes them learned; but that the fruit of a tree should confer learning—this is a rare thing indeed." This is the current of the whole book to which he has given the title, "La Bible enfin expliqué,"—The Bible explained *for the last time.* We will not follow longer in this strain. But for truth's sake we must say, that the previous experiences of Voltaire were such as to well cause him to believe that religion was an invention of priests and a source of intolerance. He had been educated among the Jesuits, had learned the whole vast scholastic theology of the Catholics, had taken legends and the biblical history at the same time and confused them all together. He lacked also that quiet and comprehensive reasoning power, which would have enabled him to discriminate the bad from the good, and perhaps we ought to add, he lacked that simple honesty and that strict conscientiousness, without which no one attains to truth. Protestantism he had only become acquainted with on a dry, hard side, as represented by the Calvinists of France; yet for the more genial side, as represented among the genuine Lutherans, he, a man without soul and without a quick fancy, had no adaptation. The selfishness and vanity of his nature were a barrier to his entering into the individuality of others. Religion he wanted to have, but only *his* religion. In some passages he commends the morality of Jesus, but in others he heaps on it bitter scorn. On the other hand he prided himself continually on his belief in God. But what a God was Voltaire's! An exalted Being, about whose existence the reason was always in warfare with itself—a lofty cloud-inhabiting abstraction, without heart and without love, without any fixed relations to the world and to man, only to be sought and found by the understanding of the learned, but not approachable by the heart, making no manifestation of himself in human form, and still less taking interest in the petty affairs of our life.

This is called deism, because it has no substance, but a bare belief in God, and He, too, a distant God, a Deus, "an unknown God," as the Athenians called Him when they erected an altar to Him. This faith is sometimes called naturalism, because its God is only known in the ordinary courses of nature. He is debarred from any miraculous powers. This deistic, naturalistic belief found many adherents during the eighteenth century, particularly in France. There were two schools of them, widely apart. There were those who had mocking, negativing no-faith, who rejected everything which was not plain to their common sense, and who advanced by quick steps from deism to atheism; and there were others who were really filled with serious longings to know the truth, and to test the dignity of the human soul, and its power to exist without a divine revelation. The first are represented by the Encyclopedists and their adherents, the last by Jean Jacques Rousseau. The Encyclopedists were a school of French writers at the time of Voltaire, who proposed to arrange and present all human sciences in one grand work, which should be written in view of the wants of the popular mind. Such a work, well executed, would have many good points, but it would have some bad ones. The writers might, if not strictly conscientious, take advantage of the credence given to them, to instil in the public mind opinions which would be dangerous. The Jesuits had employed similar means to impress their own distinctive ideas upon readers, and from them the Encyclopedists learned their skill.

Diderot and d'Alembert are to be named as the leading men who instituted and carried into completion the work referred to in the last paragraph, bearing the title, "Dictionnaire universel et raisonné des connaissances humaines," the first two volumes of which appeared in 1751. The spirit of these men is not only to be traced in religion, but also in other things. The men who imagine that music has its source in our need "of making a noise," could not have a very deep insight into religious truth. Of real philosophy, that is, a power of withdrawing the mind from the external world, and concentrating its activities upon the world of ideas alone, they had no conception. They were good mathematicians, especially d'Alembert. But all that transcended time and space lay beyond their province. The author of the "Système de la Nature," and also Helvetius, had the same quality of mind with the Encyclopedists. The authorship of that work has been attributed to different persons, but it is commonly ascribed to the Baron von Holbach. This book, which appeared in 1770, goes far beyond anything that Voltaire had ever written. The latter had not attempted to destroy the belief in God, and among the Encyclopedists had acquired a name for superstition, and for clinging to outgrown ideas, but in the "Système de la Nature," God is not treated of as a personal existence. His control of the world is denied; everything is ascribed to the rankest naturalism, and all that we call the attributes of a human spirit,—justice, freedom, honour, conscience, modesty, sorrow, are held to be only the mutual play of the senses. Helvetius held to the same doctrines, and traced all the noblest deeds of men to selfishness, which appeared to him the spring of human action, and must only be held in control by prudence. Virtue, according to Helvetius, is nothing but the habit of so ordering our acts, that they shall be to the advantage of the largest number of men, and the true function of morality consists in reconciling in the best manner what profits us and what profits others.

Thus deism advanced to atheism, and naturalism to materialism. The fruits of this infidelity showed themselves only too soon. Not indeed that the easy morals, which first diffused themselves among the higher classes, and then reached to the common people, were the first results of these abstract theories. Theory came in this case after practice. Long before, even in the pious age of Louis XV., the principles which Helvetius taught, had been largely adopted in life, they now received their sanction, the stamp of philosophical evidence was now set upon them. Singularly it was a German, in whose salon at Paris a select circle of freethinkers chiefly assembled, Baron von Holbach, a native of the Palatinate, the reputed author of the Système de la Nature, and the publisher, through his wealth, of many such works. It is not our purpose to look into these productions here. We pass over Condillac, and the men of that class, and turn to the man in whom deism displayed itself in a more earnest and serious manner, who sought to make of it a real religion, and whose soul was full of it, even to fanaticism, Jean Jacques Rousseau.

If Voltaire, as well as the Encyclopedists, had their training in the bosom of the Catholic church, Rousseau stands nearer to us, from the fact that he was a son of the city which was the mother of French Protestantism, Geneva. His life is well known to us from his own "Confessions." We learn from that book, that although born of Protestant parents he went early to a Catholic church, but afterwards returned to the Calvinists, although the system which he framed was just as far from Calvin's dogmas as it was from the creed of Rome. On its negative side, in its denial of all historical authority in religion, in its view of the Bible, the ideas of Rousseau agreed entirely with those of Voltaire and the other deists; but not in what would be substituted in place of what was denied. Here he stood in complete contrast to them, and in no special alliance with them, he despising them as much as they ridiculed him. What they put great value upon, a glittering career in the world of fashion, was to Rousseau, until his death, a most unattractive thing; and while they set their hopes of their age, and the regeneration of the world on what they called science, fine art, and general enlightenment, he held to a return to simplicity, to nature, even to barbarism. It is singular that here the decided deist strikes hands with the most rigid pietists, who saw in science and the highest mental culture only peril for the moral life, although the results which followed these narrow premises were different in both cases. The mass of the French freethinkers were materialistic, but Rousseau was a thorough idealist; and while the former sought a kind of epicurean delight in refining their pleasures, the latter sought, like the Stoics, to make himself entirely independent of what ministered to sensual delight, and to pay no regard to the opinions of men regarding him. Certainly more in theory than in fact! For in getting a real mastery over himself in a Christian sense, or even in a stoical sense, he made no great progress. What Christianity would gain through the love of our fellow men, he would attain through hatred to them and a dark fanaticism. And with all his efforts to be the servant to none, he remained his whole life long the servant of his own whims and passions. His own confessions, his domestic life, reveal this most clearly. But so far as it is possible to pass a favourable judgment on the principles of a man, viewed from his own life, we must do justice to Rousseau's theory, and confess that it proceeded from a more noble desire than did that of Voltaire and his friends; and though it is not free from great errors, yet it is more adapted to promote the aims of an earnest and an aspiring mind, than the sophisms of Holbach and Helvetius.

In his Emile, Rousseau has propounded a scheme of education, containing some novel views, but much that is worthy of consideration; but in his work called Confessions of a Savoyard Vicar, he has expounded his religious faith. In it we see the sharp lines of separation between a strict deism and atheism, or materialism, on the one side, and a positive Christian faith on the other. In antagonism to the former, Rousseau makes his vicar affirm in the most eloquent terms his belief in the spiritual part of man, in his higher destiny, in a divine Providence and government. A denier of God and a denier of the soul, is in Rousseau's eyes a man to whom is lacking one leading sense; and while Diderot leaves to a man born blind the advocacy of his scheme, Rousseau compares an unbeliever to a deaf man, who only sees the vibration of the string without knowing anything of the dulcet sounds which it is giving forth. Man, according to him, is a free being, and is accountable for his acts. Not God and Nature, but he himself, is responsible for his sufferings. What Schiller said later in his harmonious verse,—

> "The world is everywhere a perfect thing,
> Where human discords no confusion bring,"

Rousseau expressed in his neat French prose: God, the eternal God, can only will what is right. Do thou, man, do what thou knowest good, and thou wilt be blessed in it. Desire not thy wages before thy service, God *owes* thee nothing. In another world everything will be made right, there a great system of compensation will be revealed. Let the contradiction between soul and body be ended by death, and the riddle of our being will be solved. Thus Rousseau declared his belief in personal freedom, in immortality, in a Beyond, at which the materialists all flung their ridicule. With the pietists, he regarded the union of soul and body as an unnatural one; the soul is in a prison, and will sometime be free; it will first breathe that air of heaven when, freed from this body, it shall arrive at its home. To link the destruction of the soul to that of the body as the materialists do, would only be true philosophy, if soul and body were connected in that close and inner sense, which the leaders of this school have taught. But the soul is the true man, on which the body hangs as a heavy weight, and therefore the man only half lives while here in the body; his true life does not begin till the Pysche freely unfurls its wings and sails away from earth. Regarding the manner of our future existence we can know nothing. The highest happiness which a reasonable mind can ask for itself, is, that instead of receiving any reward, it may know God and live conformably to its own nature. For the rest we have our judgment pronounced upon our actions in our own souls. The conscience, the law of nature, which God has not denied to the most savage tribes, and which seems more fresh and outspoken with these than with the educated and accomplished, is a heavenly voice, the safest guide that we have to follow in the dark course of life. Through the conscience we are exalted and made like to God. The conscience transcends all far-reaching ethical speculations, and makes needless all the discussions of philosophers. Yet not all *know* the voice, but all *wish* to know it; for it is a soft and gentle voice, and is easily drowned by louder ones. Yet it never dies wholly out, it always sounds forth its appeal to enter on the battle of life, where alone is the field for virtue. And this battle is one of the sad conditions of our human lot.

These are the fundamental principles of the so-called natural religion, as the Savoyard priest lays them down, speaking for Rousseau in direct antagonism to theory, which ascribes everything to accident, to the senses, to selfishness. God, Freedom, and Immortality, constitute the holy triad of Rousseau's religion of reason. And who would not prefer such a faith, to that comfortless faith of the Encyclopedists, degrading mau to a mere brute? A question arises indeed, namely, whether this desire of Rousseau retains all that the Christian religion gives to its disciples; more than this, whether such a faith would be conceivable without Christianity and without a revelation; or whether, on the contrary, these views he so decisively set forth, and with so much apparent conviction, are not, after all, the reflection of the light which we owe to Christianity, and which Rousseau had received in his youth, without giving due credit to its source.

After the vicar has laid down the first principles of natural theology, he comes to speak of a revelation. Here, too, we meet a kind of language entirely unlike that used by Voltaire and the Encyclopedists. It seems as if the recollections of his childhood came back afresh upon him, and wrung from him a confession of their truth. His words about Christ are well known. He compares him to Socrates,—" but what a difference," he says, "between the son of Sophroniscus and the son of Mary! Socrates dies with honour, surrounded by his disciples, listening to the most tender words—the easiest death that one could wish to die; Jesus dies in pain, dishonoured, mocked, the object of universal cursing—the most horrible death which one could fear. At the receipt of the cup of poison Socrates blesses him who could not give it to him without tears; Jesus while suffering the sharpest pains, prays for his most bitter enemies. If Socrates lived and died like a philosopher, Jesus lived and died like a God." Of the historic truth of these, even Rousseau is entirely persuaded. "Such an event," he says, "is no invention of men." The history of Socrates is not so credible to him as the history of Jesus. They who deny it, he thought, only increased the difficulties of the case. "It would be more incredible," remarks Rousseau, "for a number of men to fabricate such a book, than that it should contain the account of a real life. No Jewish writers assumed the tone, none expressed the morality of the gospel. It has such striking marks of truth, such inimitable marks, that the writer of such books would be a greater wonder than their hero." But now comes the other side. This very gospel is so full of things which are incredible, which repel the reason, that no intelligent man can accept it.

This continued and unsatisfied doubting had for Rousseau, according to his confession, nothing painful. His belief in the truths of natural theology remained unshaken, and so too did his reverence of Christ, although the acceptance of a Revelation was never assured him. All religions he regards as so many helpers of mankind, and they recommend themselves to different peoples according to their geographical conditions and the extent of their intellectual and spiritual cultivation. The main point with every man should be, to accept that faith which best answers the needs of his own conscience. True worship is not that of the head but that of the heart. It is this last which expresses itself in every outward form and which brings a blessing. And so the Catholic vicar confesses, that since he gained this heart religion, he officiates at all the rites of the church with more true satisfaction than ever before. Everything now has for him life, significance; everything becomes the symbol and the expression of some unspeakable feeling. He has become zealous in his work, full of love, patience, humility, happiness, and contentment.

Some years before Rousseau, in 1738, Maria Huber, a Genevan by birth, but a resident of Lyons, had published her letters on the "Essence of Religion," in which she traced all religion to the moral necessities of the heart, and considered a Revelation as a mere auxiliary to natural theology, a means of interpreting it to our consciousness. Natural theology, as given to us in the conscience, is the beginning and the end of all religion, and it is for man to attain to its full possession. To aid in this, Revelation, *i.e.*, the historical statement of natural theology, has its function. But Revelation only attains to its true purpose when it leads, unfolds, and stimulates, but is not an indispensable thing; and as no teacher fulfils his highest duty when he puts into his scholars' hands the tasks all completed, so revelation does not commit to unreasoning minds God's great lessons all wrought out into elementary principles. God needs no service of men, no honour from us. Always happy in himself, he wishes only the happiness of his creatures. That is the goal of all religion. God can receive no injury from men; the immoral man injures only himself, when he degrades himself, and, therefore, God cannot be angry, he cannot punish eternally. Neither our own nor others' good works make him complacent towards us, but everything which we have is the gift of his free grace, or to use simpler language, of his good will towards men. This doctrine is the central truth of Christianity and of the Scriptures, but men must separate the husk from the kernel, and only retain the latter.

Thus far Maria Huber. And who will not confess that this mild and kindly faith, full of love and good-will, has not something attractive in it, compared with the stiff, and cold, and damnatory orthodoxy with which she had to deal. And when we look back over the systems of Rousseau and Maria Huber, can we fail to see that there manifests itself in them a desire to attain, in the lack of what is merely historical and traditional, something real, something living. In Bolingbroke and Voltaire we have seen a deism which, with hatred and scorn of all that is Christian, yet recognised a personal God, a Being exalted, but without any action upon or relation to the heart of man; a pure religion of the understanding, which, in the author of the Système de la Nature, and the Encyclopedists, issued in pure atheism and materialism; but in Rousseau and Maria Huber, there comes to light a deism united to human feelings, in sympathy in some respects with Christianity, and in other respects antagonistic to it. All of these views have found acceptance with the more cultivated classes of the European world since the middle of the eighteenth century. Men had tired of the old strife between Catholicism and Protestantism, between orthodoxy and pietism. The hostile parties having fought to nakedness, what wonder that there should be a wish for something newer and more satisfying? And it is noticeable in this view, that in the very countries in which the deistical tendencies showed themselves, the old churches had sunk into decay and feebleness, and had little to offer. Neither the Church of England nor the Catholic clergy of France, having no more a Bossuet or a Fénélon among their number, could interpose barriers to these tendencies. Puritanism on the one side of the channel, and Jansenism on the other, were exhausted, and Protestantism in neither country had any great names to point at among the living. Even Genevan theology was not, in the times of Rousseau and Maria Huber, what it had once been; the mildness and the conciliatory spirit of an Osterrald and a Turretin, could not stem the newly-rising stream. And so deism soon gained control of literature, and Pope, Swift, and others, only diffused it wider, using the effective channels of satire, didactic poetry, and light periodicals. History, which Bossuet had treated solely from the theocratic stand-point, was subject in England to the method of Hume, in France to that of Montesquieu, and was then given to the great susceptible public. A free man must be free from all authority, his judgment must be unfettered by any tradition, and all the past must lie as a wreck at his feet, useless and unused!

In Germany a more definite remainder of the old historic Christianity existed than elsewhere, as our brief account of pietism has shewn. Yet the one-sidedness of the pietistic theology, the multiplicity of sects, showed that a crisis and a change were at hand. Great men were rare among the German theologians, and so the imported deism soon swept through the rifts of the church, and gained supreme control of literature. And it is Frederick the Great who comes before us as the representative of Voltaire's ideas in Germany, and who therefore must rightly interpret his age to us as his father has already done for his.

VI.

FREDERICK THE GREAT AND HIS AGE.

WE purpose to present Frederick the Great as the representative of his times, after the same manner in which we portrayed Frederick William First as the representative of his own. It is not the victor at Mollwitz, at Rossbach, and at Leuthen, upon whom we wish to look, but the philosopher of San-Souci, the friend of Voltaire, the author and the king, so far as his authorship and his royalty were related to religion and ecclesiastical affairs. We must hold ourselves strictly to these limits, if we will not wander too far from our purpose. Yet with all the limitations which we will lay upon ourselves, we cannot wholly pass over the youth of Frederick, because it offers to us the key to his whole subsequent career. It only proves the truth of what a noted preacher of Berlin afterwards said, "The ship was so heavily laden with religious ballast, that it was not possible that it should not go down."

In speaking of his father, we have already spoken of Frederick's education, or rather of the plan according to which it was conducted. We need only refer to the compulsory prayer which he repeated every morning, and the rigid orthodoxy in which his young heart was so strictly drilled. To complete that picture I need only say that the prince was often compelled, by his father's command, to learn by heart and repeat penitential psalms, and extracts from the Catechism, as a punishment for youthful indiscretions.

We leave behind us the boy Fritz, for whose welfare these well-intentioned arrangements were made, and look into the fiery eye of the young man. We regard him in quite a different light from that in which his father saw him. He discerned in Frederick only a weakling, a mere flute player, "a fifer and poet," useless for war or for a throne; and that set the father's heart against him. He blamed him because he took no delight in hunting and in meeting with the tobacco parliament, called him a selfish bad spirit, who lived only to oppose his father; an effeminate rascal, without the pluck of a man; a proud, imperious, hating, exclusive, and all this after the prince had written an humble, filial letter to his father, and assured him of all a son's love and dutiful respect. The animosity of Frederick William to learning, when it did not stand in direct relation to practical life, has been already referred to. The prince must be trained on the same principle. But the son shewed an inclination for everything which aided culture, taste, and enlightenment, and early displayed a receptive mind, as did also his sister Wilhelmine, afterwards the Countess of Baireuth. His friends were chosen after his own tastes. Quandt, the flute player, and Lieutenant von Katte were his most intimate companions. It was the last, whose tragic fate was so closely woven in with the fortunes of the Prince Frederick, who, in order to escape from the incessant and even public harshness of his father, formed a plan to fly to England, in which von Katte was accessory. Through some mishap the design was disclosed; the prince was arrested, and barely escaped his father's dagger, who had drawn it in his first rage, by an officer thrusting himself between him and the prince, and saying, "Sire, strike at me, but spare your son." Frederick and Katte were tried before a court-martial. The decision was favourable to the prince, but it decided that the lieutenant be dismissed from the army, and be imprisoned for life. But this decision was too mild for the king. Although he was not accustomed (he wrote to the court) to complain of lenient verdicts, and to try to get them made more strict (which was not quite true), yet in this case he must say, *Fiat justitia et pereat mundus.* In perfect justice Katte ought to be torn apart with hot irons, yet out of regard to his family, he would be content with his simple execution by beheading. The king was very sorry, but it was better that he should die than that justice perish from the earth. Such was the monarch's decision, and in addition was set the cruel clause that Frederick must be the witness of his friend's death; it occurred in 1730. Katte was twenty-two years old, the prince but twenty. The latter remained in close imprisonment by the king's order. To be strictly watched, his warders being under fear of death if they showed him any clemency, to be meagrely fed, to be denied all society, and even paper and ink, and a dread of even a harder fortune yet, if his father's caprice should dictate it, was his hard lot. But for the soul of the young man, the king made excellent provision. The Lutheran chaplain Müller was ordered to expound to him the word of God, and to warn him to repent of his sins. Frederick paid good heed to the clergyman's counsel, and discussed the doctrine of Election with him, taking the Calvinistic side, and sorely perplexing his antagonist, who spoke freely of the prince's penitential spirit, and so by degrees the father's heart softened. "The Almighty God," he wrote to the chaplain, "give His blessing; and as he often brings men by wonderful paths into the kingdom of Christ, may the Saviour give his help, that this wretched son may be brought to a sense of his unworthiness, his godless heart be touched, softened, and changed, and he be torn out of Satan's claws." On Frederick's taking an oath, without any reservation, he was released from his hard imprisonment. He sealed the oath by a public acceptance of the Lord's Supper. Still he was obliged to remain in Küstrin, and be under spiritual charge. The morning and evening prayers must, by the king's order, still be kept up. The prince, moreover, was compelled to pay attention to practical branches, political economy among them. In another year he was released from

Küstrin, on the occasion of his sister's marriage; and soon after, in 1733, he was himself joined in the same relation to the Princess Elizabeth of the Brunswick family. It was as a political convenience solely that this marriage was dictated, and it is well known that there was never any congenial sympathy between the two. In the little city of Rheinsberg, where the king gave him a home, he first began to live a life congenial to his tastes. He assembled artists and scholars about him, invited distinguished foreigners to share his hospitalities, and in these circles, quite unlike his father's tobacco parliament, he felt truly happy. He gave himself to study in all his leisure hours. On the 10th of February 1738, he writes, "I am buried in books deeper than ever, and how gladly would I make chase after the time which I lost in my childhood; and so far as I can I gather around me a group of knowledges and truths."

In his retirement he prosecuted the study of Wolf's philosophy, and began his Correspondence with Voltaire, sending him a translation of the charges made against Wolf, and the defence, and thus awoke the interest of the French philosopher in the German one. Voltaire felt flattered by these unexpected advances of the Crown Prince, while Frederick conceived a new admiration of the author and wit. "Nothing is wanting here in Rheinsberg," he writes to Voltaire, "to make my happiness complete, but you. Your portrait adorns my library; it stands directly over the case which holds my Golden Fleece, and your works, and exactly opposite to the place where I sit, so that I can have you always before me." He writes to him again, 1739: "There are but one God and one Voltaire in the world, and God had need of a Voltaire to be the ornament of this age." "Were I a heathen," he says again, "I would worship you under the name of Apollo: were I a Jew, I would assign you a place beside the kingly Prophet and His Son; were I a Papist, I would make you guardian saint and my father confessor: but as I am no one of these, I can do no more than content myself with admiring you as a philosopher, loving you as a poet, and honouring you as a friend." This style of advice, which sounds like what we call in this day the worship of genius, and from which the truly Christian spirit shrinks, and which is not too hardly condemned as frivolous and idolatrous, we can only comprehend and excuse by recalling the sad history of the Prince's childhood. It is the spirit of youth, breaking away from its fetters, and exulting in its freedom, as the horse stamps on the ground when freed from the constraints of the stable, and snuffs the free air in a wild liberty. In Voltaire, Frederick worshipped an idol, but behind this idol he really paid unconscious adoration to the Unknown God—to the spirit of a new age—an age for which he was preparing the way, and which, through a thousand battle fields, must come to a clear knowledge of itself. That the issue *must* be different from what it was in Frederick-William's time, is plain. What better thing should come, Frederick could not know nor suspect. He served merely as the instrument in a Higher Hand. Yet it would not be right, with all the Prince's fanciful admiration of genius, to reckon him among the opponents of positive Christianity. He expected rather to reach his ideal of spiritual freedom, of mental breadth, and human welfare, through the medium of a more enlightened Christianity. He honoured the ministers of the Gospel, and asked of them instruction in the mysteries of their faith. He confessed to the pastor of the French colony that his faith was unfortunately weak, but that it was his earnest desire to strengthen it, and to see decisive proofs of the truth of Christianity; and, like all the better Deists, he confessed his admiration of the morality revealed in the Gospel. He was so deeply affected by the preaching of an aged French minister, Isaak de Beausobre, a learned and clear-minded man, that he showed him particular attentions. He had a great respect for Reinbeck, his father's chaplain. He read with great eagerness the works of the great French preachers, Flêchier, Bossuet, Massillon, Bourdaloue, and the Protestant Saurin. Yet it was the oratorical power, the logic, the moral element and the principles of universal religion, which most attracted him. The strictly Christian phases, which had appeared so decisively in the Reformation, and (though rather one-sidedly) among the pietists, had no charm for his mind, struggling for what was broad, general, cosmopolitan. The time had not come when a sense for what is strictly Christian and for what is thoroughly human, could be joined in the same person. Since the death of the old Protestant orthodoxy, there was left to an earnest, vital soul like his, only a choice between a rigid pietism and deism. Half-way measures were foreign to his nature, and it was not his calling to organize a third system of doctrine. He was a warrior, not a theologian. So he made his decision for deism, and was committed to it wholly when he ascended the throne. Yet Frederick the Great comprehended perfectly his calling, as a descendant of the Great Elector, to be a Protestant king. When he transferred the bones of his ancestors to the crypt of the new cathedral of Berlin, in 1750, he had the coffin of the Elector opened, took up the withered hand, covered it with tears, and said to those who stood by, "Messieurs, that man did a great work!" Yes, he did a great work for the Church of Christ. And although we cannot say so emphatically of the great-grandson that *he* did a great work, in its direct relations to the Church, yet we cannot exclude that wide-reaching influence which he did exert for the history of Protestantism. Not through a positive faith, but from a political position which he assumed, as counterpoise to the Catholic powers of Europe, Frederick's place in history was thoroughly Protestant. He it was who set Prussia at the head of all the Protestant interests of Germany. And without him, who can tell how Protestantism would now stand? And his labours in behalf of personal freedom and toleration, his abolishing of the rack and other cruelly severe modes of punishment, as well as many abuses in government,—his restoring Wolf to his Chair at Halle, and raising philosophy to its rightful place,—all these things are worthy of a place in the life of a Protestant king. The injuries which his secular and sometimes unchristian manner of thinking diffused among the higher orders of society, we will not dispute; but these injuries were transitory, and were neutralised at a later day by the counter movement, while the benefit which accrued from his victories, and many of the institutions which he established, and his wise regulations, have remained, and we ought to rejoice in them.

The great care of the king was for universal freedom of conscience. Did Frederick-William I. burden the Lutheran clergy of his time by forbidding the wearing of surplices, the lighting of candles upon the altar, in order to promote ecclesiastical union, Frederick II., soon after ascending the throne in 1740, issued an order freeing the Churches of this burden, and leaving open to themselves and their ministers to adopt whatever form of service they might choose. The Lutheran preachers praised him, therefore, as a second Solomon. He exhibited the same tolerance to the Catholics. In the summer of the year when he ascended the throne, a petition was made to him for permission to found a school for the children of Roman Catholic soldiers. Upon the margin of this petition he wrote, "All religions must be tolerated, and the authorities must only see to this, that one sect does no harm to any other, for every man must get to heaven his own way." And so he gave to the Catholics a larger measure of freedom than they had ever enjoyed before. He took their church in Berlin under his own protection, and erected for it the edifice which it continues to use, which was built in imitation of the Pantheon in Rome, and which is one of the chief architectural beauties of the Prussian capital. A professorship of medicine was vacant in the University at Breslau, and the candidate was not only a Catholic but a supposed Jesuit; yet an old regulation only allowed a Protestant to fill the place. "No matter about *that*," said Frederick, "if the man is skilful, but the physicians are too good doctors to need a religion." Yet with all his tolerance of the Catholics he was careful that they should be just as patient with the Protestants as the Protestants should be with the Catholics. In a letter written in 1756 to the Bishop of Breslau, he expressed his decisive will, that all controversial sermons should be forbidden in churches and convents. The forbearance of the king went yet further, he gave the Greek Christians a place for worship in Breslau, and he shewed the same favour to the Unitarians in Lithuania, and in East Friesland. He laid no opposition on the efforts of the Moravians and kindred organizations. All that was imposed was, they should be quiet, and not try to proselytize. The grand principle which he laid down for his conduct in all these matters was this, to shun the disturbing of people who were satisfied with the sect to which they belonged, by showing that you have such a regard for them as even to compel them to abandon their errors through the strong arm of the law; since experience has always shewn that when people are dealt with compulsorily in matters of belief, they grow more opinionated than ever, become fanatics, and come at last to fancy that there must be something very wonderful in what has to call out the powers of the state to repress it. On the other hand, when such people are let alone, are shown that they are worth no attention, that they deserve pity rather than contempt, if the government only look to it, so far as to make the leaders leave the land, and see that the followers only discharge the duties of good citizens, they generally become ashamed of their folly, and either come back, or make no impression on the minds of others, and see no growth to their ideas. So when in 1743 a carpenter was accused before Frederick of preaching at the corners of the streets, the king said, "If he does nothing against the laws and good morals, let him preach."

Yet it was a very easy thing for Frederick to enjoin toleration, for he had no conception of the power of a real spiritual life on the one hand, nor the strength of religious hallucinations on the other. All those things which separate men into sects, and make differences of theological opinion, seemed to him to be nothing but the working out of a folly to which he was altogether superior. And, mild as he would seem under some circumstances, under others he expressed his indifference to religion with a cutting severity, which pained pious and sensitive souls as much perhaps as open opposition would have done. In an order which he issued in 1781, with reference to the hymn book to be used in the churches, he wrote—"In my dominions any man can believe just as he pleases. As for the hymn book, let any one be free to sing, 'Now rest the peaceful forests,' or any other stupid foolishness he likes. But the priests must not forget that no permission is allowed them to be intolerant." He spoke always very depreciatingly of the clergy. He called them parsons, even in public documents, and was careful that they should have as little influence as possible over affairs, and especially over education. Theology seemed to him to be a foolish branch of study, and the theologian was compared to a beast with reason left out. He made incessant ridicule of the pietists, and in a manner which did not consist very well with his vaunted toleration.

There was an instance of this in one of the first years of his reign. When, in 1745, Professor Francke of Halle raised an opposition to the theatre, as injurious to good order among the students, the king wrote on the margin of the report, "That is the work of these wretched psalm-singers. They *shall* play, and Herr Francke, or whatever the rascal is called, shall go to the theatre and make a public retractation before the students, of his miserable meddling, and the manager of the theatre shall be the attest that he goes and does it." Elsewhere, he writes—"The Halle parsons must be held by a tight rein, they are evangelical Jesuits, and not the slightest power must be trusted to them." The authorities to whom was committed the affair of Francke, pleaded with the king to commute the sentence, but for a long time he was firm; yet at last he yielded, and changed it to a fine of twenty thalers, which he must pay for the benefit of the poor; and Francke paid it. Had a deist been compelled to go within a church, or be fined, what an outcry would there have been among the friends of toleration!

When the expressions of Frederick the Great about theologians and pietists are compared with those of Frederick William about philosophers, poets, and artists, the same roughness is remarked in both: and unlike as were father and son in the objects of their censure and approbation, yet there is a striking similarity observable in both, a certain fitful and despotic humour, which can exist with a rigid orthodoxy as well as with an assuming and arbitrary scepticism, but has not part in a truly Christian spirit.

But Frederick's conduct must not be looked at too much in detail—the true light is only thrown upon it, when we examine it as conditioned by the circumstances of the time. If we look at these, and especially at the men by whom he was surrounded, we discover that it was not Voltaire alone, by any means, who exercised influence over him, but that he was on intimate terms with many refugees from France, who had been mostly summoned from Holland to Berlin. The chief of these was a physician named La Mettrie, one of the most bold and pronounced ridiculers of religion, who even propagated a system of open immorality. The Marquis d'Argens, who belonged to the same circle, said of him, that "he preached the doctrine of blasphemy with the shamelessness of a fool." La Mettrie died in 1751 of a surfeit caused at a dinner given by the English Ambassador to Berlin, and Frederick honoured his memory by writing a eulogy, which was read in the academy.

Yet while Frederick gave a home to these French refugees and encouraged *their* free-thinking, he did not seem willing, early in his reign, that this new tendency should reach his own people, find expression in the German language, and become the popular belief. A German, Gebhardi by name, had published two works in 1743, in which he attacked the biblical miracles. By the king's command these books were suppressed, and in 1748 a young man named Rüdiger was sent to Spandau for six months in consequence of a like offence. Still the diffusion of sceptical principles could not be prevented, and, without being published, they found their way even more quickly with the mighty help of example in high places. And in later times Frederick put no check on any means to spread his ideas abroad, as we learn from the free expressions in his letters to Voltaire. These two strengthened each other in the effort to make an end of Christianity, or as they expressed it, "d'ecraser l'infame." Both wished each other success in the work; both hoped to live to see the time when the strangled thing should be buried never to rise again. And how idly they laboured, how foolishly they dreamed, and how fleeting their triumph! That religion, which Voltaire likened in a letter to Frederick to a loaf of black bread, that at the best is only good for dogs; that religion still lives, and kings and wise men eat from it, and all are satisfied with this bread of life, and how many have turned back hungry to this bread, after dulling their teeth to no purpose on the old and hard-baked white bread which Voltaire gave them! Yet historic truth compels me to say, in justice to Frederick, that while he combatted Christianity, he meant only to combat a religion of intolerance and superstition; that he pursued the ever-enlarging shadow, while he sought the true light elsewhere,—in philosophy. Frederick held with Voltaire to a belief in a Supreme Existence, in contradistinction to the atheists and the materialists, while he repudiated wholly the "Système de la

Nature," and even wrote a paper against it, which Voltaire praised. He conversed with scholars and thinkers on the immortality of the soul, yet he could not bring himself to accept it fully, and held that virtue was a sufficient good in itself even without reference to reward in another life. He once replied to a member of the academy, who wanted to read him a long argument for the immortality of the soul: "How so? You want to be immortal. But what have you done to deserve it?"

In the main, it was the insufficient proofs with which men tried to defend Christianity, and the false premises from which they proceeded, which called out Frederick's keenest wit and satire. What he found fault with often rested upon the confounding of what was essentially Christian with what had been assumed by the orthodox and the pietists. In order to get a true view of his character, we must continually go back to his education and to the impressions which he had received in his childhood. A multitude of his contemporaries thought and felt as he did, if they did not speak, or if they did not dare to speak it out as he did. We must beware, therefore, of misjudging the man. Nothing is easier, in our secure and easy possession of what we have, than to fall into false judgments of those who, in their time and amid their surroundings, and in altogether different mental conditions, have had a harder road to walk than we. This comfortable cherishing of a proud orthodoxy, while we look down upon our erring brothers as on the firebrands of hell, without a suspicion of the groans which the dagger of doubt has drawn from souls struggling after the truth: this easy enjoyment of the pillow of an inherited faith, which brushes away old doubts as it would brush away the flies from the body in order to sleep the sounder, and then rise refreshed to attack more stoutly those who would gladly disturb such pleasant slumbers, this truly is not the faith which is well pleasing to God, the faith that "overcometh the world." We will not go so far as to say that Frederick was a man who fought great spiritual battles for faith's sake, he was rather a hero on the field than in theologic warfare. He was no calm, systematic thinker, but he was no sleeper and dreamer as his father supposed him; his was a powerful, conquering nature. It was only natural that the doubts which lay in the bosom of his times should harden into graver errors in him rather than in weaker minds, and that what began in conquering would end in annihilating. That he sought his enemy in the wrong quarter, that he formed a dangerous alliance with double-minded friends, that he pulled down where he ought to have built up, that he wounded where he ought to have healed, that by the side of the fair plants which we owe to him he trod down the far fairer ones, which had been so richly blessed in the reign of his great-grandfather the Elector, instead of cherishing them, these are faults, they are deeds of violence, they are, if you will, sacrilege—I grant even this. But if we judge in this (and the judgment has been pronounced in history), let us guard ourselves from taking God's place in sitting in trial upon men who have themselves appealed to a higher measure of their lives than a mere human verdict. Frederick the Great shall be to us the expression of his age. God did not set him without a purpose in the period in which he lived. In him the spirit of his age found its picture, and the scepticism which had long been working among the roots of church life, come in him to the light, the smouldering spark burst into a clear flame.

Yet it would not be right to say that the age of Frederick the Great was wholly represented in him, so that when we have studied his character we have exhausted his age. We must recognise counter currents which he himself had to meet, such, for example, as the pietistic movement. But these were rather the relics of past days, and not what expressed the real spirit of the times. And this spirit of the times, too, had its own modifications, and we should present an untrue picture if we should say that deism, as held by Frederick and Voltaire, was the religion of most of their contemporaries. It certainly was not, for with only a very few had it come to this. But we shall not lead astray if we say, that for forty years there had been spreading over Germany a mode of thinking which, if it seemed to stand on the same ground with the old orthodoxy, yet bore in itself the germs from which, although perhaps years later, the deistical, critical, and rationalistic tendency would spring. One only needed to have eyes to see that the times were changed. There meet us other forms, other faces, other costumes, other customs, and, which is the chief thing in Germany, another use of language and another literature, another mode of educating, another way of seeing and judging of things. With all that remained of the past clinging to its skirts, the age was changed, was modernized. There is nothing more difficult to describe in words than a new epoch so thoroughly made over, for that which is commonly called the spirit of the age is seldom a definite and comprehensible thing like a sequential system, it is a fleeting cloud picture in which the beams of light fall apart ere they hardly have completed their image. All these varying colours do form unmistakably the representation of an age, and, when blended, they constitute its distinct though evanescent expression. So there are formed, under the influence of one great and paramount influence, a nomenclature, a method of reasoning, a style, which exert uncontrollable influence on contemporaries, and which even throw their spell over those who stand in opposition to the great tendencies of the age, so that, although they may in outward affairs seem to follow the old ways, in spirit they are radically changed. As in the times of the old orthodoxy, there was an orthodox phraseology for those who were far removed from the living faith which had been the mother of that language, so since the middle of the eighteenth century there has been a language of freethinking, of infidelity, which has entered more and more into literature, for just as coins sometimes change their value, so do words change their meaning. As in the olden time, men spoke of faith, of justification, of sin, of salvation and sanctification, of the kingdom of God, of enlightenment and grace, so in the time of Frederick they spoke of virtue, honour, freedom, manhood, human right, reason, and toleration. Even the language of the pulpit had to be adapted to this new nomenclature, if it would not stand like a decaying and deserted ruin. Only few have the power to oppose such a stream, and to stand upright like a mossy monument of solid rock. Not all have a call to do and be this. What with one man is true power, acknowledged power, with another is mere caprice and folly, and such a one makes himself a laughing-stock if he tries to turn or stop the current of the age. The most allow themselves to be borne unresistingly on by this current, but here and there are seen some children of the age, and its leaders, too, who will not suffer themselves to be swept blindly away, but who, keeping their senses alert, let themselves be gently borne on by the tremendous current, but keep the shore always in sight, and press on, accommodating themselves to present troubles, but at last reach the distant land. Such men are the heroes of their age.

It has been charged as a fault on Frederick the Great, that he, who would seem to be so specially the man to develope the capacities of the German literature, should have neglected it so signally in behalf of the French. But it is not in every one's power to detect, with prophetic eye, in the opening bud all the beauty and excellence of the fruit which is to come: to do this needs experience; and there was little reason for Frederick to see such richness in the hard German of his time. And if it was his misfortune that he did not detect its unopened capacities, the German literature is all the more proud that it never had a Maecenas or a Louis XIV. to cherish and give its authors a princely patronage. The German Reformation, too, does not ascribe its beginning to princes, but to the grace of God, and Luther and Klopstock can only be proud one of the other. The history of the German literature and poetry is intimately linked to the history of that stirring, progressive spirit of discontent with the past, and of hope for the future, or as I may say with the history of religion and philosophy,—in one word, the history of Protestantism.' One is mirrored in the other.

It is worthy of remark, in the national German character, how the new phase which the poetry and literature of the eighteenth century put on, was in the beginning thoroughly religious in its aspect, although later it was so hostile to positive Christianity, and so lenient to theological indifference. What a quickening to spiritual life Klopstock's "Messiah" gave, first published in 1748, is well known. Klopstock remained, in relation to religion, orthodox and conservative, although he cast his poems in an antique Greek form, and so, by making an epic of the simple gospel history, he contributed to a more secular view of what is distinctly Christian, and thus all unconsciously gave an unfortunate bent to what he would gladly have retained in its old expression and purport.

It was not long before the new poetry hung to the Bible by only a very slender cord. Gleim said openly that Bacchus and Amor could help us sooner than Moses and David. This sounds, perhaps, more frivolous and wanton than was originally meant. Biblical truths stood in plain antagonism to the fermenting spirit of the new school of letters. And so Wieland soon laid aside the theological mantle, and began to exercise his talents in an altogether different field than that of religion, and in a graceful and easy way to show himself a modern Lucian, offering the keen point of his dagger to positive Christianity.

Wieland and Lessing are the two men who, after Klopstock, opened a new epoch for German literature. Of these Lessing has struck the most directly and strongly at the theology of his times. In a history of Protestantism in the eighteenth century, his portrait should not be wanting, even if we had to pass hastily over other great names in the world of letters. Yet in order to justify his destructive criticism, which struck to the very marrow of theology as it existed then, we must first look over the field, and see the condition of that science, as it existed during the first half of the eighteenth century, up to the time when Lessing commenced his career.

VII.

THEOLOGICAL SCIENCE, INCLUDING BIBLICAL CRITICISM, IN THE FIRST HALF OF THE EIGHTEENTH CENTURY.

STATE OF THEOLOGICAL SCIENCE.—BIBLICAL CRITICISM.—WETTSTEIN.—ADVANCE AFTER HIM.—MICHAELIS—MOSHEIM.—ERNESTI—SEMLER.

FROM our brief excursion into the domain of general literature, we turn back to the province of ecclesiastical history proper, and briefly trace the progress of theological science, which Lessing so fiercely assaulted down to his times.

The old polemical theology, represented in the seventeenth century by learned and able men, had outlived its strength. Pietism had dealt a heavy blow at the old orthodoxy, and its poor dried scholasticism, and had substituted in its place an active, stirring, religious life. But pietism had from the first brought less of scientific than of practical interest to light. Science was to it only a means of appropriating for its own use what material was useful for edification, and by means of a skilful and even learned study of the Bible, to put itself in command of means for working beneficially upon the churches as a whole, and upon individual hearts. The deeper inquiry, which had to go through doubts to reach its end, and stablish doctrine, was farther removed from it, it even looked upon such investigation with distrustful eyes.

Yet this method of inquiry could not be stayed. It was awakened by all external causes. The English deists had brought a mass of charges against the Bible, which could not be met by mere loudly-sounding deprecations and disclaimers. They had disclosed a great many tender spots, they had called attention to the weakness of a great many proofs; it was demanded of them that much that was blindly accepted should be subjected to a new and unbiassed investigation. The question was not now merely whether a doctrine was grounded on the Bible, but whether the Bible itself, the sacred collection of books, to which Protestant theology makes its final appeals, was worthy of reception as the last test of truth. The point at issue was no longer the arrangement of the books, but what went before any possible arrangement of them, the history of the Bible, its formation, its fortunes, and the relations of its parts to the whole.

For the Christian, who sees something more in the Bible than a mere human book, who recognises in it the traces of the living word of God, the ground of his faith and of his hopes, the thought is somewhat distressing to see this book surrendered as a corpse is given to the anatomist, for every one to try the sharp edge of his scalpel. But this dissecting process could not be stayed. It was for the interest of truth that it should be so. We cannot help seeing that the

Bible has two sides, one divine, the other human. We take hold most readily of its divine side, and view the book in its unity, as the one unchangeable word of God, the pledge of the Father's love, and His gracious purposes with us, the expression of the divine will to man, and the living witness of all that which He was to our fathers, and of what He has been in Christ to us. Luther and the reformers took hold on this divine side, and every evangelical Christian must so take it, if his faith have a strong and secure basis. The Bible has also its human, external and historical side; and Luther and the Reformers have taken hold of that side, too, and so must we, if our faith is not to fall at last into a blind and dead worship of the letter. Comprehended in its human aspect, the Bible reveals diversity rather than unity, and appears as a collection of books made at various times, from various authors and in various styles, based upon various historical relations and circumstances, which we must study in human manner if we would understand the Bible. And then there is added what is purely external to the subject matter, the variations which have come in by copying, and the duty is superimposed upon the critic to ascertain the first and only true reading. And lastly we cannot fail to observe that the Bible, like all works of antiquity, has been viewed through various eyes, now in a simple childlike spirit, now with fanciful playful wantonness, and again with a dry prosaic common sense. The duty was, therefore, imposed upon science, to lay down fixed principles of exegesis, to see the Bible in its own colouring, and to understand it from its own point of view. It was necessary to study similar uses of language, similar words, pictures and comparisons, in other works of antiquity, especially of the East, and so by the hold of this new lore, to set the reader in the same relations to the Scripture in which they were who lived in the times when it was given. That this manner of treating holy writ was not only useful and instructive, but also favourable to the furtherance of the study of the Bible, every one will confess, who has himself known the difficulty of understanding it without any help, and we will all gladly confirm what Goethe has said, that "the Bible becomes more beautiful the more we study it—that is the more clearly we see that every word has received a certain distinct character, according to the separate conditions of time and place when it was given. We must regard it as a beneficent Providence, therefore, that from the beginning of the eighteenth century a new activity was manifested on this domain of theological science. Yet many, with greater or less reason, saw danger in this. As in all human affairs countless mischances arise till the truth is found, so it is here. Some spoke of the candour of the investigation, as contrasted with the old orthodoxy, and many sought to attain that candour; but it was soon apparent that here, too, in spite of the old narrowness in the old opinions, a new narrowness was rising, which did homage with equal servility to the opinions of the present; and that if the fathers converted apostolical Christianity into the orthodoxy of the seventeenth century, the sons were on the way of either carrying the scepticism of the eighteenth into the Bible, or of taking that away from it which did not agree with it. Yet before we judge we must look at these efforts to clear up biblical difficulties, and on the threshold we meet two men, who were the first to devote themselves with remarkable success to the clearing up of difficulties in the Greek text, and restoring it in its purity, John Albert Bengel and J. J. Wettstein. Of Bengel's efforts in this field we purpose to speak later, when we come to discuss him as a man.

Wettstein was the pioneer in the work. He devoted a long and most diligent and devoted life to the preparation of his Greek Testament, a work which is a standard yet, and which, published in 1751, but four years before his death, was the summing up of the labours of his life. As a professor and preacher at Basle he met with much unfounded and unrighteous opposition on the alleged ground of heresy, and was compelled to accept a professorship at Amsterdam, which became the centre of his European reputation. His work is still confessed to be one of the richest repositories of biblical learning.

The critical study of the Scriptures found other representatives as the age advanced. We may name as one of the most eminent, J. D. Michaelis, who did so much to give note to the rising university of Göttingen. He became professor in 1745, and was constantly employed there until his death. Frederick the Great tried in vain to induce him to enter into public service. During the Seven Years' War, Michaelis busied himself with preparations for a journey to Arabia, which he did not make after all, but which it was left to Carsten Niebuhr to carry out. Michaelis confined himself to biblical researches. He may, indeed, have looked at the east too much from his study, and so have handled with almost pedantic fingers the rich flowers of oriental poesy, but no one will deny him the praise due to vast learning. Dr. Tholuck thinks, however, that Michaelis has done much to favour the later neological efforts, not by yielding to the attacks which were made on the sacred canon, but by the want of a true religious life, lacking which, he had but the outer husk of orthodoxy, without its living kernel.

A greater light than the indeed somewhat dry and hard Michaelis was Laurentius Mosheim, a clergyman of Göttingen, a man whose noble character is just as lovely as his learning was thorough and comprehensive. There is almost no domain of theology which he did not live to adorn and bless. Mosheim is the father of modern church history: in the study of morals he, for a time at least, created an epoch, and in the history of German pulpit eloquence, a new period dates from him. He has been termed the German Tillotson, the German Bourdaloue. What Michaelis wanted in fine taste was largely present in Mosheim, and gave to all his learned works, as well as to his sermons, an indescribable charm. Mosheim in faith was thoroughly orthodox, yet mild and patient towards others, and, in this respect, really unlike many of that school. In his "Ecclesiastical History" he has laboured with a candour which grants to all who differ from him an impartial presentation of their views, and ensures justice to all; he has subjected their systems to a thoroughly scientific treatment, and in this he has been very happily likened to Melanchthon.

If Mosheim freed ecclesiastical history from a fierce polemical warfare, and gave it a place as a pure branch of science, Ernesti and Semler were the men who sought to make biblical interpretation independent of the creed which had been in general acceptance. It had been, indeed, always a fundamental principle of Protestantism that doctrine should be drawn from the Bible, and not the Bible made to harmonize with an established creed. Yet it had gradually become customary to think that the doctrine of the reformers and their successors was authoritative truth, and to accept the Bible upon their interpretation alone. The theologian read the Scriptures through the glasses of a dogmatic system, the layman through the glasses of his catechism, and it was held to be wrong to indulge in other interpretation of the Bible than that which came from the fathers of the Reformation. That was unprotestant. J. A. Ernesti, professor, first, of ancient literature, and then of theology, in Leipzig, is regarded as the founder of a new exegetical school, whose ground principle was simply this: to interpret the Bible according to its literal verbal sense, and to let that volume suffer neither at the hands of any assumed authority of the church, nor of the feelings and wishes of individuals as to what they might choose to believe, nor of a sportive and allegorizing fancy, such as the mystics used to indulge in, nor of any philosophical system. He adopted in this the main principle of Hugo Grotius, who in the seventeenth century had similarly intrenched himself. Ernesti was a philologist. He had employed the same principles in the interpretation of the writers of Greece and Rome, which he employed later in the interpretation of the Bible. And he was right in this; the Reformers had aimed to do the same thing. But he overlooked too much, perhaps, this fact, that in order to apprehend the *religious* truths of the Scriptures, there is needed not only a knowledge of their verbal and historical characteristics, but a spiritual appropriation of those truths, so that one can enter *livingly* into the very heart of the Bible. Who would deny that in order to understand an epistle of Paul there must not be a very different manner of approaching and viewing it, than would be needed with the letters of Cicero, since the whole circle of ideas is different in the two. Religious writings can only be truly apprehended by a penetrating spirit, which can strike through the whole web of grammar and logic to the fundamental truth. And this certainly comes not with a mere arbitrary and scientific dissection of the fabric, only with a comprehensive all-sidedness on the part of the expositor. When, therefore, Ernesti replaces a wilful, fantastic, but often spiritually rich method of interpretation, common among the mystics, by a verbal, dry, and unimaginative exegesis, it was a useful counter work, but it did not cover the whole ground. The suspicion would easily arise that the Bible was merely a literary work, and that its function was merely to minister to the wants of the understanding. There was danger that in rating the book among the lists of classics, the great help of the Divine Spirit, which could alone guide the mind to its deepest truths, would be overlooked. Ernesti himself, like Michaelis and Mosheim, was orthodox. He even defended the Lutheran view of the Lord's Supper. And yet these men differ from the older orthodox in their strenuous efforts after independence, after mere truth, after dry truth, if you will; but there was in them a certain mildness of judgment which had been unknown to their predecessors. They laid out the way, without knowing it, which leads to that theological method of thought which came soon after them. The man in whom these later tendencies first took a neological direction was J. S. Semler. This eminent theologian, who has written the narrative of his own life, deserves to be regarded with more than a passing glance, for we see in him that this effort after what was new did not necessarily proceed from a frivolous spirit of scepticism, but could come from a pious and honest search after the truth. In Semler, too, the university of Halle recognises the man in whom terminated the reign of pietism, and the reign of neology commenced.

Semler was the son of eminently pious parents, his father being a clergyman, his mother a woman of great devotion to her children. He was early indoctrinated in the principles of the pietists, but while he leaned very much towards them in respect to spirituality, he could never sympathize wholly with them in their unwillingness to study theology in its scientific aspect. At sixteen he entered the university of Halle, but the spiritual conflicts which he had undergone during his boyhood still remained, and he tells us that in his terrible stress of mind, he has often gone out at night upon the great square in front of the Orphan School, and in his heart wished, "O that I were a lump of ice! O that I were but a piece of wood!" This contrariety in his feelings lasted for a long time: he could not adopt the language of the pietists, although he leaned to their peculiar heartiness and mysticism. At last he began to define the limits of theology and religion, and to separate them from each other. He reckoned many sciences within the domain of the former, which were needful for the preacher to understand, but which were not essential to the soul's happiness. He believed that a man might be a true Christian in heart, and yet not receive with the understanding all the doctrines which are revealed to the intellect. This separation of a private religion, as he called it, and the generally received theology, ran through Semler's whole history. There lies an element of truth at the bottom of this, that is, the separation of knowledge and belief, of that which forms the basis of every one's happiness, and that which serves for the making clear and intelligible the processes of the religious life, and for the exchange and expression of religious thought. Whoever has considered this spiritual life, must confess that all our conceptions of divine things, all our designations of them, are insufficient to convey wholly what lies in the heart. The very language of the Bible does not bring truth in the same guise to every one : it is variously understood : every one interprets the Bible after his own manner, and each takes it home to himself according as it commends itself to his own necessities. One prefers the living pictures to the difficult thought, another even translates the poetry of the Bible into his prose. There is a great deal in this matter dependent upon the natural constitution, the degree of culture and the personal experience of the individual, and up to a certain point it may be said that with a common ground work of religious belief, yet every one has a special creed, a separate theology, a treasury of inner experiences and views different from those of any one else. And this is in no wise to be regretted. A universal, objective religion, which has the same value for all, like the formulas of mathematics, has never been given us, and wherever there has been an attempt to fasten such a religion of men, there has been the skeleton of a dead conformity, rather than the living soul of an active and growing faith. And it is only because the religion which the Church gives us, became our own possession, converted into our flesh and blood, assimilated to ourselves, yes, repeated in us and reproducing its kind, that Christianity has its greatest worth to us. And the older school of mystics felt this, and then after a long reign of outward conformity in theology, Semler felt it, and so, too, I may say, did his time. Indeed this modern epoch, which opened with him, may be characterized as the epoch of Subjectivity; and each one must see with his own eyes, and comprehend with his own understanding, and examine with his own judgment all things, in the political, literary, and religious world. That phrase of Frederick the Great, already quoted, "that every one shall get to heaven his own way," was the watchword, in one sense, of the age: it was far more than a flash of wit. Yet even Subjectivity can be abused, and it has been abused. The Subjectivity of the individual can be carried to a point, at which the bonds of fraternity may be severed, the *general* welfare impaired, the *higher* authority which ought to rule over all personal thought, put in peril. There is a double evil to shun: either a strong and earnest spirit seeks to *impose* his own opinions on others and exalt himself into a magistrate of thought, or, the individual can withdraw wholly within himself, and secede from all fellowship. The first leads to what is virtually a new papacy, the latter to the disintegration and ruin of the Church. There remains one way yet to be followed, viz., that a man indulge in his own private belief, and yet conform in theological speech to the common phraseology: seem to belong heart and soul to the great company of believers, and worship wholly with them, yet without an inner reception of what is meant in the language of worship. This is assuredly the most dangerous way of all, because when this separation has reached a certain point, it leads necessarily to a two-faced use of words and so to hypocrisy: and this is what has been charged upon Semler: who certainly was the father of what has been termed the theory of *accommodation*. Yet, assuredly, Semler was no hypocrite. He did not advance far enough along this way to fall into the fatal error where it must, and in his successors, did terminate; and he lived in the hope of seeing the day when all that was effete in the doctrine of his age should be cast aside, and that the old language should still be the conveyancer of this purified theology. But it was not for Semler to accomplish a mediation between the "private religion," as he termed it, which he held, and the general orthodoxy of his times: his was a critical, negative nature, not a positive, creating nature. He was not the man to breathe a new life into theology: like Michaelis, he was too hard and dry, and looked too much at religion from the standpoint of his study. He tells us that when he was a boy his father attended an auction, and bought a number of books by the foot, as they stood on the shelves—so that when they were taken home, there were a number of sets which contained the first but not the last volumes. And this was in a certain sense typical of the mind of him who studied this strange collection: there was an incompleteness and want of grasping the whole subject which prevented his ever attaining a high place, except as a critic. He was no constructor of systems. And yet his life, in a Christian sense, was beautiful. Few men have lived in a frame of more constant dependence on God. Not an important step did he take in life, without looking up for guidance. His family was trained in a truly pious manner, for he held strictly to the value of a religious education. He was a man of true domestic turn of mind, and wrote his books with his wife sitting by him, and his children prattling at his knee. His literary labours were large and various. In the history of the early Church, he employed a trenchant pen, destroying many things which had been firmly established. In the history of doctrine he showed the variations which had crept in with the lapses of time. He was the true father, indeed, of this department of theology. In the study of the Bible he felt that it was right to discriminate between that which had any relation to the Jewish people, their faith and their economy, and that which he considered had a permanent and eternal value. Among the former he reckoned the views given of the devil, and of the being possessed with devils, and he sought to conceive of what was said of the Messiah and sacrifices from their Jewish meaning, and to knit on to the pure idea as it remained, the Christian conception. And yet with him in all this effort to follow the course of dogmatic development, and to throw aside what seemed to be the old and useless husk, there was nothing of levity, or scorn, or a bad temper: he had a profound desire to apprehend the truth, and he always laboured in the service of that desire. And though he limited what was *permanent* in Christianity merely to what is of practical service in bettering the human race, and although he may be rightly charged with opening the way which led to regarding our religion as merely a system of available practical ethics, yet he had a fund of feeling in his heart, which found little or no expression in his books, but which was seen in his daily life, and is recorded in his biography. This seeming discordance lasted to the end of his career. In sympathies he grew nearer and nearer to the mystics, while his bold negativing criticism did not cease. In his heart he grew more simple and childlike, but in his theology more bold and unsparing. He was at once a pietist and a rationalist. He united in himself what now, more than a half a century since his death, has fallen widely apart, and what could not perhaps be again united in any single man.

VIII.

LESSING.

THE WOLFENBUTTEL FRAGMENTS.—DISPUTE WITH GOTZE.—RELATION OF THE BIBLE TO CHRISTIANITY.—LESSING'S NATHAN.—THE EDUCATION OF THE HUMAN RACE.—A FEW WORDS OF LESSING'S FATHER.

IN the domain of scientific theology, as in that of literature and poetry, we have seen, in our progress with our subject thus far, a revolution beginning, whose results we perceive year by year, and whose rich harvest is not yet completely gathered. Both of these domains lay, then, widely separated from each other, the cleft between, no man had then been able to span, and those who tilled the one paid no regard to those who tilled the other. But now we meet a man who wrought confusion both in the dramatic and the theological worlds (using these words in the largest sense), who, with his powerful understanding, struck into them both with great effect, and called into being polemics in art as well as in religion, without bringing to us a system in either: a man who, in the closest sense of the word, was neither a poet nor a theologian. He was always and everywhere a critic. Gotthold Ephraim Lessing, born January 22, 1729, in Upper Lusatia, the son of a Lutheran preacher of much piety and of extensive historical knowledge, received when a boy an education which was intended to be religious as well as scientific. His parents early taught him the importance of prayer and of Bible reading; and besides being carefully instructed in all the commonly received doctrines of Christianity, he committed to memory a large number of hymns, which awakened in him early an appreciation of devotional poetry. Yet the age of enlightenment, so called, had already begun, and he was instructed not only *what,* but *why* to believe. Very early a spirit of independence was awakened in the boy, and the consciousness of what was to be his future sphere of life. Once, when a painter wanted to paint him with a bird in his hand, as a boy would appropriately be represented, he said with decision, "No, paint me with a heap of books around me!" At school he soon began to make remarkable progress. Even there the love of independent thought was his most marked characteristic. The customary school duties did not suffice to keep him busy, so that the master wrote to his father, "That is a horse who must have a double allowance of provender. The lessons which the others find too hard are to him but play; we shall not be able to keep him here much longer." The boy acquired at school the title of "the admirable Lessing;" the fitness of which we shall not dispute. The parents of the youth wished to make him a clergyman: the mother, especially, cherished this desire. But Lessing showed no inclination for this, nor indeed for any so called "bread science." In Leipsig he heard the renowned Ernesti: the other professors did not attract him much. Lessing soon collected around him a number of young friends, who practised themselves in poetry, and not long after, the first effusions of these aspiring youths appeared in a weekly newspaper at Hamburg. He was just as resolute in making his body strong and capable of endurance, as he was to give power and edge to his mind. He learned to ride, to dance, to fence—accomplishments which his mother called childish, and which his father declared superfluous, costing much, with no return. Yet to these little cares there was soon joined a weightier one. Among the friends of Lessing was one who had already gained some name as a free-thinker, in consequence of his attacks on miracles—Christopher Mylius. The intimate acquaintance with such a man, as well as with play-actors, was injurious to Lessing, and the report of his friendship was a great grief to his parents: it tried the good mother, that her son should eat up the cakes which she had sent him for Christmas at a wine-supper with comedians. Lessing was too kind a son to let his mother be tried by such acts. In the extreme cold of winter he obeyed a summons home, and attempted to quiet their doubts by his personal representations. He had long and serious conversations with his father about theology; and in order to show his mother that he could become a preacher at any time, he wrote a sermon. He remained at home till Easter, and it seemed that a perfect reconciliation had been effected. But directly after he had arrived at Leipsig again his inclination drew him to the theatre. It was not a mere love of dissipation which drew him there; it was the desire, and I might almost say, the calling which he felt within himself, to take the drama, which was just in its infancy, into his charge, and to raise it to the high plane of an art. About this time he commenced his career as a dramatic writer. In the meantime, with the sinking of the zeal of the Leipsig actors, his own also sunk. He left that city and followed his friend Mylius to Berlin. But this step excited the anxiety of his parents again. Berlin stood then (it was Frederick the Great's time) at the height of its reputation as the centre of free-thinkers, and Mylius was one of their leaders. Lessing received a letter from his father, filled with reproaches, and ordering him to return home at once. But instead of going, he tried to satisfy his parents by writing them, and making them understand that a love for the theatre need not be inconsistent with an intelligent reception of Christianity. In order to give them a proof of this, he wrote a drama, in which he lashed the actions and words of the free-thinkers unmercifully, and made a laughing stock of them. In sending this piece to them he wrote also these lines, which are of significance: "Time shall show whether he is the better Christian, who, retaining the principles of Christianity in his memory, and often having them on his tongue, without understanding them, goes frequently to church and conforms to all the customs of the place, out of mere habit, or he who has contended with grave and well-put doubts, and has arrived at conviction through the channel of investigation, or at any rate, has sought to arrive there. The Christian religion is no work that a man can take from his parents on trust. Most people inherit what they have, as they do their property, but they show by their living what kind of Christians they are. So long as I do not see that one of the chief commandments of Christ, to love our enemies, is not better observed than it is, so long shall I doubt whether those who give themselves out as Christians are really such."

At the wish of his parents, Lessing, after remaining some time yet in Berlin, went to Wittenberg, where his brother was then studying theology, and took a Master's degree without ever making use of it afterwards. Among other things he translated Klopstock's Messiah into Latin, in order to make it clearer. After remaining there a year he returned to Berlin, where he edited a newspaper, and so brought upon himself new reproaches from home. A writer for the press, and a writer of plays, were interchangeable terms with Lessing's father. But these reproaches soon ceased, with the growing reputation of the son. He then let him go quietly on according to his bent. During this second stay in Berlin occurs Lessing's acquaintance with Nicolai and Mendelssohn, who both belonged to the deistical party, and were among its leaders, yet the young man shared by no means in all the opinions of his elders; on the other hand it had a great charm to him to dispute with them and enjoy their perplexity. He became co-editor with these two of the "Biblothek der schönen Wissenschafter" in 1757, and in 1759 he published the "Litteraturbriefe," which created a new epoch in the development of German thought. In 1760 he became a member of the Berlin Academy. About this time appeared some of his finest dramatic works. In 1767 he accepted an appointment in Hamburg, which brought him again in contact with the theatre, for whose entire reform he heartily laboured, and out of which he wished to drive wholly the dominant French taste. But in the midst of his activity in the dramatic world, he made the acquaintance of Götze, the senior pastor of St Catherine's church, with whom he afterwards held a notable theological controversy. Götze, who, though rigidly orthodox, was a learned man, and in particular a thorough historical scholar, was not a little surprised to discover in the theatrical critic and play writer, a man who had gained a footing in the whole domain of science, and who was, moreover, better versed in the Augsburg Confession, and in theological matters, than many a candidate. He acquired a greater liking for one whom he had shunned before as a half heathen, and did not hesitate to break a bottle of Rhine wine for the sake of holding conversation with a man so gifted. And Götze remarked, with great satisfaction, that Lessing did not fall into the light and flippant tone which characterised many of the new sceptics, and that he could do justice to the real nature of orthodoxy. It was a great relief to the good man that Lessing showed no taste for the ministrations of Alberti, the junior pastor of the same church, to whom all the fashionable and cultivated Hamburg world were flocking, and whom Götze valiantly opposed.

The transfer of Lessing to Wofenbüttel in 1770, where he was appointed librarian of the ducal library, removed him from the dramatic world to that of theology, and led to his break with Götze.

Lessing had begun to publish a number of hitherto undiscovered treasures which he had found in the library, among which was the celebrated work of Berenger of Tours, written in the eleventh century, and relating to the Lord's Supper, and which all had been greeted with enthusiasm by the theological world. But it did not stop with those harmless, learned relics of a past age. Lessing sought out what was newer, and published over his own name what others had not dared to do over theirs. The sending forth of the so-called Wolfenbüttel Fragments, in 1774, raised a general commotion among all minds, not unlike that which in our day has been excited by the publication of Strauss's Life of Jesus, although the books are very unlike, and set out from diametrically opposite points of view. The Fragmentist established himself not on a mythical but on a historical foundation. To him all that the evangelists wrote was not the mere poetry of an allegorising time, but the real and purposed narrative of history; but the Bible in his hands becomes not only Holy Writ but profane history, and the writers are men who were concerned in a secret plot, and not mere weaklings imposing on us a mythical tale. This point was presented the most forcibly in the ablest of the Fragments, published in 1777, under the title "Of the Aim of Jesus and his Disciples." According to this paper it was the object of Jesus to reform Judaism, and, in defiance of the Roman power, to establish an earthly Messiahship. Only when this plan had failed, when the designer of it had perished on the cross, did the disciples give it a spiritual signification, and added to the narrative the story of the Resurrection. In another fragment the want of connection and the contradictions in the account of the Resurrection, were discussed, the origin of the story and its lack of authenticity. As, according to the hypothesis of Strauss, the evangelical history is treated as a proof of pious simplicity, so by that of the fragmentist it is treated as the result of a cool, deliberate calculation, but the impression which they both produced was the same.

Very well worth looking at and refreshing our memories with at this time, is the picture which Semler has left to us. A kind of amazement was the result, even with many politicians; dissatisfaction, with many men in prominent position, with some a light and trifling levity, and a deliberate working out, in the same line, the heresies stated in the fragments; and the latter method first gaining ground with young scholars, widened its sphere, and at last got abroad among citizens and plain people, on whom the unknown fragmentist had not counted for support. Many serious youths, who had devoted themselves to the work of preparation for the ministry, found themselves in great perplexity in consequence of this shattering of the foundations of their faith; others resolved to change their calling, and not to enter upon a sphere of labours where there would be so little stable ground left them to work upon. In many a city there were readers, who insisted that the fragments *could* not be answered, and that although the theologians might write and preach against them, yet who could say whether they believed all they might assert? Many wondered whether Semler would try to confront the fragmentist; yet he did, with the whole enthusiasm of his heart, and a number of distinguished theologians adhered to him, and laboured to second his efforts. There arose a strife for the very life or death of Christianity, although the battle was fought with various weapons. That Lessing was only the publisher and not the author of the Wolfenbüttel fragments, is generally conceded; who the real author was is not to this hour fully determined. Many have attributed them to Samuel Reimarus, who was a distinguished advocate of the religion of Nature; yet this has been denied again by others. Still this is certain, that the whole weight of opposition fell on Lessing their editor. Pastor Götze now appears in the front rank of the antagonists. It is certainly a deplorable thing, that when great and solemn questions are tried, little matters of personal bearing thrust themselves in to embitter and disturb. Whether it be true, as is asserted, that the sensitiveness of the Hamburg minister arose at not having a letter answered which he wrote to Lessing, we will not inquire. But this we cannot help seeing, that Götze measured weapons with an adversary who was his master in dialectics. In his "Anti-Götze," he overcame the clergyman by his superior weight, and hence may have arisen the popular impression, that the Hamburg pastor was a weak, ineffective and ignorant man, which he was not; had he been, this Lessing would not have expended so much power on him. Among other things which he ascribed to Götze was a sheer unbelief in Christianity, otherwise he would not be so prompt to imagine that a system, whose author was God, would not bear investigation. But Götze would not suffer this reproach. He granted that Christianity had nothing to fear from investigation, however apparently strong the arguments brought against it, yet he believed it best that theological controversies should remain in the hands of the learned, and not become the discussions of the people. He did not fear for "objective religion," as he called it, which in spite of all the attacks on it, will assert itself, but he believed that "subjective religion" would be periled, since weak minds would be thrown into perplexity regarding what they were to hold. And who could deny this? Even Lessing did not deny it; but he asserted that it was always a good thing to let a fire have air: and he compared himself to a physician who, when a pestilence is approaching, does not conceal its existence, but announces it to the proper sanitary officers. A clergyman and a librarian, he said, are two entirely different things, they bear the same relation to each other as a shepherd and an herb collector. The shepherd's indispensable duty is to guide his flocks to safe pasturage, and to keep them away from all poisonous plants if he can. But the collector of herbs searches everywhere, and even gathers up the poisonous ones for the uses of science. *Truth* rises above everything, and for it even the quietness and peace of individuals must be sacrificed. "Always," says Lessing, "must the few who never were Christians, who never will be Christians, who, merely under the name of Christians, breathe out their thoughtless lives, always must this despicable class be pushed aside from the place through which the better class is to pass to the light." A hard expression, and one that chimes with that view which claims that the mere enlightenment of the understanding is the highest good; and according to which the *individual*, with his devout feeling, his struggles and doubts, his longings and his scruples, counts for nothing, if only the *race* advance in power of *thought;* a view which, if we follow it to the end, conducts us to a pantheistic conception of the world, into which no consideration of the individual enters, and the sparing of the weak counts as weakness. The truth does rise above all things; but what truth? Not that alone which satisfies the mind and gives mere knowledge, but that which makes us free, which betters us, which sanctifies us, and ennobles our whole nature; the truth, which, like a common good for all, raises even the lowliest above the limited domain of their own cares and troubles, and which enjoins humility upon the wisest, and bids them be silent and learn where the frontiers of the understanding lie. That the "unthinking Christians," as Lessing calls them, are therefore no Christians, or the most despicable class, who may say that? How long has mere thought been the measure of religion, the measure of Christianity? The distinction which Christianity makes between men is not between the thinking and the unthinking, but between believers and unbelievers. Sensibility of spirit, longing after divine qualities, hunger and thirst after righteousness, it demands at the outset, and then it turns to give itself alike to learned and unlearned, to the deepest thinkers and to the simple minded. And that this great body of unthinking ones shall be offered up to the thinkers, this harsh, and with all its appearance of liberality, this most illiberal and despotic demand, is neither Christian nor Protestant; for here may be applied the word of Christ: See that ye trouble none of my little ones. Lessing happily compares the storms in theological criticism to the storms in the natural world, which tear down many a neat little cottage with its trim hedge, but at the same time free the whole atmosphere from noxious vapours; and yet it pains us none the less to see the little cottage perish, and we cannot think that this is only an egotistical pain, lest we see *our* house fall and *our* flowers torn up the roots, as Lessing insists. Lessing was a passionate gambler, and played high, risking all on a single throw.

We speak here simply of the impression which such storms make upon us when they arise in the theological sky. Keep them off, forcibly hold them back, we certainly cannot. And we must undoubtedly concede to Lessing one Protestant principle, the hushing up and concealing of doubts in religious matters is never a good thing, for when the fire is believed to be subdued in one place, it is certain to break out more violently in another. We believe with Lessing that the fire must have air, and we must approve his keen sagacity in condemning the use of the Latin language for theological discussions, on the ground that a knowledge of Latin is not in our time the true criterion of mental development equal to the needs of scientific argument. But we also believe that air should be supplied for the fire in the most careful way, that one should not make a passionate and random move, and should be on his guard not to overrate the often one-sided merely conjectured value of scientific discovery at the expense of the general religious and moral welfare of men. We will do nothing to impede the collector of herbs in his search for the poisonous ones; yet the shepherd must be none the less on his guard lest the sheep eat what is baleful to them, and which would kill them rather than do them good. And if we cannot prevent the people from becoming acquainted with those critical studies which were not intended for them, but rather for the study of profound students, yet we must seek to ward off the harm which might result from what was used so much out of place. And we know of only one means to do this. It is not the raising of an untimely cry of horror which can do this so much as the bringing of counter arguments: let weaker reasons be met by stronger ones. Where theoretical doubts have had great weight, there the life-giving power of a practical, working faith has often overthrown them; but where this has been wanting, there scepticism has had free play. By a living piety, by exercise in righteousness, by communion with God and the working of an active love, the Christian is daily reassured of the true strength of his position, and is able to reassure others, and the issue of all argument, if one be firmly entrenched, is certain. And Lessing knew this, knew it better than the most of his contemporaries, and, indeed, than most of his opponents. "Whoever sits securely in his own house," said he, "will let any one say what he will about the foundation, the house will not fall for all the talk. It is only a fool who would go to work to dig beneath to see whether it is strong!" But in religious matters zealots have committed the error of not guarding the error in practical wise, but of throwing suspicions on scientific inquiry, and by this unreasonable depreciation of it they have lost more than they have gained. Certainly, by the untimely bringing of theological disputations before the public eye, by the reference in the pulpit to books which are only to be perused in the study, the evil has often been done, of transplanting the poisonous herbs into the meadows, and disturbing quiet minds without any good effect. In this thing Götze may have done wrong, and justified Lessing in saying as he did, that "no one has made more unbelievers than the believers themselves." But in all this storm serious and calm theologians did not lose their courage. "The Christian religion," said Semler, "does not need to beg for pity or mercy: it need not fall on its knees and cry out imploringly for life: the day will reveal whether it has gold and silver or straw and stubble to oppose to these devastating flames."

And as every controversy on the domain of religious thought, besides the bitterness which it occasions, conducts to new phases of truth, and opens new points of view, so it was here. The discussions which Lessing had with Götze led to another theme of great moment in Protestantism, the relation of the Bible to Christianity. As the Protestant Church, in contradistinction to the Catholic, had asserted that the Bible was the foundation of all religious inquiry, Lessing sought to show that Christianity was older than the Old and New Testaments, which had their rise within the Christian Church, he went directly back to the most primitive doctrine, framed by the earliest fathers from the verbal sayings of men, and an oral tradition. On this living spiritual power which linked the early believers to each other, rests, according to Lessing, the framework of the church, while the Bible is but the plan of the church on paper. And when fire overruns the edifice it is better to extinguish it than to rescue the paper plan, and carefully search in it in what part of the house the fire is raging most severely. And fortunate would it be if that which is taken for a conflagration is only the Northern Light! And this reasoning of Lessing was not without some good foundation, for Protestants had let a belief in the *living* power of the Spirit withdraw behind their belief in the *written* Word, and always cried of the danger of the latter being attacked, while they let the former sleep. Many pious and thoughtful Protestants, particularly the mystics, had spoken of this, and tried to remedy the evil, but they could not gain a hearing. Lessing went too far in the opposite direction, and fell into an equal extreme. Christianity, indeed, is not the Bible, nor the Bible Christianity; but in the Bible are recorded the traces of the primitive Christianity, which, under the influence of the Holy Spirit, continually displayed the signs of life. But yet the Bible is something else than the mere framework of the building: it is far more, and if we do not call the Sacred Writ itself our corner-stone, yet we thus call *Jesus Christ in it*, and we only know Christ in and through the Bible: and likewise those apostles who have left their records to us are the pillars of the temple, and the doctrine which they held is only revealed to us in what they wrote. Should the Bible perish, the whole framework of the temple would perish : and here is where Lessing has not gone deep enough, has been too idealistic. In the first days of the church, when the spirit of fraternal love was so powerful and so widely diffused, that every member was interpenetrated with it, there was no need of Holy Writ, for, as one of the fathers has said, that without ink and paper, faith was written in the heart. But how soon this living faith was lost, how soon the first traditions disturbed it, is known too well from the history of the church, and it is Holy Writ alone which rectifies the evils which arose, and carries us back to the primitive faith, and discriminates between apostolical Christianity and the fabric of human minds. The Protestant Church would cease to be if the Scriptures were given up, although it were to be wished that we were not content with the mere dead possession of Holy Writ, but laid more stress upon the living Spirit, which Holy Writ not only makes us understand but accept with the heart. And that we may attain to this, we need just such storms as the Wolfenbüttel "Fragments" excited.

It is a difficult task to co-ordinate all of Lessing's religious ideas into a system. He had none. His was a critical, not a systematic nature. The search after truth occasioned him more joy, as he himself confesses, than its possession did. His bold remark is well known, that "if God held all truth in one hand, and the searching after truth in the other, and gave him his choice, he would accept the latter, even if it led him into error whose consequences should be eternal."

It would be an error to class Lessing with any theological thinkers who had gone before him. It would be doing him a great injustice to class him with Voltaire and his fellows, or with any deists or freethinkers of the common sort. Lessing was of a great and noble nature. His desire for truth is unmistakeable, his directness honourable to him, though it be coupled at times with roughness. How idle sounds that story which his enemies tried to fasten upon him, that he received a thousand ducats from an Amsterdam Jew to encourage him in his attacks on Christianity. Need we wonder that with such attacks made upon him he showed some venom?

Not only was Lessing unselfish, he was sincere and serious-minded. Never does he trifle with sacred things; he is bitterly in earnest, even in his ridicule. It was not the gleam of his sword but its edge which his adversaries had to fear. Wit was indeed at his command, in larger measure, perhaps, than in Voltaire, but his wit was not that frivolous French kind, it was a lightning flash, behind which a cloud of weighty and fruitful truths was revealed. That trifling but superficial scepticism which began in Lessing's time to break out all over Germany, was not shared in by Lessing. He knew the orthodox system too well to give in to those who disowned it, and yet wanted to raise something untenable in its place. "In this," he writes to his brother, "we agree that the old system is false, but I could not say with you that it is the mere botchwork of ignorant men. I know nothing in the world which has so exercised human acuteness as that system. A botchwork of ignoramuses is that system which assumes to put itself in the place of the old one, and to demand that recognition from human reason which was given to the latter.

If we comprehend among the Deists those who have no positive religion, Lessing must be ranked among them, if we assume that the Jew, in his own drama of Nathan, gives utterance to Lessing's own ideas. And that this was so the author himself confesses. But certainly Lessing found no intrinsic difficulty in accepting a divine revelation, as the other Deists did. According to his own expression, "It must be rather a proof of its truth that a pretended revelation rises above human reason: it is no reproach that it does so, for what sort of a revelation would it be that reveals nothing?"

But Lessing did not believe that revelation was a thing past and wholly closed, but considered it as a constantly progressive development of God's plan in the education of the race. The idea of the gradual unfolding of our knowledge of the divine economy is very attractive, although it is fraught with the peril of bringing man's own plan into the great creation which God is going on with. This idea has been often presented. We must here discuss it in some of its elementary phases.

What education is to the individual, revelation is to the race. Education is a revelation made to the individual, and revelation is the education which has been and still is granted to the human race. Education gives a man nothing which he could not have of himself, but it gives it sooner and more readily. And revelation gives nothing to the race to which human reason could not attain, but it gives it earlier. As in education it is not a matter of indifference in what order it unfolds the powers of men, so is it in revelation. As education leads the mind on by a gradual process, step by step, so does revelation. Yet God must pursue in this matter a fixed and definite course. He chose for His purposes a single people, one of the rudest and most primitive, in order that He might begin at the very beginning with them. To this people, of whose religious ideas in Egypt we know nothing, God revealed Himself as a Father, in order to habituate them to the thought of a Deity interposing in their behalf, and through miracles He displayed Himself more powerful than any other God. So He accustomed them to the thought of one Divine Being. And as children are trained to obedience by means which appeal to the senses,—by rewards and punishments,—so God dealt with this people. The promises and threatenings related entirely to this life. The knowledge of immortality was concealed from them. But among this people God trained the future educators of the race: for as the child comes to years of understanding under the mingled agency of chastisements and caressings, and then goes forth into the world, so this people, after being reared in like manner, was driven forth into the world, as it were, and then first knew and felt what a Father it had enjoyed. Most other nations were far behind it; very few were in advance of it: just as with children—many, left entirely to themselves, remain rough, while a few display wonderful capacities. Yet just as slight as is the argument which children thus mature, despite the absence of training, oppose to the value of household discipline, is the argument from the existence of nations, which attained a large measure of spiritual knowledge without a direct revelation from God. Even the fact that the immortality of the soul remained unknown to the Jews, when it was known to other nations proves nothing adverse to the divinely arranged plan of the Hebrew development. The knowledge of immortality was not fitted for them in their primitive state: they had to learn, first, the lesson of obedience; and the heroic observance of the law of God, *because* it *was* the law of God, had in it an element of greatness which must be regarded as the fruit of a divine economy.

Up to this time God was rather an object of fear than of love. And now came the era when the conceptions of Him should be widened, ennobled, and purified: and this was done when, during the captivity, the Jews became acquainted with a nation which had a more spiritual conception of God than the Hebrew people itself had. Although revelation had heretofore been the guide of reason, yet now reason threw light upon revelation. That was the mutual service which they did each other. The child sent away from his home saw other children who knew more and lived more true to their convictions than he did, and asked himself with shame, Why do I not know as much; why do I not live as true to what I know? Ought I not to have received a perfect instruction in my father's house, as those children have attained without any father at all? Then it brings out its elementary instruction books, which it had thrown away in disgust, and lays all the blame on them. But the fault is not in those books; it lies in the child. The Hebrew nation came back from the captivity wiser than it went. The Jews became acquainted with the Greek philosophy, then in its palmy pride, at Alexandria, and brought thence by the Persians and the Chaldeans, and heard for the first time the doctrine of the immortality of the soul. The time of books of elementary instruction was over with them; they could no more go back to those rude records which once satisfied them, than a growing lusty lad can go back to the clothes of his childhood. In the fulness of time Christ came. He became the accredited, the practical teacher of immortality: accredited through the prophecies which were fulfilled in Him, through the miracles which He wrought, and through His resurrection from the dead. And practical, because He did not teach the doctrine of immortality as a mere abstraction, but brought it into the most intimate relations with morals. The disciples propagated this doctrine, and reduced it to writing. Their records became the second book in the series for the instruction of the race. For seventeen hundred years they have occupied the human mind more than any other books, and have enlightened it more, yet only by the light which human reason brought to the interpretation of them. It was needful, indeed, that every people should have the Gospel for a season as the *ne plus ultra* of its religious knowledge: as the school-boy must have his book to check his impatience to advance to higher things, before he has fairly mastered the lower. And the more thoughtful, indeed, who think that they can look beyond the confines of the Gospel, may perhaps find, on longer acquaintance with it, that there is more in it than they expected. And in time, the revealed doctrines, which were first received as mysteries, become at last the possession of human reason, and have their own self-founded existence; such doctrines, for example, as the Trinity, Original Sin, and the Atonement.

All education has a *goal.* Whatever is trained, is trained with reference to some end. And, according to Lessing, the end of all this progressive development of the race is the attaining of that era when men will do good, because it is right, and not because of any arbitrary rewards: then will come the reign of a new, everlasting Gospel, hinted at in the records of our present dispensation.

Judge this book of Lessing as we may, its general spiritual import and Christian tendency, as illustrating Paul's statement that the Law is our Schoolmaster to bring us to Christ, cannot be denied, although bound up together with this ruling thought is much sharp and rash criticism, which will not escape the reader.

We close this chapter with Lessing, who died in 1781, and in the next shall consider the further development of scepticism during the closing years of the last century, which, beginning with him, and building on his foundation, was so soon firmly established and carried to the last extremes of speculation.

As a last word, however, we quote a passage from the excellent father of Lessing, of whom we have already spoken, and who, in 1770, even before the publication of the "Wolfenbüttel Fragments," wrote as follows :—

"The unmerited goodness of God has brought me to the seventy-fourth year of my life, and nearly to the fiftieth of my pastoral labours. During this long career countless changes have occurred, largely affecting men within and beyond the pale of Christianity, but not, as it seems to me, for the better. Persecution in matters of conscience has passed away, and cruelties are unknown in matters of religion ; but, on the other hand, there is dominant an unmeasured license and a shameless frivolity in speaking and writing of spiritual things. Unbelief has seated itself upon the throne of Superstition. Every one feels as free to ridicule Holy Writ as to read it. Good and excellent institutions are established, but injustice, cruelty, ignorance, and disobedience, do not seem to be diminished. Science is fostered, but morals are not mended. Men hope to become known for learning rather than for a God-fearing spirit. This is my thought when I compare present times with past. Those I do not despise, and these I cannot wholly praise. Many things have been changed rather than bettered. What is old is looked at on its dark side, and what is new on its bright one."

IX.

INFIDELITY CARRIED TO ITS FARTHEST ISSUES.

THE PERIOD OF "ENLIGHTENMENT" IN GERMANY.—BASEDOW AND HIS EDUCATIONAL REFORM.—NICOLAI AND HIS REVIEW.—THE DIFFUSION OF SCIENCE IN POPULAR WORKS.—AIM AT GENERAL UTILITY.—BENJAMIN FRANKLIN.—MORALITY IN THE PULPIT.—RATIONALISM IN ITS INFLUENCE ON HYMNOLOGY AND RELIGIOUS SERVICES.—NEW VERSIONS OF THE BIBLE.—BAHRDT, THE THEODORE PARKER OF GERMANY.

FROM Lessing we advance to those who, building on the great foundation which he laid, have been the most largely instrumental in diffusing this miscalled "enlightenment" among the German nation. Yet we cannot discuss in detail the measures, or the men who popularized the modern infidelity and battled with the old faith. We will cite the names of the leaders merely, men doubtless better and higher in every way than the horde of servile imitators; they were men to whom, with all their onesidedness, and with all their false views, it would be just as unfair to deny a certain claim to respect, as it would be to insist that they laboured for the injury instead of the welfare of their fellow-men.

Two leaders in this infidel movement claim our special attention, one eminent in the department of education, the other in that of periodical and popular literature, Basedow and Nicolai. The education of youth, and the periodical popular press, are the two great agencies through which the ideas which agitate the times give their impulse, find diffusion and produce far-reaching effects. Both are agents on whose relation to the Church much is dependent; and if in this era of infidelity of which we write there was a papacy, as much as there was in middle ages, we must look for its popes among the directors of schools or among the editors of influential journals. Of these two mighty agencies, before which even yet public opinion bows so submissively, nothing was known before. The school stood under the sceptre of the Church, and periodical literature under a censorship. But now began a change: education claimed to be independent of the fostering care of the Church, and a broad current of literature spread over a domain of life which had hitherto been familiar only with the Bible, a few books of devotion, and some scanty and barren facts of science. The new educational system, and the new popular philosophy, played into each others' hands, and contested the right of the Church to be the only instructor of youth, the only guardian of the people. Not content with that, after they had gained an independent existence, they turned their united forces *against* the Church. The ancient edifice, with its Gothic towers and windows, with its gloomy aisles and monuments, seemed to be no longer a fitting place for the instruction of light-hearted childhood; the Church must become a cheerful school-room, the quaintly carved pulpit, with its stone staircase, must be transformed into the awkward desk. It would be hard to say, whether this great change would more fitly call out the song of triumph of one, the elegy of another, or the satire of still a third. For my own part, I consider it a matter alike worthy of joy and of sorrow, and to treat it thus, is the duty of the impartial historian.

That a great reform in education was needed, that it was a great necessity of the age, no one will deny, who casts a glance back to those times. The religious education of youth had been narrowed down to the mere committal of the catechism to memory, and the crowding of the mind with biblical and theological details, which remain entirely undigested in the brain, instead of being transformed into flesh and blood. The blame did not lie in the church as such, it lay in the ministers of the church and their ecclesiastical arrangements. There were some men among them who exercised large and wholesome influence; such were Francke and the able teachers of the Orphan School at Halle. With this exception, there was nothing in the educational field of Germany from which good could be expected. Up to the time of the eighteenth century, there was no true science of education. What, hitherto, had been left to nature, to habit, and to traditional prejudices, had to be corrected and raised to the place of an art; its good elements had to be reduced to laws, its bad elements cast away. Man must be regarded as a whole, as truly man; his education must be a gradual development and cultivation of body, mind, and soul, certainly a noble worthy task, but also a very difficult one, to accomplish which, a single century, however "enlightened," does not suffice. And certainly this could not be done without deadly offence to every conservative influence of society; and as the goal of every educational process is religious development, it is not to be wondered at that this new movement produced instant strife with the theologians—for the ground principles of education are connected in the most intimate manner with the views which are taken of the nature of man. Whoever adopts the old doctrine of human depravity must insist on education as a process from without, inward. Its work must be to break the natural will, as if it were a hard and putrified thing, and to do it, if need be, by the sternest measures. The historical and doctrinal elements of Christianity, according to this view, cannot be too early impressed upon the soul of the child, and it is of prime importance that they be held as an imperishable possession. Whoever, on the other hand, adopted the new ideas which began largely to prevail, regarded human nature as a germinating seed in which a good and noble impulse dwells, and requiring only fostering care; the educational process going on from within outward. Religion was not only to be carried into the soul of the child, but was also to be drawn from that soul, and only so much was to be carried in as was adapted to its immature grasp, and to the necessity of adequate inward stimulus. But how speedy was the transition from one extreme to the other, from the denial of human sensibility to goodness, to the denial of sin and a fallen nature, from an overestimate of historical and positive Christianity, to an under estimate of it; then came another change. The old educational system had borrowed much from the church; to promote the interests of the church was its great end. A large proportion of all the studies of the gymnasium and the University looked towards theology and the clerical profession; hence the value laid on the ancient languages; but the modernized educational scheme aimed at educating men for the world and for practical life. For what use, then, it was said, are the ancient languages and ancient history? Even men of the most rigid orthodoxy, like Frederick William First, expressed themselves against the Latin; and even Thomasius had declared the uselessness of it for those who were not professed students. And so education was transferred from a narrow ecclesiastical field to broad cosmopolitan ground, from a positive Christian basis, to a so-called philanthropical one. Rousseau had given a great impulse to this movement by the publication of his "Emile." Basedow was his interpreter and advocate in Germany. To Basedow succeeded Saltzmann and Campe; to them the more noble and reliable Pestalozzi.

J. B. Basedow, born at Hamburg in 1723, was the son of a hairdresser, who wished to educate him for his own calling, and governed him with such strict discipline that Basedow ran away from home and became the servant of a country physician in Holstein. The latter soon discovered the remarkable capabilities of the boy, and sent him back to his father at Hamburg, where he became student at the gymnasium. Reimarus, the supposed author of the Wolfenbüttel Fragments, was his teacher, and valued him highly. It was the wish of his father, a man of the most rigid orthodoxy, that Basedow should study theology. Even when a student at the gymnasium, the young man preached at some of the villages around Hamburg. He was very genial and merry in his social nature, and fond of all the boisterous amusements of youth. He studied irregularly, and displayed little inclination for hard work, while the rapidity with which his mind moved helped him easily over every difficulty. Thus, prepared neither by scientific acquirements nor by a natural taste for theology, he went to Leipsic, and began to form projects for becoming a great and celebrated man. He was soon tired of going to the lectures, and chose his own course of study. During his vacation journeys he made the acquaintance of men, and during his months of study he became familiar with books. In particular, he read all the polemical works of his time. At the close of his university career he accepted a tutorship in a Holstein family, and it was there that his natural, undeniable talent for instructing first displayed itself, in a success in making his teaching comprehensible, and in converting the process of learning almost into play. He linked his instruction to almost everything around him, in the schoolroom, in the house, in the garden, in the field, and in the workshop. His talents soon attracted much notice, and his theory was received with such favour that he soon entered upon a wider sphere. As a public teacher, and as a writer on education, he soon won applause. Laying great stress on sound understanding, and considering the attainment of a practical philosophy of life one of the most valuable subjects of human acquisition, he became a passionate antagonist of the old theology. This hostility, and certain bullying habits, which he did not lay aside even when a professor, procured his transfer to Altona, where he led an active life for some time as a leader in the new school of critical theology.

His next step was to enter with his whole powers upon educational reform. Stimulated by Rousseau's "Emile," he issued a prospectus for his great work on elementary instruction, a very profitable book in a pecuniary sense, yielding him 15,000 rix-dollars. There was no lack of exaggerated representations of educational science as it existed before, there was no lack of ambitious sentences, nor of affectations of every kind, yet the work, which appeared in 1774, met in great degree the public expectation. The feature which gave it its special success was its indifferent tone in relation to religion, an indifference evidently purposed and carefully maintained. In its view, Catholics and Protestants, Jews and Christians must be treated alike; the mental powers must be awakened, the habit of observation sharpened, and a general system of morality taught which should not interfere formally with any system of positive religious faith. The book met with universal acceptance, and whoever ventured to oppose it was held to be an advocate of superannuated opinions. Basedow became the universal favourite; he had spoken out clearly what lay in many minds confused, incomplete and unexpressed. He was very soon invited to Dessau, and, under the patronage of the prince, he established a normal school to test the practical worth of his ideas. To this school he gave the name of Philanthropical Institute. A prime object with him was to exclude all positive religious instruction, and to build chiefly upon the conception of the dignity of the human soul. Such conceptions were very attractive to many persons, in consequence of the pleasing flattery which they offered to man's nature. Basedow was not long without eager followers, of whom Saltzmann and Campe, students of his at Dessau, were the most noted. Similar institutes sprang up elsewhere, and the principles adopted by Basedow were grafted upon the domestic training of children. Immediate changes were perceived; in place of the old pedantic stiffness there came a jocose levity, and instead of religious instruction as given heretofore, there ensued a general effort to develop as from within the capacities of the soul. A universal superficiality of knowledge followed, a want of consistency in moral and religious training, and a premature scepticism among youth, yet, doubtless, despite the errors, the exaggerations, the whimsicalities, and the moral effects of Basedow's scheme, it was a needed and healthy protest against the religious pedantry of a former day, and a needful transition to the position which we fortunately occupy. We will not deny that in this revolution of educational ideas the final issue was good; and we will not subject the personal character of Basedow, and his peculiarities as a man, to an over nice analysis, satisfied as we are that the meagreness of his own scheme proved its bane, and prepared the way for the conviction that a balanced system of educational science must rest on a positive Christian foundation.

In personal appearance, Basedow was not attractive. He was pertinacious in argument, and comparatively indifferent with whom he conversed. If he could not secure the attention of a Goethe, he would thankfully accept that of a dancing-master. He was in the frequent habit of interjecting startling questions, putting every one into perplexity, and then laughing bitterly at their confusion. Himself the preacher of toleration, he was the most intolerant of men.

What Basedow was in the domain of education, Nicolai, another high priest of scepticism, was in the domain of periodical literature.

Frederick Nicolai, the most prominent publisher of his day, was the son of an eminent bookseller of Berlin. He received a large part of his early education at the Orphan School at Halle, and is another instance of what we have often marked among his cotemporaries, viz., the reaction from a rigidly formal and unspiritual religious instruction to a bold and arrogant infidelity. Not a man of positive and original genius, he early became the mouthpiece of Lessing and Mendelssohn, and the publisher of the "General German Library," the avowed organ of infidelity. This journal, which first appeared in 1765, commanded at first the services of fifty in its editorial corps, and at the height of its power there were an hundred and thirty. It was the recognised medium of attack upon superstition, fanaticism, and prejudice, upon everything which claimed a lofty spirituality, or which appealed to fancy or feeling. A bare, cold intellectuality capable of no high emotion, a heartless wit which laughs at everything which it does not understand, set themselves upon the throne of a merciless criticism, and sought to crush everything to the ground which ventured to resist their domineering sway. Not orthodox people alone, not those who are called dreamers and pietists, but Goethe and the poets whenever they left the blank level of prosaic thought, and philosophers whenever they rose above a commonplace manner of discussion, were subjected to this modern inquisition, on a charge of folly, hypocrisy and unavowed Jesuitism.

This work, like Basedow's educational scheme, was in exact union with the spirit of the age, and seemed to meet a crying want of the times. It popularised all departments of thought which had heretofore been the jealously guarded possessions of a few. Even philosophy was no longer an unapproachable theme. Such writers as Moses Mendelssohn, Garve, and Engel, brought to the discussion of philosophy a practicalness, and a clearness and purity of style, which tended largely to awaken a popular interest in it. Translations from the English periodical classics, such as the "Spectator," gave impulse in the same direction, as did also the writings of that original American genius, Benjamin Franklin, one of the most perfect representatives of the purely materialistic philosophy, the so-called "enlightenment" of the eighteenth century. Everything tended to, and was measured by, practical utility.

It was, of course, impossible for the preachers not to feel this new movement. From the stiff and formal presentation of mere doctrine, there was a reaction towards the preaching of simple ethical truth. Benevolent and eleemosynary institutions, such as those for the deaf, dumb, and blind, grew out of the practical spirit of this modernized Christianity. Instead of hearing what the grace of God can effect in the soul, people heard what their duties to their neighbours were, and the most popular preaching was that which was based on the parable of the good Samaritan; and people heard very little religious instruction excepting about what would make them happy in this world, and which would render them useful citizens and worthy heads of families: in one word, the preaching of good morals took the place of the preaching of Christian faith. The reaction was a necessary and natural one, still it was a reaction, and its last extreme was as meagre as its first had been harsh. A pure Christianity has as little to do with the one as with the other; it demands a living faith which works by love, and all good deeds which have vitality in them it perfects as the fruit of faith. Mere doctrines held by the understanding, with no application to life, are just as much opposed to the spirit of the Gospel as mere ethics without the deeper basis of a soul filled with faith. But men almost always fall into one of two extremes. Giving up a mere intellectual adherence to the old forms of doctrine, they react to a mere external morality, a method directed far more to a mere material prosperity than to the incalculable worth of the soul. Not that the preaching of morals is wrong; Christ and the apostles preached morality, and so did the Reformers, Zwingli in particular. It was the manner in which it was now preached that was deficient. It was forgotten that, besides the hands with which man earns his daily bread,—besides the feet with which he walks his busy rounds,—besides the head with which he thinks,—he has a heart always disquieted until it finds inward peace; and to these men of mere utility, the interests of the heart and the emotional nature appeared but foolish fanaticism. This was carried so far, that even in the domain of poetry Campe insisted that the inventor of the spinning-wheel ought to occupy a higher place in the temple of fame than Homer himself. With the prevalence of such crude ideas all thought of supernatural ideas, and of the unseen world, was crowded one side, even where it was not resolutely opposed to the elevation and enlightenment of the people. Sermons were preached everywhere upon such subjects as the care of health, the necessity of industry, the advantages of scientific tillage, the necessity of gaining a competence, the duties of servants, the ill effects of lawsuits, and the folly of superstitious opinions. I will not enter into an inquiry whether it is true, as has been asserted, that Christmas was taken advantage of to connect the sad story of the child born in a manger with the most approved methods of feeding cattle; and the appearance of Jesus walking in the garden at the break of day on the Easter morning, with the profit of rising early and taking a walk before breakfast. Not a word was heard regarding atonement and faith,—sin and the judgment,—salvation, grace, and Christ's kingdom. A selfish love of pleasure, and a selfish theory of life, put a selfish system of morals in the place of a lofty religion. The old-fashioned system of religious service had to be modified and adjusted to this new style of preaching, which was as clear as water, and as thin as water too. Everything symbolical, whose relation to practical life did not appear at once, was cast aside, however edifying it may have been to the growth of the soul. The sacraments were an empty ceremony, the festivals of the Christian year unworthy of remembrance, and even the person of Christ of indifferent value, provided always that the morals of Christianity should be retained. What a dry shrivelled remnant of Christian faith was this!

The next step was to purify the old and precious hymns of the Church. It did not require much skill to so modify expressions as to make them ridiculous. But more laughable still was the absurd attempt to strike out the whole poetical element from poetry, and to reduce sacred song to the level of feeble prose. Paul Gerhardt's evening song,

"Now peaceful all the forests rest,"

Frederick the Great dismissed with a sneer as stupid stuff; and the hymn-book makers of his age, wishing to retain the beautiful melody, and yet make it *practical* by linking it to life, substituted for Gerhardt's line the following—

"Now peaceful rests the entire world,"

but this would not do. Either Basedow or some of his imitators discovered that the line as it then stood was not true to geographical facts—that while one half of the world is sleeping, the other half is broad awake. The final emendation remedied that, and left the line

"Now peaceful rests a *hemisphere*."

Every element of fancy, every appeal to the emotional nature, every trace of oriental imagery was rejected. Nothing was retained in the hymns of these men, except good common sense, an excellent quality in its place, but eminently stupid in sacred song. While complaining of the meagreness of the old hymnology, they composed hymns on such themes as a Good Use of Time, on Friendship, on Frugality and Moderation. We give a version of one, as representative of the prevalent style, but not so crude a specimen as might have been selected.

"To take my body's weal in charge,
Thou hast commanded me, O Lord:
To see it injured by my fault,
Thou hast forbidden by Thy word.

"Industrious, Thou would'st have us be,
While we are tenants of the earth,
And Thou hast willed that what we do,
Should be large mutual profit worth.

"O give us mental strength and joy,
O grant a large increase of power,
That we be true to every trust,
And conscientious every hour."

The last step of all was to emasculate the strong and vigorous language of Luther's version of the Bible, substituting a weak, modern, over fine style, and making Moses, David, Isaiah, Paul, and even Jesus, speak in the same language which they would use if they were writing a trial sermon before entering the ministry. The brief and pregnant sentence, "In the beginning God created the heaven and the earth," became, in the new version, "God, external to whom nothing existed, made a commencement of all things, by calling into being the primitive constituent materials thereof."

The representative man of this crude type of German infidelity, when it had run to its extreme of frivolity, of blasphemy, of prosaic weakness and emptiness, was K. F. Bahrdt. One of the weakest of men, so far as regards symmetry of character and strong intellectual power, he reflected, in so eminent a degree, the superficial scepticism of his times, that we must bestow on him more than a passing glance.

Bahrdt, born in 1741, studied theology at Leipzig when old enough to enter the university. His manner of working was irregular, as with so many soft heads who have relied more on their own genius than on patient acquisition. To this irregular method of labour, he united a want of moral principle, and so led a wasted life, made the more wretched by unbounded vanity. This moral defect, and the last named defect of character, begot in him a spirit of disquiet and a want of fixedness, which followed him like an evil demon his whole life. Bahrdt was not without talents, but he drew prematurely upon them and checked their power of growth. He wrote and preached a sermon in his sixteenth year. Vanity, forwardness, and confidence in his own powers (so he himself tells us), combined with his desire to please his parents in driving him to this step. He wrote the sermon with the greatest rapidity and while engrossed with thoughts of a most worldly nature, and even while leading a life of great irregularities. The success in preaching it was so soothing to his vanity, as to increase his confidence in himself from day to day, and to strengthen his determination to shine as brilliantly in the professor's chair as he had already done in the pulpit. The external covering of professed orthodoxy served him for a while; but soon he was betrayed into public disputation which revealed the extent of his ignorance. It was about this time that his doubts, his religious doubts, began to press in upon him. But it was not theological doubts, but his sad morals which compelled him to leave Leipsic in 1768. He removed thence to Erfurt, where he was appointed Professor of Philosophy. Here he began to express publicly his dissent from the commonly received doctrines of the Church, though modestly as yet; awakening the opposition of theological men, yet calling out a reactionary protest against such opposition in the form of the degree of Doctor of Divinity, conferred upon him by the university of Erlangen. A thoughtless unhappy marriage served to embitter still more a life already wasted and desolate. He left Erfurt and came to Giessen. The report of his heretical views had already preceded him; Bahrdt strove to dispel it, by having recourse to a subterfuge, which does not give a very favourable impression with regard to his honesty. He tried, as he himself confesses, to give his opening sermon an orthodox cast of expression. "One only needs to pronounce the name of Jesus, a la Lavater, very often, and with a very solemn tone, to convince the crowd he was sound in the faith—so I did what prudence dictated, and preached a sermon very full of Jesus, as the old ladies say."

His eloquent manner was of large service to him, and on his style he expended great labour. He not only preached but gave theological lectures, and was largely engaged in literary plans. Still, he was not yet persuaded in regard to the central truths of religion. After a certain sort he believed in the Bible, or, at least, persuaded himself that the Bible was the source of divine truth; but he sought to make it useless for the purposes of orthodoxy. He translated the New Testament into a dialect peculiar to himself, and afterwards confessed that this translation, "made in the fair presence of this beautiful outward creation," viz., in the back garden of a spirit-dealer, was a financial speculation. It was not so profitable, however, as Basedow's work on education, and Nicolai's "Review." A few bottles of old wine was all that the dedication to the Catholic Archbishop of Wurtzburg brought him. On the other side the storm arose. The Protestant theologians, Götze of Hamburg at their head, declared themselves his opponents, and Bahrdt found himself compelled to seek a new field of activity. Here Basedow came to his rescue. For some time he was engaged in educational labours. But publishing a second edition of his translation of the New Testament while the head teacher in an institute at Worms, a Catholic centre, he aroused the indignation of the clergy of that church, and his book was confiscated. After travelling to Holland and England for an institute elsewhere, he was suspended, by an imperial edict, from exercising any clerical function in any part of the German empire. He hoped upon this to find a refuge in Prussia, and in 1779 he came to Halle, but here Semler met him with his whole weight of authority and influence, Semler, upon whose protection he had confidently counted. He now made the acquaintance of the philosopher Eberhard. It was he who drove the last relic of faith out of Bahrdt's soul. Eberhard, formerly a preacher at Charlottenburg, was the author of a work called an "Apology for Socrates; or, the Final Salvation of the Heathen," a field which attracted some attention. If the earlier hyper-orthodoxy condemned the heathen to perdition without reservation, and almost without pity, neology placed Socrates on the same level with Christ. Both views were partial, and, therefore, both untrue. But to an unscholarly and light-headed man like Bahrdt, it was not hard to prove that Christ laid down no important principle that Socrates had not announced before. "Now," says Bahrdt, "the death-knell of my faith was struck. But this does not fall from his lips in sorrow; he glories in the same breath that he has at last come into the free air, that he has shaken off the fetters which had clogged his feet so long. The past he regarded as the time of growth, the present as the time of ripeness. "I looked upon Moses and Jesus," he himself confesses, "upon Confucius, Socrates, Luther, Semler, and—myself, as the instruments of Providence, through which He is working for the welfare of man." With the third edition of his New Testament appeared also his notorious letters upon the Bible, written in a popular style, and having for their object to strip from the Word of God and the person of Christ every mark of the miraculous and the mysterious, under the pretence of recommending Christianity more favourably to men of philosophic mind. Christianity must have fallen very low to have needed the recommendation of a Bahrdt; a Bahrdt who, in his almanac of churchmen and heretics, spoke of the most of the theologians living then as hypocrites or stupids; a Bahrdt who, after giving lectures on morality for a while to a mixed audience, became the dispenser of wine and beer in a tavern at Halle, till at last he was imprisoned at Magdeburg for writing some scurrilous lampoons, and released from there dissatisfied and embittered against the whole world. He closed his sad life at Halle in 1792.

With the career of Bahrdt we have carried the denial of Christianity to its last stage. We must hereafter turn to the positive side, and watch the process of reconstruction, not merely asking what was doubted and destroyed, but what was reaffirmed, defended, and established.

X.

THOROUGHGOING PROTESTS AGAINST INFIDELITY.

TWO PARTIES, THOSE WHO WOULD CONCEDE ALL NON-ESSENTIALS, AND THOSE WHO WOULD CONCEDE NOTHING.—THE ABLEST CONTENDERS FOR ORTHODOX DOCTRINE NOT THE CLERGY BUT MEN OF SCIENCE.—EULER THE MATHEMATICIAN, AND HIS DEFENCE OF CHRISTIANITY.—ALBERT VON HALLER THE PHYSIOLOGIST.—GELLERT THE POET.

We now turn from the negative to the positive side. We have traced infidelity to its lowest and crudest forms. Further it is not necessary to go. Instances of a reckless profanation of everything holy might be easily cited, and proofs of the concordance between unbelief and levity abound. But even in this time of darkness a pure Christianity was not without zealous and able defenders, men of large attainments in knowledge as well as of blameless life. Even within the philosophical and literary world, with all the efforts to destroy Christianity, we find an unfaltering desire on the part of some to sustain it, to strengthen troubled spirits, to solve doubts, to dispel reproaches, and to restore peace. Not all who ranked themselves among the defenders took the same course. While some were firmly resolved to surrender nothing of what had been considered the principles of a biblical faith, others manifested a willingness to give up all that was not essential, and to guard with double constancy what should remain. Of course, there could not fail to be misunderstandings among both these parties of defenders of a common faith. Indeed, Tholuck says of the latter of the two classes, that they were like some foolish man who cries out that his house is on fire, and throws the best mirrors out of the window to save them. Great differences of opinion existed as to what was essential and non-essential in doctrine.

We need to make two observations in advance. It has often been said that theologians have a special interest in defending Christianity. They must defend it because it is their calling so to do. Were it not for this they would fall in with the general voice of the times. But if we look at the most eminent defenders of Christianity in the eighteenth century, we find that they were not theologians, they were not clergymen, nay, more, they were men who, if actuated by religious motives, would have gained far more repute and consideration if they had chimed in with the general voice of the times. This is the first observation. The second is, that in view of the great advance in natural science, such a blow has been given to a belief in revelation that it is no longer possible for a thorough physicist to believe in miracles in the seen, nor mysteries in the unseen world. And yet it is observable that the most able defenders of Christianity, Euler and Albert von Haller, were not theologians, but the leaders of science in their day, Euler in mathematics, Haller in physiology. We must speak briefly of the labours of two such men.

Leonhard Euler was born in 1707. He received his education in Basle. He displayed very early his remarkable genius for mathematics, and gave promise of the eminence which he afterwards attained. In 1741 Frederick the Great called him to Berlin. Under the very face of the free-thinking king he published his "Defence of Revelation against the Attacks of Free-thinkers." This admirable book was so marked for ability that we sketch its main features. Euler rests our need of a revelation not so much on human knowledge as on human will. The completeness of man lies in the harmony of his understanding and his will. Only where the understanding and the will agree,—where the understanding rests upon a knowledge of God's requirements, and the human will is in subjection to the divine, is happiness to be found. The want of this harmony produces unhappiness. "The understanding," says Euler, "can attain to a high degree of knowledge, and the will be not bettered. Experience proves this: for very often men of the keenest intellects are the most deficient in goodness, and yet oftener a high degree of virtue is commensurate with a mean understanding." A revelation which should merely increase our knowledge without healthfully influencing our will, would be an injury to the race; and in the fact that the Christian religion, by introducing the love of God, as its most active element in subduing the will of man, lies the main burden of proof that the Bible is the Word of God. It not only enlarges our knowledge of duty, but it also gives our most needful help. Such a book *cannot* be an imposture; and not to believe in it because it contains difficulties would only plunge us into difficulties greater yet. And using geometry to illustrate faith, he shows that the alleged difficulties in the Christian religion are not greater than those with which the mathematician contends. And he shows conclusively that the refusal to accept the Bible as a revelation of God, is an offence of the will; else why do those who stumble at everything which they find in the Bible so readily believe everything else? Euler was a thoroughly practical theologian, with a profound knowledge of human nature. He rested his whole plea for the Bible on the necessity of a spiritual regeneration of the soul and of a change of the will. The life of this great man was full of sadness, but thoroughly simple, patient, and Christ-like. He lost his right eye in 1735, he became entirely blind in 1766. He lost his house and his library by fire, and bore all this with a resigned and cheerful spirit, and died in 1783.

As Euler stands among mathematicians, so does Albert von Haller among naturalists. Every one knows that the science of physiology owes its foundation to him. And it is this science most of all to which unbelief has made its appeal, asserting as it does, that the spiritual part of man is only the result of his physical organization, and that with the body's dissolution it ceases to be. But precisely here Haller took issue with the materialists, making a sharp discrimination between the mortal body and the immortal soul—between the ground in which the plant takes root and the plant itself—just as he discriminates between the plant and the unseen hand of Him who created it, and who trains it up for heaven.

Albert von Haller was a Swiss by birth, and descended from a noble family. He displayed a remarkable genius, even in his childhood, and early entered on the study of medicine, beginning as a pupil of the world-renowned Boerhaave, in Leyden. In 1736 he was appointed Professor in Gottingen, and entered on the enjoyment of an reputation which soon became European. The greatest Academies of the century, those of Upsala, Stockholm, Berlin, Bologna, Paris, Florence, Padua, Copenhagen, and St. Petersburg, accounted it an honour to reckon him among their members.

His diary has been published, and gives us a thorough insight into a spirit always struggling to perfect itself in a knowledge of God. In the midst of his profoundly scientific career he writes, at the close of the day, such words as these: "O soften my hard heart; teach me to know Jesus; not to confess Him merely with my lips, but to appropriate His grace. O teach me, when I am sad at heart, not to turn to worldly consolation, but to Thee! O give me another heart, that shall not flatter, that shall love Thee, and be wholly Thine!" Again he writes: "O that I might think, in this still hour, on eternity, and prize the pitiful joys of this fleeting life at their true worth! O that I might not only know, but feel, that out of peace with God there is nothing for me, and that the most pleasurable life is only a sad dream, which eternity will end." And again; "Without God the heart of man is a sea in constant storm; and so long as we find our happiness in vanities, so long will we live without peace and joy."

When the Emperor Joseph II. of Austria once honoured him with a visit, he recorded in his diary, "My vanity and pride have been flattered to-day. But let me not forget, O my God, that my happiness does not depend upon man, from whose favour or disfavour I shall have in a short time little to fear or to hope. Keep me in mind that this alone is true happiness,—to know Thee, to love Thee, to be assured of Thy grace, and to find in Thee a reconciled God and Judge." When, a few days after this visit of the emperor, some one was congratulating him on the honour shown him, he answered in the words of Jesus, "Rejoice, if your names are written in heaven."

That a man who was so rigid in his self-examinations should feel an inward call to become a defender of Christianity, will surprise no one; and more especially since there was at that time such demand made upon men who united scholarly acquisition with Christian experience, to defend the faith once delivered to the saints. Haller, therefore, wrote and published his theological letters. In the first one of these he takes the ground that religion, in order to become a solace in time of trouble, must be *felt*, embraced with the heart no less than with the understanding. In his views of human depravity Haller differs widely from those who gloried in an unsullied lofty nature. He was very clear and positive in his estimate of sin. The externals of honour and benevolence with which men disguise a nature deeply guilty, did not prevent his seeing the depravity of the heart, and dealing faithfully with it. Where Bahrdt and Voltaire gloried in their virtues, Albert von Haller repeated the publican's prayer, "God be merciful to me a sinner. Assuredly there is a philosophical and rationalistic phariseeism, as much as there is of any other kind. And this Haller opposed with the whole strength of his genius. The fundamental principle of his theology is the depravity of the heart; and he advances from this as Paul advances from the same great truth to the mystery of redemption. "The first view of this mystery," says Haller, "is like that of a mountain height, and human reason, human wisdom, and human understanding, sink into nothing before it. The Eternal One, the incomprehensible God, manifests Himself to the people of one of His smallest planets; He pities the poor creatures who live upon this earth, and He unites Himself to their life as a God only can, taking up their thoughts and their deeds, and running through the whole course of a mortal career to a sad and ignominious death." It is a touching spectacle to see a great and brilliant genius like that of Haller bow before the more majestic greatness of the plan of salvation, and look on in silent adoration where the spirit of infidelity stood unabashed. Of the workings of divine grace in the heart of the believer, Haller somewhere says decisively, "No one has truly given himself to God who does not discover as plainly the working of grace in the heart as he feels the power of sin. I am truly convinced that in the grace of God we have an Almighty helper, who can free us from the bonds of sin, and lead us on to lofty and consecrated purposes."

A third eminent defender of Christianity was Gellert, the Christian Poet and Professor at Leipsic. His life was entirely uneventful, characterized not less by persistent and faithful efforts, than by protracted and painful physical sufferings.

As a teacher he exerted a silent but eminently healthful influence over the young men of Germany, four hundred of whom were sometimes under his instructions at once. As a poet he was the Watts of his country, and was largely instrumental in preventing the growth of that prosy utilitarian kind of sacred poetry to which rationalism gave rise. Inferior to Lessing in keenness and to Euler in scientific attainments, he yet filled a large place in the eye of his countrymen; his hymns were universally read, his piety was praised by nearly all; the king, Frederick the Great, honoured him with a special audience, and treated him with great respect, and even the Roman Catholics tendered him their homage.

Thus much for the efforts made to protest, root and branch, against the rationalizing tendencies of the times. We now come to the men, many of them most worthy and amiable, who deemed it the soundest policy to conciliate the enemy by timely concessions of all that was unessential in faith.

XI.

HALF-WAY RATIONALISM.

THE HALF-WAY RATIONALISTS.—EFFORTS TO COMPROMISE BETWEEN THE ORTHODOX AND THE SCEPTICS.—CONCESSIONS TO THE OPPONENTS OF CHRISTIANITY.—JERUSALEM.—SPALDING.—ZOLLIKOFER.—THE ENDING OF ALL THESE EFFORTS IN THE THOROUGH-GOING DEISM OF TELLER.—THE EDICT OF GOVERNMENT TO CHECK THE GROWTH OF INFIDELITY.—ITS FUTILE RESULTS.—BENGEL AND HIS WORK.

We pass from that able class of minds, of whom we spoke in our last chapter, to another class of defenders of Christianity, not less honest and sincere, although widely different in their method: men thoroughly imbued with a religious spirit, and having no sympathy with the coarse and frivolous scepticism of their cotemporaries, and who felt it their mission to rescue what was holy from impious hands, and to commend what was fundamental in Christianity to the most enlightened thinkers of their day. These men were, however, somewhat tinctured with the spirit of the age in which they lived, and their efforts were mainly directed to such a system of accommodation and concession of unessentials, as should disarm the opposition of avowed infidels, give a quietus to disturbed and sceptical minds, and yet not displease thorough-going believers. These men must not for a moment be confounded with such light-minded triflers as Bahrdt, although they may have shared some of their opinions. The point always to be regarded in such comparisons is the spirit out of which religious differences grow. But this point was not held distinctly enough in view in the last century. And the result was, that men of Christlike temper, perfect honesty and sincerity of purpose, drew upon themselves a suspicion, a hatred, and a misunderstanding, which lasted even to the third and fourth generation. Is anything more painful to bear or to think of as borne, by men of guileless motive and gentle spirit? Because it is our custom to measure the faith of a man by the language of his religious confession, the error has been often made of bringing into undue prominence errors of the understanding, and of passing a hasty judgment upon the heart, which certainly has often been far sounder than in many who set no value upon a pure heart, but only on an accurate intellectual statement of religious truth. It makes me sick in my soul, when I hear men, who were the leaders of their times in morals and religion, called unbelieving, unchristian, and even antichristian, when I know that many of them, in spirit and in deep religious feeling were far superior to many speculative thinkers of our time, who probably have a more digested and a more thoroughly comprehensive grasp of Christian doctrine, but no more of a deep spiritual experience than they. I would not be understood as speaking in approval of their theology, for their theology was a mirror, poor and broken, of their age; I do not deny their errors, nor the dangerous defects of their theological system, nor the one-sided consequences to which it led; least of all would I commend their writings for the edification of Christians now; I believe we have advanced far beyond them in Christian truth, and I rejoice at it; but we must not forget that it is our duty to prize and to acknowledge truth wherever we find it, in Catholics and Protestants, in Orthodox and Heterodox, in Mystics and Pietists. We name first a man who was a cotemporary with Gellert, and an intimate friend of his, Dr. Jerusalem.

J. F. W. Jerusalem was born in 1709, and was the son of a clergyman. He early became a student at the University of Leipsic, and afterwards at Leyden. Later he made a journey through Holland, and became acquainted with men representing all religious rites, and learned how to prize what was good in each. He sought, as he himself tells us in his biography, to become acquainted with every man of high Christian principle, and the nearer he came into terms of intimacy with such, he enjoyed their society the more thoroughly, and saw that the fundamental principles of Christianity, despite all the differences in expression, bear the same fruit.

Jerusalem led an active influential life in the Duchy of Brunswick, advancing from the position of private tutor in the ducal family to the prince. His life was in every way a blessing to Brunswick. The eminent school called the Carolinian, and the institutions for the benefit of the poor, owe their existence to him. His observations, both on education and the treatment of paupers, were the result of a large experience, and have value even now. Some words of his on religious instruction I cannot forbear quoting. "It is in the highest degree sad, that according to present arrangements, instruction in religion ceases at just that time when the understanding begins to attain some maturity, and that therefore young people, have no further knowledge of Christianity left them for their future life, than what remains of their meagre instruction during youth. Sermons can never make this want good, and yet it is these very young people who, on account of their varied employments, will exercise a large influence over society." This deficiency, in a thorough religious course of instruction, Jerusalem ascribes to the almost universal underrating of the value of religion and the worship of God, and, on the other hand, to that external form of rigid belief which, lacking the very spirit of religion, causes men to react towards scepticism and unbelief. "We have," says he, "altogether too little Christianity: people enough who bear the name of Christian, but too few who have the truth within themselves, who can bear witness to its blessedness, and speak with assurance of its testimony in themselves."

While Basedow and his followers sought to divorce education from religion, Jerusalem sought to make strong the bond between church and school, and to contribute to the furtherance of that, he desired, that the church should share in the light which the school was flinging out in new profusion. He criticised the purely theological training of the clergymen of his day, and insisted on the need of a broader and more harmonious culture. Without wishing to proscribe the dead languages, he condemned the one-sided devotion to their attainment, and tried to bring into new prominence the study of natural science, and a perfect mastery of the German. The development of the resources of his mother-tongue was a favourite theme with him, and his weight was largely influential in giving this direction to the studies of young men.

Not only upon education, but upon the condition of paupers, Jerusalem exerted a vast control, and to him his country is indebted for services in behalf of the poor which can hardly be overrated. Public charity had heretofore restricted itself in great part to the mere giving of alms: Jerusalem exalted it to a science: he founded institutions which should stimulate to industry, and give paupers an opportunity to earn a part of their living at least; and more than all, he sought to invest their children with a cordon of religious associations, that they might, in their future life, have some memory of holy things, and be able in all the possible adversities of a career of poverty, to look upon the cross of Christ and bear their burden in patience. It is clear that the Christianity which such a man possessed was not learned by rote, a mere system for the brain, but faith for the heart. And this devout and earnest practical piety he displayed in all his relations to others, and in all the provident trials of his life. A hard blow to him was the death of his only son, the staff of his old age, and a young man of promise. Soon after this he lost his wife. "Both of these bereavements were a sore trial to him," says his biographer Eschenburg; "they sank deeply into his soul, and made his friends apprehensive for his life; but his spirit soon nerved itself, and religion came to his support with its most potent consolations. Peace gradually crept over him, and in all his sorrow not a murmur of discontent escaped his lips. When his own end approached, he exclaimed, "If I shall go now to my higher home, how happy I shall be!"

Jerusalem's faith was simply biblical, as distinguished from that which the later speculative theology had grafted upon Christian doctrine. Those presentations of divine truth had the most weight with him which brought out most distinctly the wise dealings of Providence, and the value of love to our fellow-men. He was a devout believer in the divinity of the Saviour, without feeling a necessity of accepting the commonly received doctrines regarding His person and the Trinity, as essential parts of religion. With all good Christians he regarded the death of Jesus as the greatest blessing ever conferred on the race, as the ground of our salvation, yet he did not agree to all the statements of the doctrine of the atonement, thinking some of them harsh and repugnant. He says himself, "How sad it is that so many people are held back from a confession of Jesus, and even converted into enemies of the Gospel, in consequence of our insisting upon certain formulas, and so they who ought to be Christians are prevented from acknowledging God, from following a virtuous life, and accepting Christ as a divinely appointed messenger of peace and goodwill. Must the Christian religion, which was assuredly meant to be so simple as to be suited to the wants of all men, to lead and comfort even the unlettered, be clad necessarily in strange and artificial dogmas, and in phrases which are not found in the Bible?" He carefully avoided, therefore, in his sermons, all those expressions which he judged would call up false and crude ideas, unworthy of God, and rather employed the simple, natural style of common life. And even now, a hundred years after, Jerusalem's sermons are remarkable for the simplicity of the style, the clearness of the thought, and an earnestness which gives them great value. Although many expressions which are sacred and precious in the eyes of most people may be missed in them, yet not without great injustice would they be denied the credit of many Christian excellences. Above all, it must not be forgotten, that, next to Mosheim, it was Jerusalem who first introduced, in opposition to the false taste then prevalent, a more simple and truly German style of pulpit eloquence, a style which, although lacking the primitive strength and originality of Luther, and approaching more the tone of the essay, was yet in entire contrast to the inflated, tasteless, canting method of preaching which had been in vogue during the seventeenth century, and which still continued on, even into the eighteenth. Jerusalem complains strongly of the tastelessness of those preachers, who, although talking in general society in the same tone and manner with all sensible men, no sooner ascend the pulpit than they break into a brawling tone, such as watchmen might use at night in calling the hour, or roving pedlars vending their wares along the streets. This manner, they think, is more impressive. The returning from such a false style to a more simple one was of great moment; and it brought into religion something of the same gain that the return to more naturalness introduced into the domain of education and literature. It was possible, indeed, that simplicity might lead to jejuneness, and that what is grand, sublime, and solemn in religion, might be made bald and pitiful by too meagre a presentment in the mere language of common life, and so in the end the noblest themes be reduced to bare common place. Yet with Jerusalem, and the best preachers of his school, this was not the case. They knew how to combine simplicity with dignity, and thus to give to their sermons, despite all their deficiencies, a certain classical worth, in contradistinction to that fanciful and tasteless lawlessness, into which so many of our modern preachers have fallen, in their struggles after originality. In other words, Jerusalem was a representative of the best tendencies of his time. He aimed to be serviceable to that class of men, whose employments do not permit them to enter upon close and learned investigations into religious truth, but who ought, in consequence of their intimate relations with the world, and the general frivolity which sets all serious matters aside, as unworthy of attention, to be acquainted with the fundamental principles of religion, and the applications of Christianity to life.

And, therefore, Jerusalem met a real and general want of his age. The time was past when thoughtful and educated laymen would be satisfied with what they had learned in the catechism; sermons would not cover the whole ground with which they wanted to be familiar, nor had they leisure for pure theological works, and there was needed a new type of religious literature, which should be interesting and instructive at the same time, and which should stand midway between rigid metaphysics and mere declamation. And Jerusalem laid the foundation for just such a literature as this, and in conjunction with Sack, a court preacher in Berlin, he did much to diffuse a genial unsectarian spirit, and to throw a religious spirit over common life.

Another man who contributed much to this new type of religious life was J. J. Spalding. He has left us his life written by himself—the record of a career singularly wanting in eventful incidents, but active and peaceful. He lived to a great age, and was engaged in high ecclesiastical functions in Berlin during the larger part of his career. His life was free from any of those storms which tossed such souls as Augustine, Tauler, and Luther, and made their life so fruitful in struggle and passionate experiences. And Spalding's theology was the reflection of his peaceful, uneventful life, a superficial theology, in the best meaning of the word, a faith which, though not disowning the unseen sublimities of revelation, yet mainly ignored them, because it felt no special need of them. He laid great stress upon uprightness, and sincerity, and the common virtues of life: he had little or no sympathy with an emotional type of religion, if divorced from the understanding; he had no sympathy with the rich and gorgeous language of the Oriental books which enshrine our faith, and sought to translate it into the familiar language of daily life, overlooking the fact that, according to all experience, the Bible is one of the most intelligible of books, and to no classes more so than to the rude and the simple. Spalding was a gentle, genial, affectionate soul, but his faith was too arid to meet the wants of men of stormier life; and while he won universal respect, and the love of even his theological opponents, he did much to encourage the unsettled temper of his age, to make religion common place, to degrade the clergy into mere teachers of the understanding, instead of prophets of the truth. He was a man not without emotion himself, but the resolute foe of emotion in religion, particularly when the offspring of appeals to the senses. In this way he gave, as Tholuck remarks, a colder and yet a purer character to religion; colder, inasmuch as he laid more stress upon intelligent conviction than upon impassioned feeling, and purer, inasmuch as he encouraged the growth of the more homely virtues, when heed is given only to a deep emotional type of piety. Spalding preached oftener on honesty and happiness, on the faithful performance of duty, and the contentment that ensues, than on a new birth, salvation, and redemption; more on the *religion* than the *person* of Christ; more on the fruits of a virtuous disposition than of the Holy Spirit. He did not see that men, in changing the form of expression, often surrender the object expressed,—that in pouring wine from one vessel into another, a large part might be spilled and lost. And yet no man was a more sincere friend of religion than Spalding. So far as he went he was perfectly true to himself. His creed was limited, meagre if you will; yet, such as it was, it was the expression of his own nature. He never spoke a word on religious things which did not testify to his own experience. It is the people who do not trouble themselves deeply about religion, who do not hesitate about accepting a doctrine more or less in their creed; but Spalding would take nothing on trust; he must always know for himself, and feel for himself, what he acknowledged as true.

Zollikofer, an eminent preacher of Leipsic, was another leader of this half-way school. His congregation consisted mainly of intelligent tradespeople; and at a time when the prevailing tone of all talk was in mockery of religion and Christianity, he endeavoured to awaken an appreciation of what was high and noble in them, and to develop their moral aspect. He carried morality, in his preaching, to its farthest limits, where, perhaps, the roots out of which the Christian life should spring, were lost somewhat from sight. His themes were such subjects as the Worth of Manhood, Friendship, Education, Social Life, and the like. Yet the one-sidedness and unformity of Zollikofer's discourses being granted, it is not hard to find in them proofs of a noble and even character. He lived in the universal respect of all who knew him.

We have tried to do full justice to the good intentions of the class of men of whom we speak in the present chapter, and to show that, despite a rather meagre appreciation of the essential principles of Christianity, their aim was to cultivate and diffuse a catholic and gentle spirit, and to promote the best interests of religion. Notwithstanding, we must confess that the results of their labour were not so happy as they expected. Their piety, clear as it shone out in them, was too much the manifestation of their personal character, it was too subjective, to make a deep impression upon the great mass of men. A Christianity for the mere thinking, corresponding, reasoning, and philosophizing world, was not the glad tidings, which were meant for all. The fair, blue, philosophic heavens, which, as Herder expresses it, was seen everywhere through the church roof, was only the cold northern sky of abstraction, and the blessing which fell from it was far more poor and meagre in good, than that which had followed the labours of a Luther, an Arndt, a Spener, and the hymn writers of the sixteenth and seventeenth centuries. As the gifted Steffens says: "The well-meaning writers of this school did not observe that all religion is a primitive thing,—that it demands the first place in the heart,—that it will allow nothing to stand between it and its possessor,—and that, if its inner kernel is gone, it can no more be made living and effective, than life can be breathed into some of the products of chemistry." And we must also assent to Steffens, when he asserts that the works of these half-way men have opened a path which eventually led to rationalism; instead of conducting the minds of their age away from infidelity, they aided, in the end, the general movement of their age." This result was most signally displayed in the life of a man who stood in terms of the closest intimacy with Spalding, and whose personal character had many excellences, but who carried the temporizing and accommodating spirit so far, that the vital differences between what is distinctively Christian, and what is Jewish or Mohammedan, faded almost out of sight in his teaching. This was Teller, an ecclesiastical dignitary of considerable eminence. He was one of the strongest advocates of a version of the Bible which should eliminate its Oriental features;

and in arranging a system of faith in which all might agree, he arrived at something very little different from deism; and although he clung to the orthodox rather than to the neological school, yet his name was caught up by those who were endeavouring to overthrow the old faith; and at his death, his eulogists went so far as to say, that if the world had a few more such men as Jesus, Luther, and Teller, all would go well with it. Thus the circle was complete, and the two arcs, the one ending with the frivolous Bahrdt and the other with Teller, united.

The death of Frederick the Great caused a reaction. The course of frivolous scepticism and of the half orthodox, half sceptical rationalism had been completely run, and the love of novelty had been satiated. On the accession of Frederick William II., a religious edict was published, in which the orthodoxy of past days was loudly vaunted, and the stern religious discipline of the older Prussian monarchs loudly extolled. This edict, while repudiating any interference with conscience and with individual beliefs, yet rebuked severely the blasphemous tone everywhere prevalent, reaffirmed the need of a revival of the old orthodox faith, and forbade the preaching of infidelity. It conceded all the former privileges to the Lutheran, Calvinistic, and Catholic Churches, but it enjoined a strict adherence to its old formulas and symbols. It appointed a commission for the examination of candidates for the ministry, and its actions were to be decisive, though courteous and fair.

Yet this edict, in one sense so much needed, utterly failed. It was soon found to be impossible to make religion a matter of police, and to prescribe for the faith of a great nation as one would prescribe for the cutting and fitting of a uniform. It was soon seen that it was not possible to have binding guarantees from those whose duty it was to enforce the edict itself, for the stream could not rise higher than the fountain. There was hardly an effort made to enforce it. A single clergyman only was set aside from his office in consequence of his infidelity, and the government gave him a good civil appointment at once. And despite the approval of Semler, and the bitter scorn of Bahrdt, the edict speedily became a dead letter.

But what police ordinances could not effect, the great law of reaction could accomplish. While rationalism was advancing, bóth in open and in covert forms, pietism was making steady advances too. Men who could see to what this half way method, this compromising spirit, would lead, were steadily working in the interests of deep and yet enlightened piety. Through all the stormy days of Frederick's career, while a blasphemous infidelity reigned at Court, and a compromising and accommodating rationalism was preached from the most popular pulpits, they quietly worked on and awaited the time of reaction, a reaction of which the above-named edict was rather the exponent than the avenging minister. And at length the reaction came.

The most prominent name among those who, with wise yet steadfast moderation, resisted the spirit of the times; was John Albert Bengel, whose name is well known to English and American biblical students as the author of that critical commentary on the New Testament, called Bengel's Gnomon.* This keen, thorough, and scholarly work, after passing into disuse, is again brought forward, and ranks among the foremost of exegetical productions, and is regarded as indispensable to students of the Bible. Yet this work, voluminous as it is, formed but a comparatively small part of the labours of its author. Bengel was a native of Würtemberg, and spent his life in Southern Germany and exerted an influence which, wide and deep as it was there, hardly extended at that time to the north. The school which he founded cannot, therefore, be regarded as of the most marked power and prominence in its relation to the vast problem of German infidelity. Yet it would be unjust to the great man of whom we speak to lead any reader to the inference that the circle of his activities was a narrow one. He towers in a most marked manner above the men of his cotemporaries. Superior in keenness to any other theologian of his time, a chaste, forcible preacher, using the simple Bible truths in the plainest and most sternly practical way, genial and winning in all his relations, and so bound to all the rising young men of his native kingdom by strong ties; an active, vigorous man, largely controlling the educational and the religious affairs of Würtemberg;

* First translated into English quite recently, and published by Messrs. Clark of Edinburgh, in five volumes 8vo.

a man of varied learning, and so writing on many subjects, and on all well; a man of unceasing industry, and so accomplishing the labours of many common lives in one; he may be regarded by us as not only one of the greatest and best, but as one of the most effective men of his age, preserving the flame of pure Christianity alive during a period almost wholly given over to a reckless infidelity; a firm and sure anchor to many souls less sure and steadfast than his. He was not a pietist in any technical sense, for he lived a long way from Halle, which pietism called its home. In the narrow use of language prevalent at that time, he might perhaps be called a pietist, for all were called by that name who believed in anything higher than the mere objects of sense, and whose religion sprang from anything deeper than a mere desire to discharge correctly the common duties of life, and to practise the virtues which give an irreproachable reputation. More strictly he was a mystic, and yet not a mystic in the sense of being so drawn into the current of religious speculation, as to have nothing left for the purpose of an external activity. Religious men are usually exclusively workers, or exclusively thinkers; few unite, as Bengel did, a large share of the speculative with an equally large share of the practical element. Like many of his countrymen, his domestic life was singularly rich and happy, and his whole career is one which, did our space permit, it would be profitable to present in more than this meagre outline. He founded a school, not, indeed, on any set system of doctrine, but moved rather by his broad and genial spirit, and the influence of his followers was widely beneficial. Under the conduct of men of this school, the first scheme of an alliance of all Evangelical Christians was carried into effect, and the basis of union, the broad yet distinctive features of salvation through Christ, has been retained even until our own time, and is reproduced in the Evangelical Alliance of to-day. To Bengel, therefore, Germany owes a debt which it would be hard to pay, not for successfully stemming a tide which no man could stem, but for keeping alive a flame free from all the fluctuations of caprice and overwrought zeal and ignorance, yet bright and cheering and invigorating to the most healthy Christians of his age. Amid most depressing influences, he stands out in the full soundness of a complete, graceful, effective, Christian man.

XII.

ZINZENDORF, THE FOUNDER OF THE MORAVIANS.

ALLUSION TO HIS BIOGRAPHERS—HIS YOUTH AND MARRIAGE—CHRISTIAN DAVID—FOUNDING OF THE MORAVIAN COLONY AT HERRNHUT—ZINZENDORF'S JOURNIES, FORTUNES, DEATH, AND BURIAL—SKETCH OF HIS PERSONAL APPEARANCE—EXTENT OF HIS LABOURS AND INFLUENCE—HIS CHARACTER AND MENTAL CONSTITUTION—HIS THEOLOGICAL VIEWS OF CHRIST, OF THE ATONEMENT, AND OF THE BIBLE—HIS POETRY—ZINZENDORF AS AN ORGANISER: THIS HIS MAIN STRENGTH—RELATION OF THE BROTHERHOOD TO THE CHURCH.

THE remark has been made that it has not always been the distinguished theologians, in contrast with men of the world, who have most ardently espoused the cause of Christianity; but that, on the contrary, where the theologians have been imperfectly guarded, or have too readily surrendered their sacred trusts, laymen, pious and gifted, have risen, who, partly by their teachings, partly by their organising power, have largely influenced the development of religious life. This is plainly to be seen in the founding of the Moravian order, and in the history of its founder. We meet there a most notable instance of that constructive talent, often missed in the deepest thinkers, the greatest scholars, the most genial and fruitful minds, and which yet makes an impress on history hardly second to that made by conqueror or statesman. In the midst of a colony of poor artizans, descendants of those old Hussites who left their homes for their faith's sake to dwell upon German ground, rises the figure of a distinguished and accomplished man, and, by his side, a wife no less conspicuous. This nobleman and his countess we see, in conjunction with these simple people, able to organise a church—one which shall serve as a model, and out of which a new life shall grow—a church which in its branches has been found throughout the Protestant world, and which finds to-day both outspoken and secret friends among people of all ranks and all varieties of education. I wish to give an unbiassed account of the life of so remarkable a man as the founder of such a church must have been; to narrate rather than to sit in judgment. Zinzendorf's life has been written by many. I will refer only to the biographies by Spangenberg, Schrautenbach, John George Müller, and Varnhagen von Ense. In them the curious reader will find larger detail, and the most varied criticism of the man.

Nicolaus, Count of Zinzendorf and Pottendorf, was born at Dresden, May 26, 1700. The house of Zinzendorf, from a remote period in possession of large estates in Austria, had been raised to the rank of a barony by Leopold I., and, in some of its branches, had early embraced the Protestant faith. The grandfather of our Count went to Franconia for the sake of his Lutheranism, and two of his sons, among them the father of our count, came to Saxony. He, when prime minister of the country, married Charlotte Justine, Baroness of Gersdorf, who bore him the son, the subject of the present memoir. Six weeks after the birth of the child the father died, after having given it his blessing on his death-bed. The mother was not only pious but accomplished; but the little one enjoyed her care for only a few years. After the death of her husband the baroness left Dresden and lived upon her estates in Upper Lusatia, and marrying a few years later, she removed to Berlin, and committed the bringing up of her child to her mother. So, in his grandmother's house, his susceptible heart received the first impressions of that piety which was through life his most marked characteristic. The aged Spener, who had been the godfather of the child, always remained his fast friend; and, in one of his visits, he gave his blessing to the child, predicting for him great eminence as a promoter of Christ's kingdom. Under the mild discipline to which he was subjected, he early became acquainted with that old treasure-house of spiritual books and poems, which, in those times, stood next to the Bible as a means of edification; and though a stormy and passionate nature sometimes broke out in him, he took great comfort in devotional works, and there soon was developed in him a desire to enter into a living and inner union with the Saviour. "Be thou mine, dear Saviour, and I will be thine," was his cry. He communed with Jesus for hours at a time. He even wrote little notes, which he threw out of the window, in the hope that his heavenly friend would find them. From his childhood he felt, as fire in his bones, to use his own expression, a desire to preach the eternal godhood of Jesus. And even when a child of six years, he was fond of going into an empty hall, and gathering the chairs around him as listeners, to preach to them. In 1706, a troop of Swedish soldiers came to Grosshennersdorf and pressed into the manor-house. Astonished, the warriors stood and listened to the young preacher, and forgot the object of their coming.

A desire to do good seemed to be kindled at the same time with his love of prayer. All money which the young count received he gave immediately to the poor, and displayed a strong desire to be of service to the needy. The whole mental development of the boy seemed to be directly dependent upon the predominant spirituality of his nature. For mathematics he shewed little taste, and for languages he had little aptitude. On the other hand, he committed to memory in early childhood all the most quoted verses of the Bible, and showed a remarkable sensibility for devotional poetry. He himself tells us how full of joy he was weeks before the celebration of Advent and Christmas; and he entered so fully into the songs then mostly sung, and into the sermons which treated so exclusively of the Saviour, that he was able almost to transport himself back into the past, and make himself a witness of Jesus' life.

When ten years old, Zinzendorf came to Halle to enter the High School, then under the charge of Francke, its eminent founder, who took him under his special charge. Francke subjected him to a rigid discipline, and sought to break down in him a pride of rank which he supposed to exist in him. That Zinzendorf had faults he himself confesses, alleging that he was subject to a prying curiosity, and was not disinclined to enter into the usual rogueries of school boys; but, continues he, "I stood under the restraint of a discipline of which my comrades knew nothing, and I was not merely held back from doing wrong, but was so blessed of God as to be the means of bringing to the Saviour many who sought to lead me astray." He not only succeeded in calling his school mates to meetings for prayer, but he even established an Order, the Order of the

Grain of Mustard-Seed. The insignia was merely a gold ring, on which was engraved, "None of us lives for himself." In the spring of 1716 Zinzendorf returned from Halle to Grosshennersdorf, and soon after entered the University of Wittenburg; for his uncle, who conducted his studies, did not wish him to remain in Halle, fearing that he would become a complete pietist, of which there were already marked indications. Zinzendorf must study law, and the nephew obeyed, although theology lay much nearer his heart. He paid attention to systematic training even, rather out of obedience than natural inclination. He conformed to the discipline of the schools for fencing, dancing, and riding; but he prayed the Saviour to deliver him speedily from these enforced studies, and to grant him freedom to devote some hours each day to what was more consonant with his natural tastes. He learned some games, but only those which sharpen the understanding, like billiards and chess; and, if he played for money at all, he gave what he won to the poor, or laid it out in Bibles for general distribution. Among the theologians of Wittenberg, he was specially attached to Dr. Wernsdorf, who roused in him the desire to become a minister of the gospel. But there were many hindrances in the way of this, especially his noble rank. But Zinzendorf cared very little for the humbleness of the preacher's calling. He was willing to become a simple catechist or village pastor, so far as he was himself concerned, little as his friends would enjoy it. Yet he left it all with God. "Will God grant me the power to be useful," he writes, "I will bid defiance to a world in array against me. But if he grant this not to me, yet am I not forgotten of Him; and he has work for me to do, even if it be to keep my own heart and life pure in these evil times, and prepare for a blessed eternity."

The year 1719 the Count devoted to the tour then usually taken as a part of the education of a young nobleman. His route took him first to Holland. In the picture gallery at Dusseldorf, an *Ecce Homo* made a very powerful impression on the youth. Below the painting were the words, "All this I have done for thee, what hast thou done for me?" He was ashamed to confess to himself how little he had done, and he wished that the Saviour would *compel* him to become a participant in His sufferings, if he could not himself reproduce their keenness. And so through his entire tour over Holland, Belgium, and France, his soul was drawn with almost passionate yearnings to Jesus: and in Paris it was not the showy displays, not the operas and the theatres, the fine buildings, the gardens, and the fountains which claimed his interest: what he sought in that great capital was the Christians, the children of God: and it was the pious and benevolent institutions which called for the most of his attention. France was then an interesting field of view for a person interested in ecclesiastical affairs. The philosophy of Voltaire and the Encyclopædists had not yet been promulgated. The names of Bossuet, Pascal, and Fenelon shone out in undimmed glory. The conflict with the Jansenists, received as an heirloom from the seventeenth century, still existed, and had been recently revived by the Papal bull Unigenitas. Zinzendorf made the acquaintance of a number of the Jansenist clergy, and became on intimate terms with Cardinal Noailles, whose simple, pure piety won him to the man without making a Romanist of him. Zinzendorf returned to Germany by way of Strasburg and Basle. The impression which this tour left upon him was not of wonder at the extent of worldly splendours, but, on the contrary, he writes to his brother, "You cannot believe how distasteful the world now looks to me. The littleness connected with the things reputed high is pitiable, and there is no one so grand who is not miserable if another be grander than himself. Half of the world is dying of envy to-day. O splendida miseria!"

Zinzendorf spent some time in intercourse with the pietists of Halle, and some time on his grandmother's estates, and only after many appeals from his friends could he be persuaded to enrol himself as counsellor-at-law at Dresden, and then only under the condition that he should undertake no longer round of duties than should be agreeable to him.

But although engaged in secular pursuits, he could not abandon a spiritual calling. He was and continued to be a *preacher*, obeying his parents' wishes out of filial respect alone, but living with his whole heart in another sphere. Every Sabbath he used to call around him in his own house assemblages to worship, and what was the most remarkable, even

Löscher, director of religious affairs in Dresden, otherwise rigidly orthodox and severe towards the pietists, tolerated these meetings, and assured Zinzendorf of his sympathy.

But the time had now come for the Count to break away from the old conditions of his life, to sunder his connection with pietism, to which he had been allied, and to transfer his hopes and his energies to another sphere, to become the founder, not of a new sect, but of a new church, one distinguished from any pietistic associations heretofore formed, and which should stand forth as a new feature in the history of that century.

Zinzendorf, satisfied neither with the orthodoxy of his time nor with the ruling pietism, had long contemplated the union of all friends of the Saviour on common ground, and to this end he was willing to use his noble birth, as giving him a larger measure of personal influence. He purchased of his grandmother the estate of Berthelsdorf, and in May 1722 took oaths of fealty from its tenants. He established Andrew Rothe, a young minister, who had his full confidence, as pastor of the domain, and in September of the same year he was married to Erdmuthe Dorothea, the sister of his friend the Count of Reuss. Of her, Zinzendorf testified twenty-five years later, that she was the only one who could have adapted herself to every winding and corner of his nature. "Who could have lived," he asks, "less subject to the world's criticism? Who could have aided me so much in laying a bann on mere dead morality? Who so thoroughly comprehended the lifeless Phariseeism which had ruled for years? Who saw more clearly into the hearts of the impostors who would gladly have joined their fortunes to ours? Who could have lifted from my shoulders more completely the burden of household cares? Who could have administered all my business affairs in so prudent and successful a manner as she? Who could have lived so economically, and yet so well, as she? Who could have been so humble, and yet so dignified? Who could better have taken now the place of servant, and now mistress, and yet discharged her duties in both situations with equal honour? Who could have borne such pilgrimages by land and sea with more heroic endurance than she?"

The establishment of the new brotherhood was simultaneous with his entrance on domestic life, and his coming into the possession of his estates. But already in the seventeenth century some members of the Bohemian Church which Huss had formed even before the great Reformation, had left their former home in Moravia, and had gone forth to form new colonies in Poland, Saxony, and Prussia.

Christian David, born in 1690, at Senftleben, Moravia, had been awakened while a boy, tending his father's sheep; then, travelling as a valet, everywhere seeking peace for his soul, he had at last, while at Gorlitz, in company with the pastors there, come to a deeper insight into evangelical truth, and to a certain degree of satisfaction and comfort. He then was anxious to impart to his brothers in Moravia the same blessing which he had enjoyed. He made them a visit, told them what he had experienced, and awakened in them a desire to leave their own country and to settle down with Christian people, that they might be better taught in these things. In a subsequent interview with Zinzendorf, he disclosed to him the necessitous circumstances of his brothers, and the Count was willing to give them a home on his own estates. David retraced his steps to Moravia with the good news, that God had touched a nobleman's heart, and had inclined him to give them a home. The brothers fell on their knees, and thanked God for opening this path to them. They immediately started for Upper Lusatia, Christian David at their head. It was but a little company. On the 17th of June 1722, the first tree was felled for the building of their village. The chamberlain of Zinzendorf delivered the address at the dedication, and he it was who gave the name Herrnhut[1] to the colony, taking it in part from the name of the hill on which the village should be built. Two years later the name thus given began to come into common use. Towards the end of December the Count made his first visit to the place. When he arrived he entered the newly-built house, fell on his knees, thanked the Saviour for bringing the newcomers thither, and recommended them to the grace of God.

From this time the desire grew strong in Zinzendorf's mind of realizing Spener's idea of benefiting the Church, by founding a Church within itself. He connected himself with

[1] Herrnhut, the Lord's Protection. The hill was called Hutberg.

his chaplain Rothe, his friend Wattewil, and with Schöfer, the pastor of Görlitz, and called it the Union of the Four Brothers. These men, thus associated, made it their special charge to exert a healthful influence on the Christian world, as they might find opportunity, especially by the agency of edifying publications, several of which Zinzendorf himself wrote. The regular meetings, which soon drew together other friends, were called Conferences. The Count often preached at Berthelsdorf: he regarded himself as the spiritual colleague of Pastor Rothe and on the Sabbath afternoons his habit was to go over the sermon which had been preached in the morning and have a kind of catechizing. Soon people from the neighbourhood began to take a part, and other Moravians arrived and increased the number of the colony. On the 12th of May 1724 the foundation-stone of a church was laid. In the course of the address which Zinzendorf delivered on the occasion, he said, "May God suffer this house to stand no longer than while it shall remain the home of love and peace." The bystanders felt the weight of his words; for even then the seeds of discord had been sown in the little colony. From the beginning the Moravians were not of one mind. Lutherans and Calvinists had their contentions about the Lord's Supper; others had even brought in Socinian opinions; others, especially the later comers, wished to enforce a rigid system of discipline, which the older members steadfastly opposed. Zinzendorf was the more troubled about these contentions, since the errors and exaggerations which came to the public knowledge were attributed to him, and it was not long before the most injurious reports were disseminated regarding the new society. In the year 1727 the Count had given up his dwelling in Dresden, and had taken up his abode with the colony. For a time he took the post of superintendent, and gave the people a constitution and a more permanent organization, and wrote, journeyed, worked, struggled, and prayed for them incessantly. For himself, he was content to remain a Lutheran of the Augsburg Confession, yet always anxiously keeping himself from any intolerance towards Christians of other denominations. Yet this, and his kindly intercourse with pious Catholics, gained him a repute for indifference to religious distinctions. The very manner in which he expressed himself on religious subjects gave those who detect heresy behind all unusual forms of speech, a suspicion of his soundness in faith. Even the pietists of Halle were not satisfied with him, since he dwelt less than they upon the atonement, and more upon the extent of salvation than on the power of sin; more on the love of God and joy in Him, than on the fear of God. "He makes religion too easy," they said; and because he did not profess to have felt that inward struggle over the atoning blood, of which they spoke much, they even denied him the right of being called a Christian. The Catholics also looked at him with an evil eye, and the Jesuits went so far as to accuse him to the Emperor of being a plotter against him, of setting his subjects against him, and winning them over to a new faith. And so, while Zinzendorf was entering upon a course of activities quite enough to absorb his whole energies, a series of attacks began upon him from every quarter, even from the very body which he was engaged in founding. With all this his spirit remained strong and his faith unbroken.

With a view to live entirely to the great purpose of his life, Zinzendorf finally concluded to take upon himself, formally, the functions of the priestly office. He submitted his plan to the oldest members of the colony; but they, and his wife still more, found difficulties in the way. So, to solve these doubts, he determined to have recurrence to the lot, the usual way with his people for settling all doubtful questions. The lot confirmed his own choice. It so happened that about that time a merchant in Stralsund sent to Zinzendorf for a Moravian tutor for his children; and the Count resolved to take the place himself, and travelled to Stralsund under the name of Louis von Freidick, to avail himself of this opportunity to be examined and ordained. On the way he was compelled to hear many unpleasant things of himself and his colony. On the 11th of April 1734 he read his trial sermon at Stralsund with great applause. He completed his examination and returned to Herrnhut with a fine reputation for soundness of faith, and laid aside the advocate's badge for ever. The same year he was ordained with all the formalities of such occasions. But other means were required to put the other members of the community in a position so that they could go forth as missionaries to the heathen, and celebrate the ordinances of baptism and the Lord's supper. The candidates were mostly artizans, men without education, who could not pass through a theological examination as Zinzendorf had done, and there was no ground for hope that a Lutheran consistory would admit them to ordination. They must get help elsewhere. Just then the old custom of the Moravians came to their relief. From remote times they had had bishops who could consecrate, by the laying on of hands, any whom they might think worthy of the pastoral office; and so it only became necessary to find a bishop in order to make the thing complete. In Berlin there was living the oldest of the Moravian bishops,—Jablonsky, preacher to the king. Zinzendorf applied to him, and recommended David Nitschmann, one of the most active members of the community, a man who had already preached to the negroes in the West Indies, with the request that he would consecrate him to ministerial labours. This met Jablonski's instant approval, and was done.

We pass over the journeys, more or less extensive, which Zinzendorf undertook in the furtherance of his work—the associations which he formed in North and South Germany, in Switzerland, Denmark, Sweden, and Holland—the opposition which he encountered—the humiliations to which he was subjected, the conversions which were the result of his preaching, and we recount only the leading events of his life. Among these is to be reckoned the edict of King Augustus of Saxony, issued in 1736, driving him from that kingdom in consequence of his teaching false doctrine and promulgating dangerous principles. Zinzendorf accepted even this in a worthy spirit, and felt no bitterness towards the king, whom he recognized as his rightful lord. Yet he had to look him out a new home. This he found in a half ruined castle on the Ronneberg. Hither he took his wife, and a handful of his best co-workers. Soon he collected new assemblages from the neighbourhood, as at Herrnhut, and the seed of the new doctrine, driven from Saxony by the storm, was only wafted a little further away, to take new root in the Rhine country, and bear the same fruit anew. Zinzendorf himself did not remain long there.

He journeyed eastward as far as Livonia. The new colony of Salzburgers in Lithuania drew his special attention and interest. He had previously enjoyed himself much with these simple people, and had addressed a memorial to Frederick William the First, King of Prussia, regarding them, but now he took occasion to commend them in person to the favourable notice of that singular and capricious monarch. Zinzendorf was formally presented to the king at Wustershausen. Frederick William had imagined Zinzendorf to be "a merry or a melancholy fanatic, a fellow half ridiculous and half formidable," but the interview with him displayed him in so different a light, that he confessed to his court, "that he had been purposely deceived and lied to about the Count, that there was nothing the matter with him about heresy or state affairs; his only sin was, that being a nobleman, and having a polite air, he had given himself to the preaching of the Gospel: in short, the devils in hell could not lie worse than he had been lied to about Zinzendorf."

The favour of the king was of this advantage to him, that it secured him the same service from Jablonsky which had before been conferred upon Nitschmann. The ordination did not take place, however, till a year subsequently. Meanwhile, Zinzendorf's wife and friends had left Ronneberg, and had gone to Frankfort-on-the-Main, where he soon after met them. Here he entered, as elsewhere, upon the functions of a preacher, and made the doctrine of reconciliation, or, in his words, "the grace founded on the blood of the Lamb of God, which does not admit of one spark of self-righteousness to be mingled with it," the ground thought of his sermons. It was a serious stumbling-block to many, when he insisted that the most devout citizen of Frankfort could not be justified on any other ground than the highway robber broken on the wheel. In the neighbourhood of the city, at the castle of Marienborn, the Moravians held their first Synod, near the close of the year 1736. Soon after this, Zinzendorf undertook a journey to Holland and England, and not long after he received official permission to enter Saxony again. Thus he could once more look upon his beloved Herrnhut: but soon after, on declining to sign a declaration which he could not honourably agree to, he was once more driven from the country.

Zinzendorf, after this second repulse, turned his steps to Berlin, and there delivered lectures in a private house, first twice a week and then four times. The press to see and hear him, even of the most noted in the fashionable world, was so great that, at one time, forty-two coaches were counted before the door. In 1739 he went to the West Indies in order to visit the Islands of St. Croix and St. Thomas, where the Moravians had established missions. At St. Thomas he found his brethren in much trouble, brought on them by the planters' resentment at their preaching to the negroes. From the West Indies the Count went to Switzerland; and, while at Basle he wrote to a friend, under date of January 28, 1740, from which letter I will quote some lines which illustrate happily Zinzendorf's mode of thought and expression, and give us some insight into the great purpose of his life.

"It is now somewhat over thirty years since I first experienced the power of divine grace drawing me to the cross of Christ; but in all that I have attempted and done, I have laboured entirely for Jesus' sake, and never for any side purposes whatever; nor was it at all to my taste that my name should be glorified in preaching Christ. Naturally, I was fond of horses, of show, and was enamoured of the reputation of a Xenophon, a Brutus, or a Seneca. The ambition of my parents and of my grandparents conformed to my own inclination—my education ran in the same line, and I well knew that no government had ever been founded on truly Christian ideas. Yet I gave all up for Jesus' sake. My training was tedious and confused. . . . As to my general plan, I have none, but go on from year to year, following the Saviour's direction, and do with my whole heart what I can do. I have, indeed, marked out certain leading courses; I have had, for example, as one object of my life, the preserving of the Moravian church as pure as possible, and safe from the attacks of any plundering wolf; another object which I cherish is the sending the gospel to as many heathen as I can, and make them share in the benefits of the blood of Christ; another wish of my heart is to fulfil the prayer of the Saviour contained in John xvii., and to bring the whole children of God into fellowship, not by making Moravians of them, but by enjoining unity upon the whole church: another purpose of my life is to bring as many souls as possible to a conviction of sin, and to the grace in Christ; and, for this, I labour earnestly, and have sometimes travelled over three hundred miles at once to preach his blessed gospel; and now, after following these great purposes so long, from 1717 to 1739, I am compelled to surrender them, and to leave them all with God, not seeing myself the end of all these things, but confident that divine Providence will cause them all to result in accordance with His great plans."

The following year he visited Switzerland once more, taking Geneva in his route. Then he turned his thoughts to an extensive tour, being no less a one than to North America, accompanied by his daughter, then sixteen years of age. On the Delaware river he found a Moravian colony already planted, out of which grew, at a later period, the villages of Nazareth and Bethlehem. In America he formally laid down his title of count, and in the presence of some eminent witnesses, among them Benjamin Franklin, he took the name of Thurnstein; but he was generally known under the title of Brother Lewis or Friend Lewis. The numerous sects in the United States furnished many points to which he could easily make an attachment, but, on the other hand, their existence raised many difficulties in his way. He first directed his energies to the Lutherans, whom he consolidated into an organization; he also preached to the Calvinists; but he could make little impression on those of New England descent. As an example of their dreadful intolerance towards Zinzendorf, it is said that he was once fined for breaking the Sabbath, in consequence of transcribing on that day a hymn which he had composed.

He afterwards journeyed into the interior to preach the gospel to the Indians: and, while on this tour, he at one time fell into danger of being killed, but, at another, was treated with the high honour of receiving the belt of beads, which was given by the Indians as a token of amity. He soon returned, however, to the Continent by way of England.

Not yet wearied with travelling, Zinzendorf cast his glance upon Livonia and Russia; but he was forbidden to enter the last-named country, as his wife had gained an evil name there as the founder of a sect. The count was arrested at Riga.

The Empress Elizabeth, to whom he then applied, gave him the short answer, "The sooner he took himself out of Russian territory the better;" and when he requested an investigation into the evil reports spread about him, he was told that "her Majesty did not find it necessary to enter upon one." And so he was conducted to the frontier by a military escort, and there tarried for some time in Silesia, where there was a number of Moravian settlements.

We omit the recital of his many journeys, his plans, the institutions established—the obstacles which met him both among the Moravians and outside of his own people—the uncounted writings which he put forth, and those which appeared against him. We need only say that, in the year 1747, the sentence of banishment from Saxony was withdrawn—that he passed the period between 1751 and 1755 in England, where his influence gained from Parliament a recognition of his brotherhood—that, after losing his son Renatus and his wife, he was married, in 1757, to Anna Nitschmann, a friend and helper of long standing; and that lastly he died the 9th of May, 1760, at Herrnhut. An attack of catarrh had impeded his speech; but, although he could hardly speak, he called his son-in-law to him and said, in a feeble voice, "My dear son, I am now going home. I am wholly reconciled to God's will. He is content with me. I am ready to go, nothing now stands in my way." When he had closed his eyes, his son-in-law said, "Lord, now lettest thou thy servant depart in peace;" and, as he pronounced the word "peace," Zinzendorf drew his last breath. His decease was announced in a manner common among the Moravians, by the notes of a trumpet. The whole colony assembled at his deathbed, and, with bended knees, thanked the Saviour for the usefulness which he had so signally blessed in the departed. On the next day the body was robed in a gown, such as the Moravian bishops wear, and, placed in a violet-coloured coffin, was visited by the whole brotherhood present in procession, the children leading the way, and all uniting in a sacred song. A week after his death he was buried. Two thousand strangers came to witness the funeral obsequies, and walked behind the body; and thirty-two ministers and missionaries, some from England, Holland, North America, and Greenland, who were present, bore the bier, the whole convocation joining in the choral—

> "How blessed now thy sleep,
> How sweet thy peaceful dream."

At his left hand his first wife was buried; at his right the second, who survived him only a month. By his first marriage he had six sons and six daughters; only three daughters survived him, and they laboured for the brotherhood to the end of their life. Zinzendorf died without means. "I sought," he could well say, "not yours, but you. No one shall say that I have made myself rich. I have not for years laid out a hundred dollars annually for ought excepting the bare necessaries of life."

In figure Zinzendorf was large, slim in youth, but in later years stout. His carriage was free, and indicated a gentle bringing up. As to the common saying, that he had a way of hanging his head, it is enough to remark that, so far from this being the case, he always carried his head remarkably erect. His features were regular—his forehead high—his eyes blue and gentle, and full of lambent flame—his nose slightly Roman—his mouth expressing a fine blending of seriousness with amiability. "He had," says his biographer Schrautenbach, "a manly, pleasant, full-toned voice, adapted alike to speaking and to singing. The difficult art, or rather the high gift, of laying the accent with exact discrimination, and the accompanying his voice with the appropriate gesture, was natural to him. Life, soul, and a happy blending of the best qualities, characterised all that he did. If he consecrated a bishop, or presided at an ordination, and raised his right hand to pronounce a blessing, it produced a visible sensation throughout the audience. Especially impressive was his bearing while administering the sacraments. His appearance was noble, and the stamp of power was on his every motion. He was a noticeable man when seen in the company of the most polished, or walking quietly along the streets of London or Amsterdam; and the respect paid him, the stepping out of his way as he approached, the involuntary bowing to him, and the desire to do him service, were always marked. He uniformly dressed in the most simple and unstudied way, was never sumptuously lodged, indifferent to furniture, never valued merely external things, and ascribing little worth to the trifles of life. Of all things which concerned his person, clothing, food, and the like, strangely inconsiderate. . . . In conversation the count was lively, sociable, and uncommonly entertaining ; a lover of mirth and of an innocent joke, even if he himself were the subject of it. Yet no one was on terms of familiarity with him. . . . In professional matters he had nothing of a dictatorial tone, as though absolute master of affairs. He could chide ; and it is the case, perhaps, that once in a while he had better have suppressed his feelings, yet he never said what would lower him in any eyes. . . . In respect to his scientific attainments and general knowledge he was only a self-made man, and therefore not amenable to criticism on these points. He read little, the Bible almost exclusively, and, in the last twenty years of his life, perhaps no other spiritual book ; he wrote much and meditated much. His writings and sermons are not elaborate productions ; for his mind was far too lively to dwell very long on a single theme. The active life of a man who thought much, wrote, preached, composed hymns, builded, made all kind of business arrangements, visited remote places, is like the sight of a new and great city rising in the midst of the waters, here a palace, there a hut—a large and confused picture, not to be studied in detail, but to be looked at in reference to the composition of the whole." So far Schrautenbach.

The extent of Zinzendorf's labours was very great. He planted his colonies in Norway, Greenland, and Lapland, in Ethiopia, Guinea, and among the Hottentots, in Russia, Persia, and Palestine : he scattered his ideas throughout North and South America and the West India islands, and sent missionaries to almost all parts of the globe, to labour for the glory of that Saviour for whom he lived. The names of the chief Moravian colonies still existing are well known : Barby, Niesky, Gnadau, Gnadanfrei, Gnadenfeld, Christiansfeld, Königsfeld, Neuwied, Neudietendorf, and Ebersdorf. These are mostly in Germany, the great scene of his active labours and his chief triumphs.

Zinzendorf and the Moravian brotherhood, whose history we have now briefly sketched, have from the first been variously judged. It was not people of the world alone, professed unbelievers, who discovered stumbling-blocks in the Count himself and in his doctrines, nor was it the orthodox alone, bound to dead forms; but learned and pious men, among whom I mention even Bengel, found much exception to him and his views. Even the brotherhood itself was not always satisfied with its founder, yet it never took offence at what occurred within itself and went forth from itself: and so we are often surprised at a want of coherence between the judgments passed on Zinzendorf himself, and the system which was his own plan and work, and which bore in every part the imprint of its designer's mind.

Beginning with the man, we have already drawn a sketch of his personnel, as his cotemporaries have given it to us. They evidently did not consider the Count free from faults, and he himself, least of all. In his Reflections on the year 1742, he has thus painted himself, and given this testimony. "From my childhood up I have had but one object, the glory of the Lord Jesus Christ, the crucified; and I have always been unwilling to enter into discussions which touch on other religious themes. Other foundation know I not, save Jesus Christ, the Son of the living God; but I can bear well with all who build on this foundation, though they build differently from me. I am perfectly free from crookedness of mind, I always live in fear before God, in love to all men, and on terms of perfect confidence with the brethren; I am most open to my own censure, and on account of my free manner of speaking, I do not put the bridle on my tongue when I should, and so sometimes say what I ought not, but always say from my heart what I say. In most matters of opinion very liberal, in action severe and almost intolerant: in the doctrine of the divinity of Christ sêt and unchangeable: in religion a friend of every name, order, or persuasion: in the brotherhood an advocate of a community of interests, of order, and of rigid discipline, yet without wishing to enforce these outside of my own domain. It is not my object to establish one visible church, but many churches. They who draw themselves off from the great church, do wrong, and they who separate from the smaller churches among which they live, are selfish or visionary. It is the wish of my heart to establish the Moravian brotherhood on the freest, most simple, most orderly basis, and to make myself one of the lowest among the brethren, for I hate all lordship in this matter. All else that is said about me is a slander and a lie. God and the Father of our Lord Jesus Christ knows that I lie not." "I have only one passion," he writes in another place, "and it is He, only He." And yet Zinzendorf confesses very frankly that his genius often leads him into extravagances, and his friend Schrautenbach, already quoted, expressly begins his biography with these words, "Count Zinzendorf was not a man without faults," and elsewhere confesses that the fire of his nature, and his glowing imagination, sometimes led him astray.

Schrautenbach discriminates a number of periods in the life of his friend. "In his childhood he was obliged to yield to others. So we find in all that is left of his between the age of twenty-seven and forty-two, a quiet, contented spirit; from that period to the age of fifty-five, we detect a self-exalted spirit, but thence to the age of sixty, we find him drawing back within himself, and testing his system by the probe of experience. His life has confirmed his own ground principle, which he put forth as chief of all, that no one is good save God alone, but it also showed the power which a system, embraced by the heart, can have upon the whole actions of a man, and how the life of faith in Christ can change the will and soften the heart."

That Zinzendorf was a man of earnestness, no one will doubt. And who shall be his judge, how far human weaknesses may have had dominion over him? But though we acknowledge the noble direction which his nature took, and the piety and purity of his motives, although we confess that his appearing in the age in which he did appear, was a necessary and useful phenomenon, for which we ought to be grateful, yet the task remains to us, after the waves of passion have swept by, and the act has appeared in the heavens, of subjecting the man and his doctrines to the impartial scrutiny of history. To this end we must first inquire, what was his own aim, what he purposed to effect. It was not a reformation of the world, but a bringing of men's souls to the Saviour, and the preparing of them for His second coming. This we recognize as his chief service, that in a time when so many were scattered, he drew them together, and when so many hearts were cold, he awakened in them the glow of a new spiritual life. Zinzendorf was no dogmatic theorizer, he was a practical organizer, and in that his great strength lay. Unpractical as he was in external things (often lost in reverie and sunk in thought even while on his walks, unable to reckon money and the like), yet in all religious affairs he was thoroughly practical, and his power displayed itself in most of his arrangements. It was not Zinzendorf's theology, not his language and presentation of thought which made him great; on the contrary, these helped to make his name a laughing-stock with the world, and an offence even to orthodox Christians: they are not what was durable in his work. Yet it is our duty to make a brief exposition of Zinzendorf's religious views, becoming, as they did, with more or less change, the doctrines of the Brotherhood. We will pass over all the unworthy and venomous attacks which were made upon him, embracing not only the charge of all imaginable heresies, but of atheism itself. From his opponents we will select only the worthiest one, Bengel, whose name and whose praise are on every lip.

It needs only a superficial glance at the doctrines of Zinzendorf to see that Christ, Christ the Crucified, was its middle point, its great summary of contents. Taken in its general aspect, no one can say aught against this: on the contrary, this must be confessed to be the primitive, apostolic doctrine. And further thought will only confirm the happy conjunction of events which at the time when Voltaire was imposing on himself the task of banishing all thought of the Crucified One from the hearts of men, a man arose, who although from his position he might have lived in the enjoyment of all the pleasures of life, gave up everything, shunned no shame, no loss, that he might raise the Lamb of God to his throne, and make His sufferings the basis of all theological theory and practice. But if we look closer at the teachings of Zinzendorf about Christ and His sufferings, especially if we weigh the expressions which he used, we need not wonder if he caused unbelievers to be repulsed rather than to be attracted, and if believers like Bengel considered it a duty to put men on their guard against him. As is often the case, that those whose duty is to reaffirm a rejected truth, carry it to an extreme which is itself an error, so was it with Zinzendorf. The doctrine of the divinity of Christ had been cast aside, first by the

Socinians, then by the deists, and even the milder rationalism which was then just coming into being, but which has since become so formidable, left Christ's person, work, and suffering, in the back-ground, bringing morality into undue prominence, and exalted the human element in Jesus above the divine. The conviction that a belief in God, the Creator and Sustainer of all things, and that a virtuous life crowned with its due reward, were the only valuable truths of religion, was a conviction which had become widely prevalent, and had found lodgment in many excellent minds. This conviction Zinzendorf met with his whole power, and against the one-sided doctrine of God the Father, whom many supposed they could approach without the Son, he brought the equally one-sided doctrine of God the Son, whom he placed undeniably in the place of the Father. Although the Scriptures so fully show that through the Son we are led to the Father, and name the Father Creator of the heaven and the earth, and bid us pray to him *through* Christ, and in Christ's name, Zinzendorf bids us to know no God but the Saviour. It is true that he gained more power over the heart by bringing Jesus so prominently forward, than those had who went no further than the abstract idea of a higher Being. Still he went further, and not only ignored the existence of God the Father, but employed expressions of great harshness against what he called the God-Father religion. In this way he lost the great doctrine of the Mediatorship of Christ, and obscured the full significance of the Trinity. It is without doubt a great defect in his teaching that he made so little account of the attributes of God the Father. As Bengel says in his naive way, "We ought not to leap over the Son; nor ought we leap over the Father: and if Zinzendorf supposes that they are enemies to the Saviour who do not assign to him the Father's place, he too could be charged with enmity to the Father, on the same ground, which would assuredly be doing him a great injustice."

No less one-sided was Zinzendorf in his representation of the sacrifice of Christ. Here, again, is a deep religious necessity, which had driven him from his childhood up to the suffering Saviour, and in this strong love to Jesus the Crucified, the one great and absorbing passion of his life, there is something grand and beautiful. In this Bengel was entirely at one with Zinzendorf, for he, too, would acknowledge no basis of salvation save Jesus Christ and Him crucified. But it was this which Bengel so severely criticised in Zinzendorf, that he did not make the sufferings of the Saviour merely the central point of theology, but its sum total. Nor did he relish the dwelling upon those of His sufferings appreciable by the senses alone, the exclusive allusion to the blood, the wounds, the print of the nails, the piercing of the side. It did not escape the observation of so close a student of the Scriptures as Bengel, that the sufferings of Christ are always united in the closest union with His life, His actions, His teachings, on the one hand ; and with His resurrection and glorification on the other, and that only in this mutual connection has the cross its true significance. Nowhere in the words of Jesus, nor in the apostolical writings, did he discover an effeminate tone and a dealing with the cross as a pure object of sense, and he wished an equal purity and strength in those who wish to preach the cross with power. Nor did this able and yet truly pious critic consider the expressions which are called forth, and the tears which are shed at the representation of the physical sufferings of Jesus to be the most truthful token of a reconciled spirit: he feared that thereby men might fall into a false security and fail of a true conversion. "The mere hearing and speaking of the wounds of Jesus," says Bengel, "ends in nought but words. There are those who only *name* Christ, and never *know* him. Even they who always bring prominently forward the sufferings of the Saviour make them common, and cannot ward off a misuse of what should be so rare and precious. They make of the blood of Christ an opiate to apply to their consciences, thinking that thus they may better distinguish between right and wrong. Through the supremacy which the Moravian scheme of doctrine grants to the imagination, the Scripture itself is made to pervert itself; the cross is buried beneath itself, the heart is made the instrument to lead itself away, human freedom becomes its own betrayer, and the sensibilities blunt their own native delicacy." Bengel brings also as an especially serious charge against Zinzendorf's teachings, that all religion is narrowed down to the feelings: that the great questions of duty are determined by the feelings alone. The Moravian doctrine wholly casts out fear: it does not subordinate it as a motive, it ignores it wholly, and rests all law, and all impulses to duty, simply on looking ever to the Saviour's face.

Zinzendorf was a devout believer in the Holy Writ. Without going so far as to accept a verbal inspiration, or to claim that there are no historical nor chronological errors in the Bible, he did insist, with all sound Protestants, on the sufficiency and the divine origin of the Scriptures.

In close correspondence with what has been said respecting Zinzendorf's doctrines, stands his spiritual poetry, which has been the fruitful source of much of the ridicule which has been heaped upon him. That he had a genuine appreciation of what was beautiful in the old lyrics of the church cannot rightfully be denied, but so far as concerns his own writings, it must be confessed that they are of various quality. Some of his hymns do not rise above the level of rhymed prose. He had great facility in verse making, or, to use Herder's expression, "that pliancy of speech, and that wealth of bold images, and tender, devout phrases which often surprises, often deceives with a false sense of beauty." Zinzendorf has written some hymns which should be excluded from no collection, and yet it must be confessed that the later Moravian poets have far surpassed him.

The following may be taken as an example of his most successful efforts in sacred poetry:—

Jesus go before,
Open heaven's door,
Not much longer will we tarry,
After Thee our cross to carry,
Lead us by the hand
To the promised land.

Though we prosper not,
Stand we in our lot;
Even in the darkest days, Lord,
Sad complaints we will not raise, Lord;
For through Sorrow's sea
Leads the way to Thee.

If some painful smart
Anguishes our heart,
If another's grieving move us,
Let the fiery trial prove us;
Thy own patience give,
Patiently to live.

Order all our way
While on earth we stay;
Rough the paths through which we're faring,
Ne'er withheld our Father's caring:
Jesus, go before,
Open heaven's door.

We now advance to the consideration of the constitution and the interior organization of the Brotherhood, in relation to the church universal on the one hand, and to Protestantism on the other. In the capacity for organizing such a community, the greatness of Zinzendorf appears not in his dogmatic theology, nor in his poetry. It is not Zinzendorf the theologian, it is not Zinzendorf the poet who calls out our wonder: for as a theologian he was far surpassed by Bengel, and as a poet by Freilinghaus, Tersteegen, and Hiller, but the Zinzendorf who created an epoch in history is the founder of a Brotherhood. Whoever casts a glance back at the beginnings of the Moravian movement, at the varied and contradictory elements which cross each other, and then looks at the edifice as it now stands, which has been created in so brief a time out of the older Moravian, Lutheran, Calvinistic, and Pietistic materials, and has become so fair, so united, and so strong a Church, must admire the skill, the patience, the power, and the prudence of the man who could do all this. A one-sided, prejudiced, confused, and fanatical sectary would never have accomplished it. For this work there was needed a man of tact, a man of the world, a man of large observation, and having a thorough knowledge of men: there was wanted a nature made to command, which works in perfect quietness, with the gentleness of the dove, and yet with the wisdom of the serpent, which goes in meekness to take possession of the earth, which knows how to employ every gift of God with an eye single to the winning of souls to its great object. It may, indeed, be said of Zinzendorf, that circumstances combined to further his designs; but to look through and control the circumstances of one's lot, is the work of a man of mind and power. This power of winning the souls of men to one's self may become a dangerous one, as the history of the Church abundantly shows; and there have not been wanting those who have charged Zinzendorf with a desire to establish a Papacy within the Protestant Church. But every one is exposed to this charge who undertakes to organize any new movement in the church. Luther and Calvin even were called minor popes. It depends entirely upon the fact whether the power of controlling the minds of others is usurped, or the result of natural gifts. That Zinzendorf would usurp no lordship over the consciences of men is evident from what he has left on record, in a passage which we have quoted—"I hate all lordship among the brethren." But when people willingly gave up to his judgment, and yielded implicitly to him, it was a matter of their own choosing. How often Luther warned his friends not to become Lutheran, and not to take his words as the Truth, and yet all in vain. And so Zinzendorf, though not anxious to become a spiritual hierarch in any bad sense, could not prevent men from becoming, to use Bengel's expressive phrase, "a lump of wax in his fingers, to be shaped as he might please." There have not been wanting those, too, who have not hesitated to institute a comparison between the Moravian Brotherhood in the Protestant, and the Orders in the Catholic Church. The Jesuits even have been cited, not without some show of reason, as not unlike Zinzendorf's Brethren. And, indeed, whoever looks at the external forms, and at the mere machinery of the religious orders, at the prompt obedience to authority, at the immense influence which the *esprit du corps* gains to every association, and at the great geographical extent under command, will not wonder that such parallels should be instituted. But whoever looks deeper, whoever goes to the bottom of things, and marks the fundamental difference between Catholicism and Protestantism, sees that, so far from having a common goal, they run to opposite poles, as nothing has more conclusively shown than the missions established respectively by the Moravians and the Jesuits. It was foolishly said, that "over Herrnhut lies the way to Rome." As according to the old proverb, all "roads converge at Rome," it might be true that some Moravians, among others, were led thither, but surely their number was not greater than those who have found their way thither through other paths not so severely criticised.

"But," it may be asked, "is it not true that Moravian colonies have always assumed a cloister-like character?" Yes, it is the fact that to many a soul the entering the Brotherhood has been as the entering a cloister to Catholics. But when such a soul feels constrained by the pressure of its hard circumstances to withdraw from the world, to flee from its stormy lot to a safe harbour and spend the remainder of its days in religious meditation, is there, we would ask, anything unprotestant in it, anything which opposes man's natural freedom? I, at least, have heard of no solemn vows which permit no return to the world. And there have not been wanting words of regret that in the Protestant Church we lack those places of retreat in which those who long for perfect retirement and for sweet religious communion with those like-minded with themselves, can have this natural wish gratified: and is it not a matter of congratulation that the Moravians have met this want, and given us in so simple a way those places to which men may withdraw and be at rest and commune with God, and yet be free to return to the world when they will?

In contrast with the Catholicising tendency which has been ascribed to the Moravians, is the charge of sectarianism. How far the Brotherhood can be regarded as a sect is a matter which has been largely discussed. Zinzendorf very plainly declared that he would be the founder of no sect. He differed widely from Spener, who proposed to exert an influence upon the State Church, by establishing many minor churches. Zinzendorf, on the other hand, did not believe in founding a number of small churches, but of establishing a Brotherhood, and so of introducing into the bosom of the State Church, a new and productive force, which should renew it, working like leaven within it. Such a fact not only disproves in an instant the charge of sectarianism in Zinzendorf, but shows the extent and grandeur of his scheme. He had clearly seen, by the gradual decay of the Pietist Churches established by Spener, that that was an ineffective method, and so he had come to the great and fruitful conception of implanting his Brotherhood in the very heart of the Church itself.

That Zinzendorf kept this great conception always in mind is manifest from the care with which he always sought to maintain the different religious orders, and not have them blend in one and lose the old distinctions of sect. By keeping the Lutherans distinctly Lutheran, the Calvinists distinctly

Calvinistic, and so forth, he hoped to affect the different persuasions more effectually by the reaction of all these agencies upon the churches which they represented. Unfortunately, this great conception of Zinzendorf has been too much forgotten or ignored by his successors, and the Moravian Brotherhood has taken a position more outside of the Church than its founder intended that it should ever occupy. I dare not venture on a decision how much this unfortunate result is owing to the peculiar customs which the Moravians have adopted: the deciding of important matters by lot, the wearing of different coloured ribbons to designate among the women differences in age, and in domestic relations, the partaking of the "love feast," and the washing of each others' feet in connection with the Lord's Supper. But this is certain, that to the Moravians we owe a large measure of that practical Christian spirit which had so largely disappeared from the world, but which has of late awakened so much activity and beneficence. I need only refer to the missionary efforts and the diffusion of the Bible, which, though not primarily proceeding from the Moravians, have been so greatly due to the preparation which was the work of Zinzendorf and his successors.

We close by quoting a few words from one who, although a leader in the theology of the nineteenth century, was himself trained in youth among the brotherhood. Schleiermacher writes in this strain, while on a visit to the Moravian colony at Barby in 1802.

"Here it was that for the first time I awoke to the consciousness of the relations of man to a higher world. Here it was that the mystic tendency developed itself, which has been of so much importance to me, and has supported and carried me through all the storms of scepticism. Then it was only germinating, now it has attained its full development; and I may say that, after all that I have passed through, I have become a Moravian again, only of a higher order."

XIII.

SWEDENBORG, HEINRICH, STILLING, AND LAVATER, THE MYSTICS.

In formidable antagonism to German infidelity was the school of mystics, headed by Swedenborg, Heinrich, Stilling, and Lavater. These men we may call theosophic mystics, if we do not go so far as term them visionaries. Within the pale of the pietists, and even among the followers of Zinzendorf, there had appeared tendencies to a belief in this phase of supranaturalism, but with them these tendencies were merely fortuitous and transitory. The field which the pietists and the Moravians chiefly tilled was the domain of the practical. The miracles of the moral world, and mainly those connected with the conversion of the soul, excited more wonder with them than miracles in the natural world. Zinzendorf did not claim to have visions, nor did he believe that newer revelations would ever supersede the Bible. In this he differed from Swedenborg, who insisted upon the fact of a continued revelation, a power of communicating still with the spirit world, and of the possibility of miracles even now. And yet there were wide differences in the views of this school of mystics. While Swedenborg was very far removed from the common views of the church, and from the reception of the letter of Scripture, Stilling and Lavater, with all their lawless fancies, clung to the Bible and to Christian doctrine as generally accepted, and were rigid advocates of practical righteousness, and so were bound by some ties to the pietists. Indeed, Lavater was so many-sided, and united so many contradictions in himself, as to be very difficult to classify at all. We must begin with Swedenborg.

Immanuel Swedenborg was born in 1689 at Stockholm. His father, a Lutheran bishop, educated him in the principles of rigid orthodoxy. Even when a child, people caught up his expression that angels taught through his lips; and, up to his tenth year, he used to speak continually of such subjects as faith and love. In 1710 he commenced a series of travels through England, Holland, France, and Germany, and visited many of the most celebrated universities in those countries. Mathematical studies engaged his interest most. Charles XII., with whom he had frequent interviews, appointed him assayer at the mineralogical college, where Swedenborg made some important investigations, and published a number of scientific productions. In 1719 he was raised to the nobility, and visited the mines of Saxony on professional business. Later he published valuable treatises, not only on mineralogy but on philosophy and zöology. Up to 1741 we see him only in the light of a distinguished naturalist, whose attention was devoted to mines, machinery, and other practical matters. But observation and inquiry into the world of sense were merely the foundation for his speculations on the spirit world. It was in 1743, during his sojourn in London, that, as he stoutly affirmed, the Lord appeared to him, opened to him the mysteries of a higher stage of being, and brought him into communication with angels. In 1747 Swedenborg relinquished his office, but continued, at the king's desire, to receive his full salary. After this time he lived exclusively to his new calling, that of a spirit seer and an investigator into heavenly mysteries. His home was alternately in England and Sweden, interspersed (in good faith, according to Swedenborg) with journeys to heaven and hell, during which tours he had interviews with antediluvians, as well as with men of the Old Testament and of the early Christian epoch. The theological works which he wrote, he published at his own cost. The sceptics ridiculed him, the orthodox laid their bann upon him, but the favour of the king protected him against them both. Yet his book gained him some friends as well as enemies. With all his close relations to the spirit world, Swedenborg was always a wellbred man of the world, and knew how to conduct himself to equal advantage among gentlemen and ladies, and with disembodied forms. With all his peculiarities he was a man of humane disposition, rigid morals, and unaffected piety. He lived in perfect health to an advanced old age. He died in London in 1772.

To give a sketch of Swedenborg's doctrines would be difficult, as there is an inner connection in what seems torn apart; and the separate threads which bind the whole are often entangled in a knot, while their loose ends are lost in a mystical cloud. Beginning where he began, we find that the Scriptures alone were by no means the whole source whence he drew religious truth, least of all the Scriptures read according to the letter. The angels, he asserted, *i.e.* the spirits of the departed, were his instructors; for Swedenborg accepted no other angels than these. The teachings of celestial beings he did not hold as antagonistic to those revealed in the Bible, but supplementary to them; indeed the angels help me, said he, to a right understanding of the Bible. Our present Holy Writ, as we have it, is only a coarse copy of what was written by angels; and, therefore, we need the help of those celestial beings to guide us to a correct interpretation of the counsels of God, and to help us to ascertain that inner sense of the Bible, which ought to beam forth as the soul does through the body, as the thought does through the eye. To every expression in that book, as well as to every external expression in the world of sense, there is something to be expressed, an inner something, and to trace the correspondences between the two is the task of the true Scripture expositor. In this way names, numbers, and the like, which otherwise would have no meaning for us, have their true significance. In the most ancient times this science of correspondences was thoroughly understood in the Orient; the wise men who came to adore the Saviour were versed therein; but the Jews had lost the key, and held only to the letter of Scripture, and so could not interpret the truth. This was the reason that they did not see that Jesus was the Messiah. Even in the time of the primitive Christians this science of correspondences was not understood, nor, indeed, was there need of it, because of their simple faith. Not even to the reformers was it revealed. But now, *i.e.* the time of Swedenborg, it is understood once more.

One of the beautiful poetic fancies of Swedenborg is this, that when innocent children read the Scriptures the angels are edified more than when older persons read. Swedenborg's doctrine of the church harmonises with his views of the Bible. The true church, the new Jerusalem, is only to be looked for when there is a thorough appreciation of Scripture, which can only be attained at the second coming of Christ. Much of what the church has received before is false; among other things the doctrine of the Trinity. According to Swedenborg, or rather according to the revelations made by angels to him, there are not three persons, as the orthodox maintain, which is but saying that there are three gods; but the whole Trinity is embraced in the single person of the God-man Jesus Christ. And this idea he has in common with Zinzendorf, that there is no other God with which Christians, as such, have to do, excepting God incarnate in Christ. According to him Christ is Father, Son, and Holy Ghost at once. He himself is the triune God. No less decisively did Swedenborg cast aside the commonly received doctrine of the satisfaction of Christ. That men should be justified by the service of another, by what was purely external to them, seemed to him contradictory to sound sense. In this point he approached the Socinians and the sceptical writers of his time much nearer than did Zinzendorf. Yet the death of Jesus had more import in his eyes than it had in theirs. Swedenborg saw a purifying power in all suffering and sorrow, lifting man above himself; and hence, in the sufferings of Jesus Christ, he traced the advance from the battle to the victory; and in this advance he discovered, as he supposed, the building of the human character up to the divine. In his death Christ solemnised his own glorification. He was perfected through suffering. He did not take away once for all the sins of men; but he takes them away (from us, in the present time) by imparting a new divine life. Salvation is, according to Swedenborg, an inner, spiritual work, and is identical with the work of renewal of the heart and sanctification. In the whole doctrine of repentance he stood on entirely different ground from Zinzendorf, who was firm in his advocacy of the appropriation of the merits of Christ as the great fundamental truth of salvation. In this matter Swedenborg was widely apart from most Protestant theologians, and nearer to the Catholics, who hold that sanctification and justification are one, and who demand works *with* faith.

Especially singular are Swedenborg's views of life after death, claiming, as he did, to have communications direct from the departed, and apparently convincing himself of the reality of these communications. Every person transfers his life here unchanged to the other world; what he was and did here, he is and does there; what he wished and strove after here, he wishes and strives after there. That is the foundation of his views of the future life. He complained of it as a fundamental error that, after death, we expect a great change in our nature; and that the life after death is something entirely removed from life as we understand it, something ideal, abstract, peculiar. He regards life there as only a high potentiality, as it were, of life here. "Many learned Christian men who shall see themselves in the future world invested with a body, clad with clothing and living in houses, when they shall recall what they used to think before death about the soul, about spirits, about heaven and hell, will be filled with shame, and confess that those who were simple and unlearned were wiser in divine things than they." "That the spirit of man, after its separation from the body shall have a human form has been perfectly known to me [says Swedenborg] for many years; for I have seen those spiritual bodies a thousand times, and have heard them converse." "The spirits heartily pity us, because there is so much ignorance about them not only in the world but in the church." To this ignorance Swedenborg ascribed that abstract idea of the learned, that the spirit is and will be immaterial, mere being, without corporeal substance, and that the doctrine of the church does not recognise a spiritual body till after the resurrection. According to him, this union of soul and body is essential to life, and must be continued in another world, because just as essential then as now Heaven and hell are peopled with beings who once lived on this world, for Swedenborg acknowledged no other angels than the souls of the good who once lived on this earth, and no other devils than the souls of the bad who also once lived here. What is meant by the devil, when spoken of as a person, is only the collective being of damned souls. So, too, he throws away the commonly received view of the last judgment. According to him, that judgment is already past; he himself had seen it, and it occurred in the year 1757, occupying nearly the whole of that year. We have from his pen the following description: "All nations and peoples who were subject to judgment appeared in the following order; in the middle were those who were called Protestants, arranged according to countries—the Germans, where it was almost perfect darkness—the Swedes, where it was like evening—the Danes, in the twilight—the Dutch, where it was quite light—and the English in the broad glare of day. Around the Protestant group of nations stood the Papists, the greatest part in twilight gloom, a fragment in the broad light. Around these were the heathen in vast numbers, forming the outmost circle. Outside of all was what seemed like a great sea. That the nations were arranged in this order had its ground in the varied degree of receptivity for divine truth. The evil minded among the Mahommedans were in swamps and bogs, and the like class among the heathen were thrust into two great abysses, while the pure-minded among both were allowed to join the Christians. In that way the prophecy was fulfilled, that they shall come from the morning and the evening, and shall sit down together in the kingdom of heaven. The Papists, represented by the word Babylonians, had gone on until the day of judgment with their masses and their worship of images, had had their churches and cloisters, had sent monks to convert the heathen, had their councils, &c. In consequence of their formal and outside sanctity they have a place in the lowest ranks of heaven; but, in consequence of their inward impurity, they have a portion with the hosts of hell. But after the judgment in 1757, those of the Romish Church who lent their aid to suppress the truth were thrust down into the abyss referred to above, while those of pure life and of sincere desire for the prevalence of truth were accepted, and sent into a certain locality, where they enjoy Protestant instruction, and then are received into heaven. As to the representations of heaven and hell, the subjoined quotation will show what Swedenborg believed. "In the spiritual world," said he, "is everything which is in the natural world; there are houses, and palaces, and gardens, and in these trees of all kinds; there are fields, and meadows, and cattle, great and small, exactly as upon the earth, with this difference, that the latter have a spiritual origin. The people who are inclined to what is good and true, live in palaces surrounded by beautiful gardens; those who are inclined in an opposite direction are shut up in hell, within prisons which have no windows, or they live in deserts or in huts, surrounded by barren land, filled with snakes, dragons, owls, and whatever corresponds to their inner bad nature. Between heaven and hell is a middle place, called the spirit world; hither comes every one directly after death, and there is the same freedom of intercourse between people that there was before on earth. Everything there, too, is in correspondence with what we are accustomed to here. There are gardens, forests, shade-trees, and briar copses, flowery and grassy fields, animals of various kinds, wild and tame. I have often seen [says Swedenborg] sheep and rams in a contest of strength; I have seen rams with horns bent backwards and forwards too, terribly goad the sheep; I have seen rams with two horns butting the sheep with fierce impetuosity; and, as I looked to see nearer, I discovered others who were quarrelling with each other about faith, and that love that works by faith, which I interpreted to mean that the ram signified faith separated from love, and the sheep the love out of which faith springs. And when I had seen such contests several times, I felt assured that those who are trying to live by faith separated from active love are indeed the rams."

Swedenborg's writings were not universally known till after his death. He founded no sect; but after his decease there were formed in London and Stockholm the philanthropic exegetical communities bearing his name. These were joined rather by the learned and the affluent than by people from the masses: just the reverse of what had been the case with English Methodism. It is very natural that a faith which concerns itself far more with a future than a present world, and which expects to find that world only this one glorified, would not meet the feelings of those who feel themselves burdened and cramped by the hard conditions of life. Besides, such a faith would mainly find its advocates among those who have leisure and taste for speculation. And although the church-forming spirit was not pre-eminent among the followers of Swedenborg, it was not wholly lost sight of by them, and in 1787 they first organized themselves into a church, with a definite statement of polity and doctrine. The three countries where Swedenborg's views were most acceptably received were Sweden, England, and North America. His followers early sent missionaries to Africa, with the expectation of finding their own church already fully established there. The success of Swedenborg's doctrine of late years has been a remarkable phenomenon of our times. Perhaps the very mixture of what is fanciful and what is rational, and the spiritual arrogance with which it puts forth its pretensions to acquaintance with the land of mysteries, may have a special charm for an age which displays such a marked taste for whatever is piquant. That great ideas, such as those relating to the connection between the seen and the unseen world, lie at the foundation of Swedenborgianism, and that its views antagonistic to those commonly received by the Church were not wholly without ground, we will gladly confess. This recently-begotten faith, this mixture of rationalism and mysticism, is a proof that the times, unsatisfied with all that has been offered to it as the pure doctrine of the Church, sighs for something new and fresh; and that those who could not coincide with the views of the modern sceptical school, could just as little find satisfaction in the thoughtless imitation of orthodox forms.

Somewhat similar was it with Stilling and Lavater. We rank these two men, who had much more in common with our times than Swedenborg, with him, not because they accepted his system, but because they shared with him the tendency to speculate on the mysteries of the unseen world, and believed with him, in the close connection and correspondence of this world with the next. But while in Swedenborg there is nothing but this dreamy and insecure and fanciful speculation, and nothing of the practical, with Stilling and Lavater a lawless mysticism forms but a part of religion. They stood with firm foot upon the earth, and displayed so much activity among their fellows, that their career would be remarkable even had they not displayed their marked mystical tendencies. Especially true is this of Lavater, whose character in its practical phase, in regard to piety and moral worth, is well worthy of study. Both men (Stilling and Lavater) are so well known as to the external course and conditions of their lives, that we need enter into no detail. "Stilling's Life" is in all hands: not only has it been largely read in Germany, but, in its translated form, in England and America. That autobiography makes plain much that was peculiar in him. When we trace the career of this man, born in 1740, from the lowest classes of society, advancing first to the position of a schoolmaster, from that to the chair of a professor and privy councillor, and ascribing every step of this advancement to the special leading of God in answer to prayer, we must feel an interest in him. Stilling was brought into intimate connection with the pietists, without having his whole energies absorbed by them, and without being claimed by them. In his "Theobald, or the Fanatic," he has treated of some of the wild vagaries of faith in his day, characterizing them so soberly and at the same time so keenly, that no one, after reading that book, will expect to find a fanatic in the author. That simple, child-like piety of his, which rested almost solely on "an undisturbed faith in God, in help coming directly from Him," and which found its confirmation in the experience of many years, was highly valued even by those whom we are accustomed to think of as the enemies of all religious enthusiasm, such as Goethe for example.

His belief in God's power and willingness to answer prayer, Stilling shared with a number of pious contemporaries. Stilling is but the representative of a class not insignificant in influence, embracing even Bengel within it. The same belief we find in Lavater, even during his childhood, and we read of him, that after making a blot in his writing-book, he prayed to God to erase it. This was but typical of his universal reliance on the power of prayer. It may be thought that such a belief might lead to superstition if applied to all the petty troubles of life, yet it must be confessed that in an age when philosophy was separating God more and more widely from the world, reducing him to a mere abstraction, and waving him away into the vast emptiness of space, a belief in a God who can hear and answer prayer was the only bond which united the truly pious and godly to that distant Being: it was the shortest way to arrive at the comforting conviction that God has *not* deserted His people, that He is near to all who call upon Him. Had Stilling and Lavater held to no other valuable truth than this specific theory of prayer, they would have largely compensated for the dominant unbelief of their time. And, fortunately, they had on their side men who, in respect to historical Christianity, had far less positive belief than they. It was that firm belief in what Zinzendorf called a God-the-Father religion, that belief in a Providence which controlled even the details of life, which was peculiarly strong in the pious men of that day, and which supplied in some measure the want of a more definite and strongly based confidence in a historical Christianity. It was this belief in God as a Father which brought Lavater into such intimate relationship with Spalding and Zollikofer. Many a childlike soul could assent entirely to God's power of working in the present, and his ability and willingness to hear prayer, and yet stagger over the doctrines of the Trinity, original sin, and the satisfaction of Christ. That is a remarkable phenomenon of those times. And it is in this that that age was so widely different from ours, in which a belief in a personal and prayer-hearing God stands on a weak footing, while there is no lack of strict orthodoxy in other points.

But Lavater and Stilling were not content with that mere God-the-Father religion. The former tells us, indeed, that when a boy he had no conception of Christ: that the New Testament affected him far less than the Old. "Christ," he says, "had as Christ neither attraction nor repulsion to me. He was for me a wholly non-existent person, so far as drawing out any attachment from me. My heart then wanted no Christ, it only wanted a prayer-hearing God." Thus he as a boy stood on the same step with many pious men of his time. But when he became a man he looked at the matter differently. As a man he still stood on terms of the closest communion with God; but it was only when he attained to manhood that he saw that Christ had procured him that intimate approach to the Father. In a conversation which he once held with Zollikofer, on a journey, he expressed himself thus: "Men need not only a God worthy of worship, but one who can enter with them into all the conditions of life. The eternal, invisible, supreme, ever-present Being of all beings can be adored without Christ, but He cannot be approached in real supplication. In Christ the incomprehensible and infinitely exalted God has brought himself within the circle of the finite, and come within our call. Christ is the face of God in which all the attributes of God, hitherto hidden from view, were fully mirrored.

This reconciliation of divine and human elements in Christ was to Stilling and Lavater, and particularly the latter, the source of a living and active faith. For them the chain of mystery and miracle which appears in the Bible history, and has its beginning there, continues on to these later times, and in this they differed from the most of the orthodox who limit the period of miracles to the times of the apostles. In their sight the spiritual world is not far removed from view, it is only thinly covered, and it merely needs faith to have the veil removed. They were, therefore, drawn into fields of speculation as Swedenborg was, and it must be confessed that they did not fail to carry their notions to some degree of extravagance. Each had his own pet theme: with Stilling it was the world of spirits, with Lavater, it was wonders in the physical world rather. Both busied themselves with the Apocalypse, and Lavater, in his "Views into an Eternal Future," propounded a number of conjectures similar to the views of Swedenborg, but with this important difference, that Lavater speaks of what he conjectures, while Swedenborg speaks of what he claims to have seen.

And yet, strange and crude as were Lavater's material ideas of employment, houses, and the cultivation of art in the spirit world, unworthy of so great a man, and unsanctioned by Scripture, yet it would be unjust to him to refuse to make the concession, that such views as his and Swedenborg's had a very different reception at that time from what they would have now. Thère was prevalent a far more personal and distinct idea of future life then than now. They were conservative men for their time, and though in many things they were fanciful, yet they were not proscribed for their definite conceptions of man's future life. And notwithstanding Stilling's mysticism, yet he was remarkable for his practical piety, and his singularly beneficent life, his unwearied charities and labours of love in behalf of the poor and afflicted; while Lavater, with all his fanciful speculations on the houses, and gardens, and pursuits of the heavenly world, always stood with his feet firmly planted on this earth, and was to the last a faithful pastor and an earnest preacher. While Stilling seemed to think mostly of the heavenly home, and even went so far as to write in the family register of a friend, "Blessed are they who are home-sick, for they shall come at last to the Father's house." Lavater rejoiced continually in this life, and worked faithfully and truly to bless the earth. Lavater was in every point of view far more many-sided than Stilling, and his Christian faith far more joyful and less morbid. "Can it be repeated or thought upon enough," says Lavater in his "Manual for the Sick," that joy, nothing but joy, is the purpose of the great Leader of men, joy, nothing but joy, the only end of all that we suffer. Jesus and joybringer are words of the same significance. Whoever considers Jesus as anything but a joy-bringer, and the gospel as anything but tidings of joy, pain as anything but the source of joy, knows neither God, Christ, nor the Gospel."

This marked emphasis of joy was closely connected in Lavater with the most definite idea of Christ. This idea was the richest fountain of all his experiences. It governed his entire life. The divinity of Christ, his almighty power on earth and in heaven, was the theme on which he most loved to dwell. He was able to say with Zinzendorf, I have only one passion, and it is He, only He. Like the founder of the Moravian Brotherhood, he wanted to be on terms of personal communion with Christ, to be bound to him by a strict and literal tie. He never seeks to draw Christ down to bimself as Zinzendorf had done, but would rather be lifted up to Christ. Such a conception of the Saviour, which did not in extreme idealizing tear him from historic grounds, and yet just as little remained content with the mere historic Christ, which let Jesus become man anew, from day to day as it were, which did not lift him above the stars, but let him live in the breasts of men, which did not make him once for all the curer of the blind and the healer of the sick, but which raised him up as the Light of the world, was like a new gospel to men. What we are accustomed to regard as the very *essence* of Christianity, as something peculiar, as its distinguishing mark from all other religions, the blending of the divine and the human through Christ, appeared to the men of that time as foolish fanaticism, and many spoke it plainly out, that "the good man would suffer far less if he were not so believing, if he did not hang so to his Christ." While foolish and superficial sceptics ridiculed the spirituality of Lavater (I need only refer to Nicolai, who abused him shamefully), others, like Goethe, spoke approvingly of it as a most desirable gift, even if they did not share in it. "It lifts the soul up," writes Goethe to Lavater, "and gives the most cheerful thoughts to see the zest with which you raise the clear crystal to your lips and quaff the divine drink in such liberal draughts, even letting it pour profusely over the sides of the goblet." Goethe, of course, did not sympathize with Lavater in his views any farther than to look with appreciation upon the spirit and work of the man. Yet it is indeed wonderful to see the hold which both Stilling and Lavater had upon Goethe as friends, sceptic though he was.

XIV.

JOHN GODFREY HERDER.

HERDER TILL HIS APPOINTMENT IN BUCKEBURG.—GOETHE ON HERDER.—HERDER IN HIS OFFICIAL LABOURS IN BUCKEBURG.—THE COUNTESS MARIA.—HERDER'S LITERARY LABOURS.—CALL TO WEIMAR.—HIS LITERARY CLIMAX.—JOURNEY TO ITALY.—HIS DEATH CHARACTERISTIC OF HERDER.—HIS GREAT MENTAL POWERS AND VIVACITY.—HUMANITY.—ITS RELATION TO CHRISTIANITY AND PROTESTANTISM.—HERDER AS THEOLOGIAN.—HUMAN MODE OF VIEWING THE DIVINE.—HERDER'S POETIC VIEW OF THE WORLD.—SKETCH OF A JOURNEY.—HERDER'S CHRISTIANITY.—HIS THEOLOGICAL CONVICTIONS AND THEOLOGICAL CHARACTER.—HIS VIEWS ON THEOLOGY AND THE MINISTRY.—HERDER AS PREACHER.—HIS TALENT FOR RELIGIOUS POETRY.—HERDER'S POSITION IN REFERENCE TO PROTESTANTISM.—HIS CONSERVATIVE TENDENCY.—STRICT VIEWS OF CHURCH DISCIPLINE AND FREEDOM OF THE PRESS.—HIS POSITION IN REFERENCE TO PHILOSOPHY.

JOHN GODFREY HERDER was born at Mohrungen, East

Prussia, August 25th, 1744. His father, a poor chorister and teacher of a female school, is represented as a man strict and conscientious in performing his duties, very regular and methodical as well as good-natured and taciturn. Herder, however, appears to have inherited more of his mother's than of his father's nature. There was something very tender and sympathetic about his mother which, together with her quickness of comprehension and inclination to ceaseless activity, was transmitted to the son. She was a zealous Christian, and had, as her pastor Trescho testifies, a good knowledge, without, however, making a display of it, and was one of the most attentive and most easily affected hearers in the church. In this household the old spirit of family-worship and pious habits still prevailed. The day, which was spent in industry, was finished by singing a hymn. A deep and lasting impression was made on Herder's mind by these pious evening hymns. He frequently thought of them with emotion and melancholy longing, and in later years the remembrance of them still impelled him to play on the clavichord, and to sing the old chorals in the stillness of the night. A considerable part of the small family-library was composed of books like Arndt's "True Christianity," and it is said the leaf of this book still exists on which the father wrote the names and birth-days of his children, and a wish for their welfare added to each.

Herder's first education at school was very strict; much was learned, though not according to the best and easiest method. A boy like Godfrey Herder would, however, soon have surpassed the other pupils whatever method might have been used. His peculiar talents soon manifested themselves. Even in his early youth his greatest enjoyment consisted in music and poetry. He was fond of ancient history and ancient languages, and his talent for poetry developed in a wonderful manner. As his poetical taste was, next to the classics, awakened chiefly by the Bible and sacred hymns, it is quite natural that his first attempts at poetry were formed according to these sacred models. His reserve and bashfulness made it difficult for those who directed him in his studies to see clearly what his future career would be; and it happened that Herder, as well as some other eminent theologians (even Luther and Calvin), chose some other pursuit of life before he was led to the study of theology. After he had sighed away a good part of his youth with the pious, but rather melancholy and peevish theologian, Trescho, and had consumed many hours of the night in study, he fell into the hands of a regimental surgeon, who took him from his kind parents, whom he never saw again, to Königsberg, in order to teach him the science of surgery. But the fact, that at the first operation witnessed by the tender youth he swooned, was decisive. Herder was as little fit for a surgeon as a soldier, which he had dreaded to become even from his early boyhood. He, therefore, turned to the quiet study of theology and philosophy, of history, of languages, and polite literature. But difficulties increased with this change of studies, for the surgeon withdrew his assistance. Königsberg, whose grand architecture had at first astonished him, now became, with all its splendour, a school of severe trial, his poverty, connected with modesty and timidity, only formed so much the greater contrast to the grand impression he received from external objects. Dependent chiefly on himself, and assisted by only a few noble friends, the genius, pressed and restrained on all sides, was now to break his own way. The struggle, however, soon led to victory, and the path which had at first led through rough and gloomy places, soon conducted him cheerfully to the temple of fame.

Kant and Hamann, men of very different minds, were particularly prominent, in their respective spheres, among the men who at that time adorned the University of Königsberg. Lilienthal, the defender of the good cause of revelation, taught theology. Herder always spoke with the greatest respect of this worthy theologian, as well as of Kant, though, as we shall see further on, he could not agree with his philosophy. Being appointed teacher in the gymnasium (Frederick's College) of Königsberg, his circumstances gradually improved. Herder was an earnest teacher, who insisted on diligence and attention in his classes, but was just as strict with himself; and with such a course of conduct this position resulted in inward as well as outward advantages. "I am indebted to teaching," he says, "for the development and clear understanding of many ideas, whoever wishes to acquire these on any subject, let him teach that subject." When his relations had afterwards changed and taken him from the profession of teaching, he often wished that he could teach several years in a university, in order to get rid of his thoughts and ideas, and to give them expression in a living manner. This ardent desire to communicate is very important to us in Herder. His was an electric nature, easily receiving and easily emitting sparks. Thus the fiery soul of the timid youth gradually matured to the clearness and firmness of manhood. His natural bashfulness decreased, and he "to whom formerly a man with a collar seemed fearful, could now fearlessly look upon badges of honour and diadems."[1]

Of his friends in Königsberg, J. G. Hamann was one of the most intimate. "He found in him," Herder's wife says, "what he sought and needed, a sympathizing, affectionate and warm heart for all that is great and good, and a spiritual piety, the strictest moral principles and a genius high and consecrated both in mind and heart. He bore Hamann in his heart, and the deepest sympathy united them for time and eternity." Hamann was, as Herder says, "a good handful of years" the older. He exerted a great influence on Herder's life, whilst Herder in return made him known to the literary world as the *Magician of the North.*

Owing to his removal to the school of Riga in the autumn of 1764, Herder's relation to his friends soon changed. He was twenty years old when he became assistant teacher. Till this time he had worn his own uncurled hair; but now, according to a strict observance of the school custom of the day, a wig was to give the youth an older and a clerical appearance. But more than by the wig, was this done by the character of the man, which was able, not only to give him the proper appearance, but also to gain the confidence and affection of the scholars. "His method of teaching," one of his former pupils says, "was so excellent, and his intercourse with the pupils was so friendly, that they recited no lessons with greater pleasure than those assigned by him."

In Riga, Herder found quite a number of old and new friends, and his free, aspiring mind readily adapted itself to

[1] Thus his teacher, Trescho, who had visited him in Königsberg, wrote in 1764.

the still cherished relics of old Hanseatic customs and institutions. His views were enlarged, and his ideas of political freedom and prosperity, on which he had long been reflecting, now received form and distinctness, and became to him truth and reality. His external circumstances also improved from day to day. The bookseller. Hartknoch, Herder's student-friend while at Königsberg, published his works, which at this time already excited attention, among which the Fragments on German literature and Critical Wälder awakened by their bold spirit many new friends from the literary world on the one hand, and on the other many who envied and opposed him. In order to avoid the unpleasantness which is almost necessarily connected with literary disputes, Herder determined to travel to some foreign country, and in this he was encouraged by his friends. He resigned his position, and first went by way of Nantes to Paris, at that time the seat of the "encyclopedical" philosophy, from which the deistical tendency proceeded and gradually spread over the whole of Germany. He became acquainted with several leaders of this philosophy, and spoke of some of them with great respect, though he did not like their system; for he generally looked for the man, and then knew how to make a distinction between him and his views and opinions. Though his character was thoroughly German, he was still able to appreciate the good qualities of other nations, without overestimating or recommending them for servile and spiritless imitations; and it was from this standpoint that, among other things, he judged of French poetry. After having also visited Holland and the Netherlands, he returned to Germany by way of Hamburg, and in this journey made the acquaintance of Lessing, Claudius, Bode, Reimarus, and pastor Goetze. Of these, so very different men, Claudius, "the Wandsbecker Messenger," obtained the privileges of that intimate friendship which Hamann already enjoyed, and which, with all the external changes, continually struck deeper roots within.

In accordance with a request which had been made to him in Paris to travel with the Prince of Holstein-Oldenburg, Herder proceeded to the court of Eutin where he was well received and preached several times in the Castle-Church. The journey with the Prince led him through Darmstadt.

Here he formed the acquaintance with the lady who afterwards became his wife, a Miss von Flachsland. "He preached," his wife relates, "in the Castle-Church. I heard the voice of an angel and words which moved the soul, such as I had never before listened to. I have no words to express this unprecedented and unparalleled impression. He stood before me like a heavenly being in a human form. I saw him in the afternoon, and expressed my gratitude with a faltering voice; from that time our souls were and are one; our meeting was God's work." He made the acquaintance of Goethe and Jung Stilling in Strasburg, where he spent some time to have an operation performed on his eyes, as he was suffering from fistula lachrymalis. Each of these men gives an account of the impression Herder made on him. Goethe witnessed the resolution and patience, manifested by Herder during the painful and, unfortunately useless, operation. A disagreeable part of Herder's nature appeared very repulsive to Goethe, and even at this time occasioned a slight feeling of uneasiness between them. Jung Stilling, on the other hand, gained Herder's entire affection and soon liked him better than he did Goethe. "Never," says Stilling, "have I admired any one more than this man." He acknowledges, that he received from him an impulse to *perpetual activity.* "Herder," he says, "has but one thought, and this is a whole world."

In this confession of Jung Stilling, that he received from Herder "an impulse to perpetual activity," we have given not only the confession of a single individual, but of many, even of whole generations. How many to whom life has appeared in its great importance, are there still who with Stilling received their first impulse to perpetual activity from Herder! And has not the age itself received from him this impulse, this incitation and activity so multifarious, and in extent unlimited? And yet when Stilling made this remark, Herder had scarcely done anything in public life. He was still a youth, full of impelling ideas and plans. "What a motion there must have been in such a mind," says Goethe, "what a fermenting in such a nature, can neither be conceived nor expressed. Great, however, must have been the hidden striving, as will be readily acknowledged, when we consider how many years he afterwards laboured and how much he accomplished." This testimony is so much the more reliable, because the disagreeable part of Herder's character appears to have affected Goethe more than the attractive. Goethe continues to say, that Herder had "in his youth something tender in his manner, which was very becoming and agreeable, without, however, being very smart. He had a round face, a considerable forehead, a nose a little flat and a pouting mouth which was, however, peculiarly agreeable and lovely. Under black eye-brows a pair of jet black eyes, which never failed to produce an effect, though the one was generally red and inflamed." So far Goethe.

We now approach the manhood of Herder, and will follow him in his public official capacity in the Church and school. It is often painful for great minds, who feel that they are adapted to accomplish so much, to be taken suddenly from the free course of genius, developing without all restraint, and to be confined to the narrow limits of a circumscribed sphere, and yet this faithfulness to one's calling, and this activity of a great man, in apparently small affairs, is the test of real greatness of mind.

Herder received an honourable call to Bückeberg, the small residence of the Count of Schaumburg-Lippe, as counsellor of the consistory and superintendent, which call he willingly accepted, since his relation to the Prince of Holstein and his train began to be burdensome. He entered on the duties of his new position in May 1771. The Count, a man of a scientific education, of modern enlightenment, and not without noble traits, hoped to find in Herder as clever a friend and good companion as he had found in Thomas Abbt, author of a work on "Merit." The Count manifested his low views of the ministerial office in expecting that Herder would devote himself chiefly to him and regard the affairs of the Church as secondary. Herder, who had a different notion of the ministerial office than that of a sinecure, was unwilling to do this. He, who afterwards in the Provincial papers contended so strongly, that "a tutor's or carver's place at the lower end of His Excellence's table" should not be regarded as the surest road to clerical offices, would not degrade himself to become a mere clever table companion and literary carver.

This occasioned much discord between him and the count. But the Countess became the more intimately attached to her "teacher," as she was accustomed to call him with great respect. This excellent woman, Maria, born countess of Lippe and Sternberg, who seemed to Herder "like an angel from heaven," lost her mother on the day of her birth, and received her first education in the house of her father with her twin brother whom she called her Jonathan. She was afterwards committed to the charge of an elder sister in Silesia, and came under Moravian influence. It was perhaps owing to this fact that a certain anxious and painful feeling was connected with her deep piety, from which feeling Herder's pure and frank mind gradually relieved her, not by unseasonable enlightenment, but by kindly studying her feelings, by friendly assistance, by progressive instruction, and by bringing to bear the advantages of his scientific education and superior intellectual powers.

The correspondence of this countess with Herder is very instructive in a psychological point of view. As the mists which cover a beautiful landscape are scattered by the sun, so before the penetrating rays of Herder's clearness we see the doubts vanish, which had at first enveloped the tender spirit in gloom, and we behold the image of her soul, the image of a tender feminine nature, becoming more and more friendly, more clear, more confident, and more secure. She unfolds herself to her teacher as a flower to the light of the sun, and in doing so gains more inner worth in our eyes. Indeed, I might say that the reformatory calling of Herder, the calling to illuminate without destroying, to pour light into the soul without disquieting and confusing it, but rather making it firmer, manifested itself in this relation to the countess Maria in such a way, as it ought properly to have done, wherever his spirit came. But for this the relations were, of course, not always as favourable as in this case. Many prejudices opposed his activity from without, and much internal uneasiness prevented him from being as free in his actions as he desired, which occasioned him much sorrow. "A pastor without a congregation! a patron of schools without schools, counsellor of the consistory without a consistory!" These were intolerable thoughts for Herder, during the first years he spent in

Bückeburg. To Miss von Flachsland he writes: "All my favourite notions of the ministerial office are in part destroyed here, are at least always destroyed when I think of this place and my sphere of activity in it!"

Herder also preached to the congregation, but at first his discourses were too philosophical for the majority of his hearers. Gradually he, however, brought his expressions within the comprehension of all, for which he was universally approved. It thus happened, that even the farmers of the parish listened to him with the greatest attention. And Herder, indeed, spared no exertions to make himself generally understood and to avoid all difficult expressions in his sermons. "My sermons," he writes to Miss von Flachsland, "have as little of the clerical in them as my person; they are the experience of a full heart, without any forced or confused matter, the use of which I am spared here." Especially the sermons on the Life of Jesus, preached in Bückeburg, made a great impression on his congregation. They are like a field full of the sown grain which awaits the fructifying influences of heaven. His office still gave him sufficient leisure for writing books. The freshest, the most stirring and most ardent effusions of the fancy and the heart came from his pen while in this place. Such, for instance, are the "Oldest Records of the Human Race" which as it were flowed from a feeling, a gush and a breath, in the morning hours of the longest summer days. "They were unparalleled, blessed, memorable days!" says his wife, who shared these intellectual joys with him. Such, too, are the Provincial Letters and the Philosophy of the History of Humanity, being the preparation for the later ideas on the same subject.

An attempt (in which the distinguished philologian Heyne was particularly active) to bring Herder to Goettingen as fourth professor of theology and university preacher, failed after various negotiations; for Herder, in order to end these negotiations, which began to be annoying to him, immediately answered the question of Goethe, Whether he would accept the appointment of general-superintendent in Weimar, if offered him? in the affirmative. There were at first difficulties in the way of this appointment. Herder's orthodoxy was questioned, his learning was undervalued, and the report was even spread that he could not preach. An estimable member of the town-council of Weimar even requested a trial sermon, with which request Herder, for evident reasons, did not comply.[1] After many negotiations he entered on the duties of his new office, having first, however, preached the funeral sermon of the deceased Countess in Bückeburg, and thus in a very significant manner ending and, as it were, sealing his labours in that place.

By means of his removal to Weimar, Herder was placed in the most intimate relation with the men from whom the new intellectual life of Germany chiefly proceeded, with Wieland, Schiller, Goethe, Jean Paul, Knebel, and others. Whilst before this Herder had paid considerable attention to literature besides his theological labours, he was now in danger of being drawn entirely from theology to literature. His comprehensive mind was, however, able to accomplish much, and the author of the "Cid" and various æsthetic and philosophical works, and the zealous and judicious compiler of national songs of different nations, found sufficient time and strength to fructify theological science with his new and animating ideas, besides the labours connected with his office which he did not neglect, and besides his manifold other labours in the Church and school.[2]

[1] So his biography. The matter, however, appears to be different from the communications in reference to Herder's call to Weimar, viz.: that a trial sermon was indeed required according to the old custom of the consistory, but Herder was excused from preaching any, by a rescript of the Duke.

[2] It may be seen from Herder's first sermon in Weimar, how earnest and anxious he was in the performances of his ministerial duties. "Methinks," he says, "the spirit of Luther hovers around me and exclaims: 'Look upon that which I have attained by my exertions; see how difficult it was for me and those whose bones rest here (in the Castle Church) to place the light of the gospel, which was buried in ashes, on the candlestick! Here thou enterest a sphere where everything reminds you what doctrine to teach, whose word you are to proclaim, to what an extent and in what an age! You are called to be a shepherd of souls at a time when it is frequently doubted whether there ought to be such a thing as religion, whether it ought to be regarded and cherished, and when, at least, the stream of thought flows against it and threatens to sweep over it with its furious waves; it is said that it ought not to be thought of, that we can least of all things take care of ourselves by being religious, and that it is the duty of each one to take care of himself, that, therefore, the ministerial office is useless, a remnant of old customs which only continues because of the prejudices in its favour, and, to say the least, is so difficult and obsolète that its duties cannot be fully performed in our day. And, behold! such an office thou enterest upon here! Their souls shall be required at thy hand! Whatever is born of

His work on "The Spirit of Hebrew Poetry," and his "Letters on the Study of Theology" (which gave valuable instruction and proper direction to so many young men) exerted a great influence on the views of the age, and scattered seed to be developed in the distant future. They were not only a blessing to Germany, but also to Switzerland. As Lavater had at one time made a pilgrimage to Spalding, so in 1780 J. G. Müller, brother of the historian, travelled on foot from Gottingen to Weimar for no other purpose than that of seeing Herder and asking advice of him about his studies. Herder received him very cordially, and soon the conversation turned on the arrangement of theological studies. A cheerful smile spread over Herder's countenance ; he arose and brought from his book-case a volume, which he handed the young man. It was the first part of the "Letters on the Study of Theology," which he had received from the publisher but an hour before ; and what must have been Herder's joy to find in the very next hour a youth, for whom the book had, as it were, been written, and who, as he himself assures us, received it from Herder's hand with a desire to be instructed, and with sincere gratitude. From this hour the friendship between the Weimar and the excellent Schafhauser theologians was formed for ever.

We will not now follow Herder in his literary activity in connection with the distinguished men of Weimar. We expect, however, to resume the subject in another place. A journey to Italy, which country Herder had in his early youth longed to visit, reinvigorated his body and recreated his mind. His taste for art and antiquity was exercised, and rendered still more acute, and nature, and the customs and manners of

God through thy instrumentality shall be thine, and shall prepare eternal habitations for thee ; whatever is neglected by thee, and falls away or goes astray, shall grieve thy soul for ever.' Methinks those words of Luther—or, why do I not rather mention the Lord of lords, the King of kings, the Holy one and Protector of all human souls, Jesus Christ, to whom Luther pointed, whose doctrines he preached, why do I not mention Him, as he stands here, where more than two or three are gathered in his name and call on Him, as he stands here, in our midst, pointing to His word and His congregation saying: 'I have bought and gained them with my blood. Take care of these, and all over whom thou hast been placed as shepherd and guardian, that none of those may be lost whom I commit to thee, who are like stars in my hand, are written in my heart and on my breast.' "

the country found in him a keen observer. Whilst in Rome, he received another call to Gottingen; he was very much inclined to accept it; his own spirit seemed to advise him to go, but the reigning duchess, Amelia, succeeded in keeping him in Weimar for life. The latter part of his stay in Weimar[1] was unfortunately disturbed by much unpleasant experience, and also by ill health, and it really makes a sad impression upon us when we hear, that on account of this as well as on account of the frustration of earlier plans, he exclaimed with grief: "O my disappointed life!" The distinctions conferred on him, the elevation to the vice-presidency, and afterwards to the presidency of the consistory (1801), were only a small compensation for what he in vain demanded of himself, and besides involved him in many new difficulties, from which he found the best relief in the family circle. The soreness of his eye increased continually. The treatment of the disease both in Aix-la-Chapelle and Egra did not realise his hopes. The three weeks spent in Dresden were the last bright days of his life. He returned to Weimar, September 1803, and on the last day of the month held an examination on angels with an unusual elevation of spirits; he himself was soon to be transported to the invisible world. "It appeared," says John von Müller, in the letter written to his brother on the death o Herder, "to bear the impress of another world, and to be about beings to whom he felt himself related." In his last years he longed for nothing more earnestly than for some great high thought on which he might live. Klopstock's "Odes," Young's "Night Thoughts," and Müller's "Relics" were, next to the Bible, especially the Prophets, the last food of his soul. He died December 18, 1803, shortly after he, whom inner nobility of soul had always elevated above what is low and ordinary, had been raised to the nobility

[1] There was no lack of collisions between him and the other great minds which adorned the court of Weimar. It is really humiliating to see what a little, often malicious, spirit of backbiting could enter such a circle, which fact must have embittered his life as much, as he on the other hand may have been the occasion of annoying others with ill humour. Only compare the malicious representation of Herder's matrimonial life in the "Letters of Schiller and Koerner," vol. i., p. 166. The respect for genius in general decreases, when we see that with all cultivation the rudeness of the natural man, which can only be removed by Christianity, remains in full force.

by the Elector of Bavaria. So much in reference to his external life.

In turning to the characteristics of his inner life, I will quote a few sentences from Jean Paul in reference to Herder: "The noble spirit (of this man) was not appreciated by different times and parties, though not entirely without a reason; for he was so unfortunate as not to be a star of the first or any other magnitude, but an aggregate of stars, from which each man formed a constellation, according to his own pleasure. Men of many various powers are seldom appreciated, those of one particular talent nearly always." This was the case with Herder. Those who only estimate the greatness of a man according to his specific performances in a particular department, who only ask, who was the greatest poet? who the greatest philosopher? who the greatest theologian? will not chime in with the praise of Herder. They will prefer Schiller and Goethe as poets, will place Kant, Fichte, and Schelling infinitely higher as philosophers; and as far as theology is concerned, they will ask, whether Herder really accomplished anything extraordinary in the department of exegesis, of church history, of dogmatics, anything which equals what Mosheim, Michaelis, Semler, Ernesti, Döderlein before him, what Griesbach, Eichhorn, Spittler, Plank, his contemporaries, as the most distinguished in their respective spheres, performed? We answer: greatness in a particular department, however necessary it may be to science in general, and however beneficial to learning, is still not the only greatness worthy of admiration. It is, indeed, most easily measured, and therefore (as Jean Paul intimates) generally receives its merited admiration, but where life is to be influenced, where new intellectual and moral conditions are to be produced, where new points of view, not within the fixed limits of an art or a science, but within the whole sphere of life are to be disclosed, there it is not so much the men in a particular department of learning, who break out a new course, as those universal minds, to which Herder belonged on one side, and Goethe on the other.[1] Goethe was certainly still more universal than Herder, but he lacked one thing, which is the most

[1] An ingenious comparison between Goethe and Herder may be found in Wm. Humboldt's "Letters to a Female Friend," vol. i., p. 232. Among other

important to us, that deep religiousness, at least the definite relation to Christianity. But in this we find Herder's strength. Whilst, therefore, Goethe's influence on the development of a consciousness of the world, which we do not esteem lightly, was greater than that of Herder, the latter has led the consciousness of God, which is infinitely higher than that of the world, back to its lowest depths, and has not mingled it with that of the world, but has in various ways brought about a mediation between the two. Let Herder, then, be inferior to Schiller and Goethe as a poet, still, we have not only the poet in him, but also the theologian, the public, popular speaker and the preacher; and this union of the religious-theological genius with the poetical, of the author with the minister of the church, makes Herder what he is, and assigns him a place which no other mind can fill. Therefore we regard such an appearance as Herder peculiar in kind, one in which an old period ends and a new one begins; for even if theologians of that time might be mentioned who surpassed Herder in learning, in extent and profundity of knowledge, whose investigations in some one department have led to more lasting results than many of the bold views and ideas of Herder's mind, still none of them has exerted so great an influence on life. They have been of more benefit to the school, he of more to the people, especially the more educated part. But Herder has also influenced the school and theology by giving them new life and new tendencies. Or (I ask those who are capable of judging in this matter) of what advantage to the study of the Bible was that lifeless learning of Michaelis, which lacked all poetry, and therefore all deep truth, when compared with the impulse which Herder gave to the investigation and interpretation of the Old Testament! In philosophy, Kant, Fichte, and Schelling have, of course, taken the lead, so that their names, like mile-stones, mark the stadia in the history of modern philosophy, of which Hegel may be said to form the terminus. But from them the

things he says (quite in accordance with our views): "Herder was certainly inferior to Schiller and Goethe in compass of mind and poetical talent; but in him there was a blending of soul and fancy, by means of which he accomplished what they could never have done." Is it not this blending of soul and fancy which constitutes the religious genius?

school gained the chief advantage. From them, too, originated that forced, unusual language of the school which Herder opposed so violently, since he valued the self-dependence of the mind more than the prevalence of coined and imitative forms. And, indeed, the time has come when another Herder ought to appear to purify the temple of science from the trash of the new scholasticism. In the history of archæology some may have brought to light more profound knowledge than Herder. But who like Herder has really awakened so many and such great ideas, and scattered intellectual sparks where formerly there had been mostly only dead matter cemented with dead matter, where only numbers and names had been strung together, and only registers and commentaries to registers had been made!

We must not confound Herder's variety of knowledge with a superficial polymathy and a meddling disposition, which know a little of everything, but nothing thoroughly, and trip lightly over all the departments of learning. No one was more opposed to a mere smattering of knowledge. Whatever Herder studied he studied completely and thoroughly, and penetrated to the roots, and was never satisfied with gathering flowers for the sake of adorning vanity. Everywhere the points of his mind touched the heavens, whilst the weight of the mind sank it to the depths, everywhere his genius appears, and never, never, when it knocks, is the sound hollow; and when he spreads his pinions he never sinks to mediocrity. One may miss in his writings the close deduction, the careful completion, the mature investigation and connection of thought; one may take offence at his harshness, at apparent contradictions, at groundless, doubtful assertions, especially when he presents them with that confidence which denies the right to all contradiction; but never by the side of the stubborn will the shallow head appear, which says a thing only because others have said it, and only wants to reap where it has not strewn. Nor is his the chaotic variety of the polymathist that has accumulated in him as an undigested mass, which might more probably be regarded as the case with his friend Hamann; we rather see that all that Herder has gathered is immediately changed into sap and blood, is all united harmoniously, and is then again properly distributed and arranged, and becomes, as it were, Herder. This his contemporary and opponent also observed, for he remarks in his review of the "Ideas for a History of Humanity," rather blaming than praising. "It seems as if his genius does not only gather the ideas from the wide field of science and art merely for the sake of adding them to others, but it appears as if he changed them, according to certain laws of assimilation peculiar to himself, into his specific mode of thought." We should like to understand this expression of Kant in a manner favourable to Herder, and to add: The beautiful, the peculiar and admirable in this is, that by means of this process of living personal appropriation nothing essential is lost, but that the idea which passes through his consciousness gains in clearness, in truth, in internal beauty for others, and consequently also in universal validity for all, since he gives back what he has gained, cleansed from all dross. Herder thought and felt *in* his age, *with* his age, and *for* his age. He expressed what was on the tongues of many who, however, could not utter it, because they lacked the proper words. The age was mirrored in him. In him humanity found and recognized itself in its humanity. Therefore he was the prophet and representative of *Humanity*. Hence we only understand Herder as poet, as philosopher, as theologian, and preacher, when we at the same time understand him as a man. As he gave everything in a living manner, it must be comprehended in the same manner; I might say, must be personally perceived and understood thus. He who wants to receive, as it were, only goods from him, to gain a definite profit from him, results which he can carry home in his pockets, will not seldom find himself disappointed; he will at first think that the load of wisdom he has found in him is heavy, but in the end he will find but little in his hands. But whoever seeks in him a living fountain, a strengthening fragrance and inspiring breath, will never come to him in vain. It is not always the bright noonday sun, which beams from Herder's pages; frequently it is a subdued light, a twilight. But we never become gloomy in this twilight, we only cling so much more closely to the guide, who boldly leads the way with the torch in his hand. Though we may often wish that he were clearer to us, still we never suppose for a moment that he himself does not clearly comprehend the matter. There, too, where we miss plan and order, where he leaps rather than walks, we do not fear; and where we least expect it, we are placed on a point from which an extensive prospect opens to our view.

Let us now, however difficult it may be to keep the particular sides apart, still take up the various sides of his nature, and in such a manner, that we may never lose sight of the main object we have in view. We intentionally do not begin with that which is connected with this main object, the theological life and activity of the man, but with those talents which supported this life, with his poetic talent, his position in reference to philosophy and the literature of his age; with that, in general, which Herder comprehended in the one word, *humanity* (die Humanität). As far as Herder the poet is concerned, we have already observed, that many might prefer Schiller, Goethe, or some other of his cotemporaries (for he must only be compared with these). We will not dispute about such a preference. I readily admit that much, perhaps the most, of the earlier poetry of Herder, has something harsh, unpliant in it, which can only be read with reluctance. Herder's poems neither recommend themselves by the sweetness of the rhyme (the most are blank verse), nor by the beauty of the rhythm, nor by that peculiar charm, which Schiller's and Goethe's poems possess. But that concerns us less here. The poetical works of Herder, among which his "Cid," his legends and cantata, are distinguished as poetical productions, are of less interest to us, than his pure, noble, grand poetical taste. To him, as his wife says, poetry was no empty jingle of words, but the language of God; and Jean Paul appropriately says of him: "Even if he were no poet, he was something better, a poem, an Indo-Grecian Epos, made by some one of the purest gods; for all flowed together in his beautiful soul, as in a poem, and the good, the true, the beautiful, were inseparable in it." Herder was as it were poetized in the Grecian manner according to life. Poetry was not a horizon-appendix to his life, as we often observe a rainbow-coloured cluster of clouds on the horizon in foul weather, but it flew like a light rainbow over his clouded life as a gate of heaven." This poetical disposition of Herder, so deeply and heartily prized by Jean Paul, was of infinite value to his theological views. The ability to comprehend religion poetically, to enter into the spirit of the Scriptural-oriental, Old Testament poetry, and to interpret the sacred books ingeniously from the spirit, was of great value, furthered the cause of interpretation, and suddenly removed many serious difficulties; for in my opinion the reconciliation of theological extremes lies to a great extent in this ingenious poetical view; whence do these extremes mostly originate, if not from an intelligence too dry, freed from all poetry of life, from a prosaic, insipid consequentness? from misunderstanding of the symbolical? Herder at once cut the thread of rabbinical-scholastic subtleties, when he tore the holy things from profane hands and bore them to those regions, into which only a consecrated taste, one susceptible to the beautiful, the peculiar and strange, such as poetry nourishes, can enter. He penetrated to the depths of religious life, as it appears in the history of nations, and especially in the people of God, whilst others were wallowing, with a learned air, in the slime which had accumulated on its surface. To make poetry like Herder's more is necessary than mere versification. Just as he gathered the songs of the most different nations and wove them into one garland, and with the same susceptibility and mobility of spirit inhaled the fragrance of Grecian poetry, with which he imbibed the songs of Job and Ossian; so, too, did he make history the ground on which his sublime views of life, his philosophy, rested.

Herder was a philosophical poet, and a poetical philosopher; but he was neither of these in that superficial generality, in which pretended geniuses love to wander, without foundation, without nourishing roots. Poetry and philosophy were the blossoms of his spirit; the trunk, however, had its roots in history, not indeed in the history of one people or age, but in the history of the human race. The thought first seized by Isaac Iselin, to show "the progress of humanity from the lowest degree of ignorance to continually increasing light and prosperity," was farther developed by Herder in his "Ideas for a philosophy of the history of humanity." Already, in the title of the book, Herder's mind reflects itself, which does not want philosophy and history to be separated, but to be studied in their most intimate connection and relations to each other. He had as great an aversion to a philosophy which, regardless of history, forms its system from abstract propositions, as to a history, which only accumulates a mass of materials, without letting philosophical ideas shine and waft through them. In this joining of the historical with the philosophical, which forms a higher unity by connecting itself with the poetical view of the world mentioned above, lies the secret of Herder's genius. "*Poetry, philosophy,* and *history,*" he says himself, "are, in my opinion, the three lights which illumine the nations, the sects and the generations; a holy triangle! Poetry elevates man above all separation and partiality by means of an agreeable, vivid presence of the objects; philosophy gives him firm, lasting principles in reference to them, and, if he still needs them, history will not refuse to give him maxims."

Just as formerly his poetical view of the world, so now too his historical-philosophic sense gives the means of judging of the influence to be exerted on the formation of the religious ideas: for, since the error and partiality of *Rationalism* consisted in this, that, with a disregard for an historical foundation and development, it wanted to set a religion of reason in place of the existing religion; and the error and partiality of the *Orthodoxy* of that time in this, that it only clung to the historical as dead precepts. Herder had already made progress towards a real mediation between the two, in not being able on the one hand to conceive of anything developed and really present in man, which had not been acquired through instruction, through history, through divine communication and revelation, nor, on the other hand, of anything which had come altogether to and into him from without, unless there is something analogous in man himself, with which he recognises that of which he may obtain a knowledge (which exists for him), receives it, reflects on it, developes and advances it, as much as he is able. He thus, for instance, attacked, in his prize essay on the Origin of Language, the apparently pious, but really mechanical view, that man received language altogether as a divine communication, whilst he himself thought that the origin can only be properly regarded as divine, in so far as it is human. In general, there was not that contrast between the divine and human for Herder, which is usually thought of in connection with these words, according to which God lacks all that is human and man all that is divine, or at least only an external approach of the one to the other takes place; he wanted to see the divine brought about or mediated through the human, and the human glorified and ennobled by the divine. To him all was divine and all human, according to the view you take of the matter. We have called Herder a priest of the purely human, a priest of humanity. We will pursue this thought farther, before we contemplate him as a theologian.

Let us now embrace poetry, philosophy and history, which we have thus far contemplated as separate branches of his nature and activity, in that one word which he emphasized more than any other, which he continually had in his mouth, but still more in his soul, in the word *Humanity.* This word, like the word tolerance and similar party words, became a shibboleth of that age, and therefore it is necessary that here, with the representative of humanity, we also obtain a clear idea of the word, with which a great part of modern history is connected, that we consider the relation which this modern humanity has taken to the Christianity and Protestantism of the age. We properly ask in the first place: What did Herder himself understand by the word? Herder knew very well that a word does not decide a matter, and that an odium is easily cast upon the word; but still he knew none that was better.[1] The dignity of human nature, he thought, is a characteristic of our race, to which it must first be brought by education. The beautiful word philanthropy, he thought, had become so trivial that the human race is mostly loved, so as really to love no one among men. He, therefore, chose the foreign word humanity. In it he sees the character of our race which, however, is only potentially innate, and which must properly be acquired by cultivation. "We do not bring it," he says, "really with us into the world, but in the world it ought to be the aim of our striving, the sum of our efforts, our dignity. The divine in our race is therefore cultivation, leading to humanity; all great and good men, lawgivers, in-

[1] See especially the letters on humanity, and the ideas for a history of the philosophy of the human race (Werke zur Phil. und Gesch., vol. iii., p. 217).

ventors, philosophers, poets, artists, all noblemen in every rank of society, have aided in this work, by the education of their children, by the performance of their duties, by example, conduct, precepts and doctrines. Humanity is the treasure and profit of all human labours, the art, as it were, of our race. The education, leading to it, is a work which must be carried on unceasingly, or we sink, higher and lower classes, back to rude brutishness and barbarity." He does not regard humanity as old as the human race. Whilst the notion of man brings to mind his weakness and frailty, it also calls to mind his human nature, his sympathy with his fellow men. Knowledge of human nature, development of man's powers and talents in a manner conformable to this nature, the gathering of all, called man, into the one city of God which is governed by only one law, the law of common (universal) reason, this is, according to Herder, the task to be performed by humanity. "I wish," he says, "that in the word Humanity I could comprehend all that I have heretofore said about man's noble education, leading to reason and freedom, to the filling and dominion over the earth; for man has no nobler word for his design than he himself is." So far Herder himself.

Now, we may ask, is not all this the object of Christianity? Certainly. Herder, too, regarded it in this light. "*Christianity*," he says, "*commands the purest humanity in the purest way.*" But why, then, we ask further, beside the preaching of Christianity, that of humanity? The answer to this question can best be given historically; and, therefore, permit me to give this historical explanation of the relation of humanity to Christianity and Protestantism, as a supplement, as it were, to Herder's life. Christianity is, of course, the religion of the human race. Christ, the Son of Man, is also the best friend of man, and his spirit the true educator of humanity. But we know how soon these simple ideas were lost sight of, how the Christian doctrine had been alienated from man by the accumulation of heterogeneous precepts, and how from a misunderstanding of the doctrines of natural depravity, it was believed, at one time, that man ought to be deprived of his human nature, whilst at another the superhuman was demanded of him. Christianity, of course, requires more than the mere cultivation of the natural man; it wants the *restoration of man to the image of God.* In this respect it differs from humanity in the ancient, ante-Christian sense. It knows an old and a new man. We are to lay aside the old man, destroying himself with his lusts, and are to put on the new man, formed after the image of God, in righteousness and holiness. But this new man created in God's image is again to become natural for us through God's grace; Christ is to live in us, the inner man is to renew himself day by day, and this new man is not to fit us merely as a new dress, in which we move stiffly and feel uncomfortable, but is to become a second nature to us, is to conquer the old that is in us, and to permit us to take sure free steps, as those that are regenerated, called, and illuminated, even as the sons of God. For a long time, however, Christendom did not comprehend this becoming natural of the supernatural, this entering of the divine into the human, and the elevation of the human to the divine. The old variance between the human and the divine always appeared again, persons always thought they were accomplishing something particularly holy by stifling, dislodging, and wrenching human thoughts and impulses; hence the excrescence of monkish piety in the middle ages which disowned human nature; hence the abortion of scholasticism, which turned the mind away from a healthy contemplation of itself and nature. These phenomena, though they had grown on Christian soil, were in opposition to humanity. The Reformation restored the divine as well as the human to its rights. Indeed, even before this, the interest in human affairs, for human life and efforts had been awakened by the restoration of the sciences, and the revival of the study of the ancients; still this *humanism* (as we call it, to distinguish it from the modern "humanity)" was not sufficient, since it connected itself too much with the old world of the Grecians and Romans, and only externally with Christianity. A greater revival, proceeding from the deepest religious experience, and a regeneration, proceeding from faith, were necessary, which actually occurred in the Reformation. But how was humanity related to this work of the Reformation? We do not deny that Luther had a sense for the purely human, for it often appears in him in its most lovely *naiveté.* But this very *naiveté* indicates that the purely human never came to consciousness in him. His sense for the human, as such, recedes far behind his enthusiasm for the divine purposes he served, and in his position this was very proper.[1] The harshness of his natural disposition may also have hid many pure expressions of the humanity in him, whilst the calmer, more refined Melancthon rather makes the impression of a human theologian. Afterwards humanity was, however, again driven from theology. Rough, heartless quarrels frightened it away, and only a few noble men, like Valentine Andreae (a favourite of Herder), projected, with their bright human physiognomies, above the heads of the combatants. Neither was pietism, though it accomplished much good, compared with the old orthodoxy, exactly distinguished for humanity. It is true that, in its earliest period, in the days of Spener aud Francke, and, still later, it developed a great deal of active philanthropy, and its grand institutions are in the highest degree institutions of humanity, and noble witnesses of the same. But the other, the more ideal side of humanity, that open sense for the most various human developments, for the cultivation of all talents, the artistic, too, in one word, the sense for the beautiful, was wanting in pietism. It was, therefore, reserved for the eighteenth century to understand, to cherish, to exercise and vivify this sense, which then awakened on every hand, and manifested itself in all the tendencies; and in this century it was Herder who took the lead and opened a new way. What the philanthropy of Basedow had commenced awkwardly and in a rough manner, and what the noble Iselin had already attempted in a finer way but only in timid intimations and to a more limited extent, that Herder now accomplished through his deeper truth, his nobler tendency and the greater extension of his works, and thus Herder promoted the cause of Evangelical Protestantism, since he, as it were, introduced humanity into it, and humanized the Reformation.

But everything has its shady side, and we dare not close our eyes against the fact that the enthusiasm for *Humanity*, every where met with, at that time, could easily take a wrong

[1] Schenkel in his "Wesen des Protestantismus" has shown that in Luther's Christology the human does not receive its due.

direction, and that that which was intended to occupy a place in the history of the development of Evangelical Protestantism produced disagreeable effects, when, severed from the whole, it developed in a poetical manner. From the very effort and zeal to seek only the man in man, man could finally not be found, and what Herder said of the beautiful word philanthropy could soon be said of Humanity—that many had it on their tongues, without even showing themselves human in life. The charm which always lies in the sound of a new word led many away from these simple Evangelical truths, and to look down upon Christianity as a lower grade of Humanity, if indeed it did not appear to their eyes like barbarity. What was called Humanity of course was opposed to the limitations of nations and confessions of former times. Every one was to feel himself a man, and in this feeling all was to vanish, that separates the members of one nation from those of another, and the professors of one religion from the professors of a different one. If this were so understood, that it is only the partial, the selfish and the wrong which separates man from man under the garb of nationality and religion, and which leads to contracted reserve and senseless hatred towards others, then the preaching of humanity was quite in place. But how easily this lauded humanity became indifferent to all that is popular and religious, and produced cosmopolitanism in politics and indifferentism in religion! How soon did the ideal love for the Patagonians and Iroquois supplant the active love for the neighbour; and how soon did the professors of humanity withdraw from the Christian community, in heart at least, and revile, in the most inhuman manner, all that was accomplished by the Church or proceeded from it! Whilst it had formerly been demanded that the man should be put off in order to become a Christian, it was now demanded that Christ should be put off in order to be—man. From what has already been said, it must be evident that this was not Herder's view. As far as the national is concerned, none had a more German heart than his, however susceptible and open his sense for all the different nationalities; and in reference to Christianity it might perhaps be acknowledged that in the latter part of his life he permitted what is *peculiar to Christianity* to disappear too much in its historic and dogmatic distinctness, before the idea of the purely human, as he called it. But of this we cannot judge, till we have learned to know Herder the theologian more fully. Let me here quote the proposition which Herder regards as the watchword of both Humanity and Christianity: "Whilst bad morality is satisfied with the proverb, 'Every one for himself, no one for all;' the saying, 'No one for himself, every one for all,' is the watchword of Christianity"—and also of Humanity in Herder's sense of the word.

We have considered Herder the poet, the philosophical historian, or, if you prefer it, the historical philosopher, Herder the prophet and representative of Humanity, and have also attempted to explain the nature of humanity as a co-operating power in the department of mind. We now come to speak of Herder the theologian. The above remarks had to precede in order that the present view we take of Herder might have a foundation; for Herder the theologian stands on the foundation that we have seen spread out before us, on the foundation of a general human education, on the foundation of humanity. His theological were not separated from his other labours; he was not a scholar, who occasionally wrote poetry as a recreation; not a preacher who, when he had no preaching to do, gave himself up to the study of history as a favourite occupation. All was, as we have seen, the same to him. He was a theological poet and a poetical theologian. Poetry and prose, the spiritual and the natural, the scientific and the popular were given in and with one another by him. In his works, not theological, he was just as apt to appear too theological for the worldly-minded, as on the other hand too little theological to stiff professional men in his theological works, and to the anxiously pious too worldly. He has also drawn Theology into the sphere of what is purely human, into the sphere of Humanity. Bible and Christianity, divine in their origin, have been humanized to a certain extent by him. Persons may be frightened at this thought of humanization, but the fear will vanish or at least decrease, when we explain ourselves more fully. All depends on what you understand by the human, with what measure you measure man. If by the human you understand the bad, the frail, the sinful, the miserable, then, indeed, it sounds like blasphemy to call Christianity a human religion and the Bible a human book; then it would amount to this: What you have regarded as divine till now, and venerated as such, is an empty human work, a human invention, an arbitrary despotic command, sheer deception. Such language was indeed made use of already before Herder's time and has been used at all times. But whoever thinks that Herder, in the least chimed in with such language would only show his ignorance of the thoughts of the great man. Herder wanted the very opposite. The Bible which so many laboured to remove as an obsolete, incomprehensible book, as an arsenal of old prejudices, this very Bible he laboured to place as the candle in the centre of the sanctuary, just as Luther had done in the days of the Reformation. The despised, the reviled form of the Son of Man which the meanest souls ever thought they had a right to deride, he wanted to revive again before the eyes of the world and so present in its innate glory, His majesty in the form of a servant, and (of course in a different sense from that of Pilate) to exclaim, "Behold the man!" He wanted to proclaim the fact that he too knew no other name, by which men can be saved, than the name Jesus Christ.

All the efforts of Herder appeared to be apologetical, and displayed a fresh courage to defend the divinity of the Bible and Christianity in opposition to the spirit of freethinking. This we find especially in Herder's earlier writings, in the most decided, most powerful language, even at the risk of being regarded as a blockhead by the "illuminati." But it must certainly have grieved Herder, when the theologians, by their awkward defences, gave weapons into the hands of their opponents, when they sought the divinity of the Bible and Christianity, where it ought not to be sought, when they were zealous for the letter, whilst they suffered the spirit to vanish, or again, when they, on the other hand, too easily abandoned what ought not to be abandoned, and when they themselves assisted in bringing the Bible into disrepute by their artful and forced interpretation. Herder required of every person who wanted to have an opinion to express about the Bible and Christianity, that he should understand them clearly, and should not cling merely to given words and conceptions, but should read the Bible, as it ought to be read, as a book which, with all its divinity, with its divine origin and divine ends, is still written by human hands for human beings, for a human eye, a human heart, a human understanding; as a book which, though written for all times, even for eternity, still refers to certain times and occasions, and must be interpreted from these given times and occasions. This genuine, purely human view of the Bible, which Luther had already laid great stress upon, and in which light only it gains the favour of man, was again made conspicuous by Herder, and in this sense he began his letters on the study of theology with the words: "It is true, my dear sir! the best study of divinity is the study of the Bible, and the best reading of this divine book is human. The Bible must be read in a human manner, for it is a book written by men for men. The more humanly we read the Word of God, the nearer we come to the design of its Author, who created man in His image, and acts humanly in all His actions and kindnesses, in which He manifests himself as our God." Each one must see that this human was not to be in the way of the divine, but was rather to serve as a support for it. And in how childlike a manner, how humbly did Herder himself open his heart and his mind to the divine Spirit which speaks to us through the Bible! "As a child," so he writes in his letters to Theophron, "hears the voice of its father, as the lover hears the voice of his bride, so we hear God's voice in the Scriptures, and perceive the sound of eternity in it. . . . Whilst God's Word in the hands of the critic is like a squeezed lemon; God be praised! it appears to me now again as a fruit, which flourishes on the living tree." However necessary Herder regarded a scientific method of treating the Bible and scientific inquiries in reference to it and its history; and however little he desired to check labours of this kind, to which such as Wetstein, Semler, Ernesti and others, had given an impulse; still he was decidedly opposed to all hypercriticism, to all artificial and distorted interpretations, with which many at that time began to martyr the Bible.

He who was the first to hold the principle that the Scriptures must be comprehended and enjoyed with a poetical sense, strongly opposed the levity of those who wanted to make the historical part of the Bible mere poetry. "Then," he says, "I would rather wish all poetry away, and in its place the most naked and driest history." Thus here, too, his historical sense balanced the poetical. "Truly it is," Herder continues, "a fine thread which passes through the Bible, Old and New Testament, especially in those places in which figure and fact, history and poetry are blended. Rough hands can seldom follow it, much less unroll it, without tearing and tangling it, without injuring either the poetry or the history, which are spun by this thread into one web. Then, indeed, interpreting belongs to God, or to that man on whom the spirit of the gods, the genius of all ages, and, as it were, the infancy of the race rests. If persons attempt it, who know nothing of this spirit, to whom nothing is more foreign than a poetical feeling, especially that of the Orient, and though they are the greatest dogmatists and critics in the world—the plant grows pale at their breath and withers in their hands." Truly golden words, which ought to be placed in large letters over the judgment-seats of many critics of modern times!

This poetical feeling of the Orient, demanded by Herder, he himself possessed in the highest degree, and it assisted him in all his labours. It was not, however, a feeling acquired by study, but was experienced. Had Herder been so fortunate as to make a journey to the Orient, what a profit might then the Occident have gained! But even in the Occident Herder felt Oriental, because he everywhere looked for the key-note of nature with the susceptible feeling of the Orient. Thus his voyage from Riga to Nantes was a living commentary to him, partly for understanding Ossian, partly, too, for understanding the Bible. "What great spheres of thought," he exclaims, in his journal of travel, "does not a ship, hovering between heaven and earth, open up to the mind? Here all gives thought wings, and motion, and atmosphere! The fluttering sail, the ever-moving ship, the roaring waves, the boundless view! On the earth, one is fixed to a dead point, and is confined to a small place. Frequently the former is the student's chair in a gloomy room, the seat by a plain table, a pulpit, a lecturer's chair—often the latter is only a small city, with a uniformity of occupation. . . . . Let one now suddenly step out, or rather let one be cast out without books, writings, or occupation—what a different prospect! Where is the fixed ground on which I stood so firmly, and the small pulpit and the student's and lecturer's chair on which I felt myself proud? Where are those whom I feared and whom I loved? O my soul! how will it be with thee when thou leavest this world? The narrow, fixed, limited centre has vanished, thou flutterest in the air, or swimmest on a sea—the world vanishes from thy view—is gone! . . . . A philosopher he even who has learned to philosophize from nature but poorly, without books and instruments! Could I have done this, what a standpoint, sitting under a mast on the wide ocean, to philosophize on heaven, the sun, stars, moon, air, wind, the ocean, rain, storm, fishes, the depth of the sea, and to discover the physics of all these. Philosopher of nature, this should be thy standpoint with the youth whom thou instructest!" And this standpoint Herder also sought to gain for his interpretation of the Bible. "The crew," he says, among other things, "are always a people who are chiefly attached to the superstitious and wonderful. Since they are necessitated to pay attention to wind and weather, to little indications and foretokens, and since their fate depends on phenomena in the heavens, sufficient occasion is given to notice little signs and forebodings, and also to inspire them with a kind of reverential awe, and induce them to study omens. . . What man will not pray during a storm in a fearfully dark night, in tempests, in places where pale death dwells? Where human aid fails, man always falls back on divine aid. . . . Whoever believes and prays will, though he were in other respects a rough, wicked fellow, in view of the objects on the sea have pious words in his mouth, and not ask how was Jonah in the whale's belly? for he considers nothing impossible for the great God, although he may think himself able to make his own religion, and may reject the Bible. The entire ship-language, the waking, the change of the watch is therefore in such pious expressions, and as solemn as a song from the belly of a fish." Thus Herder studied his sublime philosophy, but also his exegesis and theology in the sea-breeze among the sailors, as Luther in the Wartburg once reflected on his Bible, and pursued theological thoughts while in the chase. Such studies of nature, in the higher sense, have always promoted a sound divinity more than mere book-learning. The ideas which Herder laid down in his "Oldest Records of the Human Race," in which he took the Mosaic account of creation from the hands of those who want to see a mere compendium of physics in it, are indebted to these powerful impressions from nature for their origin. To him sunrise, as it appears anew every day, is the living picture of the first morning of creation, and, as then, nature gradually awakes, as fogs and vapour vanish, and the earth and firmament continually become more definite and distinct; as gradually the vegetable kingdom unfolds itself, as the animals leave their hiding-places and man awakes to consciousness—this was to him like the theme of Genesis repeated daily; herein he found the eternal truth of the six days' creation. In a similar manner Herder viewed many other parts of the Old Testament. The poetical, living contemplation is always the most prominent, as it appears so beautifully in his work on the "Spirit of Hebrew Poetry," through which he gave a new impulse to the study of the Old Testament.

But Herder's theological character is only half understood if we see in him only the ingenious interpreter of the figurative language of the Old Testament, and the eloquent defender of the oldest revelations. We are particularly concerned to know Herder's Christian convictions, and his more definite relation to the Evangelical Protestant Church, to its doctrines, its government, its entire development. Herder wrote no system of Christian doctrines,[1] he only explained isolated books of the New Testament, the Epistles of the brothers of Jesus, James and Jude; he has almost left entirely untouched the great treasure of Paul's Epistles, which properly form the dogmatic foundation and kernel of the doctrines of the Evangelical Church, though he esteemed the Apostle and his teachings very highly. He, however, understood more clearly than many in his day that Christ himself is the centre of Christianity, not only the doctrine, but the *person* of Jesus

[1] Such a system was afterwards formed from his works with the title, "Herder's Dogmatics." Jena, 1805.

Christ, whose image he was anxious to stamp on the souls of his hearers and readers, just as he bore it in his own soul.[1] Here Herder again followed his own course as might be expected. He had an aversion to all learned disputes about the divine and human nature of Christ and their union, because in such learned definitions he saw the death of all religion. Still, he was fully convinced that in Christ, both the divine and human must be viewed, and these again in the most intimate union. The two works, "Of the Redeemer of Man," according to the first three Evangelists, and "Of the Son of God, the Saviour of the World" (according to the Gospel of John), are supplemental to each other, so that in the one the Son of Man, the teacher, the prophet, is more prominent, and in the other, the Word of God revealed as man, Logos made flesh. Whilst those who made Christ a mere popular teacher took offence at the Gospel of John, and regarded it with suspicious eyes as the mine of mysticism, Herder on the other hand said, "that little book is a still, deep sea in which . . . the heavens with the sun and stars are mirrored, and if there are eternal truths (and such there are) for the human race, they are to be found in the Gospel of John." He did not fear the depth of the Christian mysteries; he required, however, that persons to enter them must be provided with an anticipating spirit, and must be prepared to look into their depths, and not to approach them with the vain presumption of human criticism, which touches holy things with rough, unskilled hands. Here, again, he was assisted by his Orientalism. He attempted to explain the mystic expressions and sacred figures of the New Testament by means of the newly discovered oriental source of Zoroaster's teachings. But he did not stop with the figures; he insisted on the kernel, the contents, the fact, lying at the basis of the figurative expres-

[1] "The kingdom of God," he says, in the sermon at Weimar, mentioned above, "and Christ's feast, are not intended to be word and figure, but to become truth and reality: we are to taste and see what joys God has prepared for us in Jesus Christ, and in the entrance into his nature, to his feast of noble equality. In every act, every circumstance of life, we ought to feel ourselves as brethren at the same table; in the will and love of the great King of the world we should rest as in the bosom of the Father, at the feast of our beloved. The elevated, quiet joy of Jesus, the spirit which breathes in the eternal kingdom of God, ought to speak through us, pass over to others, and silently to testify of us."

sion. "It is evident," he says, "from the entire New Testament that Jesus must be regarded as the first active source of the purification, of the deliverance and of the blessing of the world, not with an 'as it were,' or 'that was only so and so,' but in reality."

As Herder gave the advice that the Bible ought to be read in a human manner, so he also preferred to make the human in Christ conspicuous, that is, the divine, as it appears in human relations and circumstances. Everywhere he calls attention to the fine, tender shades in Christ's character, as represented in the gospels, and lets us, as it were, obtain glimpses of the divine through the human. As Jesus is to him the revealer and representative of divinity among men, so he regards Him also as the representative of humanity, always laying perhaps too much stress on the expression "Son of Man." It may be that, if the sum is taken of all that Herder said about Christ, the human mode of view preponderates; yes, that this sometimes passes over into cosmopolitanism. Thus it may surprise some, when Herder says in various places, that Christianity would still continue, though the name of its founder were forgotten. But there is certainly a difference between living under the shadow of a tree, yea, feeling ourselves branches of the tree and absorbing its nourishing sap, and merely receiving the fruit from a third person. This Herder must have known and felt. But why shall we conceal it? A thoughtful and impartial reader of Herder's writings cannot easily fail to discover that the author in his later theological works, and exactly in those which are entitled "Christian writings," has here and there sunk from the height of that enthusiastic contemplation on which we behold him in the writings of his younger days; that he has approached very much the level regions of a mode of contemplation, which makes all even, wipes out all sharp outlines, without, however, which is to be well marked, becoming flat himself.

Whoever reads this author with attention, and does not merely admire and echo his sentiments, must find it possible to refute Herder with Herder; so that Gervinus in his "National Literature of the Germans," justly remarks, that with all love and regard for him, one can frequently not be a follower of his without at the same time becoming his opponent.

This was the case with the most intimate friends of Herder, as Hamann, who accused him of leaving his former principles. But we would as little like to say, on this account, with Niebuhr, that Herder ever ceased to be religious, as to denote with Gervinus this period of greater sobriety as his brightest period. We rather agree with the editor of Herder's works, J. G. Müller, when, in his preface to the Christian writings, he says, "The spirit in which these writings, too, have been written is pure, open, honest, noble, towards the holy, reverential, and in this respect certainly, truly Christian. As in all his other works, so here, Herder never dissembles. Christianity was to him a matter of the heart from his youth. Every reader of these writings will feel this, who has an ear for the language of the heart and of conviction. Love of God and of the truth are the spirit of Christianity, and he who has these perhaps loses nothing, if here and there, in less important matters, his views do not quite correspond with the truth. Who ever knew it fully?"

What interests us particularly in Herder, and also enables us to overlook the change and shades of his views to a certain extent, is this, that he did not place the essence of religion in dogmas as such, but separated it from them. Whilst others still made religion a matter of the head, or an empty external show and performance, he made it a matter of the heart. "Dogmas," he says, "separate and irritate, religion unites. Let words and syllables be idolized, and the intoxication will last for a while; then it ceases, and the naked scaffold remains. Religion, on the other hand, is a living fountain; though it be dammed up and obstructed, still it will break forth out of its depths and purify itself, will quicken and animate." "Religion is (this Herder knew distinctly before it was confirmed by Jacobi and Schleiermacher) a matter of the soul, of the inmost consciousness; . . . it is the marrow of a man's disposition, the most careful conscientiousness of his inner consciousness, the altar of his heart." We will not, therefore, stop to learn Herder's dogmas one by one, or to harmonize them, where they appear to contradict each other. He was not a school-dogmatist and did not want to be one, though he knew how to estimate the scientific value of exact definitions in their place. He regarded the *character* more than knowledge in the man as well as in the scholar, in the

Christian as well as in the theologian. "I think," he says, "the most important thing in our being is *character*, not knowledge and science. These are only finely ground instruments, with which much good, but also much that is useless and injurious may be done; it depends on the hand that uses them. It is, for instance, immaterial for practical purposes, whether I understand a moral truth symbolically or in a general form; it is sufficient if I understand it in a living manner and obey it."

Let us therefore examine Herder's theological character more closely, whilst we see him moving in his practical theological sphere as preacher, as pastor, as superior of the Church, and as schoolman. Certainly no one has ever called Herder a pietist. But still he had this in common with pietism and its founder, Spener, and also with Luther and the other reformers, that he required more of the minister than a mere scientific or learned preparation, or speculative mis-preparation, since he regarded piety—a Christian piety, nourished by Scripture—as the soul of theology. "A theologian," Herder says, "ought to be reasonably well educated, and ought to learn from childhood the Bible as practical religion. He ought early to have the example of pious, active parents, and to use all diligence, like Timothy, to become an active man of God, skilled in doctrine and in life. Boorish, rough, and wild manners, low aims of avarice, of pride, indolence, and other wrong motives, on account of which theology may be chosen, are injurious to an understanding as well as to a feeling and application of the truth. No ray of light can pierce through a hard earthen vessel; much less can such a vessel be made a mirror to reflect light to others." "Let prayer and reading of the Bible," so he advises the young theologian, "be your food morning and evening." "A taste for God and divine things, this is the genuine study of theology." . . . "A quiet fervour, a heart warm, innocent, modest, but still high and noble in its aspirations!"—this he valued above all other things in young men who devoted themselves to the ministry. And how high and noble were Herder's ideas of this office! I have already mentioned in my former lectures, that the tendency of the time was to make all things practically useful, and that even the pious and well-meaning Spalding assisted this tendency in his work, "On the Usefulness of the Ministerial Office." Herder esteemed the author himself highly, and indeed never attacked the book directly; but it was the occasion of his forcibly attacking low views of the ministerial office. This he did in the provincial papers. The patriarchs of the old covenant, the priests and prophets, Christ and His apostles—these he regarded as the patterns for all ages, whose example even the poorest preacher of the Word ought to follow. He ought to imitate them, and not pliantly accommodate himself to the requirements of an effeminate and secularizing age. These were Herder's views on the duties of the ministry. He regarded the office of the preacher as God's office. To him all real wisdom rests on theology as its deepest root. It was a very repugnant thought to Herder, that preachers ought only to be teachers of wisdom and virtue, as the spirit of that age asserted. "Why then," he asks, "do you not come down from your pulpits, which are clumsy chairs for teaching? . . . . Of what use, then, are these Gothic buildings, these altars, etc. No! religion, true religion must return, or a preacher will continue to be the most indefinite, the idlest, and most indifferent thing on earth. . . . . Teachers of religion! true ministers of the Word of God! what a work have you to perform in our century! The harvest is great, but unfortunately the labourers are so few." . . . "But in order to aid in this matter," the animated speaker continues, "it must be believed that there is a *revelation of God in the Bible* and also in the course of the human race, and thus we must naturally always and everywhere come back to the great centre, around which all revolves and arranges itself—Jesus Christ, the Corner-stone and Heir, the greatest Messenger, Teacher, Pattern, but also according to His person the Corner-stone of salvation, on which we must found all that the other world will approve."

Whilst it was the tendency of the times to separate religious instruction from history, and use the latter merely as a collection of examples for morality, Herder recommended as strongly as possible the history of religion as the foundation of religious education, on which all must be based. For him the beautiful plant of God grows from the living seed of the facts of history; its soil is revelation—its main sap and power, faith. Interpretation of Scripture is, however, to be the principal business of the preacher; not mere preaching and reasoning on morality. "If morality," he says, "is the chief business of the preacher, and the Bible and words of Jesus are mere quotations which come from God, just as all truth comes from Him, then farewell Christianity, religion, revelation—the names become polite masks, and that is about all." Then, he thought, we might as well preach from Seneca and Epictetus as from the Bible. Therefore Herder also disapproved very much that pulpit eloquence was modelled after worldly heathen patterns, after Demosthenes and Cicero, who treated entirely different subjects, had different audiences, and aimed at results also very different. He, therefore, rejected all those theories of pulpit eloquence, with which the literature of the day began to teem, as a miserable invention of the age. He himself in preaching, despising all vain display, adopted the simple form of explaining Scripture, the oldest form, the homily. According to the testimony of those who saw and heard him, his appearance in the pulpit was very imposing, though he did not assist in this with gestures, but on the contrary stood almost motionless; but the expression of his voice must have been powerful. Let us hear an unsuspected witness on this subject. A witty author of those days, Helfrick Peter Sturz, a man by no means agreeing with Herder's writings, says the following in a letter: "I have heard Herder preach in Pyrmont, and I wish all good Christians who, incited by their leaders, hate him so orthodoxly, could hear him. Our aristocratic congregation was not in as susceptible a spirit of devotion as the primitive churches, and yet you ought to have seen how in a few moments he changed the bustle of distraction, curiosity, and vanity to the stillness of a Moravian congregation. All hearts were opened, every eye was fixed on him and rejoiced in unaccustomed tears, only sobs of emotion were heard in the affected congregation. My dear friend, no one preaches in such a manner, or religion would be to all what it ought to be, the dearest, most confidential friend of man. He preached on the text of the day, without enthusiastic extravagance, with that enlightened, high simplicity which does not need the figures and arts of the school to transcend the wisdom of the world. Nothing was explained, because all was clear; no reference was made to theological metaphysics, which neither teach how to live or die, but how to quarrel scientifically. It was no exercise of devotion, not an attack on hardened sinners, divided in three blows, nor any other of the current articles of pulpit manufacture; neither was it a cold, heathen morality, which only looks for Socrates in the Bible, and can therefore dispense with Christ and the Bible, but he proclaimed the faith of love, proclaimed by the God of love, which faith teaches us to be patient, to suffer, to persevere, and hope, and which rewards with its own peace and satisfaction, independently of all the joys and sorrows of the world. So, I think, the followers of the apostles must have preached, who were not examined in dogmatics, and did not play with systems and compendium words, as children play with counters. You know how differently I think of Herder the author. We only go together a short distance, then he escapes from me rushing, shining, and quick as a rocket; but as a *preacher* and a *man* he is a true man, and on the short way which we can journey together, he is my dearest companion."

Herder did not write his sermons, but made mere sketches of them, and from these the most is taken which we possess of him under the name of sermons. Herder's sermons are very peculiar, and cannot be compared with others. His intentional deviation from the pulpit language goes so far, that he brings into his sermons all the expressions of common life, all foreign words, altogether adopts the language of common conversation, and even gives free course to satire. Of many of his sermons we can scarcely believe that they have ever been preached. If they were to be read before an audience for edification they would shock every moment, but one may very appropriately read them alone. Herder's language in his sermons is so peculiar, and so intimately connected with the relations in which he was placed, that it can by no means be recommended as a model for imitation. But the sermons recommend themselves so much the more; they elevate themselves above what are called model sermons, for their excellence does not consist in the regular, the methodical, but in the original, the individual, the characteristic, and these qualities can never be imitated.[1]

Herder's manner of preaching and sermonizing was connected with his views of worship in general, and in this department he also exerted an influence with his reformatory spirit. He had a great aversion to mere forms and ceremonies, no matter how fine and beautiful externally. "It has, alas!" he says in one of his sermons, "become so usual to confound devotion and a sleeping of the soul, piety and sluggishness of thought, that no one wants to think with the preacher, but each one wants the Spirit of God to think for him." Whatever, therefore, was not calculated to rouse the thinking mind and the moral powers of man, but only indistinct, gloomy feelings, found no advocate in him. He was most fond of the simplest, the truest, clearest, and the most powerful in the divine service. Herder did not, however, regard public worship as a mere exercise of thought or a dry moral institution, but his poetical disposition led him to the truth here, especially in reference to church hymns and spiritual songs generally. . . . Of his numerous poems few are intended for use in public worship, and of these but a small number can be sung by the congregation: they are cantata, hymns or poems, free in their form. Herder never attained the proper spirit of church hymns, because he lived in a time to which this spirit was foreign. He was unwilling

[1] "Herder's sermons," W. von Humboldt writes in his letters to a friend, "were very interesting. They were always thought too short, and were wished as long again. But those which I heard were not edifying; they touched the heart but little." Schiller, in his correspondence with Koerner, says: "The entire sermon (of Herder) was like a conversation which a person carries on by himself, very plain, popular, and natural. It was less a discourse than a rational conversation. A proposition of practical philosophy, applied to certain particulars of common life, doctrine which would as soon be expected in a mosque as in a Christian church. The delivery was as simple as the contents of the sermon: no pantomime, no play of the voice, but an earnest calm expression. It can easily be seen that he is conscious of his dignity. . . . . *Herder's sermon pleased me better than any other I have ever heard;* but I must honestly confess that no sermon pleases me." With this confession the criticism loses much of its force. Afterwards he accused Herder, that he preached of himself after his return from Italy, and had a *Te Deum* sung on himself of which he (Herder) had composed the words, and had them scattered through the church. It is to be hoped that this belongs to the gossiping mentioned above, in which Weimar life was rich; poor miserable wealth!

to imitate, and the most gifted cannot create if the age does not support him.

We have now gained the standpoint from which we can view Herder's position in reference to the history of the development of Evangelical Protestantism, and from which we can also determine what link he forms in the chain of this development.

As we have already found the essence of Protestantism to consist in this, that the spirit striving for progress, greater freedom and clearness, boldly follows its course in spite of all the enmity and suspicions of erring judgments; that with all this progress, however, it looks back to the foundation once firmly laid, that it does not only find pleasure in protesting, but rather builds on and alters than destroys, and therefore opposes, as far as possible, all violent and forcible reforms and revolutions with calmness; we have in Herder the picture of a true Protestant, a Protestant adapted to the age in which he lived. We find in him both a man of progress and yet conservative, a man of ancient and modern times, in so far as he was adapted to bring forth things, both old and new, out of his treasure, and to mediate the two in an intellectual manner. This must be evident from the representation of his theological system and his theological mode of thinking and acting, with which we have been occupied in the previous Chapter. Compared with the violent modern minds and the illuminati, Herder is orthodox, and compared with the stiff orthodox he is a bold modern mind. Vulgar Rationalism will make him out a mystical supernaturalist, and vulgar Supernaturalism a dangerous rationalist, against whom one cannot be too well guarded. But it must be so, and always will be so, where a genuine reformatory spirit lives and acts. It was so with Luther, who, in opposition to the Pope, appeared an enemy to peace and order, even as a rebel, and in opposition to the rebels as a servile subject of princes and a despot in matters of religion. There will always be men for whom genuine Protestantism goes too far, and again others for whom it does not go far enough. But it would be very unjust to charge Herder with a characterless *halfness.* The true medium, to which Protestantism and also Herder belong, differs from the false medium, which of course often calls itself the right and true medium, in this, that it does not vacillate, without principle and character, between the extremes, but that it holds a firm definite position above the extremes; that it moves neither to the right nor the left; that it does not reject every means of reconciliation harshly and peremptorily, but yields where it ought to yield, and clings at the peril of life to what it ought to hold, and that it is conscious of what it does, and with all apparent inclination in this or that direction, neither loses sight of its object, nor its centre of gravity.

In order that we may estimate Herder's Protestant disposition, we must still view him in his practical sphere, in which we have just left him. We have learned to know him as preacher and religious poet. In his views of church hymns his genuine Protestant spirit revealed itself; on the one hand his Lutheran heart, which felt itself intertwined with the roots of Protestantism, felt itself one with the vital nerve of the Reformation, and would not permit itself to be robbed of the faith of its fathers by the first whim of the custom and taste of the age; on the other hand, however, a free, open, calm view, which knows how to discover the errors of the old as well as the good of the new, and which therefore knows no close in the productions of the Christian life and spirit, but always expects further developments in the distant future, and assists in producing them. With the contemplation of Herder, as preacher and poet, we have not yet exhausted the practical activity of the man. The large field of church-direction, which was open to him as general superintendent, the management of the church business, and especially the reform of the school system, for which he laboured as part of the duties of his office, and also from love, are still to be considered. Here we come in contact with the preserving spirit of Herder, which protected the old and authentic in all its greatness, in a time, too, which thought it could not remove too much of the old.

We have already seen from Herder's relations in Bückeburg, how conscientious he was in his pastoral duties. But in Weimar, too, in the city of polite scholars, he ventured to advocate the old church discipline, which had become unfashionable. And in this matter he placed himself directly on the true foundation of old approved Protestantism. What had made the Reformation necessary, but the sale of indulgences, the redemption of sins through money? What had at that time proceeded from the Pope now proceeded from the haughty, frivolous spirit of the age. Many of the rich and educated thought they could redeem themselves from church discipline through money and fines. Herder protested against this. Regardless of the judgment of the members influenced by rationalistic tendencies, he says: "The penance and censorship of the church, taken purely in the Scriptural apostolical sense, according to which public stumbling-blocks are removed from the communion of the church, and repenting sinners are received again, ought by no means to be laid aside, nor to be changed into anything which it is not intended to be, as long as the Bible exists and we believe in a communion of saints, which consists in forgiveness of sins, according to the third article of the Apostles' creed, or pretend to believe it. From this no rank is to be excluded, no one is to be excepted; for there is no rank in Christianity. Soldiers, court-officers, princes, and ministers are Christians; no sin can be redeemed with money, and no prince can except sins and excuse them."

Strict as Herder's views were on this subject, they were just as strict in reference to the licentiousness of the press and the abuse of the so-called freedom of instruction. At this time, in which the free word and free press are the party-words of an unbounded reformatory tendency of the age, it may not be amiss to hear Herder's views on this subject. "That all which calls itself science," Herder says, "ought to be suffered without inspection and direction in a state; I believe no old lawgiver would ever have thought of such a freedom. It is undeniable that there are abuses of science which can only adorn themselves with impudence, wantonness, and licentiousness, and which are certainly injurious to the morals and thinking of a community. Whoever will, let him excuse public blasphemy, or, which is just as bad, a reviling of sound reason, honesty, and virtue; even praise it, if he like; but the State is not only at liberty, but in duty bound to defend and preserve its members against these. In respect to the soundness and blessedness of certain points in thinking all are agreed; the government must not suffer itself to be driven from these points or it will go to destruction. This is the more so, because the very seed of such insects is corrupt, and is anxious to lead the whole to ruin, in which it frequently results. The body, which has been left by the regulating spirit, whose pulse has ceased to beat, and whose consciousness is gone, is unquestionably the prey of corruption. Let us suppose that blasphemous, wanton, scandalous writings are allowed to be published by the State, whom will they influence? None but the weak, the sick, and unprotected part of the State, the very persons on whom the influence will be most injurious. The steady man, the thinking, honest, industrious citizen, scornfully casts such things aside, and nothing is to be feared on his account. But the idle tenderling, the weak woman, the inexperienced youth, perhaps even the innocent child, will read them; the more elegant, more beautiful and attractive they are, the more they will be read by these persons, and the worst influence will be exerted on this class of readers. . . . *The State is the mother of all the children,* and ought to take care of the health, the strength, and innocence of all." "Every science," Herder continues, "has its abuse. . . . *Philosophy may lead to such bad results by false reasoning; criticism may become so rude, impudent, and villainous;* history so false and distorted in its application, that the government ought not always to remain indifferent to see so much talent misused, true science decreasing and the false increasing, so many impediments placed in the way of the former, and so many retreats offered to the latter, and finally to see all the good influence of literature destroyed." Does it not seem to every one as if Herder spoke in *our* age and to *our* age? I, at least, can find nothing illiberal in this nor in his dramas which he wanted placed under a strict censorship, and cannot, therefore, agree with Gervinus when, in his National Literature of the Germans, he compares these and similar severe lectures with the blustering polemics of the superintendents-general of the seventeenth century. I, of course, recognise in it something of the same spirit of discipline, of order, of lawfulness, which, however, belongs to the spirit of Protestantism; I even recognise in it the spirit of Luther. Herder knew that he agreed with Luther in this respect, and appealed to him with a good conscience, where he attempted to show that change of government is not necessarily an improvement of it, that ochlocracy is the worst tyranny, and that it ought to be the pride of the Germans not to imitate the French in reference to loyalty and faith, and old discipline and customs. Herder properly attempted to form this feeling of loyalty from the very foundation, and to lay its basis in the schools ; for he regards education as the impelling power of the nations.

We shall have occasion hereafter to form an estimate of Herder's pedagogical views which he developed most fully in his school-addresses, and in which he was far from agreeing with the philanthropy of *enlightenment.* We now leave Herder for some time, without, however, losing sight of him, for he will frequently be of service to us, as a magnitude with which we are acquainted, and by which we can measure other magnitudes, as a person whom we have placed at the entrance of the garden, by whom we may find our way out again in its various labyrinths.

We now turn our attention to another subject. As we must follow the course of modern German philosophy, we must now turn to that point where this development commenced in Kant. It may appear strange that we speak of Kant *after* Herder ; for, though they were cotemporaries, still Kant was the older, and was Herder's teacher. I have, however, done this intentionally, for Herder was far from being a follower of Kant, he rather appeared as an opponent to him, and then, in his entire education, a greater influence was exerted on him by ancient times than on Kant, who tore loose from it as much as possible. Besides, Herder, though the younger, had already gained a literary reputation before Kant's Critique had excited much attention, so that as an author he has seniority in his favour. But finally, and this is the main reason, Herder's personality seemed much better adapted to be first contemplated, because it is so multiform and interesting, whilst with Kant the system, separated from his personality, will more especially require our attention. I had some scruples, too, about commencing with a system that is, with both lifeless and abstract. I wanted to lay a foundation of another kind first, and this Herder afforded. Strengthened and warmed by him, we may now approach the marble bust of the great thinker.

In 1769 Herder wrote an essay on the ideal of a school, in which he agreed with Basedow in some things, and, of course, attacked others. Like Basedow he censured the exclusive prevalence of the Latin language in the schools, and called it Papistic-Gothic. It was his principle, as well as that of the new pedagogical science in general, that in the elementary instruction the child's attention must first be directed to what surrounds it, before the memory is burdened with names of things farther removed from it, and that, therefore, all instruction, if possible, must be in some way connected with life and the things surrounding the child. "It should be one of the principal objects of a teacher to give the boy living conceptions of all that he sees, speaks about, and enjoys, in order to place him in his world, and to impress him for life with the enjoyment of the same."

But however much Herder agreed with Rousseau and Basedow in reference to that part of education merely human, and referring to the development of the consciousness of the world, he differed widely from them in reference to the awakening of the consciousness of God in the principles of religious education. In this respect he stood on the positive foundation, and wanted to have nothing to do with the arts, by means of which the children were prepared to approach God, and of the tender roundabout way on which it was thought they ought to be led to heaven. In direct opposition to the untimely philanthropising and reforming, he says: "*Luther's Catechism must be thoroughly learned by heart, and must remain for ever.* Explanations of it are a treasure of duties, and of the knowledge of human nature. Basedow may say what he pleases about the Jewish character of the ten commandments, they are a fine morality for children." He also defends the use of Biblical accounts, only select portions of which he wants, however, to be used for the first stages of instruction. Herder is firmly convinced that good Biblical instruction produces high regard for and a knowledge of religion for life, and this he regards as the best means of creating a new Christian public. Just as Herder thought more deeply of religion than the realistic pedagogues of that age, so he also thought more profoundly of language and philological studies. How could he who, so to speak, regarded language and reason as the same, value philological studies lightly; and, though he opposed the excess of Latin, he estimated the study of the German very highly, and gave excellent hints for its improvement. Herder laid down his chief pedagogical principles later in the school addresses delivered at Weimar, which have been published under the name of "Sophron." In them there is, here and there, an echo still found of the ecclesiastical tone, which continually became less and less in the new school language. Thus Herder is not ashamed to designate the schools the workshops of the Holy Spirit. "Our ancestors," he says, in one of those addresses, "called the schools workshops of the Spirit of God;" an old-fashioned appellation, and it will, perhaps, appear strange that I repeat it in our day and do not rather speak of the temple of Apollo, of the Muses and Graces. The appellation, however, properly understood, expresses something far more noble, true and deep than all those idol-expressions of the temple of Apollo, of the Muses and Graces can possibly do.

According to Herder, all education is to aim at giving the man an inner power, an indwelling wisdom, a pure eye, a clear understanding, the Holy Spirit, without which all acquired knowledge and skill become idle apparatus or means of destruction. "How beautifully," he says, "does every trial of moral culture adorn the child and the youth!" Is there a more lovely brow and more beautiful eye than those in which modesty and shame, uprightness, confidence, humility, and love, the Spirit of God, dwell? Is there a more beautiful charm of the gestures and limbs than when they are anointed daily, with pure innocence and mild complaisance, as it were with the oil of joy for beautiful activity? The expression of the Hebrew youth in whom the Spirit of God dwelt from childhood, "How then can I do this great wickedness and sin against God, the holy thing that is in me?" has something so beautiful and powerful, that it alone is able to keep a youth who has this holy thing within him, who recognizes himself a temple of the Holy Spirit, from all that is low, common, and wicked. . . . . All distinguished men had this noble feeling, which was the very thing that distinguished them from the common man, and preserved them from all that is base and low. He was their shield and buckler, their counsellor and guardian, their warning friend, their ruling genius, which impelled them to take the narrow way, and to press through the straight gate, instead of taking the broad road of wanton fancy and concupiscence." . . . "Spirit of God," he exclaims, "return to our schools to lay a good foundation in the minds of the young, to form in them a firm and pure character, which cannot be led astray by wild immorality, bold impudence and saucy importunity, which now prevail in so many books."

"It is not good," he says in another place, "to moralise much with youth in religious instruction; but it makes a living impression to explain the doctrines and the proofs clearly, and to support the rules of morality with reasons and examples from common life, and with biblical and other anecdotes." According to these principles he revised Luther's Catechism, which he preferred before the new-fashioned Catechisms, which moralised and reasoned much. "Of the twenty or thirty catechisms," he writes to a colleague, "which I had before me, I have used much, but I could not make one the basis, because in the most an unnatural, compounded, theological language prevailed, and in the rest the most shameful recklessness." Finally, Herder was also active in the arrangement of a seminary for teachers in Weimar, and it will most likely not be without interest for our times, in which so much is said about public schools, and reforms in them, to hear the views of a man whom probably no one has ever numbered among the blockheads.

"The object of a seminary is not to give young persons, who want to prepare themselves to become country schoolmasters, *a useless kind of enlightenment,* with which they will think themselves overwise, and with which they will sooner be of disadvantage than benefit to their future pupils; for too much clearness and argument spread carelessly among ranks of society, in which they do not belong, promotes neither the welfare of the State nor the happiness of the individual, but chiefly not of the private life of the poorer class. Still less is its object to procure young persons a comfortable living, etc. It is rather its only object, far from all the ostentation and pedagogical playthings of our age, to give young persons, who devote themselves to the profession of teaching, a convenient opportunity of learning from instruction and personal application what is *necessary* and really useful for their future calling, for the best ability of a teacher is only acquired by *method* and *exercise*."

Herder, the great proclaimer of humanity, was far removed from all the effeminateness of the so-called philanthropinism. *School discipline* he regarded as a necessary requirement of a good school. A great number cannot exist together without order, without a strict arrangement and regulation. "A school which has much discipline, many and strict exercises in good, and all kinds of good, to which children are to be trained, that is a good school. A gymnasium which daily becomes a wrestling place, both in virtues and abilities for noble young souls, which wrestle and practice diligently, and with emulation, that only is a true and a good gymnasium. Where there is not this discipline, this good exercise in scienc and morals, there is a dead sea, though in and around it dwe all the Muses."

XV.

IMMANUEL KANT.

SKETCH OF HIS LIFE.—"CRITIQUE OF THE PURE REASON."—POSITION OF THIS PHILOSOPHY IN REFERENCE TO CHRISTIANITY.—THE RAPID INCREASE OF KANTISM.—HERDER'S POSITION IN REFERENCE TO THE KANTIAN PHILOSOPHY.

IMMANUEL KANT, son of a saddler, was born April 22, 1724, at Königsberg, and received from his parents a strict, and, especially from his mother, a pious Christian training. Kant expresses himself thus in reference to his mother:[1] "She was an affectionate, tender, pious, and upright woman, who led her children to the fear of God by pious instruction and a

[1] Jachmann's "Life of Kant," p. 99.

virtuous example. She often took me out of the city, and directed my attention to the works of God, expressed herself enthusiastically in reference to His omnipotence, wisdom, and goodness, and infused into my heart a deep reverence for the Creator of all things. I shall never forget my mother, for she planted and nourished in me the first germ of the good, she opened my heart to the impressions of nature, she awakened and expanded my conceptions, and her teachings have had a lasting and salutary influence on my life." According to some, his mother connected herself with the existing pietism, which also Pastor Schultz, one of the first teachers of Kant, embraced. At all events, that strictly moral conscientiousness, for which the system of Kant, in spite of all its deficiencies, is distinguished; may have had its root as much in these first impressions of his training, as in the later order of the thoughts of the man. The father had always insisted on truthfulness, and had regarded lying a sin worthy of death, and this likely influenced Kant in forming the strictest view of the value of the truth. It was the mother, however, who besides truthfulness also demanded *holiness*, and thus (as Kant's biographer remarks) the requirement of his practical reason, to be *holy*, was perhaps very early made of him by his good mother.[1]

On the advice of the pious preacher and director of the gymnasium, Schultz, the parents permitted their son to study, and Schultz assisted them nobly in this matter. Kant soon displayed an extraordinary memory. He knew large portions of the classics by heart, and also made considerable progress in mathematics. In 1740 he entered the university of his native city. It was intended that he should devote himself to theology, on which he actually heard several courses of lectures; but his course of life soon took another turn. He occupied the post of family tutor in the country for a time; but this neither suited his talents nor inclination. He was utterly incapable of letting himself down to the conceptions of the children, and afterwards was accustomed to remark, that a worse tutor than he was could perhaps not have been found in the world. He used this quiet stay in the country so much the more for his studies, and here already the basis

[1] Borowski, "Life of Kant," p. 23.

of his later system was laid in his mind. He had not yet abandoned theology entirely, he even preached several times in country churches, but soon abandoned the pulpit and all ministerial labours, and turned himself to the academical course of life. Having returned to his native city, he took the degree of master of arts in 1755, and began to deliver lectures on philosophy. For fifteen years he continued in the precarious position of a lecturing master of arts, till in 1770 he became professor in ordinary of mathematics, which he soon, however, changed for logic and metaphysics. Long before this he had already distinguished himself as an author, mostly in the department of the practical natural sciences; and in philosophy, too, he had already struck out his own course, deviating from the prevailing method of Wolf. In 1787 he became a member of the Royal Academy of Berlin; other distinctions were less frequently conferred on him than on many other learned men of his day; nor did he place any special value on them. His life, in general, was very simple, and in outward events was very meagre. He had never made long journeys; had never been more than thirty miles from Königsberg; was acquainted with no large city but this; he never visited even the neighbouring Danzig. He was never married; saw even his nearest relations, his brothers and sisters, but seldom; gathered around him only a few select and tried friends; he lived with his man-servant according to a strict, orderly disposition of his time and domestic affairs, from which he did not easily deviate. He showed but little taste for the polite arts. He neither paid attention to portraits and engravings, nor loved music. He even considered music an injurious amusement. He thought it would be better for young ladies to take lessons in the art of cooking, than in music and dancing. On the art of cooking the great philosopher placed a high estimation. He preferred conversing on this subject with women, and avoided philosophical conversations with them. He was fond of ombre, and in social circles manifested a cheerfulness and versatility elevated above all pedantry. Toward the close of his life his mental powers decreased perceptibly. The man, who had given the thinking world new laws, sunk into a kind of imbecility, so that he could not even write his name properly. He resigned his professorship in 1794, and died on the 12th of February 1804. His lean body was at the time of his death dried up like a potsherd; his ingenious, blue eye, which had animated his unimposing form, was extinguished. The lifeless body was interred in the vault of the University Church.

As far as his character is concerned, his honesty, veracity, and high sense of what is becoming, are to be praised. Although he gathered a considerable fortune during his single and simple mode of life, yet he did not set his heart on earthly riches. An enemy to all idleness and begging, he was beneficent to the worthy poor. He seldom attended public worship, as he considered it, according to his whole mode of thinking, a mere incitement to morality. He, the educated man, believed that he no longer stood in need of it, while he insisted that the unthinking masses, who do not educate themselves, should make use of the institution of the Church. He therefore still esteemed all religious institutions; and with all his liberal views of government, he still remained a conscientious friend of public order, and abhorred all that is violently revolutionary. We shall estimate his religious convictions more fully in connection with his system. Only this much here. "Gentlemen!" he said once, "I do not fear death, I shall know how to die. I assure you before God, that if I felt this night that I would die, I would raise my hands, fold them and say: God be praised!"[1] When unreasonable admirers of Kant placed him on a level with Christ, he opposed this idolatry, and confessed that he bowed reverently before *this* name, and regarded himself, placed beside Him, as a bungler interpreting Him according to his best powers.[2]

We must now endeavour to unfold the system of Kant, which is, of course, of more importance than those characteristics to which we have just alluded, and we feel the difficulty of the task, which is so much the greater, since even Kant himself despaired of ever making his doctrines popular, and always avoided introducing them into circles of educated women. I believe, however, that a development of his system would not only be unnecessary, but even im-

[1] Wasianski, "Life of Kant," p. 52.
[2] Vorowski, "Life of Kant," p. 86, note.

proper in this place, and therefore I shall content myself with imparting the results of his system in so far as they relate to a moral and religious life; for only these results have exerted an influence on the development of that which belongs to the Church, and on the formation of the Protestant faith in other individuals.

Though till then the theologians and philosophers of all confessions had speculated upon, and discussed at a venture, divine and human things, and, from premises generally received, had drawn conclusions, about which they disputed the more warmly the more each one believed that he had the truth, still Kant bore no lance in this war. While these men were fighting with each other, he went circumspectly around the lists, and first examined the field of battle, to see whether the ground was solid—reviewed the weapons to see whether they were fit to cut and stab, and asked how far the darts would reach, and how deep the swords would cut. He subjected (according to the example of the English philosopher, David Hume) the intellectual powers to a new investigation, in asking himself the question, *What can man know?* How far does the power of his reason extend? To what regions does she bear him safely? How far may he trust himself to her guidance?

In his work entitled, "Critique of pure Reason," he chiefly carries on those investigations which lead to this result, that nothing that lies outside of time and space, outside of the forms of our sentient faculties of perception, can be an object for pure thinking. As once, in the visible world, the discovery that our earth is not the centre of the universe, around which the sun and stars revolve, but itself only a small point in the universe which, like all others of its kind, revolves around its sun, was followed by a not insignificant humiliation on the part of man; so it was also with this discovery in the realm of the invisible world, the kingdom of thought. It now became necessary to fold the wings of speculation, which till then had been spread out above the heavens; to recall the active forces which had been employed in all directions, to muster them, to accumulate and concentrate the entire force on the one clearly illuminated point, on that, namely, which lies within the region of thought. And who will deny that in this self-knowledge and self-limitation of reason there was more clear gain, than in all the supposed conquests in a territory which man could not call his so long as the limits were as indefinite as they had been till that time. What is certain and proved appeared in every respect preferable to the uncertain and the visionary. It is true this discovery of Kant could not be raised to mathematical certainty, as the earlier discovery of his countryman, Copernicus, since it could be followed by no external apparatus, and no other glasses could be used, except those which had been ground by the Kantian critique, by the categories which had been set up by him. The fact that the mind was directed to itself, to the examination of its own powers, was of great importance. The old inscription on the temple of wisdom, "*Know thyself*," was as it were revived, and shone like an admonishing pillar of fire through the darkness in which so many philosophers of ancient and modern times had been groping. On this account many have called Kant the second Socrates, whose not knowing reached farther than all the knowledge of the sophists. All the scholastic edifices of a reason, appeared to be shaken to their foundations by Kant's critique, and in considering the history of Protestantism, we cannot avoid seeing in Kant's critique something Protestant, in so far as it opposed the pretensions of reason, or rather the pretensions of the understanding, which had placed itself beside genuine reason, with the same resoluteness with which at one time the Reformers opposed the old scholasticism. It is a pity, however, that after the new scholasticism had been overthrown with the old, a newer one and then the newest soon took its place, and that instead of real individual thinking, the swearing on the master's word, the repeating of forms not comprehended, became worse after the time of Kant than it had ever been before. But let us hear himself first, and consider his philosophy and its application to religion.

When Kant designates that as object of *pure thinking* which is contained in space and time, he does not mean by this, that all that is outside of these does not exist, that beyond time and space there is nothing infinite, eternal, which would certainly be a gloomy philosophy, banishing man entirely into the finite. No; he only does not want the eternal things to become objects of human investigation and learned proof, and thus he leaves faith, *as faith*, essentially untouched, even if he avoids the expression, *faith*, because he has no place for it in his system. Kant consequently denotes *God* and *immortality* not articles of faith, but requirements of the *practical* reason, which he distinguishes from the *pure* or *theoretical* reason. God and immortality cannot be proved in a strict sense, but starting from the practical-moral standpoint, man is led to both. That of which man is *certain*, also within the limits of time and space, is his *moral* nature, his moral freedom, his *will*. Now in this self-determining will, the warrant of man's immortality lies, and also the evidence that a God exists, a Rewarder of the good and evil. Man, a free, moral being, has in him the calling to live in accordance with his moral nature, even in the case in which his natural inclination to comfort and happiness comes in conflict with the feeling of duty. This moral urging, which the uneducated Christian would simply call *conscience*, Kant called rather imposingly the *categorical imperative*.[1] This man has to follow unconditionally; he is to do the good purely for the sake of the good, not with a view of reward or fear of punishment in this or the other world. By this morality would be degraded to means, whereas it is intended to be the end.

We have already said that Kant did not deny immortality and retribution in another world. On the contrary, he demanded the latter from the standpoint of practical reason, and even founded on it his faith in God and immortality; for since the striving of man for morality often comes in conflict with his natural inclination for happiness, there must most likely be a compensation beyond this world, there must be an all-wise, all-righteous, all-benevolent Being who can and will effectuate this compensation.

But however clear this is to the practical reason, the theoretical reason must inexorably demand the fulfilment of the moral law, even supposing the case that no compensation would take place. Man, under all conditions, must act in a

[1] He distinguishes the *categorical* imperative, from which no one can honourably free himself, from the *hypothetical*, the inclination of a person, and the principles, from mere maxims.

manner worthy of a free moral being, and whatever he lays down as a law for others must be the same to himself. Our morality must not be made dependent on promises and threats, its worth must be in itself. Kant, therefore, did not want to reject religion as something superfluous, but he certainly wanted to emancipate morality from it, and to place it on an independent footing. The truly moral man ought not to need religion as a support, nor ought he to permit himself to be led by the religious, but only by purely moral motives. If now these religious motives were in reality nothing else than hope of reward and fear of punishment (even if the punishment and reward were eternal), then Kant was perfectly right in desiring to make morality independent of these; for Christianity also teaches us to do good not for the sake of reward, and to shun evil not from fear of punishment. It does not want the servile spirit of calculation and fear, but the free spirit of sonship. But of this filial spirit nothing is heard in the Kantian system. The categorical imperative is certainly not that spirit of sonship in which we cry, Abba Father. It is, and remains, even if not an external arbitrarily given law, still always a law, a mere "Thou shalt," a commandment of iron necessity. The Kantian doctrine, indeed, leads us to the idea, to which the Apostle Paul also leads man, that there is one law in our reason and another in our members which wars against the law of our reason; but to the cry, "O wretched man that I am! who shall deliver me from the body of this death?" no reply comes to the free man from the system, except this, "Physician, heal thyself."

Kant was certainly right in being unwilling to make religion the *prop* of morality, if by this we mean merely an outward prop, a support for the morally weak. This is not only opposed to the dignity of morality, but also to that of religion, which does not want to serve as mere means to outward ends, not as a bugbear and scarecrow for the wicked, nor as bait for the covetous. But there is a great difference between an outward prop, against which the tree miserably supports itself, and the *root*, from which it draws its nourishing sap and receives the impulse to grow, and from which it shoots forth with vigorous life. That religion is this root, and that from it morality draws its purest sources of life, is a view which the Kantian doctrine lacks. That the mere external performance of works does not justify man, and gives him no claim to salvation, and that *conformity to laws* is not *conformity to morals* (legality not yet morality) has been proved admirably by Kant. In this he stands altogether on the foundation of Christianity in opposition to legal Judaism, and on that of evangelical Protestantism in opposition to the holiness of good works of the Romish Church, and of many of the later so-called moral philosophers who regarded happiness as the highest aim of man (Eudaemonism). In this respect he has done very much. But when we inquire further after the source of morality, after the essential force and fundamental impulse of all virtue, he points man to himself. The life-producing grace, the Spirit of God imparting himself to man, elevating and supporting him, these are objects for Kant which find no place either in his theoretical or practical reason. That fresh, free life of faith, which overcame the world in the days of the apostles, and which manifested itself again in the time of the Reformation, in Luther, could not, of course, breathe under the air-pump of the categorical imperative. Whatever heaven has awakened and nourished of the heavenly among men, is resolved here into the process of rational action, working according to unchangeable laws, and one is led to think of the image used by Herder, of an automaton that moves its limbs according to the tact, as if by command, which, however, lacks the soul with the spark divine.

Kant indeed recognizes a God, a real, self-conscious, personal God, not a mere mundane soul. But this God is, in reality, too extramundane, too much beyond this world ; it appears almost as if He existed merely for the sake of future retribution, and waited till then as an inactive observer of human actions. The Kantian God is indeed the strict Judge who holds the balance on the day of judgment, but it is not He who *gives* our actions their weight. He is really like the man in the gospel who reaps where he has not sown, who demands, and inexorably demands, without giving the power to comply with these demands ; for even supposing that there are individuals who go as far in rational self-esteem and self-victory, as the wise man demands, then these individuals will wrap themselves up more closely in the philosopher's cloak of their own righteousness, and elevate themselves in moral haughtiness above the masses, while the majority, when they gaze up to the dizzy height, despair of ever reaching it, and, seized by moral discouragement, sink to ruin. And yet Kant lays this requirement on *all*, demands it with seriousness, and in this seriousness with which he demands morality of man, and according to which alone he values the *true* worth of man, there is something grand and reverential. If later philosophers appear to determine the worth of man according to the amount of his thinking, when the intellectuality, the dialectic dexterity and activity of man, his geniality, is valued more than anything else, then it is affecting to observe in Kant, in opposition to these, that he did not place the happiness of the future life in intercourse with great minds like himself, but in the intercourse with honest souls, among whom his servant Lampe, with his limited knowledge, would also be welcome to him.[1] In this there is something extremely humble and truly Christian. Such an expression would also have pleased Luther.

If, now, we inquire further into the attitude the Kantian doctrines assumed in reference to Christianity, it might be asked, whether the conviction of an *ignorance* of divine things, of the weakness of our reason, ought not to have led directly to the reception of a *revelation!* It might be said to Kant, "for the very reason that man cannot apprehend the divine with *his* reason, as thou thyself hast shown, we ought to thank God doubly when he has revealed to us what we could not discover ourselves." This conclusion, certainly bordering closely on his system, has really been drawn by several Kantians in order to bring their philosophical system into harmony with faith in revelation, but not by Kant himself; for the very notion of a *supernatural revelation*, from which these set out, belonged, according to him, to those things of which reason knows nothing. Whence, thus he asked quite consistently with his presuppositions, whence shall the human mind know that that which announces itself as a revelation is really such? which are the certain signs (criteria) by which he can recog-

[1] Jachmann, p. 123.

nise such a revelation, by which he is to distinguish the true from the false? Where are the boundaries of the natural and supernatural? where does a miracle begin? where does nature cease to be nature? For all these questions reason has no decisive answer, and therefore Kant decided nothing. The *possibility* of a revelation and miracle can, according to him, be neither proved nor denied by sound reasoning. But, for this very reason, the essence of religion cannot depend upon the reception or rejection of these. Since all depends on the *moral*, therefore, according to Kant, the *moral* contents of a system of religious doctrines are the measure of its truth and the criterium of every revelation; and of all existing religions Christianity corresponds most perfectly with the moral requirements of reason, and contributes most to promote morality outwardly, this Kant acknowledged, being fully convinced of the fact. And he did not present the doctrines of Christianity in so onesided a manner as many of his followers; its historical proofs, also, had a value for him. So it was with the *person* of Christ. It is well, he thought, that the mass of mankind have an ideal in the historical Redeemer, in which ideal pure morality appears rëalized, and to which they can adhere; it is well that, in the ecclesiastical communion, an institution is given which makes that accessible to the mass which the wise man could, of course, without this, draw from reason. The idea of a kingdom of God on earth, that is, according to the Kantian interpretation, a moral confederation of men for the attainment of the highest moral ends, was estimated highly by him, only he thought that the priesthood, and whatever is stationary in religion, ought to be distinguished carefully from its essence.

Whilst a Voltaire scoffed at the Bible, the profounder philosopher Kant recognised in it an excellent means for the promotion of *moral* truth. The preacher, the teacher of the people, ought to make this book as useful as possible. He should, however, be less concerned (Kant thinks) to establish the original meaning of the Holy Scriptures (which he may leave for learned theologians) than to explain the Holy Scriptures according to the actual wants of his hearers, even at the risk of drawing from it something different from what was originally intended. This was certainly a dangerous principle, leading to the most arbitrary use of the Bible, and which permitted anything to be made of everything, provided only that in it a moral advantage appeared,

Kant had this in common with Lessing, that, in opposition to the neology of the time, which rejected all, he discovered, even in the old dogmatics of the church, a kernel of deep truth, which he recommended to be used wisely. He, therefore, sought to bring to honour again certain church dogmas which had already been cast overboard, not only because regarded as opposed to reason, but also to Scripture. So it was with the doctrine of original sin. Kant was too well acquainted with the human heart to become fanatical like Rousseau. He could not reconcile himself to the view that man, according to nature, is good and innocent. Man is, according to Kant, rather an egoistic being, concerned only for self-interest and his own welfare. This he called the *radical evil.* The good is not innate in man, he must be trained and educated for it before he possesses it: but, of course, the Kantian and church doctrines here separate again, since, according to Kant, man must finally become, through man, what according to Scripture, and the doctrines of the church, is accomplished by God.

If, now, we sum up the foregoing, we can say: *Christ, Christianity, Bible, Church, and Church doctrines* were not to him empty sounds, not what they were to the common deists, objects of contempt and scorn; no, they remained to Kant objects of reverence, at least objects worthy of earnest reflection and the most careful investigation. He, the master, did not decide speedily what many of his disciples afterwards decided hastily. He did not want to burden his conscience with the fact that he had torn from the heart of the people that which serves as the props of its morality. He regarded these props as remaining, but, of course, merely as props, as crutches for the weak, as temporary levers for those who cannot raise themselves. The religion of the Bible and of Christianity had not come to life in him; and what was not living in himself how could he impart it to others? Let us honour this, however, that he did not take it from them, at least not intentionally. Of course, he could not prevent it, that his disciples removed that which the master had permitted to remain. Even, if it may be doubted, that one of the greatest disciples of Kant, *Fichte,* made use of the expression, that Christianity would have outlived itself in five years,[1] still there was no lack of similar expressions on the part of others. If the more moderate admirers were satisfied in placing their master on a level with Socrates, the infatuated raised him above Christ, or they applied to him the language of creation. God said: "Let there be light, and there was"—the Kantian philosophy.[2] We have already seen how Kant refused this idolatry. He, like all truly great men, had not aimed at bringing up a host of admirers to repeat his own sentiments, but to inspire the mind with new impulses. At different times he had repeated in his lectures the sentiment that he did not want to teach his auditors *philosophy,* but how to *philosophize;* he did not, therefore, want to deliver a finished system into their hands, but to exercise their minds in thinking, and to render them capable of discovering the truth themselves. But how could he govern the stream which was, with continually increasing force, overflowing its banks? It may appear strange that a system, apparently dry and abstract, like the Kantian, a system which, perhaps, scarcely one in a hundred understood, should, notwithstanding this, have received so many adherents. It was nevertheless so. The Kantian system, or the critical philosophy as it was called, was too soon raised as a party standard, around which theologians, jurists, pedagogues, and physicians flocked. A proof this, that the ideas suggested by Kant were lying in the age; that the same, which he presented in a strictly scientific form, was glimmering in an indefinite manner in the minds of men, and that but the spell of a system was needed to call up the spirits who, without this spell, would have remained in the dark. But, just as everything has its limits and its opposition, so it was, too, with the Kantian philosophy; and the man, to whom we have already called your attention, Herder, we shall next see as one of its most ingenious and most powerful opponents.

We have already seen that the Kantian system produced a

[1] Fichte's son, at least, contradicts this saying mentioned by G. Müller in the "Life of Herder."

[2] This is mentioned by the younger Fichte in the life of his father.

revolution, not only in the German philosophical world, but also in the wider field of science, that it exerted a decided influence on religious thinking, on art, morality, politics, education, &c., &c.; and, though we could not avoid remarking that the desire to keep up with the spirit of the age, and the longing for something new and peculiar, assisted to increase the number of his followers; still it would be unjust to feign to be ignorant of the great impulse given to the mind by Kant through his philosophy. A philosophy which could gain over to it, and altogether fetter for a while, though it could not satisfy them very long, such young men as Schiller and Fichte; which governed the minds more than half a century, whose traces may even yet be seen in a large class of educated and half-educated men, though it has at present but few followers among philosophers, such a philosophy cannot well be regarded as something accidental; it has a great historical importance, and on this account, ought to be mentioned with respect. In his Critique, Kant has given the thinking mind, which finds its representatives in the German nation more than in any other, a task on which the deep thinkers—the philosophers—are to this day exerting their powers. It is not yet fully determined what his philosophy has accomplished, wherein its truth, wherein its error consists; and it is not our duty to form a judgment in reference to this matter, much less to give one. It is sufficient for us to recognise the great, the significant, wherever we meet it; and though we have found that the position which this philosophy took in the development of Protestantism was onesided, that in several respects it departed from the principal root of Christianity, we only design this as a judgment of this position and relation, which alone concern us; not of the system itself, which we have only contemplated in fragments.

It however belongs to our historical task to contemplate the enthusiastic reception which Kant met with from some of his contemporaries, as well as the opposition from others. We cannot give a special history of the dispute here. It may, however, be presupposed, that as there was a number of mad followers, so also there would be no lack of senseless objections, of reviling, and suspicions of a low order. Many, whose paper houses of ingenious arguments Kant had somewhat roughly blown down, were naturally incensed against him; even the great mass of the "illuminati" who had heretofore followed a broad, limitless mode of argumentation, were dissatisfied with Kant, for however much his system was calculated to promote that which had long been the aim of neology (a limiting of the religious to the moral, etc.), still the severe discipline which Kant introduced by his critical method was uncomfortable to many, and it might also grieve the vain among them that their names were obscured by his. But it is true that besides these common bawlers other voices were raised against the Kantian system, which differ entirely from the others by their weight, their influence, and their entire tone.

We have mentioned Herder as an opponent of Kant, and now we shall be able, as intimated before, to measure another magnitude with his. Before, however, we consider the points of difference between these two men, let us turn to what they have in common. It is not only the common native country (both were Prussians), not only the distinguished name in a remarkable age which places them in an intimate relation to each other, but also their Protestantism, their acute, critical minds. Both were Protestant spirits, both men of progress, of free development; both felt an impulse for something new, something better; both wanted to elevate man above the limited views given him by birth, education, and custom, to a contemplation of self, to a consciousness of the dignity of his spirit, to the possession and enjoyment of his humanity in the noblest sense of the word. Man as man, regarded purely as a human being, was the great subject of each, and it is remarkable that the word "*humanity*," so frequently used by Herder, also became the watchword of Kant. When the strength of his mind and body had already been considerably weakened, when he roused himself just before his close, Kant remarked, "*The feeling for humanity has not yet left me.*"

It may be expected from his kindly feeling that Herder, as Kant's junior and former scholar, retained the personal regard for him, which he had for all great men of his own and other ages. Otherwise he would have been false to his own principle, when he says, "A scholar who persecutes his teacher bears Nemesis on his back, and the sign of reprobation on his forehead." In the life of Herder we have already seen that he esteemed Kant personally. He also knew how to do justice to Kant's system, and its importance to the age. He even defended it against unjust charges and false sequences drawn from it. "It is false, altogether false," he says, "that his philosophy abstracts from experience, since it rather refers to experience wherever this takes place. . . . . . It is false that he loves a philosophy which, without a knowledge of the other science, is eternally threshing empty straw; whoever does this does not belong to his class." Herder opposed those one-sided admirers of Kant, who, instead of taking his Critique as a "fan which separates the chaff of philosophical thinking from the wheat, regarded it as the contents of human thinking, and of knowledge generally." "If," says Herder, quite Protestantly, "the sketch is taken for the thing itself, the frame for the picture, the vessel, whose grooves he exposed, for the contents of the vessel, and it is then believed that all the treasures of knowledge are gathered, what a mistake! What an abuse!!!" . . . . "The intolerance with which the Kantians spoke, condemned, praised, rejected, has been as much despised by the sound part of Germany as it must have been displeasing to the tolerant spirit and great love of truth of the author of this philosophy." . . . . "Kant's own works," says Herder, prophetically, "will remain. Their spirit, even if moulded into other forms, will continue to live and to exert an influence. It has already done much, its traces are seen in almost every branch of human investigation. A new impulse was given by Kant not only to sift the old, but also to arrange in a strict, logical order the sciences properly human, the science of morality, of natural and political right. These attempts are very beneficial, they will influence action, and, if God grants it, will themselves become received maxims." "It would have been very fine and useful," says Herder in his "Letters on Humanity,"[1]

[1] "Works on Philosophy and History," xi., p. 188, where a beautiful representation of Kant is also given: "I have been so fortunate as to know a philosopher who was also my teacher. In the prime of life he had the vivacity of a youth, which I think will follow him to the end of his days. His open, thought-

"if the pure object of Kant had been understood and adopted by all his followers. The salt with which he has sharpened and purified our understanding and reason, the power with which he rouses the moral law of freedom in us, must produce good fruits." "But," he says in another place, "whilst the Kantian philosophy is to be regarded as a ferment, stupidity took the leaven for the dough, and hence this inexplicable confusion."

Herder thought it would be a praiseworthy undertaking to collect the principal propositions of Kant's writings, in order to compare them with what had been possessed by philosophy before Kant, and thus to obtain a definite idea of what new ideas he had really advanced, for only blind Kantians could assert that all was new. Justice, humanity, he thought, demanded such an undertaking. Kant's real merit was not to be taken from him, but he was opposed to the one-sided elevation of this at the expense of that of others.

Herder must have been particularly prejudiced against the universal prevalence of the Kantian philosophy, which was now also beginning to prevail in theology, from what he experienced at the examinations of candidates in Weimar. Herder's biographer, J. G. Müller, relates, that "young theologians came to Weimar to make their examination, whose ignorance, arrogance, and impudent answers both provoked and pained Herder. A young theologian of Weimar had shot himself, before or after the examination, owing to the despondency arising from the fact that he had been disappointed in his studies. Another talented youth wrote an essay against matrimony, and at the same time requested, with pressing urgency, a pastoral charge

ful brow was the seat of undisturbed serenity and joy; his speech was fertile in ideas: humour, wit, and pleasantry were at his command, and his instructive discourse was very interesting. . . . . The history of man and of nations, natural history and natural philosophy, mathematics and experience, were the sources whence he drew the material to animate his lectures and conversation; he was indifferent to nothing really worth knowing; no cabal, no soul, no advantage, no ambition, ever had the least power to influence him against the spread and illumination of truth. He encouraged and gently forced persons to reflection. Despotism was foreign to his mind. This man, whose name I mention with the highest regard, is Immanuel Kant; I hold his image before my mind with pleasure," etc.

of the high consistory. An unrestrained arrogance, with a contempt for all that is venerable, spread among the youth, so that the most sacred ties of nature were disregarded; they scoffed at the love of parents and children, of husband and wife . . . said that we are not obliged to keep our promises, and that religion, especially the Christian, is superstition. All this new wisdom was boldly expressed, and found powerful advocates. This grieved Herder. He was grieved, too, on Kant's account, for the indignation against the foolish veneration was finally transferred to the person venerated. He thought it little in Kant that he did not check this mischief, as he certainly knew what abuse was made of his teachings. It is said that Kant himself remarked, that only one of his followers understood him, the court preacher, Schulz, in Königsberg.[1] Herder, therefore, thought himself in duty bound to oppose Kant's "Critique," in his "Metacritique."

We cannot follow the dispute. It is a fact that Herder's "Metacritique," as well as his "Kalligone," which was also directed against Kant, did not produce the desired effect, and that neither of them belongs to the best of his writings. We must acknowledge that Herder here ventured to enter a field in which he was less at home than in theology, history, and literature. Speculative philosophy was not Herder's sphere. The living, poetical view prevailed over his conceptions. He himself addresses the abstract philosopher thus: "If you must peel the fruit on account of your weak stomach, you may peel it, but do not suppose that I chew the peels of your abstractions only. I eat the fruit with its beautiful colour, I quaff the cup with its pleasant fragrance." So the poet speaks, and we gladly agree with him; but it did not satisfy those who want to peel with the critical knife. If these philosophers regarded reason as an independent power, separated from all personal influences and circumstances of the individual life; if they thought that the general conception stood higher than the individual, as he lives and moves before us, then Herder's living poetical disposition was repelled by these metaphysical abstractions. "Reason," he says, "is not

[1] A similar anecdote was related of Hegel shortly after his death.

primitive, pure potence, as the philosophers suppose, but an aggregate of observations and exercises of our soul, the sum of the education of our race, which the educated individual, as a strange artist, finally completes in himself, according to given patterns. It is only by means of education that a man becomes a man, and the entire race lives only in the chain of the individuals. Genus and species are general conceptions, which are only real so far as they exist in the individuals: Herder, therefore, as we see, started from the reality of the individual in its connection with the class, from the perception of the senses, from experience, whilst Kant and the Kantians started from abstract conceptions, which they then combined like numbers in ciphering. Having thus different stand-points, a reconciliation of views was not an easy matter. And this difference between their stand-points was intimately connected with the different personalities of these two great men. Herder was educated in life, Kant in the school. This was the great difference. Whilst for Herder the ship that carried him from Riga to Nantes became the cradle of his great ideas on the waves of the ocean, we find Kant never leaving his native city. While Herder, like Luther, loved music above all other things, and found a key in its mysterious language to many things, which cannot be expressed in abstract conceptions, we know Kant's indifference in reference to it, which, in a man of his position, we are tempted to call stupidity. In other respects their ideas were also very different, in reference to the nature and object of art. Kant was unwilling to let anything pass for poetry unless it was in rhyme, whilst Herder generally wrote blank verses. Herder's prose, like Lavater's, was frequently considered too poetical, and his poetry, on the other hand, sometimes dragged too much with prosaic sentences. Kant, however, demanded (and not altogether unjustly) a clear distinction between prose and poetry. He called a poetic prose one that had gone mad.

But perhaps the greatest difference between the two men may be traced to this, that Herder lived in the family with his whole soul, while the unmarried Kant was confined to himself and a few friends. A family can as little live intellectually on abstract ideas, as physically on viewing empty dishes. The daily bread, which is intended to support, must be more nourishing than the meagre fare afforded by the philosophical kitchen. Herder, like Luther, knew how to give to his own family the bread of life which he broke unto his congregation; and as he felt himself chief priest, so, too, he recognized with a true Lutheran heart the high significance of a priest's wife. "The position of a true, noble wife, and priest's wife," he says, "is (I say it without singularity or selfishness) the most dignified, most beautiful on earth, and with good children it may become a heavenly position." Kant, who regarded the art of cooking as the greatest attainment of a woman, knew nothing of this bliss. He could not accommodate himself to the minds of children, which he clearly proved whilst tutor, but Herder knew how to talk with children in a childlike manner. If we read, for instance, the letters which Herder wrote to his children while on his Italian journey, we are naturally led to think of Luther; he can adapt himself so artlessly, so heartily to their capacities. But we have said enough to shew how the personal difference of the two men influenced their modes of philosophizing.

XVI.

SCHILLER.

SCHILLER AND HIS RELATION TO CHRISTIANITY.—HIS RELATION TO PROTESTANTISM.

We now come to consider Schiller and Goethe, in whom, according to the ideas of many, the national literature of Germany culminates. We think it best for our object to separate the two, and though Goethe was the older we speak first of Schiller, since his influence on the thoughts of the German nation manifested itself earlier in a decided manner, than that of Goethe. Schiller's views were also intimately connected with Kant's philosophy, whilst Goethe's significance for his age and even for ours can only be fully understood in connection with the later philosophical systems —with Schelling and Hegel.

It may appear strange that I take Schiller as the representative of the rationalism of his age, as it manifested itself outside of the church and outside of theological science, in life. How, it will very properly be asked, if the nature of rationalism, as we have seen, consists in a certain sterility and dryness of the understanding, how does it happen that the fiery, imaginative poet is placed here? I must, therefore, explain myself more clearly. I might first remark that I distinguish the nobler rationalism, that of humanity, from the trivial, vulgar rationalism, which existed at the same time; but this explanation would not be sufficient; for this nobler rationalism, as far as we have learned to know it, had also, on the whole, a certain insipidity of the understanding, which even prevailed in the supporters of the opposite system, as in Reinhard. Now Schiller formed a decided contrast to this insipidity of the understanding, and we really find that Reinhard, for example, could not at all chime in with the brilliant genius of Schiller, but, among other things, characterized his poem on Joy as the effusion of a scorched brain. We must therefore ask again, how does it happen that in spite of this we place Schiller in connection with rationalism? Because, I reply, with all his poetical form, which Schiller handled with masterly skill, the contents of many of his poems, and even the whole aim of his life, agreed with the rationalistic tendency, and because he knew how to give rationalism by means of his beautiful, inspiring language, that ideality, sought for and desired in vain by so many, the very thing the dry rationalistic preachers lacked. We must here distinguish the poetical genius of Schiller, (which raised itself far above the level of a rationalistic mode of thinking, and which in different circumstances would have been just as capable of losing itself in the mystical regions of fanaticism), from his philosophical education, from the religious views which prevailed in him, and which constitute the soul of most of his poems, if we except a few productions of his youth, which bear the impress of a mind still struggling with a certain degree of indistinctness.

Schiller was (and this accounts for much) a disciple of Kant, an advocate of the critical philosophy, and he did much to spread the Kantian rationalism, of course in a poetical dress, into the hearts of the people. We do not blame him for this. But, on the contrary, the world needed an impulse to higher life, a moral invigoration, something that would direct their minds to the invisible, that could not be touched with hands, though this were only a poetic-philosophical ideal, in opposition to the materialistic, frivolous tendencies, which had been promoted to some extent by the school of Wieland. In opposition to the selfish view which made virtue the servant of inordinate desires, the world needed a voice to advocate virtue and to awaken enthusiasm in its behalf, to turn the eyes of men from the dust of earth to the glory of heaven. And this was done by Schiller. Not to acknowledge this, and in some respects with joy, were prejudice, were ingratitude, were at least ignorance; and it can only be regarded as a good indication when men, decidedly Christian, like Albert Knapp in his beautiful poem, have the courage to declare before believers and infidels what the German nation owes to Schiller. We can therefore agree with the festive sentiments of the speaker, who, on the occasion of unveiling the statue of Schiller in Stuttgart, began with these words: "Lost in admiration and in reverential contemplation, but also filled with sincere joy, we stand before the unveiled image of the sublime poet, the sagacious, popular teacher, the labourer on the building of eternity, the favourite of the people, who is both our pride and our love." If we place Schiller's image before our minds, we can look with the same pleasure on that brow "which reflected on the design and destiny of man," can hang with the same deep admiration on that kindling eye, on those eloquent lips, whence flowed the riches of bewitching song, without becoming idolaters on this account, as persons are sometimes charged.

But with all this acknowledgment and admiration we cannot refuse an answer to the question, in what relation does Schiller stand to Christianity? what position does he take in the history of the development of Evangelical Protestantism? Our task itself demands this; and only in this respect have we a right to speak of him here. Besides this, the question has forced itself on the age, and the veneration for the great poet, manifested at the unveiling of his statue, led to the discussion of this question. "Schiller and Christianity" have become the theme variously treated by different authors, and the speaker referred to above, Gustav Schwab, also found it proper to give his views on this subject, and to treat the matter fully, in his biography of the poet. Let us attempt to form a judgment on this subject, by taking these works into consideration as well as the writings of Schiller himself.

Schiller was born (Nov. 10, 1759) and educated in a land in which Christianity still had a good foundation, in the kingdom of Wurtemberg. The same custom which we found in the paternal home of Herder, that of morning and evening prayers, we also find here. The father, as Schiller's sister relates, regularly read the prayers morning and evening in the family circle, and Schiller, while yet quite young, was very attentive. And, in his school days, he never went to bed without offering a *silent* evening prayer, for, hating all mere outward form, he remarked that "there was no necessity of bawling." The songs of Paul Gerhard were favourites of his. Schiller was soon transported from his home to a hot-house, which could not possibly be favourable to the religious development of the youth. Not that there was a lack of religious exercises in the military school at Hohenheim, they were indeed very abundant, but in the form of military exercises, as an external work of the law and letter, as it had been the case in the religious training of Frederick the Great. Fortunately the former influences of pious training did not fail to leave their impressions on Schiller; he still loved to read the Bible, especially the Psalms and Prophets; he still more frequently poured out his soul in prayer, and even led devotional exercises in society; he still regarded religious poetry as the highest, and his youthful fancy was already thinking of a poem on Moses, to form a counterpart to Klopstock's Messiah. At this time the ministry was Schiller's ideal, and he could think of nothing more sublime than to proclaim, from the consecrated pulpit, the heavenly truths to a people longing for salvation. No one can read, without being affected, without the deepest sympathy, those thoughts of a Sunday morning of 1777, which have been handed down to us. Here already doubt struggles with faith in a manner which can only fill us with respect for the love of truth that animated the youthful thinker.

"God of truth, Father of light! I raise my eyes to Thee with the first rays of morning, and worship Thee. Thou searchest me, O God! Thou seest the trembling of the praying heart, even when yet afar off; O then, Thou also knowest the burning desire of my soul for truth! Thou knowest, O God! that anxious doubt frequently enveloped my soul in night, my heart was often alarmed, and struggled for divine light from Thee. Then there often fell a blessed ray from Thee into my benighted soul; I saw the horrible abyss on the edge of which I was already dizzy, and thanked the divine hand which kindly drew me back. Be Thou still with me, my God and my Father! for the days have come in which fools arise and say in their hearts, There is no God! Thou, my Creator, hast reserved me for troubled days! for days in which superstition raves on my right and infidelity scoffs on my left hand. Then I stand and frequently waver in the storm; and, alas! the trembling reed would break, if Thou didst not support me, mighty Sustainer of Thy creatures, Father of those who seek Thee."

"What am I without Truth, without the guide through life's labyrinth? A traveller lost in the woods, enveloped in night, in which no friend, no guiding star shines upon his way. Scepticism, uncertainty, unbelief, ye begin with anguish and end in despair. But Truth, thou leadest us safely through life, bearest a light before us in the dark valley of death, and bringest us to heaven whence thou camest.

"O my God! keep my heart in peace, in that holy stillness in which the truth loves most to visit us. The sun does not reflect itself in the stormy ocean, but in the calm, clear surface its countenance is beautifully mirrored. Do Thou also keep this heart calm, so that it may be able to know Thee, O God! and him whom Thou hast sent, Jesus Christ; for this only is truth which strengthens the heart and elevates the soul. If I have truth, then I have Jesus; if I have Jesus then I have God; if I have God, then I have all. Shall I permit myself to be robbed of this treasure, this sublime view, by the wisdom of the world, which is foolishness in Thy sight? No! let him that hates the truth be my enemy; but him who seeks it with a sincere heart I will embrace as a brother."

"The bell rings which summons me to the temple of God. I hasten to confirm my faith there, to become strong in the truth, and to prepare myself for death and eternity. Do Thou guide me, O my Father! Open my heart to the truth, that I may become strong enough to proclaim it to those who are mine, then they will be happy. They will then know that Thou art their God and Father, that Thou didst sent Jesus Christ, thy Son, and the Spirit, to testify to the truth. Then they will have comfort for every grief in life, and the blessed hope of immortality in the hour of death."

"Now, my God! Thou mayest take all things from me, every earthly happiness that fills my heart, every charming joy; let me but keep the truth, then I shall have happiness and joy enough."

"If Thou, merciful God! wilt permit me to cry unto Thee with this quaking heart, this trembling tear in my eye, O, then, do Thou also look with compassion on the erring! Of all the miserable on earth they need Thy help the most. They cannot enjoy Thy sun nor the lovely moon, for their soul is night, and their heart is full of bitter struggles. O do Thou pity their anguish! Let them hear the voice of truth, that they may stop and tremble and retrace their steps, and follow the heavenly call of this voice. Bring us all to that place where no night, no error, no doubt can trouble our souls, but where light and truth and certainty beam upon the blessed, and where we shall know for ever that Thou art God our Father, and that Jesus Christ is the reflection of Thy glory, through whom Thou impartest every joy, every blessing."

"Preserve us, our Saviour, Jesus Christ! who sittest on the right hand of God; be Thou our shield and hiding-place! Before Thee the host of scoffers is mere dust."

"Thou hast seen from eternity how long their defiance shall last and shall snort against Thee on earth; perhaps their measure will soon be full."

"Thou hast also redeemed them, O Lord! whose mockery now reviles Thee! Grant that before the night of death they may awaken to earnest repentance. Amen."

Schwab justly remarks that the poem, with which this prayer closes, might stand in any orthodox hymn-book. The scepticism nourished by the philosophy of Voltaire, with whose writings Schiller became acquainted when only fifteen years old, kept increasing continually; but wherever this doubt is expressed, it is "*a doubt full of the holy earnestness and depth of a soul thirsting for the truth,*" more like that of Rousseau than that of Voltaire. In the philosophical letters (Julius to Raphael), written somewhat later, Schiller's anguish and doubt frequently found expression: "Blessed time, when I still staggered through life like a drunken man, my eyes being closed! I felt, and was happy. Raphael taught me to think, and I now regret that I was ever created. Thou hast robbed me of that faith which gave me peace. Thou hast taught me to despise what I worshipped. A thousand things were venerable to me before thy gloomy wisdom exposed them. I saw multitudes flocking to church, I heard their fervent devotion expressing itself in united prayer. Divine must be that doctrine, I exclaimed, which the best of mankind profess, which conquers so mightily and comforts so wonderfully! Thy cold reason quenched my enthusiasm. 'Believe nothing but your reason,' you said, 'there is nothing holier than the truth.' I obeyed, sacrificed all my opinions. *My reason is everything to me now,* my only assurance of God, virtue and immortality. Woe to me, henceforth, if ever I find this only assurance contradicting itself."

It was during this period of doubt and anxiety that Schiller published his "Robbers." But it is remarkable that in this piece, which has many esthetic and moral imperfections, in the midst of the abortions of an unbridled fancy, the firm old Wurtemberg faith in Christianity still appears as the foil from which human depravity is reflected in its most horrible forms. Or does it not appear strange that Schiller, in his preface to this drama, justifies the choice and management of the materials by assuring us that he wanted to represent the disposition that is just turning away from religion and Christianity?

"It is now," he says, "the fashion to give wit free play at the expense of religion, so that a person scarcely passes for talented unless he lets his wicked satire make sport of its holiest truths. The noble simplicity of the Bible is daily abused by the so-called witty minds and distorted into the ridiculous; for what is so serious and so holy that may not be rendered ridiculous by distortion? I hope that I do not revenge religion and morality only slightly, in delivering these wilful despisers of the Bible to the contempt of the world, in the person of my basest robbers."[1] On the other hand, he gives the picture of a worthy, not strictly orthodox, but Kantian-rationalistic minister in the same piece, in the person of pastor Moser, a picture of what the age perhaps regarded as the ideal of a preacher.[2] It is remarkable that this, with slight exceptions, is the last favourable representation of a minister in the works of Schiller. Almost everywhere else we find a settled hatred of priests, which could easily connect with itself a hatred of the Church and all positive religion. We do not blame him for finding and attacking priestly dominion in the Protestant Church. There was, unfortunately, too much of this, and it is related that the religious instructor of Schiller while a youth, is still decried by the people as a "Lutheran priest." But that he frequently made no distinction between positive religion and priestly dominion,—that in attacking the one he also attacked and designed to attack the other,—this was owing to the effect of that one-sided "illuminism" bitterly reproached in his "Robbers," but into which he gradually fell more and more himself.

It is never the insolent scoff of a Voltaire which our poet

[1] This was really done by Schiller. After one of the robbers had ironically proposed to become a pietist and to hold devotional meetings, the other answers, "Capital! and if that fails, turn atheist. We might fall foul of the four gospels, get our book burned by the hangman, and then it would sell at a prodigious rate." And as Italy is praised as the land of thieves, Spiegelberg utters these significant words: "Yes, yes, and if Germany goes on as it has begun, and if the Bible gets fairly kicked out, of which there is every prospect, Germany, too, may arrive at something respectable."

[2] The Kantian idea of retribution is the point to which Moser directs the attention of Frank Moor. "The thought of God will wake up a terrible monitor, whose name is JUDGE. The different destinies of mankind are balanced with terrible nicety; the scale of life which sinks here will rise there, and that which rises here will sink there. What was here temporary affliction, will there be eternal triumph; and what was here temporary triumph, will be there eternal despair."

adopted, nor a low utilitarian and commonplace philosophy. How would this have been possible with the ideal turn of his mind! Nor does he seek to free himself of the thought of the supernatural from pure religion, for the purpose of giving himself boldly to the enjoyment of earthly pleasures. He says, I profess none of all religions that may be mentioned, that is, none of the historical religions; and his attacks are therefore chiefly directed against the historical, the positive, which he could not harmonize with his idealistic notions of the nature of religion. "I must acknowledge," he writes to Goethe in 1797, "that I have so many doubts in reference to the historical in the Bible, that your doubts on a single fact appear to me very moderate. For me, the Bible is only true where it is artless; in everything else, I fear a design and a later origin." It is therefore the greater distrust of all that is historical, the supposition of an intentional deception on the part of the priesthood, or of some similar invention, which injured his taste for the Bible. Only the artless has still a charm for the poet, and even this was not very great. For the sublimity of Scriptural poetry, which Herder appreciated so fully, Schiller manifested little taste, or it was merely transient; his ideals of beauty were rooted only in the Grecian world. No wonder, then, that he was not attracted by Herder's personality, with which he was so closely connected in Weimar?

But the farther Schiller departed from positive Christianity, the more he became attached to the Kantian philosophy, which he studied very diligently, and the results of which he gave in his poetry. Marquis Posa, as is well known, is a Kantian in the Spanish costumes of the sixteenth century, and the "Words of Faith" of 1797 preach to us the trinity of the practical reason.[1] Schiller gives a disclosure of his relation to the Kantian philosophy in several of his letters. To his friend Koerner he wrote in 1792: "I have formed the irrevocable resolution not to leave the Kantian philosophy till I have fathomed it, though this should cost me three years." He wrote to Kant himself to assure him of his adherence to

[1] Instead of the triad—God, freedom, and immortality, we here have freedom, virtue, and God (a God "high above time and space," having no relation to, and taking no care of the world).

his system, and he did not approve of Herder's not taking the same decided ground in favour of Kant's philosophy. Schiller's own enthusiasm for Kant, however, lasted only a few years. Afterwards, he was repelled by the austere and monkish in Kant's system of morals, and though he did not return to Christianity, he still acknowledged that there was a difference between it and Kantism. In this respect, a letter to Goethe in 1795 is remarkable, in which he praises the "Confessions of a Beautiful Soul" in "Wilhelm Meister," and then expresses himself thus: "In the Christian religion I find virtually the occasion for what is highest and noblest, and the different manifestations of this religion in real life appear to me so offensive and insipid, only because they are *abortive* representations of this highest. If we cling only to the peculiar character of Christianity which distinguishes it from all other monotheistic religions, we shall find that it consists in nothing else than an abolition of the law of Kant's imperative, in the place of which Christianity wants a free inclination."

Here Schiller was on the right track to the recognition of the peculiarity of Christianity, and in the same letter he denotes it "the incarnation of the Holy One;" but he does not go any farther than to consider Christianity for this very reason, as "an esthetic religion, which is chiefly beneficial to the nature of woman, and is, therefore, only met with in a tolerable form in women."

Whilst Schiller only occasionally refers to religious and theological matters in most of his works, we have a theological essay in his "Mission of Moses," which he, however, completed before he became a Kantian. In this essay his rationalistic tendency is very evident. On the one hand, in the effort to change the miraculous as related in the Bible, and as it impresses the fancy, into the natural, the explicable; and on the other, also, in the stress he lays on the providential, which manifests itself in the direction of human destiny, and in the use and shaping of circumstances, as the kernel separated from the shell. Schiller recognises the hand of Providence in the history of Moses, "but not that Providence which interferes with the economy of nature in the violent way of miracles, but that which has itself prescribed such an economy for nature, which performs extraordinary things in the most quiet way." He affirms that Moses, being initiated into the Egyptian mysteries, attained a knowledge of the one God, that, however, instead of proclaiming this idea of the one God as an empty, abstract theory, he had connected it with the idea of the national Divinity of the Hebrews, and that he was not satisfied with making this national God the greatest of all gods; he made Him the *only* God, and hurled all gods back into their nothingness.

The truth of this notion of Schiller is perhaps this, that in the Old Testament, the Creator of heaven and earth at the same time appears as the God of Abraham, of Isaac, and of Jacob, and that in this connection of the monotheistic-universal and the national, the peculiar religious power of the Mosaic and Jewish religion in general consists. But the false, the mistaken in this idea, is, that he represents that as the work of ingenious human calculation and deliberation, which, according to the Christian belief, is the work of the divine education of the race.[1] This leads us to Schiller's views on history in general, and to his position as a historian.

Schiller had become professor of history in Jena, without any effort of his to attain the position, at a period when his soul was full of dramatic projects. Thus far, history had only been a mine of poetry to him, of the drama especially, and it was to be the same in the future. In a letter to a female friend he has expressed himself clearly on this subject: "I shall always be a bad source for a future historian who will be so unfortunate as to turn to me for authority. But I shall probably find readers and hearers, at the expense of historic truth, with which I may now and then agree philosophically. *History in general is only a magazine for my fancy, and the objects must submit to be plastic in my hands.*" A hazardous confession for a professor of history! but, at the same time, an important confession, which gives us a general view of the unhistorical nature of the wide-spread philosophical mode of thinking in that day. Kant also wanted the Bible to be so used that you can make what you will out of it for the

[1] We see how little Schiller could transpose himself into the religious thinking of antiquity from the frivolous Voltaire-like manner in which he derides the appearance of God in the burning bush, and the fact of Moses taking off his shoes.

sake of morality. Schiller claims the same for aesthetics, and thus the great and fine minds knew how to share the profits with each other, since now they degraded history to the office of a servant, as they had formerly done philosophy; and this deficiency of historical taste, I might say of historical humility, which, with self-denial, regards history as a power above the individual, pervades the history of rationalism. It has manifested itself in different departments of learning, in law as well as in theology, in politics as well as in art. We do not mean to say that Schiller lacked all high views of history. Some excellent ideas on this subject are expressed in his academical introductory discourse: "What is, and for what purpose do we study, universal history?" In opposition to the former confession so carelessly made, he here acknowledges that in history truth is the great consideration, and recognises the obligation "*to be careful that the value of truth may not be diminished in his hands.*" Here, however, it is more the generalising *philosophical* spirit for which he is zealous than the fine historical sense which knows how to seize and to estimate that which is individual, peculiar, in each nation, age, and person. This same deficiency of taste for the individual in history appears in Schiller's poems, some characters are not only arbitrarily idealised, but changed to their opposites, and persons are made the bearers of ideas which are foreign to their nature. Schiller's heroes are generally less the speakers of their age than the organs through which he conveys his philosophy; they are the mirror of the poet, not of their age: therefore the plastic, which Goethe could handle so well, is frequently outweighed (as in Racine and the French generally) by the declamatory.[1] The declamatory requires strong contrasts; and, in history, Schiller's eye is more keen for these than for the events and their connection. But there is much danger of exaggeration, and, therefore, of untruth in this. Whoever seeks either savageness or civilization, nobility or meanness of soul, humanity or brutality everywhere, shows but little susceptibility for the intermediate grades and states of transition, for the infinite blending of events; lacks the skill and patience to describe characters according to the whole truth, and will waver between the original and its ca-

[1] Wallenstein's Lager is a fine exception to this.

ricature. It is a common law of history, that the past must serve the present; but, above all, justice must be done to the past, and we must not arbitrarily measure the past by the present, and lay aside, like old clothes, whatever at first sight appears to be of no advantage to the age. Rationalism, which wanted to recoin the discoveries of history into current money, injured the historical sense, and hence the quiet, judicious industry with which Herder, like the bee, gathered the memorials of history, the reverence which he manifested for the past and for the dead was among other things highly offensive to Schiller. In harsh expressions, he charges him with veneration for all that is dead and antiquated, and with indifference towards all that is alive, and calls the diligence with which he collects the materials of the past, a miserable culling of antiquated and diseased literature.

If we turn again to his discourse on the study of history, we find occasion to rejoice in the fact that in it Schiller reveals the Protestant character of his mind, and with a certain pride says that " he speaks to Protestant Christians." " The Christian religion," he continues, " has so much to do with the present condition of the world, that it becomes the most important fact in the history of the world." But he adds, by way of limiting this remark, " that neither in the time in which Christianity appeared nor in the people in which it arose, can a sufficient explanation for its appearance be found," and he thinks the reason lies in a want of original sources of historical facts. Here, too, philosophy, and a philosophical pragmatic method, which arranges history according to its own laws, makes up for him the deficiency of sources and a want of the study of those that really exist. Philosophy must unite the fragments and transform the given materials into a connected whole.

Schiller, then, regards Christianity as the most important fact in the history of the world. If, however, those only fully can comprehend its historical position, as the redeeming power of the world, who have a deep view of the nature and historical ramification of sin, it might be objected against Schiller that this he did not possess. Even the very beginning of the history of our race he regards (in an essay on this subject), from a point of view according to which the first transgression of the divine commandment, as related in the Mosaic account, does not appear to be a misfortune, but a blessing. He sees, with the ancient Gnostics, no fall in the first sin, but an elevation of the human race to moral independence on awakening from the dreams of childhood to real consciousness. Hence he does not regard Christianity as a restoration, but at best as an element of development in the progress of the race towards humanity.

Whilst Schiller's name is perhaps scarcely mentioned in church history, much less his influence on national culture estimated in it, we have at the very beginning remarked, that we did not intend to consider merely the ecclesiastical phenomena in the narrow sense of the word, but also to draw into the circle of our contemplations whatever has influenced the formation of ideas in general, has opened new points of view in judging of moral relations, has produced new tendencies of thought, of feeling, of action, and has thus most deeply influenced the progressive development of Protestantism. And who can deny that Schiller has been thus influential?

If we examine Schiller's poems more closely, we shall soon agree that the title, "Christian," could hardly be chosen to indicate their nature, and still less shall we look for hymns there. Schiller has been blamed for not having been a writer of hymns; but it is wrong to blame him on this account. It is not the business of a single individual to write a hymn; the impulse to it must lie in the age, but in no age was the impulse for this less than in that in which Schiller lived. We would scarcely thank him, if, to redeem himself as it were, he had patched together a few religious verses, and in all the rest had still shown himself a secular poet, as was the case, for instance, with Uz, Guenther, and others. Schiller's poems proceeded from the depths of his soul, and were the full expression of his character. They all contain truth, even if only subjective truth. Nothing was more offensive to him than the appearance of hypocrisy. Whilst he himself breathed the air of the old Christian life, he might write a poem like the one we have given; afterwards he could also have done it and much better. as far as talent is concerned, but he could not have done it consistently, not without sporting with the most holy things, and this he was unwilling to do. Let us honour this disposition, and not be forgetful of it in judging of his poems.

The fact, however, must be carefully noticed, that there is an extensive field between that which is Christian in the narrowest sense of the word, and unchristian, and though we do not wish to be too free with the name "Christian," though we do not say that the *moral* is in itself the *Christian* (in which the error of rationalism consisted), still we may admit that where we meet with an excellent moral disposition, a point is found where Christianity can commence its influence, and that at least a principal obstacle in the way of Christianity has been removed. It is, therefore, the moral dignity and purity running through most of his poems, which is especially worthy of acknowledgment, even viewed from the Christian standpoint. Schiller elevated poetry from the filth of sensuality, into which it was threatening to sink from an imitation of foreign models, into the pure sphere of the ideal. Ought we not to thank him for this as Christians? Whoever walks with Schiller, perhaps treads with him on giddy heights, may pass dangerous chasms and abysses, but he does not walk in darkness, not in filthy mire, but always with his eye directed towards the sun, though this may hide itself behind the black storm-clouds of anxious doubts and powerful errors. From such a dreadful height, on the edge of an abyss, his "Resignation" resounds, and he longingly casts his eye back to the old Hellenistic land of fables, and wishes the gods of Greece back into the very midst of Christianity.[1] But in this stormy breast a noble heart beats, which longs for God, and as far as the "gods of Greece" are concerned, it is more the abstract soulless theology which banishes the living God from the world, and changes all into dead forces of nature, against which this poem is directed, than against real Christianity. Even when Schiller in his "Words of De-

[1] His correspondence with Koerner throws some light on this subject. "The God whom I place in the shade by the side of the gods of Greece, is not the God of the philosophers (?) nor the beneficial vision of the great mass (!) but it is a monster formed by the combination of many weak, false conceptions." After all, the God of philosophers; at least not the God of the Bible.

lusion" appears to doubt all truth, when he says that the truth never manifests itself to the "human understanding," when he calls that which we may attain mere "guessing and opinion:" he still has that dead, formal wisdom chiefly in view, which thinks it can imprison the mind in a "sounding word," whether it be called orthodoxy or a philosophical system; but he wants the heavenly faith to be preserved. "What no ear has heard, no eyes have seen, is nevertheless the beautiful, the true; it is not without—there the fool seeks it; it is in thee, thou art continually producing it." He says something similar in his poem on the Commencement of the New Century: "Thou must flee from the bustle of life to the holy, silent chambers of the heart; freedom exists only in the realm of dreams, and the beautiful blooms only in song."

This retiring to the inner world Schiller has in common with many noble minds who, being ungently touched by the external world and its formalities, take refuge in the quiet home of the soul. We honour the beautiful and the grand in this disposition, but will not close our eyes to its dangers. This retiring into one's self may easily awaken pride, false self-contentedness, which is never really content, and which seeks amends in despising others. The morbid in Schiller's tendency, which was communicated to many of his contemporaries, and which finds its root in the Kantian philosophy, is that forced ideality, which hovers high above us as something supermundane, something unattainable, and to which we can only raise ourselves by the highest soaring of the fancy; whilst Christianity holds to a historical realization of the ideal, which has already taken place, in reference to the religious and moral, by means of which the transformation of the human into the divine is also to be made possible, of course not through a high poetical or speculative flight of thought, but in the modest way of humble waiting and struggling. When Schiller calls to the Friends: "All in life is but a repetition, and only the fancy is eternally young; that which never and nowhere occurred, only that never becomes antiquated;" Christianity answers, "It has certainly occurred somewhere; and at a certain time, the saving grace of God has appeared to all men—we beheld His glory, the glory as of the only begotten of the Father, full of grace and truth," and *this* it is which never becomes antiquated, but an eternal rejuvenescence proceeds from the Spirit of regeneration into all the world, ever since the days of that appearance.

At other times, Schiller himself, when he descended from the ideal heights into the valley where men walk, knew how to appreciate what Christianity, as an existing reality, could accomplish in the hearts of men. "Religion of the cross, Thou alone bindest together in one wreath, that of humility and power, double palms." Thus he addresses his Knights of St. John. And is it not spoken from the depths of a Christian consciousness, in direct opposition to an understanding making all things plain, as well as against a proud idealism of reason, when in his "Words of faith" he says: "And what no understanding of the intelligent perceives, is practised in simplicity by a child-like faith." The most beautiful apology lies in these words. Christ himself has the same idea when He says, "If any man will do His will, he shall know of the doctrine, whether it be of God, or whether I speak of myself;" and, "Blessed are the pure in heart: for they shall see God." "I thank thee, O Father, Lord of heaven and earth, because thou hast hid these things from the wise and prudent, and hast revealed them unto babes." That the unhappiness of man does not lie in God, as the "Resignation" seems to indicate, but in man and his sinfulness, this was expressed by Schiller in his "Bride of Messina," with these words: "Everywhere the world is perfect, where man does not come with his griefs." And in the earnest tragical close: "This one thing I feel and clearly understand, That life is not the greatest good, but guilt the greatest evil."

Schiller, however, leaves the wound and the gap which guilt has made open before our eyes, and gives us a view of the depth of sin without, at the same time, leading us to the height where the debt is cancelled and from whence issues balm for the wounded heart.

Though Schiller did not penetrate to the heart of Christianity, of which he, however, sometimes had a faint view, still he was not a stranger to its hopes. "Even at the grave he awakens hope." Does it not appear as if we heard Klopstock in the "Song of the Bell," when it is said: "We mournfully hide seed still more precious in the bosom of the earth, and hope that it will grow up out of the tomb to a destiny more beautiful."

"These words," says G. Schwab, "through which the poet has won many thousand hearts, are the words of the mourning and hoping son and brother. Are they incompatible with the truth? Are they a falsehood and fraud of our conception? Then the Christianity of the Bible is also an invention for blockheads, as it was formerly and even lately asserted."[1]

Schiller had periods, however, in which his look into the future was dark, and when he regarded the hope of immortality as one of the supports only needed by the moral weakling; but still it appears, that if the heart of the poet himself was wounded, he liked to lean on this support, which rationalism always honestly defended as an essential part of all religion, and which the great Kant numbered among the requirements of the practical reason. In after life, Schiller, as already remarked, turned away more and more from the Kantian philosophy, and buried himself in poetry, his proper sphere. And though he apparently gained nothing by this, so far as Christianity is concerned, still he gained this advantage, that he attained a clearer view of the nature of religious revelations, or that he at least accepted a region lying beyond the sphere of our understanding, a region of believing and anticipating knowledge, in which poetry and religion meet. Thus he says in his poem "The Artists," of 1789: "What reason, growing old, discovered after thousands of years had passed away, was lying in symbols of the beautiful and great *pre-revealed* to the childlike mind."

Suppose this pre-revealing in symbols, in the artistic sense, had given the friends of Christianity an opportunity of coming to an understanding with the poet in reference to the nature of religious revelations? But there was no opportunity for this. Schiller died before he had fully perfected his convictions. What a pity he could not agree with Herder! What

[1] We do not agree with Schwab when he thinks Christ is referred to in Don Carlos in these words: "Ever since mothers have given birth, only one—one has died so undeservedly." Marquis Posa refers evidently to his murdered friend; this is quite like Schiller.

an influence these two minds might have exerted by their example, if they had used the power at their command for the living and intellectual comprehension of Christianity.

From a person in intimate connection with the poet, we learn that, towards the close of his life, the world-wide historical influence of Christianity, and the pure, holy form of its Founder, filled him with continually increasing reverence. And basing his opinion principally on this fact, the orator at the unveiling of Schiller's statue said confidently, "that the heart of the great poet may not have been so far removed from Him whose name he indeed seldom mentioned, but who still has a name above all other names." But even supposing that Schiller never came into a nearer relation to Christianity than that indicated in his works, one thing must not be forgotten, that the individual can never entirely separate himself from the totality in which he lives, and that every one, no matter how high he may stand, is borne by his age. This is true both of the errors and truths which govern an age. If we take "Christian" in its widest signification, in opposition to heathenism and antiquity, we shall find, that Schiller's poetry, in spite of all the gods of Greece and all his longing for the ancient poetical land of fables, still has its root in Christian history—the Christian, that is, the modern view of the world. A mode of contemplation, essentially Christian, lies at the basis of his tragedies, "Mary Stuart," the "Maid of Orleans," and "Wallenstein," as well as of many of his ballads and novels, and "even where the poet handles a subject taken from mythology he transforms it through his subjectivity. In short, he stands on a position much higher than that of antiquity." And for this he is indebted to Christianity. So much in reference to the question, whether Schiller is to be called a Christian poet. We must still answer the question, what position did he occupy in reference to Protestantism?

If Protestantism consisted only in protesting against false piety, against hypocrisy and priestly dominion, in struggling for freedom of conscience and of thought, for political and religious independence, who would refuse to place Schiller in the first rank of the combatants? We, too, call him a Protestant in this sense, and by this we mean an honourable, noble

Protestantism, one which, with all its partiality, may still be clearly distinguished from mere noisy and low bullying. Schiller's soul was thoroughly animated with a noble wrath against all that debases man and reason, against all that lowers the dignity of man. "I will," he writes in reference to "Don Carlos," "make it my duty to revenge the prostituted human race, and to expose its ignominious blots to shame." With these words he has not only expressed the object of that drama, but of his entire life. We have already remarked, that this is not regarded by us as the genuine Protestantism which we seek and desire to follow in our history, but that in this zeal the chastising spirit of Luther is seen to some extent, no one will deny.[1]

It appears strange to us that Schiller, as historian, should have chosen that part of modern history in which the religious contest, produced by the Reformation, is particularly prominent—the revolt of the Netherlands, the thirty years' war, and the religious wars of the French. The deep religious motives are indeed not made most prominent in these (Gustavus Adolphus, for instance, being viewed merely in a political light), still it cannot be denied, that quite a Protestant tendency manifests itself in the whole, in which we recognize bone of our bone, and flesh of our flesh. But how? did not Schiller, as poet, covet the favour of Catholicism? Has he not, in his "Mary Stuart," presented her as a martyr of that Church, and done Queen Elizabeth great injustice? Did he not, in his "Walk to the Forge," give a favourable description of the services of the mass; and in his "Rudolf of Hapsburg," does he not defend the raising of the host and the officiating priest? I do not think that any person will really accuse Schiller, from such passages as these, of a Catholicizing tendency,—a tendency which was much more common in what is called the romantic school than in him. At best you might see in it that indifferentism, which values a poetical impression above all other things,

[1] Schiller by no means sought the reformatory merely in destroying. "To destroy," he says, "is a business unworthy distinguished power, so long as there is anything left to be created." He recommends "a judicious indulgence towards opinions, feelings, institutions, which contain a germ of human dignity worthy of development."

and therefore makes every religious form subservient to it. But even this is not necessary. Genuine Protestantism knows how to value the forms of Catholic worship in their historical connection and in their proper place, and only a contracted Puritanism would expect the poet to confine himself to that which strictly belongs to his confession. Nevertheless the manner in which he has represented Mary Stuart and Elizabeth might bring the charge of injustice against the poet, since he has abused poetical freedom in general in this piece, not only in idealizing historical personages, but in changing them to their very opposites.

But enough of Schiller's person. If we now ask, what influence Schiller exerted in his age, we can only say, that it was *exceedingly great*, and is still continuing. Is it not so? To know Schiller, to have read him, to cite him,—this, some twenty or thirty years ago, was regarded as a proof that one belonged to the educated world, and in some circles is still so regarded. The learned world, of course, requires more in our day, and he who wants to pass for a man of superior education must shrug his shoulders at the mention of Schiller in order to extol Goethe, though for the most modern portion even Goethe has become too old; above whom certain young lords would like to be placed. Schiller, however, still has his admirers in all classes of society; and though it may be an evidence that one still stands in a former grade of education if he admires Schiller exclusively, still the man really educated will, because educated, rejoice at the richness of Schiller's genius, and a vigorous youth will always feel the effect of Schiller's writings. This is a proof of the power of his poems, and it would certainly evince an ignorance of the development of the national education of Germany, as well as of Protestantism and its different elements, to regard the influence of Schiller, formerly and now, as only deleterious. It is only a one-sided Christianity, which would keep itself entirely free from the influences of art and of cultivation; such, however, can never be more than a mere sect, can never develop itself to a religion of world-wide importance. Who can deny that the feeling for the beautiful and noble, as nourished by Schiller, is not only consistent with Christianity, but that it can be purified and ennobled by Christianity, and by this means can be carried farther than Schiller himself did? Just as, according to the united testimony of all sensible men, the study of the Grecian and Roman Classics must exert, even in reference to Christianity, a cultivating and refining influence under the direction of a Christian teacher; so, too, the German Classics, which, with their entire view of the world, stand on Christian ground, must, in the hands of Christian teachers, serve as means of cultivating the taste and of improving the language. The attempt to banish them from our schools, or firesides and libraries, through Christian zeal, would certainly not be advisable; this would but be making the youth lust after forbidden fruit,—it would even deprive them of an essential part of their education,—would be educating them in a one-sided manner. But the overrating of Schiller's poetry, and the universal and exclusive reign which was claimed for a while for this mode of thinking, and of writing poetry, are just as one-sided. . . .

That everything in Schiller is not to be praised,—that in many of his poems there are objectionable things, even in reference to art and taste, is now generally acknowledged, as the dispute in reference to the preference between Schiller and Goethe, sufficiently proves. The over-rating is, however, still more partial in reference to morality, and where held fanatically, may take a hostile position towards Christianity. But as every tendency developes partially for a while, till overcome, or at least confined to its proper limits by another, so it was, too, in this case. The more Schiller's mode of thinking embraced elements which were opposed to the then prevalent Christian and ecclesiastical mode of thinking, the more eagerly did the youth, longing for something fresh and new, receive his writings. "The Words of Faith" had now more influence on many young men than the Apostles' creed, which they had thoughtlessly learned from their catechism; the charm of the beautiful language transported many minds to a kind of sentimental enthusiasm, and the ideal striving for the divine satisfied, "though it might everywhere lead to stumbling," many who did not care much for the stumbling. Instead of seeking forgiveness of sins in the difficult, toilsome way of Christian repentance, and of working out their salvation with fear and trembling, it was easier to join in the song with the joyous companions: " All sins shall be forgiven, and hell shall be no more."

But we must not judge too harshly of this phenomenon. We must not see mere wickedness and hard-heartedness in it, nor always even a formal aversion to Christianity. The forms in which Christianity expressed itself had really become too narrow for the impetuous spirit of the age. Secular education had overtaken, and even surpassed the religious. There were still *learned* and *believing* theologians, but only a few who, furnished with the spirit of Herder, could satisfy, or even attempted to satisfy, both the requirements of the mind and conscience, both the requirements of the Church and of learning; and those who did attempt it were led to an awkward position, and ran the risk of falling into the bad state of being half-way between the two. Even Herder himself, as we have already seen, did not at all times seem equal to the great task of presenting Christianity and humanity in their unity. How can we then be surprised, if many preachers, who were dissatisfied with the dryness of Kant's doctrines, and who felt that more was needed to elevate and inspire the soul of man than Kant's imperative, now made use of Schiller's; that they brought before the people from the pulpit their favourite poet, whom they had applauded in the theatre, and either cited from his works,[1] or else preached in bombastic Schillerian phrases? It was, therefore, attempted to supply what rationalism lacked in depth of feeling, by sentimentality, in which there of course could be no want of hollow declamation. Frequently, indeed, the dryness of an insipid morality, and the shallowness of a flowery bombast, are mingled in the same sermon.

[1] How many sermons commenced with the words, " There are moments in human life."

XVII.

SALZMANN, CAMPE, PESTALOZZI, HAMANN, AND CLAUDIUS.

CHANGES IN EDUCATIONAL VIEWS.—SALZMANN, CAMPE, PESTALOZZI, AND HIS RELATION TO CHRISTIANITY.—INFLUENCE OF PESTALOZZIANISM ON THE RELIGIOUS MODE OF THINKING.—HAMANN: SKETCH OF HIS LIFE AND EXTRACTS FROM HIS WORKS.—CLAUDIUS, THE WANDSBECK MESSENGER.

THE changes wrought in the way of viewing all moral and religious subjects, towards the close of the eighteenth and beginning of the nineteenth centuries, were thoroughgoing. Everywhere we see the new break forth and battle fiercely with the old. What Kant had done in philosophy, utterly destroying the fabric of former days, and constructing an entirely changed science of thought, Schiller (and Goethe) had done in literature. Kant and Schiller, diverse as their courses were, and dissimilar as were the provinces of labour, brought about the same results: the one as philosopher by his rigid dialectics; the other, as poet, by his singularly attractive use of speech; the one from the professor's chair, the other from the stage. Both found common ground in the tendency to analyse, to overthrow the old ecclesiastical formulæ, and to search after an ideal moral standpoint, which, instead of resting on the positive foundations of a traditional faith, should rest solely on free inquiry, and the irrefragable results of human reasoning. Thus Kantianism led to rationalism, and Schiller's poetry prepared the way for that aesthetic sentimentalism which should relieve so gratefully the dryness of rationalism. In the same category with the new philosophy and the new poetry, stood, at least in some regards, the new theories of education. Not that these were first propagated for the express purpose of carrying to the young the novel views of the age; but without any formal union with those who advanced those views, and acting apparently independent of them, yet the educational organs chimed in with the rationalising tendencies of the times.

Even before Kant propounded his philosophy, and before Schiller's name was everywhere heard, the principles of Rousseau had gained a lodgment in German minds, and had begun to exert influence; more especially in the department of education, since Basedow had established his institute and published his views. Formerly it had been the church which took the initiative in educational affairs and controlled them absolutely, but they now passed beyond ecclesiastical control. One institute on Basedow's plan followed another in quick succession; one method of instruction speedily crowded out another. Salzmann and Campe took up the mantle of Basedow, and tried, like their predecessor, to reach theology through an educational reform, and to make the church an entirely changed, if not totally needless, institution.

We turn to a more detailed account of Salzmann and Campe, the followers of Basedow in the educational field, and who carried out, in the same line, the work that he began.

Christian Gotthilf Salzmann, born the same year with Herder, 1744, in the neighbourhood of Erfurt, had been educated for the pulpit, and had preached for a time in Erfurt; but, in 1781, he relinquished his appointment of his own accord in order to labour with Basedow in the Philanthropin, the new school at Dessau. While a clergyman, he had published a number of educational papers, in which he attacked those who held to the old routine method, and he had also published his rationalistic views of religion. He was especially severe on the orthodox mode then in vogue, of committing verses and theological statements which children do not understand, and says: "that he would prefer that a son of his should rob a bird's nest than learn the Catechism." In Dessau the department of religion was entrusted to him; and at the public worship of the school, he delivered the discourses which he published in 1783. In these discourses, morality is the main topic, although there is not lacking a distinctive religious tone, especially in those which treat of the Omnipresence and Omniscience of God. Salzmann was unquestionably pervaded with religious feeling, and this proclaims itself in all his writings, even in his romances, and most of all in his sermons.

In 1784 he left Dessau and founded the institution of Schripfenthal, near Gotha, and soon witnessed among his pupils representatives of every country in Europe. The reputation of this school was at its height at the opening of this century, since which time it has declined. During its flourishing epoch he took pains to disseminate the new principles with which he proposed to regenerate education, to overthrow the lifeless orthodoxy which opposed him. His religious style was often tainted by a kind of obscure dreaminess, and a superfluity of imagery which is almost never met with elsewhere among the rationalists, who are usually devoid of this, even to baldness. The spirituality of Salzmann is unquestionable; and though his antagonism to the church seems to indicate the absence of religion, yet he was indebted to Christianity for his tender feelings. Basedow and Campe were very different men in this regard from Salzmann, and should never be confounded with him, Salzmann had a great deal of Schiller's sentimentalism; but he ought to be always remembered, not as hard and dry, but as devout and sympathetic. It is all the more sad to see such a man thrown from religious associations and converted into an antagonist, because he was capable of better things.

Less a man of feeling than Salzmann, was Joachim Heinrich Campe, who had been educated as a theologian from his childhood, and was for a time chaplain in the regiment of the Prince of Prussia, but afterwards director of the Philanthropin at Dessau. Later still, he founded an institution of his own at Hamburg. He died at Brunswick in 1818, at the age of seventy-two. He was always in entire antagonism to the sentimentality which was inspired by the later literature of his country. He reckoned poetry as one of the unproductive arts, which had its highest mission in an age of barbarism, as a poor substitute for reason; but now poetry would be like a lantern in broad daylight. With almost puritanic rigour, he refused to allow his daughter to associate with men of letters, who, he thought, differed little from seducers of youth. Campe is well known in Germany as the great apostle of utility, and the man who knew how to make himself useful always and everywhere, was the ideal which he constantly held up. Self-reliance, too, was a theme frequently enforced by him, and the favourite motto of his Robinson Crusoe was "God helps them who help themselves." To gain the victory over oneself, he considered worth the struggle of a life. Bitter as he was in his antagonism to the old faith, he was a devout believer in a Providence which overrules all the events of life, and therefore can be a hearer of prayer.

The side of Campe's character to be kept in honour, and which has little justice done it, is his moral correctness, and the fixedness of his adherence to his own religious ideas. Despite all his bitterness to orthodoxy and even to Christianity, Campe was a thoroughgoing reformer. This showed itself even in the domain of language, in his efforts to get rid of all foreign words, which had become grossly abundant since the French rule. His effort is worthy of all praise. The purifying of language is, in a certain sense, the purifying of morals; and, in Campe, the effort to do both grew manifestly from the same root. He wished to do his work thoroughly; but he set about it in true rationalistic fashion, that is, from an abstract theory without regard to historical development. It is with speech as with religion, and with words as with dogmas. No one can sit in the study and issue mandates which will be obeyed, and impose authority upon others which will be recognised. Campe wanted to anticipate the natural development of speech, and set words of his own coinage in the place of the foreign intruders; but his right to give them citizenship was not admitted. Language, like religion, must be formed under the influence of many concurring causes; it must be born out of the needs of life, as it was with Luther; and as, indeed, it was with Goethe, who, with all his use of foreign words, did more for the German language than Campe with all his new formations. And it has been just so in religion: rationalism, with all its correct theory of progress, has never been able to dictate so orderly and natural an advance as the untrammelled developments of time.

The thing needed in the department of education was not only that theories should be advanced and institutions founded, but that a man should especially arise from the people, who would give himself with enthusiasm to the beautiful work of training the young to that for which the age longed. Such a man was Pestalozzi. If Christ says, "By their fruits ye shall know them," and "Whoso shall receive a child receiveth me;" if He praises active love as the trait by which His disciples may be known; if He contrasts the confidence in God, which takes no care for the morrow, but leaves all care to its heavenly Father, with the bustling and driving of the heathen;—then the question whether John Henry Pestalozzi was a Christian would soon be decided.[1] Public opinion has lately been divided in reference to him as well as Schiller,—some denying and others warmly defending his claim to Christianity. In discussing questions of this kind, special care must be taken to avoid all excitement, and above all, first to gain a clear understanding of the proposed question. When the Bible on the one hand admonishes us to try the spirits; and on the other, calls to us, Who art thou that judgest another man's servant? we have enough to guide us in our mode of procedure. History certainly has the right of summoning all, even the noblest of men, before its tribunal, and hence a history which proposes to give the development of Christian life in its various forms, has a right to ask in reference to every man: in what relation does he stand to Christianity, and how far do we recognize in him the Christian principle so far as this is known to us?

It is not, therefore, to be regarded as a want of love or mark of ingratitude, if in reference to men whom we must personally esteem highly and regard as the leaders of their age, we ask the question (as we do now in reference to Pestalozzi), in what relation did they stand to Christianity? We must, however, be careful not to judge the *person;* and even where we fix our attention on the *opinions* we must remember that we, as weak men, may easily err, either because our standard of Christianity is not always correct, or that we do not know the facts in the case sufficiently to form an accurate judgment. The cause of truth can only be promoted by such investigations, if con-

[1] "The peculiarity of my powers consisted in the vivacity with which my heart impelled me to give and seek love wherever it could be found, to act in a friendly and agreeable manner, to endure, to forbear, and to conquer self. I knew of no greater joy of life than the eye of gratitude and the confidential grasp of the hand. I sought the poor and gladly tarried with them." Need we anything besides this confession of his?

ducted with care and modesty, and in the spirit of Christian love and entirely for the sake of truth; for a great mind is as little really honoured by an unconditional admiration without any criticism, as it can be dishonoured by passionate abuse and a mania for censuring. We will, therefore, first consider the nature and activity of Pestalozzi, and then as far as possible form a judgment of his position in reference to Christianity. In doing this we shall make use of the sketch given only a few years ago by one of our most esteemed schoolmen.[1]

Pestalozzi was born in Zurich, January 12, 1746. He early lost his father, and was trained by his mother, whose pecuniary embarrassments were great, and under the eye of his grandfather, a pious evangelical minister of the simple old-fashioned style. His progress at school was not very great. He was awkward in his intercourse with other children, and his teacher predicted that he would never greatly excel. Thoughtlessness, absence of mind, and carelessness occasioned him many difficulties; but his rich mind made amends for the rough external impressions flowing from these sources; and a genial gaiety assisted him in overcoming the most grievous matters. When, however, revolting injustice was exercised towards him, he manifested the same defying spirit which was shown by the young Lavater.

Whilst Basedow, Salzmann, and Campe[2] all made theology their profession, Pestalozzi soon abandoned it and studied law; but he also left this study with the full determination to become a schoolmaster. And he did become such,—a schoolmaster such as is rarely seen, the "schoolmaster of the human race," as an enthusiastic admirer has called him. He commenced at the very foundation, and this is the reason he excelled so nobly. In Neuhof, by Lenzburg, where he had been disappointed in an attempt at rural economy, he founded his school for the poor in 1775, and Isaac Iselin of Basle was one of the first to assist him. This friend also helped him to the publication of his first popular work, "Lienhard and Gertrude," 1781,

[1] Heussler.

[2] These all used their influence in spreading the philanthropinic system of education.—Tr.

which Pestalozzi had written on the blank pages of old account-books in order to save paper. Pestalozzi himself acknowledged that without this noble friend Iselin, he would perhaps have remained obscure in the depths of his misery; for few knew how to estimate his inner worth, since he was early treated with ingratitude, his best motives being misinterpreted, and his unskilfulness in the management of his household affairs occasioning him many difficulties. Pestalozzi appeared in the height of his glory during the misfortunes that burst upon Germany from France, when in the year 1798, on the smoking ruins of Stanz, he, assisted by the Swiss directory, became a faithful and loving father to the orphans, shared every morsel with them, slept with them, and was neither estranged from them by their disgusting appearance nor by the unreasonable judgments of others, till the storms of war drove him away and shattered the orphan asylum. He now became teacher in one of the lowest schools of Burgdorf, and there applied his method of elementary instruction which, after contending with prejudices for a long while, elicited the first, though rather limited, acknowledgment of the public authorities of schools.

Pestalozzi's labours in teaching first began to attract general attention at the beginning of this century. He founded a school of his own in Burgdorf. "The Mother's Book," published by him in 1803 made a sensation; it became "the corner-stone of his new method," and from that time men also came from a distance to assist in the institution. The praise of the extraordinary results drowned the clamour of the opponents. Many of these changed their views by seeing the effects. Pestalozzi's name became European; how could his native land then leave him unnoticed any longer? The Helvetian government declared the institution at Burgdorf a public one, belonging to the nation, and connected with it a seminary for teachers. But soon the state of affairs changed. The Helvetian government resigned, the castle became the seat of an upper bailiff, and the institution was transferred to Iferten (Yverdon). It now grew in extent, and attained a European distinction. Pupils were sent from Germany, France, Spain, Italy, and even from Russia and North

America. Those desirous of learning flocked from all quarters to study the method of Pestalozzi, which now became the subject of the most lively public discussion. Pestalozzi was now no longer alone. Other teachers came to his assistance, who excelled him in a scientific point of view, and mingled their ideas with his. The intimate family circle increased till it became a small state in which there was no lack of warlike dispositions and manifold collisions. The confusion kept increasing, and finally the work so outgrew the founder that it threatened to overwhelm him. Let us not trace any farther the sad picture of the dissolution which still stands vividly before the minds of all; nor will we here stir up the unpleasant contests which filled our public journals before the more important political disorders engrossed the public mind. Pestalozzi has been elevated above them. After the abolition of the institution in 1825, he returned to Neuhof, where he had commenced his activity, and there spent the remainder of his days in the house of his grandchild, his only descendant. He died at Bruges, February 17, 1827, a few years before the outbreak of the political storms. On the 19th his body was buried in the snow-covered earth of Birr, with quiet, unostentatious funeral services, and the simple songs of the village youth.

We cannot here examine the method itself, which aims at the complete development of man, as its main object, corresponding with that towards which the age, with its call for humanity, was pressing. Besides, the most of us are familiar with the most important principles of this method, and much to which Pestalozzi gave the first impulse is still used in our schools and families, though very properly with many restrictions and amplifications. The aim of modern education is living instruction, instead of the dead mechanism killing the spirit, and also the conscious and skilful management of the simplest elements of our thinking in number, word, and form; and though a new mechanism has frequently planted itself by the side of the old, though the letter has attempted to gain the ascendancy over the spirit, still, upon the whole, the public schools of Germany and Switzerland have made considerable progress. We do not mean to say that this was all accomplished by Pestalozzi. It has been shown that the most of what he introduced into practice had already been advanced by others at an earlier period, as Rousseau, Basedow, and Comenius. But it has been truly said, that what Rousseau attempted only with an imaginary pupil was applied, with modifications, of course, by Pestalozzi to real ones, and that he gathered the scattered ideas into a focus. It is so with all new ideas. It can even be said of Christianity, that many of its teachings and moral laws already existed, and so, too, before the time of Luther others had thought of the reformation of the church. But who is not reminded of the egg of Columbus in this connection? The very thing that connects a memorable deed with a man and his name is that where others guess, think, doubt, expect, hope, and try, he acts decidedly, and with lightning power, and puts into practice what to others was only type and shadow and mere theory, gives the thought word, the word flesh and blood, and makes it a reality. In this matter the services of men are, of course, to be praised less than the Providence which always sends the chosen person, at the proper time, to perform its bidding, as with Pestalozzi, then lets him retire, so that others may complete what he commenced. We have yet to form an estimate of Pestalozzi's position in reference to Christianity, and especially its evangelical Protestant form.

That Pestalozzi, as well as Basedow, Salzmann, and Campe, opposed the common course of the so-called orthodoxy, which thought the whole work was accomplished when it had beaten the Catechism into the heads of the children, and which, in spite of all its orthodoxy, forgot the true faith, and, above all, true love; and that he opposed the corrupt Christianity of memory and formulas, or the "*paper-science*," as he called it, no one can blame him. In this nothing but Protestantism can be seen, which regards the essence more than the form, and the spirit more than the letter. But it is another question how far this essence was clear to his own mind, and in how far his work proceeded from the inmost spirit of Christianity.

We are permitted to express our doubts, whether he understood the nature of Christianity in its full importance, the more freely, because he himself as late as 1820 acknowledged,

"Till the end of my days I shall remain in a kind of obscurity as far as most of my views are concerned, but in a *holy* obscurity, the only light in which I can live." These words are the key with which much may be unlocked. Still in this obscurity many stars rose which inspired him with courage while journeying over the hard road marked out for him. Whoever searches in Pestalozzi for the theologian or the dogmatist, who can give an exact account of his faith, seeks in vain. He differs from Basedow, Campe, and Salzmann, since he did not attempt to theologize, or to render Christianity rational, as they did.[1] He was too little interested in this, since he wished to apply all things directly to life; and he was as little satisfied by the common rationalism as by orthodoxy.

In religion Pestalozzi was simply an emotional being, a child of impressions. The religious feeling seemed rather to come on him in moments of inspiration than in those of reflection, and failed to control his entire nature uniformly. He therefore exerted the greatest religious influence over others in such moments as in prayer; and that he could pray fervently was acknowledged by those even who attacked his Christianity. And though the religious exercises of the institution were less edifying, and for the most part confined to moralizing, still Pestalozzi did not favour this; he lamented that the Bible was so little read, and said it had been different in his day. Nor was this state of things improved; but according to an official report by a committee appointed by the Diet in 1810, it is repeatedly asserted that for those who are to be confirmed, the proper instruction in Christianity is to begin after a course of instruction in natural religion, and only by special request of the parents. By this means Christianity was, of course, taken from the institution, instead of being a light to all in the house.

But it must be remembered that at this time Christianity was in such a crisis that it was difficult for individuals, in the great confusion of opinions, to get correct notions of

[1] He taught that "Faith must proceed from faith, and not from the knowledge and understanding of the things believed; love must proceed from love, and not from the knowledge of love and what is lovely; and art, too, must proceed from ability, and not from mere talk of ability and art."

matters. Pestalozzi expressed himself variously in reference to Christianity. At one time he says, "I regard it as nothing else than the purest and noblest modification of the doctrine of elevating the spirit above the flesh, and this doctrine I regard as the great mystery, and only possible means by which the inmost nature of our being may be truly ennobled, or, to speak more plainly, the means of attaining the dominion over the flesh through the inner development of the purest feelings of love. This I believe to be the essence of Christianity; but I do not think that many persons are, according to their nature, capable of becoming Christians," and he really confesses that he is not a Christian, because he did not find in himself the ability to attain to self-perfection by that conquering of the flesh. But at another time he acknowledges Christ as the only High Priest who has taught us to worship God in spirit and in truth; he even speaks of an adoration of Christ as a necessary condition for becoming his disciple, and wishes for himself and humanity that the blessed days might return in which men could truly rejoice in the Redeemer. In his report to the public in 1820 he says, "I consider a thorough knowledge of the Scriptural histories, and especially of the life, sufferings, and death of Jesus Christ, and the study of the sublimest passages of the Bible with a childlike, believing spirit, the beginning and essence of what is necessary for religious instruction, and then above all things a fatherly care to make the children feel the worth of prayer offered in faith." It may be seen from an address delivered to his household in 1818, how much, in his more advanced age, Pestalozzi was penetrated by faith, and that he thought the salvation of the world as well as his household was to be expected only from Christ—and in this the essence of Christianity certainly consists, however differently it may be viewed by different minds. After the old man of seventy-three had held, as it were, a general confession, and had appealed to the hearts of all for the institution, already beginning to sink, he closes with these words: "'Love one another, as Christ has loved us.' 'Charity suffereth long, and is kind; charity envieth not; charity vaunteth not itself, is not puffed up, doth not behave itself unseemly, seeketh not her own, is not easily provoked, thinketh no evil; rejoiceth not in iniquity, but rejoiceth in the truth; beareth all things, believeth all things, hopeth all things, endureth all things.' Friends! Brethren! 'Bless them that curse you, do good to them that hate you, heap coals of fire on the heads of your enemies, let not the sun go down on your wrath; when thou bringest thy gift to the altar, first be reconciled to thy brother, and then come and offer thy gift.'"

"Let all relentless severity be far from our house, let it not even be exercised towards those who treat us with injustice. Let all human severity be lost in the mildness of our faith. Let no one say that Christ did not love him who was sinful and did wrong. He did love him. He loved him with a divine love. He died for him. He did not call the righteous but sinners to repentance. He did not find the sinner a believer, but made him such, gave him faith through His own faith. He did not find him humble, He made him humble by His humility. Verily, verily, it is with the sublime, divine service of humility that He conquered the pride of sinners, and fastened them by faith to His divine, loving heart. Friends! Brethren! If we do this, if we love one another, as Christ loved us, we shall overcome all the difficulties that oppose the aim of our lives, and shall be able to found the welfare of our house on that eternal rock on which God Himself has founded the welfare of humanity through Jesus Christ."

After having attempted to give a picture of Pestalozzi himself, especially in his relation to Christianity, the question yet remains how far his activity influenced the entire character and tendency of the age. At first view this influence does not appear to have been so very great, if we think only on Pestalozzi's method in its strict form. This was as much opposed on the one hand as applauded on the other. And this opposition was not only manifested on the part of the orthodox, but those even who yielded to a rationalistic mode of thinking, as Niemeyer, felt it their duty to call attention to the disadvantages and one-sided application of the method, while they were perfectly just to the person of Pestalozzi. We think the influence of Pestalozzi on his age was much greater than simply that produced by his method. It is nearly the same with him as it was with Kant and his philosophy. Relatively speaking, there were but few real Kantians adhering to the system in all its particulars; and yet we have seen that Kantism had a very great influence on the times, so that many, without either knowing or intending it, thought in a Kantian manner. It frequently seems as if certain ideas, when once suggested, dwell in the air, and are breathed by humanity. This was the case with those advanced by Pestalozzi. Although it was attempted, even during his life, to deprive him of the sceptre; and though there was much discussion about the meaning and availability of his method, still the impulse he gave to popular education was lasting, and the interest taken in it since the days of Rousseau and Basedow, became still more general, and spread into all classes of society.

Formerly education had been left to the Church, but since Pestalozzi had written the "Mother's Book," no mother wished to be behind the requirements of the age. And as parental education began to place itself more on an independent footing, public education began to do the same, on which account there were many collisions with the Church. According to report, the education of the Church had in it something contracting and obscure; now it was desired that the capacious and cheerful schoolroom should form a contrast to the Gothic twilight of the churches which, like all other mysterious things of the age, had become unintelligible, and on that account uncomfortable. It was the boast of the improvers of the world that the salvation of future ages was to radiate from the schools; they wanted the old Church to die out with the old people and the old ministers.

It may easily be seen that not only the method of education had changed, but the entire view of the life and nature of children, and thus also the notion of man's nature and the development of which it is capable. In former periods little was said of the hopes placed in the rising generations; but many complaints were heard that the times were continually growing worse, that "the young had no virtue," and similar things. It was then regarded as the chief object of education to make children old and "sedate" before the proper time, and to break the will early. In all petulancy, and frequently even in the emotions of a very happy disposition, it was thought the traces of original sin were visible, which could not be destroyed speedily and radically enough. It was thought that real wisdom dwelt only with the old, with the fathers who had grown hoary in the service of God, and under severe chastisements; but how often were old customs taken for genuine piety! What a different aspect things now began to wear! Now the old seemed to be quite obsolete; and if it was formerly attempted to make the children old, now the old were to be rejuvenated. Pestalozzi himself was a living example of this renewed youthfulness.

There is something beautiful and refreshing in this hope in youth, and it has Christ's word in its favour: "Except ye become as little children, ye shall not enter into the kingdom of heaven." This saying of the Lord had either not been heard by the good old times, or it had not been taken to heart properly, lest the doctrine of original sin and natural depravity might lose something. But it is always easy to go from one extreme to the other. What was called a juvenile sense was soon overestimated, even the impertinences of youth were considered lovely; and where formerly natural depravity had been discovered, now the germs of precocious talent were seen. Impudence and dissoluteness, which appeared in a very glaring manner, and continually increased in Pestalozzi's institutions, were looked upon as the manifestations of youthful love of liberty, and the "*Liberty and Equality*," which was more and more discussed in the world at large, was imitated in the school and family circle. The young were fondled, and told to their face, that they were wiser than the old, who had become musty, and had sunk into mechanism; they were incited to criticise, and were taught to reason instead of being taught to obey. This also had an influence on the religious instruction. While formerly Luther's catechism, the use of which Herder had still advocated, or in Reformed countries the Heidelberg Catechism had afforded the only so-called "milk diet for youth," now the old catechisms disappeared, and new ones took their places, which were, however, soon found to be more tedious and less practical than the old. Since the days of Salzmann and Campe, the literary market was flooded with writings for youth, so that, as Lichtenberg wittily remarked, the men were soon forgotten on account of the children. In the most of these writings the morality either of utility or sentimentality was made specially prominent. The sublime scriptural accounts were pushed into the background by the light stuff of fictitious stories, such as are still written by the thousand, and of which but little is distinguished for being really childlike in its sense and general tone. Even Campe, in his "Robinson," sometimes stops in the very heart of the story, to tire his young readers with moral conversations, which are of course omitted by the most intelligent. Instead of the precocious orthodoxy which it was thought had manifested itself in the former youth, a still more precocious moralism and rationalism now was likely to appear, which were more injurious than the old catechism-religion.

John George Hamann, the "Magician of the North," as his friends called him, is one of those men of whom it is difficult to give an estimate correct and satisfactory in all respects. Our estimation of his character cannot be blended with our general opinion of the age, as may be done with many other men, because he stood rugged and alone, like a rocky island in the midst of the waves of the surrounding ocean. As we cannot wholly praise or blame that age, we shall not admire, much less censure, all in Hamann. He will always interest us greatly as an original, powerful, and penetrating mind, though we shall not persuade ourselves that the obscure, the crude and strange in his works must, because we do not comprehend it, be secrets so much the greater, behind which an unfathomed depth of knowledge may lie, nor that the unpalatable shell must necessarily contain a kernel so much the sweeter. But we shall first form an idea of the man chiefly from his own confessions and writings.

J. G. Hamann was born at Koenigsberg, the 27th of August 1730. Having received a common education, under the guardianship of his parents, both in school and from private tutors, he paid particular attention to the study of the ancient classics. "Several of the principal and most difficult Latin and Greek authors were run over several times," according to his own statement; still Hamann does not extol the effect of this philological training. "I could translate Latin into German without understanding either the language or sense of the author; my Latin and Greek compositions were printer's work, mere jugglery, in which the memory was overfed, and a decay of the other intellectual powers ensued, because healthful and proper chyle was wanting." We thus find in him the same opposition to the old school system, though in other respects he did not agree with the Philanthropists. At the age of eighteen he entered the university of his native city. It was intended that he should study theology; "but," he says, "I found a hindrance in my slow speech and weak memory, and many feigned obstacles in my mode of thinking, the low morals of the clergy, and the importance which I attached to the duties of the ministerial office." He also soon abandoned the study of law, and devoted himself entirely to that of antiquity and polite literature. After completing his academic course he became tutor in Livonia, for which position, however, he seemed to have little skill; he was dismissed in a very rough manner by the gracious mother. He now spent some time in Riga, as he says, "in wild industry and idleness." After making another vain attempt as tutor, he found some noble friends here, of whom the mercantile house of Berens, and the rector in Riga, Dr. Lindner, were the most prominent. "Disgusted with the school-dust," he was now induced to study commercial science and political economy, with which he occupied himself, however, only a short period. After the death of his mother he commenced travelling. In Berlin he made the acquaintance of Mendelssohn, and then went to try his fortune in London. Here he threw himself into the whirl of a dissolute life.[1] He spent a long while in internal misery, without finding any one to whom to communicate his feelings. In this restlessness he took refuge in prayer; he asked God to show him a friend, and this friend he found in the Bible, and through it in Christ. "The more I read it," he says, "the newer the Word of God seemed to me, the more divine I found the contents and their influence. I forgot all

[1] "I ate and drank excessively in vain, was dissolute in vain, ran about in vain. Intemperance and reflection, reading and knavery, diligence and idleness, were alternated in vain; I was extravagant and wanton in both in vain. During nine months I changed my lodgings nearly every month, found peace nowhere, all were deceptive, low, selfish people."

my other books, was ashamed that I had ever preferred them to the Book of God. I found the unity of the Divine will in the redemption by Jesus Christ, and that all history, all miracles, and all the laws and works of God meet in this centre to raise the soul of man from the slavery, the blindness, the folly, and death of sin, to the greatest blessedness."

One evening, quite lost in the contemplation of Scripture, he read the account of Cain's fratricide; he felt his heart beat while reading, heard a voice sobbing and groaning in its depths, and felt sure that he was the murderer, for he had committed this crime against the only begotten Son of God. He was greatly distressed, and, with tears, confessed his sins to God; but "the Spirit of God," he says, "in spite of my great weakness, and the long opposition which I had waged against His influence, continued to reveal to me more and more of the mysteries of Divine love, and the blessings of faith in our gracious and only Saviour." He continued the reading of the Bible with redoubled diligence and increased devotion, and received spiritual blessings therefrom. "God be praised," he says, "my heart is calmer than ever before in my life. When threatened with dejection of spirits, I have been flooded with a comfort, of which I cannot ascribe the source to myself, and which no human being has the power of infusing so abundantly into the hearts of his fellow-men. It swallowed up all fear, all sadness and mistrust, so that I could no longer find any trace of them in my mind."

Hamann's essay on the fortunes of his own life extend to this conversion, which in many respects calls to mind Saint Augustine. All that remains to be added is briefly the following: Hamann returned from London to Riga with the intention of devoting himself entirely to the house of Berens. He was, however, soon called to Koenigsberg by his sick and aged father. Soon after this a difficulty arose between him and that house, which led to a complete rupture, a variance in which the charge of ingratitude must almost unavoidably fall on Hamann. It is not seldom that a negligence of all human affairs follows in the train of a religious mode of thinking produced in a violent manner, and duty to man has been forced to yield to the pressure of a devotion disregarding all hinderances! This, indeed, appeared to be the case with Hamann. It is difficult to form a judgment here, and we may call to mind the significant sentence, which is, of course, frequently applied too rashly, and in the wrong place—that Christ came not to bring peace, but the sword.

From this time Hamann lived with his father in Koenigsberg, and published his first works. Kant, whose mode of thinking was very different from that of Hamann, esteemed his superior mental powers, and numbered him among his friends. We have already mentioned his more intimate friendship with Herder. "In those blessed years," Hamann says, "I learned how to study, and have lived a long while upon the harvest gathered at that time." His external circumstances were not, however, very favourable. He divided his time between the work of copying in the Chancery, and assisting in the publication of the Koenigsberg newspaper. Afterwards, having in vain looked about in a foreign land for some occupation, he obtained a situation in the excise office, and after ten years more became the manager of a custom-house, and thus, in his own language, as an invalid of Apollo, he was favoured with the office of a publican. As, however, in 1782 a considerable part of his salary was withdrawn, owing to a change in the arrangements of the house, he lived with four children in the greatest want. He was delivered from this exigency by Lavater. This friend procured a respectable capital for him from a wealthy young man in Westphalia, Frank Buchholz, which placed him in easy circumstances, Hamann lived in Muenster part of the time with his benefactor, and the rest with the philosopher, F. H. Jacobi, in Dusseldorf. His acquaintance with the Princess Gallitzin belongs to this period. As he was about to return to Koenigsberg, the 20th of June 1788, he suddenly fell into a state of debility, which resulted in death the following day. He was fifty-eight years of age when he died. He was never married in the political-ecclesiastical sense, but lived in a "marriage of conscience" as he called it. Hamann's life in general makes the impression of a personality in which Christianity worked more like a foreign volcanic power than like an inner principle that regulated and determined the whole course of his life. From his fermenting inner nature, sublime thoughts and emotions, resolutions and bright flashes burst forth; but it never attains to a quiet development and harmonious culture. Hence, with all the piety of his heart, his life was not free from much that is objectionable. In this respect, too, he formed a decided contrast to rationalism, which places the moral conduct of a man higher than all other things, and where it finds this it is satisfied with a meagre *inner* life, while in the case of Hamann one might feel inclined to forget many moral defects on account of the fulness of the inner life. Both are imperfect manifestations of Christianity, which consists in moral piety as well as pious morality.

Hamann's literary activity was confined chiefly to short piquant articles published from time to time. For large works he had neither time nor power, both of which were very much dissipated. His contemporaries took but little notice of the northern magician. Herder regarded him very highly, because he had received from him the most powerful intellectual impulse. "The kernel of Hamann's writings," he says, "contains many germs of great truths, as well as new observations, and an evidence of remarkable erudition; the shell thereof is a laboriously woven web of pithy expressions, of hints and flowers of rhetoric." "His understanding," says F. H. Jacobi, "was penetrating like lightning, and his soul was of more than natural greatness." Hamann called his own authorship dumb mimicry, and compared himself to a miner digging for treasures in the depths of the earth; he even acknowledged that much of what he had written was afterwards unintelligible to him. Goethe, who was not personally acquainted with Hamann, says of him, "He was of course regarded as an abstruse enthusiast by those who swayed the literature of the day (Nicolai and his consorts); aspiring youth was, however, attracted by him. Even the quiet of the land, as they were called, half in sport, half in earnest, those pious souls who, without joining any particular sect, formed an invisible church, gave him their attention. Goethe, however, also hints that the satirical humour, to which Hamann gave free course in his writings, repelled the more strict.

In the history of the religious development, Hamann's greatness is of a peculiar kind, which cannot well be fitted into any existing frame. It will, therefore, perhaps be best to let him speak for himself, and we will close this sketch with some of his pithy expressions, without regarding a systematic arrangement, for his mode of writing was the aphoristic. The most of it, especially that which refers to religion, is in direct opposition to the rationalistic and shallow tendencies of that age. Thus, he says of the frequently discussed relation of reason to revelation: "Let us not judge of the truth of things according to the ease with which we represent them to our minds. There are actions of a higher order, for which no expression can be given by the elements of this world. Not only the end but the entire career of a Christian is the master-piece of an unknown Genius, whom heaven and earth recognizes as the only Creator, Mediator, and Sustainer, and will recognize in a glorified human form. Our life, it is said, is hid with Christ in God. When Christ, our life, shall appear, then shall we also appear with him in glory. . . . He will come to be glorified in His saints, and to be admired in all them that believe. How much will the joy of those who love His appearing surpass that of the wise men of the East when they saw the star." Hamann did not judge very favourably of his age. "The last century," he says, "was the reign of genius; the next will probably (?) bloom under the sceptre of sound reason. What a sad figure the knights of the present make between the two! Pretty much like that of an ape or parrot, between a buffalo and lion." "An age in which words are threshed, and small and great attempts made to feel thoughts and to comprehend feelings, is called the *philosophical*. Is this done to expose our age or philosophy to shame? Do persons, by this means, want to impose on themselves or their neighbours?" "Reason reveals no more to us than was seen by Job, the misery of our birth, the uselessness and insufficiency of life, since we have no knowledge, and many passions and instincts, whose object is unknown to us." "What is religion but pure sound reason, which was stifled and confused by the fall, and which the

Spirit of God seeks to restore in us, after it has rooted up the weeds and prepared the soil, and purified it again for the reception of the seed of heaven." "We are still incomplete. Our reason must wait and hope, must be content to be servant, not strive to be lawgiver. . . . Experience and revelation are the same, they are indispensable wings or crutches of our reason, if this is not to continue to be lame or to creep." "The revealed religion of Christianity is very properly called *faith,* assurance, confident and childlike trust in the divine word and promises, and in the progress of a life developing from glory to glory to the full unveiling of the mysteries, hid and *believed* from the beginning."

"God has revealed himself to man in nature and in his Word. . . . These two revelations explain and confirm, but cannot contradict, each other, however much this may be done by the interpretations given of them by our reason. It is the greatest contradiction and abuse of reason, if it attempts to *reveal.* The philosopher, who rejects the divine Word for the sake of reason, is like the Jews who reject the New Testament the more firmly they appear to cling to the Old. In them the prophecy is fulfilled, that that is a stumbling block and foolishness, which ought to serve as a confirmation and fulfilment of their other views. History and natural philosophy are the two pillars on which Christianity rests. Infidelity is founded on a superficial history and natural philosophy. Nature is as little subjected to blind chance, or external laws, as all events can be explained by character and reasons of state." "The treasures of nature are but an allegory, a mythological picture of heavenly systems, just as all the events of profane history are outlines of secret actions and discovered wonders." "If God intended to reveal himself to men and to the entire human race, the folly of those must be the more evident, who want to make a limited taste and their own judgment the touchstone of the divine Word. The question is not concerning a revelation which a Voltaire, a Bolingbroke, or Shaftesbury, would think worthy of their acceptance, and which would best satisfy their prejudices, their wit, and their moral, political, and epic whims; but concerning a discovery of such truths in the certainty, credibility, and importance of which the whole race would be interested. Those who have so much confidence in their own understanding, that they think they can dispense with a divine instruction, would have found mistakes in every other revelation, and have need of none. They are the whole that need no physician."

Other passages, in which he opposes the pride of his age, might be cited. Let us, however, add only a few, referring to the *contents* of Christianity, in which he uses the polemic dart less, and enters upon his subject more with his whole soul. "The Christian only is a living man, because he lives in and with God, moves and has his being in Him." "It is only through God that our hearts love the brethren, and that we are liberal towards them. Unless we know Christ, we have advanced no farther than the heathen. In that worthy name, from which we are called Christians, are centred all the wonders and mysteries and works of faith, and true religion. This worthy name is the only key of knowledge, which unlocks heaven and hell, and the heights and depths of the human heart." "Unbelief, in reference to Christ, makes our hearts cold, and confuses all the notions of our reason, while we dream of a good heart within, and a rational mode of thinking." "The righteousness of Christ is not a bodice, but an armour, to which a warrior accustoms himself, like a Maecenas to his loose dress." "Criticism is a schoolmaster leading to Christ. As soon as faith originates in us the bondwoman is cast out, and the law ceases; then the *spiritual* man judges, and *his* taste is safer than all the rules of philology and logic." In accordance with this principle, which ought certainly to be limited very much, Hamann yielded to the inclination to allegorize, in which he, as he himself acknowledges, "driving along with full sail, often lost sight of the letter." What he calls the spiritual man is frequently nothing but the suggestion of his wit and excited fancy.

Let us close with some passages of Hamann on education. Like Luther, he went back to the simple principles of Christianity.

"An upright schoolmaster must go to school, to God, and to himself, if he wants to put in practice the wisdom of his office, he must imitate God as He reveals Himself in nature and the Bible, and by means of both in our souls. . . . The law of His husbandry of time, according to which He patiently *waits for the fruit,* ought to be our rule of conduct. Nothing depends on what or how much is known, but all on *how* it is known. The means of instructing children cannot be simple enough. There is always something superfluous, useless, and perishable about them. They must be rich in results, must embrace a variety and fruitfulness for application and practice."

"Every father in the Fatherland, and every citizen, ought to have the subject of education at heart, for the seeds of evils which curse public as well as private affairs, are mostly sown and cultivated in our schools. Not only the wanton worship of mammon, and the slavish worship of arms, but also the chimera of beautiful nature, of good taste and sound reason, have introduced prejudices, which partly exhaust, partly suffocate in their birth the vital spirits of the human race, and the weal of civil society."

"It seems as if the instruction in schools was invented to make learning disgusting and useless." "The best method for instructing children consists in descending to their weaknesses, in becoming their servant if we want to be their master, in obeying if we want to govern them, and in learning their language, and understanding their souls, if we want to exert an influence over them. But it is neither possible to understand nor to practice this practical principle, unless we are fond of children, and love them, without knowing exactly why." "Whoever wants to write for children must not be ashamed to employ the wonderful Mosaic history."

Whilst Hamann gained the favour of strictly orthodox Christians less through an amiable personality, which gives pleasure by its very appearance, than by means of intellectual flashes which shine through the mysterious dimness of his inner nature, and also sustained the hope that all the *positive* contents of the Reformation were not entirely lost; in Claudius, the universally known "Wandsbecker Messenger," on the other hand, we meet a man who could open the heart, with his amiable humour as with a charm, and with his "humble, roguish cordiality" could also gain the favour, I might say, could bribe, those whose religious opinion differed from his own. Here the thought again forces itself on us, that the great contrarieties of the Protestant Christian world were not fought out exclusively, or even chiefly, by *theologians*, but others entered the contest on both sides, and assisted in giving the decision. Here, too, it was a "*homme des lettres*," as Claudius ironically called himself, who appeared as an apologist of Christianity, in spite of those other polite scholars and philosophers who attacked it *in toto* or in part. A prepossession was thus awakened in favour of Christianity; and just as at a former period it was a favourable indication that the cheerful fabulist and play-writer Gellert was also the author of such beautiful spiritual songs, so now many a cheerful man of the world would rather listen to the author of the "Rhine wine song" than to the most zealous preacher, whom he might suspect of defending Christianity only for the sake of his office, and his daily bread. A poet who even ventured to relate Scriptural anecdotes, as the story of the giant Goliath, in the grotesque-comical, ballad-singer style, was welcomed as one of their own number by minds who loved to exercise their wit on such subjects; but how soon did they discover that the man who could jest so easily would not permit sport to be made with subjects whose holiness demands the deepest seriousness. Here, therefore, was discovered, not as is so often the case, a wolf in sheep's clothing, but, behind the mask of apparent frivolity, a pure, chaste, lamb-like nature and dove-like simplicity. Claudius, like Luther, understood the high art of treating divine things with an innocent pleasantry, because he might be said to be on familiar terms with God. He was artless in the noblest sense of the word, and in this simplicity he could say much, which, if said by others, would have given offence, and which, when imitated, always becomes insipid. Thus he did not oppose those scoffing at Christianity with a frowning brow, nor the assuming "Illuminati" with a pedantic orthodoxy; he rather opposed the sickly philosophy with his sound, solid mother-wit, the stiff learning of the schools with his plain, common sense, and the insolent satire of wickedness with the cheerful irony of his child-like innocence. Of "the Wandsbecker Messenger," F. H. Jacobi says, he "is a real messenger of God; his Christanity is as old as the world. His faith is not merely the simplest and highest philosophy to him, but something still higher. He appears in life just as in his writings; sublime only in secret, full of pleasantry and roguery in social intercourse; but he does not fail to let serious words drop, striking, penetrating words, when mind and heart tell him, now is the time and proper occasion."

We will, therefore, not despise inquiring about this simple Messenger, in order to see in how far he was a messenger of God or of peace in his age pointing to the right human and divine course. Hamann said he considered him a fool who denied the existence of God, but he deemed that man a still greater one who wanted to prove His existence, and Claudius also attacked this passion for demonstration in general, this strutting about with arguments and counter-arguments in the department of religion. "No one can say with a shadow of truth that I am a philosopher; but I never go through a forest without wondering who makes the trees grow, and then quietly from afar I have a kind of consciousness of an Unknown One, and I would then be willing to affirm that I think of God, I tremble so reverently, so joyfully at the thought." But he did not stop with this natural religion. The more definite Christian feeling of the favour of redemption is immediately connected with the feeling of the nearness of God. Both are the same to him. In the forest and under the starry heavens he walks about in a Christian temple, in which the form of the Son of man meets him and offers him His hand. "I was on a journey last night," he writes in his journal on the morning of a Good-Friday. "The moon shone somewhat cold on my body; she was, however, bright and beautiful, so that I rejoiced greatly to behold her, and could not see her enough. Eighteen hundred years ago, I thought to myself, you certainly did not shine thus, for it would have been impossible for men to have injured a righteous, innocent man in the face of so friendly, so mild a moon." He also honours and loves Socrates, and would not tear from his brow the wreath he deserves. But though truth is the same at all times, still it appears to him an exaggerated tolerance to desire to make the ancient philosophers Christians. It is, indeed, true, that all true philosophers and men of God since the foundation of the world are connected with Christ, as rivers with the ocean. But even John the Baptist, who was most nearly related to Him, only prepared the way for Him. This is the reason, that he always feels like kneeling, when he reads of Christ in any of the Gospels, and confesses, that though others may be able to dispense with Christ, *he* cannot; he needs some one to raise and support him while he lives, and to lay his hand under his head when he dies. That which lived in Christ never entered the heart of man before. To him Christ is a holy, superhuman being, a star in the night, one who satisfies our deepest wants and most secret longings and desires. "One might suffer himself to be stigmatised, and broken on the wheel even for the mere idea, and whoever can laugh and mock must be insane. Whoever has his heart in the right place lies in the dust, rejoices and worships."

Claudius preserved this faith in Christ as feeling and experience, as a reality felt in the heart, and avoided disputing about the matter. "It is incomprehensible," he says, "that men enter into such extensive debates with freethinkers and sceptics, and talk so much about their freethinking and passion for doubts. Christ says very briefly: 'If any man will do His (God's) will, he shall know of the doctrine whether it be of God, or whether I speak of myself.' Whoever cannot or will not make this attempt, if he is a reasonable man, or desires to be considered such, should not say another word for or against Christianity." With his decidedly Christian convictions, Claudius was thus opposed to an intolerant mania for religious disputes, and knew how to make them ridiculous whatever form they might assume. "The spirit of religion does not dwell in the shell of dogmatics, has not its abode in the children of unbelief, and can as little be gained by wanton bounds of reason as by stiff orthodoxy and monkhood. . . . . . It is an honour to a people to be strict and zealous in their religion; but it is certainly not more than reasonable to investigate before being zealous." "To improve religion by means of reason (thus he lets Asmus address his cousin Andres), appears to me like attempting to set the sun by my old wooden clock; still, philosophy appears to me to be a very good thing, and I think much of that which is charged against the orthodox is true." He compares philosophy to the broom which sweeps the dirt out of the temple. To this cousin Andres replies: "Philosophy is certainly good, and they are wrong who scoff at it, but revelation does not bear to philosophy the relation of much to little, but that of heaven and earth, of above and below. Philosophy may, in a certain sense, be such a broom to sweep the cobwebs from the temple; we might call it a brush used to sweep the dust from the statues of saints; but when one attempts to carve on the statues with it he requires more than it can perform; and it is highly absurd and provoking to see this attempted. . . . Since the holy statues cannot be restored by reason, it is patriotic in a high sense to retain the old form inviolate. . . . In short, cousin, the truth is a giant, lying asleep by the road-side; those passing that way, indeed, see his giant form, but they cannot see him; when he removes the veil you will see his countenance. Till this is done, our comfort must be that he is under the veil, and do thou, good cousin, pass him reverently and with trembling, and do not 'criticise.'"

In his later years the tendency to preserve prevailed more and more in Claudius, and like his friend Hamann he attempted to support Lutheranism, and with it the Lutheran doctrine of the Lord's Supper against the Reformed. But neither in this matter does he lose his mildness and fairness towards those differing from him, and even acknowledges that Luther went too far in his zeal against those of a different opinion. The best proof that Claudius knew how to estimate what is really Christian in all the various confessions, is his characteristic of Fenelon, prefixed to the second volume of his translation of this excellent man's works. He expected continually less and less good from the rationalistic and destructive tendency, which wanted to resolve the positive in all confessions into something general and rational, which may be accepted by all, and hence must be unsatisfactory to all. He thought men would do better if they attempted to bring reason in harmony with faith, than if they sought to make faith rational; it would bring them more blessings, and certainly more honour. He was certain of one thing, "There is one truth and only one. From it nothing can be taken by force, and it forces itself on no one; it however, imparts itself more or less if sought with humility and self-denial, with fear and trembling, as the apostles say, Those who attempt to do it violence, and to make truth arbitrarily, torment themselves in vain, and are like a reed that is shaken by the wind. Human works, like all other things of this world, waver and change. Truth remains and does not waver." Thus Claudius wrote in 1812; he died in Hamburg in the house of his son-in-law, Perthes, in 1815, being 75 years of age.

XVIII.

FREDERIC WILLIAM JOSEPH SCHELLING.[1]

SCHELLING AND THE "NATURPHILOSOPHIE." PANTHEISM AND SEEMING ORTHODOXY.

KANT, Fichte, and Schelling are the prominent names in the history of modern philosophy. We have already spoken of Kant and Fichte. Schelling yet remains to be considered. And here, for the first time, we deal with a person still among the living (1849). . . . I had determined to avoid doing this, and shall adhere to this resolution as far as possible. But when an author survives his works, these already belong to history, even while he lives. This is true of the *older* philosophy of Schelling, to which we confine our remarks. It is a finished work, and to be regarded as an important element, separate from its author, and having passed into the history of philosophy, is therefore common property, over which the author has no longer any control, though he has the privilege of renouncing it himself. The system of Schelling, as it appeared, in distinction from the philosophy of Kant and Fichte, under the name of *Philosophy of Nature* (Natur-philosophie) the *philosophy of the Absolute*, or

[1] See Appendix A.

philosophy of identity, is a historical fact which can no more be blotted from the history of science, than a victorious battle from political history. Therefore, we will speak of Schelling's system without referring to his personal history.

The thinking mind could not rest satisfied with the idealism of Fichte. But as little as this idealism could last, so little could it pass away without leaving a trace; and whatever it had that is true and excellent, namely, the glorification of the common reality through the inner act of the spirit, remained as real gain; for, with all the reality of the world, with all the richness of its forms, with the continual change of its appearances, that it is *man* who sees it with *human* eyes, while to the animal it only appears as a shapeless mass, that it is our Ego which reflects itself in the world, as well as the world in our Ego, that we first impress nature with the stamp of divinity by discovering the kernel of the supernatural through the shell of the sensible—these are mental experiences, which can never be taken away, and which first give life a higher charm, in opposition to a spiritless, thoughtless objectivity, which contemplates life externally, without placing it in a relation to our innner self. The mind awakened from its idealistic dream turned again to nature and its phenomena; but it no longer regarded nature as a dead machine, driven by external forces; it now knew a nature intellectually animated, a nature with which God does not only now and then interfere, to work a miracle, but a nature in which God expresses himself every moment, which He really penetrates, fills and animates. In a word, God and the world, mind and nature, the life without, within, and over us, are no longer to be separated from each other by strong barriers, but in our consciousness are to be placed in a living relation, and to affect each other by reciprocal action. This was the problem to be solved in the period after Fichte, and Schelling has undoubtedly done most for its solution. As Fichte had at first attached himself to Kant, so Schelling at first attached himself to Fichte, whom he had heard in Jena; but soon he left that Idealism which regards the world as the reflection of our mind. The essence of nature is the mind itself, even if in the lower grades of development, it is still a slumbering, dreaming mind which, however, awakes more and more, till finally in the man it comes to a consciousness of itself. Nature and Spirit are, therefore, not separated things; they are but the poles of one and the same life, which appears here as moving, there as moved, here as creating, there as created, here as free, there as necessitated. That which animates and moves this great organism, is the mundane soul, which is reflected in the human. Man is the world in a small compass, in him the world repeats itself, as God recognises himself in man as God, so does the mundane soul in the human soul.

These unconnected sentences may suffice to show that Schelling, in opposition to the spiritless, dead contemplation of nature, found among the rationalists as well as the orthodox, and which prevailed in the preceding periods generally, introduced a living, poetical contemplation of nature, full of anticipations and relations, which are a riddle to the dry understanding, and must for ever remain so while they continually force themselves upon the man of intellectual activity. In this consists the merit of his philosophy. Poets and artists will agree with it most readily. Natural philosophy, too, may be on friendly terms with it, although the thoughtful inquirer will not so easily permit his glance to be prejudiced by speculative presuppositions, but will continually vindicate a solid experience and contemplation against the mere poetry of nature. But in what relation does this philosophy stand to religion and morality, to Christianity, to Protestantism? These are questions which interest us much, but to answer them is extremely difficult. It seems that a God dwelling in the world, by whom we are not only created and preserved, but in whom we live and move, and have our being, is of more advantage to religion than a God above and beyond the world. There may be moments in which it is a great comfort to feel ourselves so near the heart of God in this visible world, that our own life seems to be only the stroke of the pulse of the great all-moving mundane soul, and that, like a drop in the ocean, we lose ourselves in this One and All, wishing nothing more ardently than to be resolved into it. But these dispositions, when more fully considered, are more poetical than religious; they are not the dispositions which Christianity, which the Bible, and especially the New Testament, would cherish in us; for although the Bible reveals to us a God who is near us all, still the *difference* between God and the world, between Creator and creature, is kept very prominent, and the very feeling of the *holiness* of God, which is nourished by the feeling of the contrast between the Eternal One and the finite creature, does not permit that familiarity to manifest itself, by which we appear simply as the thoughts of God, as rays of His glory, as the breath of His being. In a word, this view, which certainly cannot long be united with a Christian mode of thinking, is *Pantheism*. It has made its appearance at various periods, and also in the Christian world, but it was most distinctly stamped by the "Naturphilosophie;" it is the doctrine of the All-One, sometimes regarded as God, sometimes as the world, and for that reason never leads to a real adoration of God, but loses itself in that poetical inspiration of nature, which forms the basis of heathen worship.

Let us hear the testimony of a distinguished German theologian, who was himself attached to Schelling's philosophy for some time, but rejected it on perceiving whither it led. Tschirner, in his letters in reference to Reinhard's "Confessions," writes the following concerning his acquaintance with this philosophy:—"I must acknowledge that the universal life which this philosophy breathes into dead nature, and imparts to the suns and planets, as well as to the worm and plants; and the union which it mediates between the Infinite and finite . . . attracted me wonderfully. Physics taught me to regard the heavenly bodies as mere masses, which, being entirely soulless, move according to the law of gravity, and probably serve, like our planet, merely as the abodes of living beings of various kinds. "Schilling's 'Naturphilosophie' animated the masses, and I looked up more cheerfully to the stars and felt happy in the thought that in them, as well as in me, dwelt fulness of life, only raised to infinitely higher powers. Kant's 'Criticism' had made a boundary, which separated the sensible distinctly from the supersensible; it had robbed me of perceiving and knowing the supernatural, and had left me only a faith in the Divine, which it had placed far beyond the sphere of my knowledge. The 'Naturphilosophie' broke down the wall of partition between the sensible and supersensible, married heaven with earth, and taught me how to view the Infinite in the finite. The 'Criticism' had resolved me into a double being, had placed reason and sense in opposition to each other, and had declared the eternal, grievous contest of duty with inclination the object of my existence here. The 'Naturphilosophie' promised me a union of the separated; the spiritual, it said, and the sensible are one, the body is the embodied spirit, and the soul the spiritualized body, reason and sense are but different manifestations of one and the same power, and it is not the object of thy existence for thee to divide thyself, but to live in peace and harmony with thyself and nature. The philosophers of all ages had taught me to separate reason from fancy, the realm of truth from the realm of poetry, and had warned me not to follow the guidance of fancy if I wanted to discover the truth, and not to mingle the plays of fancy with the ideas of reason. The 'Naturphilosophie' united reason and fancy in one faculty, the faculty for perceiving the Infinite, and placed poetry and philosophy in the most intimate relation. . . . Soon, however, this poetical disposition vanished; calm tranquillity again possessed my bosom, and I attempted to comprehend the meaning of this philosophy with definiteness and clearness. . . Then it appeared, as if suddenly, a beautiful charm was broken. I saw myself no longer surrounded with lovely poetry, but only with indefinite and airy forms without solidity or foundation; and where I had heretofore beheld happy life, there *an abyss now opened*, which threatened to swallow all that is great and sublime. By calm investigation I perceived in the 'Naturphilosophie' a want of clearness and definiteness, and a firm foundation, and discovered that it led to the most mournful results. . . . No philosophy ever promised me *more*, none ever gave me *less*. It has a lovely and bright appearance; if, however, we strip off the beautiful covering, a hollow pale form appears, whose aspect we cannot bear to behold. The philosophy, which speaks so much about beholding the Infinite, so much about the revelations of God, and of the blessed life in the absolute, ends with the result that all that exists and happens, consequently also man with his thoughts, resolutions, and actions, is but the necessary effect of a necessary vital energy, which . . . . unceasingly generates, produces, and transforms its productions, in order to let new productions proceed from its inexhaustible fulness. This is the result of the 'Naturphilosophie,' with which it takes away all that gives life, dignity, object and importance—the idea of Divinity, of immortality, of freedom, and morality. Let no one suffer himself to be led astray by the language of devotion, ... the frequent mentioning of God and his revelations. The God of this philosophy is the universe, there lives in him only life and consciousness and producing power, but no holy will, no benevolence, and no righteousness. . . . The blessed life of this system consists only in the exaltation of the mind, which, forgetting itself, contemplates the universal life. The idea of a personal immortality is entirely foreign to this philosophy. . . . It recognizes no free actions on the part of man; to it all is appearance, the Absolute manifested in a thousand different forms; and what it calls freedom and morality, is only life in increased potency. . . . Its Infinite is only an increased finite, . . . and what we call the supersensible, because it never enters the sphere of experience. *God, freedom, immortality,* is sought for in vain in this system."

We will not attempt to decide how far this criticism of Tschirner is complete; how far is rests on a thoroughly correct comprehension of the system; how far here, too, inferences are drawn, which the author of the system would himself reject; how far a certain awkwardness of passing from an old and accustomed to a new way of thinking, may have had an influence in forming these judgments; but this is certain, that the impression this philosophy made upon a thoughtful and considerate theologian is the same it has made on many other conscientious teachers and preachers of Christianity. The Kantian philosophy and the Rationalism proceeding from it had, with all that is negative in them, still retained the ideas of God, freedom, and immortality (which Tschirner missed so much in the "Naturphilosophie"), as the essential ideas of religion. With all the abstractness of their teachings, they had placed themselves sincerely upon this foundation, of which Schelling's philosophy deprived its followers. And what did it give in return? Much at first sight. The "Philosophy of Nature" even appeared to be an attempt to restore the old faith of the Church, which Rationalism had forsaken; and on this account it was welcomed by many as the restorer of positive Christianity. Men were again heard to speak of the incarnation of God, of a trinity, of a fall and redemption. Even the doctrine of Satan was again advocated by the theologians who adhered to this philosophy. There was, in general, as little lack of superabundant expressions as of bitter attacks against the shallow Rationalism. Thus the orthodox appeared to receive a new ally in this new philosophy, and mysticism, which had long been decried as nonsense, again appeared to elevate its head more gloriously than ever before. But if we examine more closely what this philosophy meant by those expressions, we shall soon be convinced that it was neither the doctrine of the Reformers and of the symbols of the church, nor that of the Church Fathers, nor, finally, that of Scripture. The fixed, inflexible dogmas of the church are now moulded into moveable pictures, which may be turned at one's pleasure, to which you may at one time give one sense, and at another a different one. There, again, an ingenious play is granted to the fancy, without gaining a firm hold and lasting satisfaction for the understanding and the heart, the proper bearers of the religious life.

As in the first centuries of Christianity, the Gnostics exhausted themselves in the production of the most extravagant theories in reference to the origin of the world and the incarnation of God, so here we find a not less fantastical, though more intellectual, philosophical myth of the development of the world, which too frequently brings to mind Jacob Boehm, from whom Schelling has adopted many ideas.

In history Schelling distinguishes five periods or ages of the world. "The first is the golden period, the time of blessed indecision, when there was neither good nor bad, when man as a creature of nature spent his time in unconscious innocence. Then follows the period of ruling gods and heroes, the omnipotence of nature, which, however, in the third place, changes to a period of ruling destiny, to a period of decline and division, till God reveals Himself according to His love and mercy. God had to become man in order that man might come to God again. Thus, in the fourth place, a new kingdom is established by the incarnation of God in Christ, in which the Divine Spirit is continually realizing itself more and more fully, till, fifthly, at the end of this period, destiny transforms itself to providence, all evil is overcome, God is realized, is all in all." In this we indeed hear a language, which, with Scriptural and ecclesiastical sounds, actually reminds us of Christian truths, which were lost at that time, especially the fundamental truth, that, as Schelling himself expresses it, God became man, that man might become divine. But if we examine the matter more carefully, we find that by the incarnation of God, Schelling means nothing else than God first coming to a consciousness of Himself in man. To him God the Father is not that Father to whom Christ bids us pray in the Lord's prayer, and whom Paul calls the Father of all in heaven and on earth ; not that Father who, before the foundation of the world was laid, out of pure mercy chose humanity as His inheritance in Christ ; no, what Schelling calls Father is only that mysterious, unconscious primeval cause, or rather non-causer, of all things, who first knows himself in the Son, and through him first comes to consciousness, a dismal paternal countenance, indeed, a Saturn, who devours his children, not God the Father, who clasps them to His bosom even before they exist. God the Son is the self-revelation and self-unfolding of the Father ; He is the divine understanding, in which God first recognizes His own essence ; and since this unfolding of God again returns into itself, therefore God is God; that is, Spirit. It is true (according to Schelling) that God is the Alpha and Omega, the first and the last ; but first, as Omega, He is the proper God, or, as it were, the God having become God. Schelling thus lets his God work himself through the entire alphabet of the development of the world before he comes to full existence. This is the secret of the trinity in the sense of the "Philosophy of Nature." But how is it with the person of Christ ? As with Fichte, so with Schelling, the historical Christ, the Jesus of Nazareth, as He lived and taught as man, is not the essence of Christianity, for God comes to consciousness in man in general. The incarnation of God is, according to Schelling's own words, not an incarnation happening once, but an ideal incarnation from eternity, and is properly the same as the mystery of nature.

That in the historical Christ, God became most fully conscious of himself, is acknowledged by Schelling, since no one before him had revealed the Infinite in such a manner; but he is by no means willing to make the idea of Christianity dependent on this peculiarity; for, even without this historical basis, this idea retains for him, as for Fichte, the same significance as metaphysical truth. When, however, Schelling speaks of a *suffering* God, it may easily be perceived that he does not mean what Zinzendorf does when he speaks of a crucified God, and of the Creator's wounds. Schelling's suffering God is nothing else than the progressive self-development of God amid struggles. Thus, (although more sensually and fantastically) the ancient Manichaeans had already called the suffering of nature, the perishing of the vegetable kingdom, and similar metamorphoses, the suffering Jesus. If this is true, it may be asked, whether the church is not better off with a rationalist of the Kantian school, who dryly and honestly says: "I cannot agree with your dogma of the incarnation of God, of Redemption, etc., I will rather cling to the simple doctrine of God, virtue, immortality, and to the great and sublime teachings of Jesus on these subjects," than with a Pantheist who, under the appearance of almost extreme orthodoxy, removes that which rationalism retains. Independent of all the unworthiness of such a deception, such a doctrine is void of all moral fruits, since it only takes the speculative head into the account, but not the heart and will of man. This philosophy differs from the earlier mysticism, with which in other respects it has some similarity in its moral results. Where the mystics transplanted history to the inner man, they had the *practical* sanctification chiefly in view, and in this sense spoke of Christ being born in us, of dying with him, of being raised with him, while this philosophy thinks of *natural* events, which depend on the law of necessity, and even if it will not admit that it destroys moral freedom, but rather asserts that it puts real in place of apparent freedom, still it cannot be denied that the inclination to know, to explain the mysteries of all life and development is far more prominent in it than the tendency to become better and to produce a more worthy state of being.[1] In

[1] Of course philosophy, as such, deals with knowledge; for this it shall not be reproached. But when Christian theology, which deals with the practical

this the philosophy of Schelling differs from both its predecessors, the Kantian, and the Fichtean systems. He also sustains a different relation to *Protestantism*. A separation in the church between persons of knowledge, and those simply believing, (the esoterics and exoterics) is foreign to Christianity in general, and especially to Protestant Christianity. A language which only the initiated understand, and which does not at all accommodate itself to the comprehension of the weak and uncultivated, is any thing but the language of the Reformers, the language of a Luther and Zwingli. But even if only compared with Kant and Fichte, Schelling's philosophy shows much less of a Protestant character than theirs. Kant and Fichte, with all their deviations from the orthodox doctrines of the Protestant Church, stand altogether on a Protestant foundation, they even have a certain Protestant prudery, carry with them a moral exactness, a corrosive critical salt, while the "Philosophy of Nature," with the poetical twilight in which it moves, may very easily be used by Catholics for the support of the Catholic doctrines, which has actually been done. The Catholic tendency in art found its support principally in the Pantheistic-poetic view of the world.

But still we will not deny the significance of this philosophy; that the living comprehension and treatment of all that lives, for which modern science is distinguished, received its impulse from the "Philosophy of Nature," even if much still needed sifting. Through this philosophy spirit and life were brought into the study of nature, of art, of history, and also of theology; for that through it attention was again called to the deeper significance of the church, its doctrines, and divine worship, is a great merit of which it cannot be deprived. It was not now considered bigotry and want of acquaintance with philosophy, if one spoke of the mysteries of faith with fervour, with reverence, and with animation. The poverty and narrowness of the so-called philosophy of "common sense," became more and more evident. Men again

religion of the gospel, is entirely consumed by this philosophy, it is a different thing; therefore, just at the right time Schleiermacher was desirous of separating the two.

searched deep, and did not even avoid the miracle, where it pressed itself on the mind. How much Schleiermacher was indebted to this philosophy we shall see in another place. We now turn to a man who had at least as great a share in the education of Schleiermacher, as Schelling, although he took a position entirely opposite to the latter and his philosophy. We speak of F. H. Jacobi.

XIX.

FREDERIC HENRY JACOBI.

JACOBI AND THE RELIGION OF THE HEART IN OPPOSITION TO ORTHODOXY AND SPECULATION.

I HAVE intentionally refrained from speaking of this pious, deep thinker, this man of childlike purity, this noble philosopher, till the phases of modern philosophy, as they appeared in Kant, Fichte, and Schelling, had passed before us, so as to permit us now to follow his life without interruption. He came in contact with all the above-named philosophers, and externally, to some extent, formed a centre, around which gathered the intellectually great of that age.

Fr. H. Jacobi, second son of a wealthy merchant of Dusseldorf, brother of the well-known genial poet, Joh. George, was born the 25th of January, 1743 (a contemporary, therefore, of Lavater and Herder). He was intended for mercantile business by his father, and in order to prepare himself for this, went to Frankfort-on-the-Maine in his sixteenth year. In the meantime, however, he showed more love for the sciences than for trade. He went to Geneva, where he formed the acquaintance of educated men, especially of the mathematician, Le Sage, and he also became familiar with the best works of French literature, and returned home in a few years. In his twenty-second year he married Betty Von Clermont of Naels, near Aix-la-Chapelle, "an excellent Belgian lady," as Goethe calls her, "who, without the least sentimentality or expression of sensuality, brings to mind the women of Rubens." Jacobi soon abandoned his business, in order to devote himself to the service of the state as member of the exchequer, and afterwards with the title of privy counsellor. His external relations were very favourable. His well-arranged house in Dusseldorf, and especially his country-seat in the neighbouring Pempelfort,[1] afforded the thinker and author a fine asylum, and the hospitable man a desired opportunity, for the reception of distinguished guests from all parts of the learned world.

His social talent and the affection which accompanied nearly all that he said, did very much to animate the intellectual society in which he moved, and this tone of affection, which was softened by his fine manners, also characterizes his writings. Some have denied his fitness for authorship, because he lacked a profound, learned education; he was, they say, rather a scientific amateur. But this very thing seems to me of the greatest significance, that a man, who kept free from all German pedantry, who had been more incited by French culture, who had no need of disputing for a philosophical chair in a university because he had more means than he needed, that such a man ventured to enter the depths of philosophy, led only by the inner impulse of his spirit, not for the sake of becoming renowned, or of establishing a school, but purely to attain a knowledge of the highest interests of humanity. This impulse had already manifested itself in Jacobi in his early childhood. "I still wore my polish coat," he says, "when I began to be anxious about the affairs of another world, and my childish thoughtfulness brought me in my eighth or ninth year to certain views, which cling to me to this hour. The longing to bring to certainty the better expectation of man, grew with my years, and it became the principal thread to which all my other fortunes were attached." Nor did this impulse leave him in later life. "I have now (so he says in his 'Conversation on Idealism and Realism') forty-three years on my head, and have been cast about by fate with

[1] An effort is now being made by the friends of learning to purchase this country-seat, so that the premises may be preserved in honour of its former distinguished owner and of the eminent men who there shared his hospitality.—Tr.

a pretty rude hand. Thousands of persons may excel me in intellectual powers, but certainly few in perseverance and zeal in struggling for knowledge and truth. I have traced the most distinguished and obscure sources of human knowledge with untiring energy till many of them lost themselves in invisible veins. I have seen other inquirers, and not a few of them were among the greatest minds of my contemporaries. I have had an opportunity, and have been obliged to try my powers in many different ways."

Jacobi has in a special manner become the philosopher of life and of the educated world, but in a higher and nobler sense than those popular philosophers, who attempted to make the thoughts, snatched up here and there and rhetorically polished, popular by rendering them shallow, and who, for the most part, only took them from higher sources. That sincere struggle for depth as well as clearness, that continual self-penetration, that demanding an account of the inmost part of our nature, that examination of the original sources in man, that humanity with which he welcomes every appearance in the department of the intellect which he discovers, and also that noble wrath with which he rejects whatever denies a personal God and dishonours virtue,—it is these that place him in the same line with Herder, and which must make him dear to all who have determined to follow the course of their own inner experience, however great the clamour of those following the beaten track may be against them.

Jacobi stood in a very peculiar relation to the philosophy of his time, as it worked its way from Kant to Schelling.[1] He was urged on by each of these systems, learned something from each, exercised his powers on each, but he was satisfied by neither, and was most repelled by Pantheism. Jacobi, with all his profound knowledge, was, according to the usual idea of philosophy, either an opponent of all philosophy, or a philosopher in that sense of the word in which Socrates was one through the knowledge of his ignorance. He was, however, a decided opponent of that philosophy, to which the

[1] This relation cannot be described easily. "Do take the trouble," says Goethe in a letter to Jacobi, "to shew me plainly in what respect you differ from our modern philosophers, and at which point you separate from them, and make me able to dispute with them in your name."

mere formal knowledge of things is the final object. He had no taste for that mere "logical enthusiasm," to which thinking itself is the highest end. The explanation of things was not his final object, but that which cannot be explained, cannot be comprehended by our conceptions, cannot be analyzed in words, the simple, the indissoluble. "The basis of all speculative philosophy," he says, "is only a great hole, in which we look in vain as in a very dark abyss." This aversion to speculative philosophy did not, however, prevent him from searching continually for the best foundation, only he dug within, while others only laboured on the hole from without. "No one," says Jacobi, "can despise the close and subtle investigation of trifles more than I do; but from this I distinguish the free exertion of the inmost original sense." And on this inmost original sense Jacobi based everything. "There is, indeed," he says, "a knowledge of the supernatural, of God and divine things, and this knowledge is the most certain in the human mind—a knowledge absolute and proceeding directly from human reason; but it can never take the form of science." Jacobi was no despiser of reason, but rather defended it. He did not, however, regard it a power which can create truths of itself, can discover, can produce them; but by reason he understood, according to the etymology of the word, that which perceives, that inmost original sense mentioned above. He did not think that reason and faith are opposed to each other, but that they are one and the same. Faith supplies what knowledge cannot reach. Jacobi followed Kant in this respect, that he acknowledged that our perceptions are inadequate to say anything purely demonstrable in reference to God and divine things. As on this account Kant had left a vacant place in his system for God and divine things, which was but imperfectly and unsatisfactorily filled by what he thought belonged to practical reason, Jacobi supplied the deficiency by his doctrine of faith. Man, of course, cannot reach God in thought, but he can *feel* and *experience* Him. We must love God, he says with Pascal, in order to know Him. This love, as we experience it in ourselves is the original, is that which proves itself in our minds superior to all thinking. We have a knowledge of God and His will, because we are born of God, are created after His image, are like Him. God lives in us, and our life is hid in God. If He were not thus immediately present by means of His image in us, what outside of Him should make Him known to us?

Consequently Jacobi believed in a revelation of God to man, but in a revelation which is continually being made to the inner man, a revelation which he perceives with reason, but cannot comprehend with his understanding.[1] However much he opposed the cold, calculating understanding, with this faith in revelation, still he did not place himself on the side of the believers in revelation, in the sense in which the word is held by the Church; and this is the point in which he differed from his friends Claudius, Hamann, Lavater, and from the friends and professors of positive Christianity. On this account it is impossible to class him with the Christian philosophers in the more limited sense of the word, however thoroughly Christian his disposition, the thoughts and meditations of his heart, and the tendency of his entire philosophy. For the very reason that Jacobi made all depend on the inner experience of the heart, because that was the divine to him, which each one has to perceive himself, therefore an external revelation, even if provided with all miracles, could as little satisfy him, as a philosophical system construed externally, and then made ours by learning it. In both he beheld the killing of the letter. As the speculative philosophy was too idealistic for him, so the orthodox faith was too realistic, too material, too positive. He indeed valued the strict faith in revelation highly, and felt himself most intimately connected with it by his living faith in God and the piety of his heart. How intimate his relation to Claudius, is evident from his book on "Divine Things and their Revelation." But it appeared to him, that the pious people deceived themselves, because they ascribed that to an external revelation, which lay in themselves and which was only *awakened* by the reading of the Bible, not originally *produced* by it. They are, he thinks, like children who, when they ride their hobby-horse, think the horse bears them along, while it is owing to their

[1] Jacobi deserves credit for having so strictly carried out the difference between reason and understanding, especially in his later writings, which difference Kant had only half conceived.

own exertions that they move at all. "It depends on your own motion and continual adherence to wisdom, bravery, and good pleasure; . . . the horse no more makes the man than the coat." Claudius, on the other hand, compared an ideal religion, without historical basis, to a painted horse which you can admire, but not ride. Jacobi made another and more ingenious comparison when he compared revelation to the consonants and the religious sense in us to the vowels, through which the mute consonants are quickened. He, however, acknowledges that both belong together, and in this Claudius had to agree with him. Jacobi bowed humbly before the warm enthusiastic representation which Claudius in his high simplicity made of Christ. "What a picture!" he exclaimed, "what sublime and touching contrasts! What a power of beauty, of grace and majesty in the united traces of this perfect ideal of united divinity and humanity." Jacobi, too, as Claudius, found all that he required of a religious and moral man united in Christ and that in the real, the historical Christ, who was more to him than a mere idea, and by no means a mere fiction, a myth. When, however, Claudius insisted, that it is only *through* Christ that we come to God, that we can only elevate ourselves to him by clinging to Christ, Jacobi thought on the other hand that we soar to God *with* Christ. The principal thing for him was, that that which lived in Christ, also become alive in us. Trusting on historical events he considered superstition, and therefore he always had his suspicions in reference to the positive Christianity in general, because he feared, and not without reason, that the external to which he was so much opposed was concealed behind it, and because he regarded every completed system as something dangerous, that is, as an idol which is worshipped instead of the living God. In this respect he had much similarity to Fichte, however much he differed from him in his philosophical principles. Jacobi, as well as Fichte, in his more advanced age, felt himself drawn towards the inner, deeper life-giving fountain of Christianity with his whole heart; therefore, compared with the cold "illuminati" of the day, he was decried as a hypocrite, and as one opposing the march of intellect; but as soon as he attempted to arrange the contents of the Christian doctrines with his understanding, to embrace what is believed in a confession, a formula, his inner sense strove against it. From this sympathy with religion and antipathy to all dogmatics and speculation, his own remarkable declaration may be explained, that with his heart he was a Christian, with his understanding a heathen, that he swam between two waters which would not unite in him.

However, this heathenism of Jacobi was not intended to be taken very seriously. We would rather say that with the heart he was a Supernaturalist, perhaps even a Pietist in the noble sense of the word, and with the understanding a Rationalist; for, however little Jacobi could agree with the doctrines more distinctly Christian, his philosophy still showed itself essentially Christian, in that it maintained against the Pantheistic fanaticism of the age the faith in a personal God, which forms the foundation of all revelation, and without which all talk about revelation is mere deception and a quibble. We cannot follow the diffuse philosophical dispute itself, which was first occasioned by the study of Spinoza, which Lessing had incited, and which received special importance through Schelling. Something, however, must be said of the disputed question in general, as it became more and more the living question of the whole period, and for its solution our own age is very anxious. If I advance it as one of the chief merits of Jacobi's philosophy, and as a characteristic token of its Christianity, that it maintained the *faith in a personal God* in opposition to the pantheistic tendencies, I do not insist on the word and conception of "personality," and I will gladly consent to another word, if one can be found which denotes with sufficient distinctness a God, conscious of Himself, different from the world, and not coinciding with it. I admit that the expression "personality" is apt to carry with it the accessory notion of limitation, which of course must be removed from the idea of God. In this sense Herder, who, in opposition to Jacobi, agreed with the philosopher Spinoza, objected to the expression "personality," and even Lavater acknowledged that the conception of a personality of God belongs to the childhood of humanity. But the same Lavater in this very matter stood on the side of Jacobi; when he writes: "that which is most vigorous in me, above me and around me, is God, and personal man must personify." Jacobi wanted to know nothing of a God who is no Helper, of a God who makes the eye and does not see, the ear and does not hear, the understanding and does not perceive, does not know, does not will, and therefore is not. Pantheism and Atheism were not the same to Jacobi; for a God who first receives his existence through the world, and comes to consciousness first in man, is no God, but an idol, just as little did Jacobi want a God merely above and outside of the world (as the Deists), who is sundered from the world and humanity, and who does not appear to be concerned about them; he wanted a God who communicates Himself to the inner man and gives us the assurance that we are of divine origin; but he did not want this God to be confined to the world, he wanted a God whom we have not only in our eyes, but before our eyes; a God whom we have not only as I—Ego—but as Thou; a God to whom we can pray, and who says to himself, *I am that I am.* Thus man, according to Jacobi, ought to recognise God as well above him as in him, and only in holding to one as well as the the other, did he regard man as having the living faith in God, as the Bible and Christianity teach, and as all that is called religion in heaven or on earth, requires and presupposes with eternal necessity. So much of Jacobi as a Christian thinker.

We will not speak of the personal contest between him and Schelling, which was carried on by the latter with much bitterness; but will only call to mind that the subject of controversy between these two men, continues to be discussed in the schools, for Hegel built on Schelling,[1] and Fries and many other independent thinkers, continued to build partly on Kant, partly on Jacobi; each one of course in his own way, and partially opposing his predecessors.

[1] It has already been mentioned that we only speak of the earlier Schelling. That the later Schelling forms the opposition to Hegel, cannot appear strange to him who observes the rotating motion of philosophy, with an unprejudiced eye. It appears to us that the return of the great philosopher to the religious standpoint, can, perhaps, not be accomplished otherwise than by an atonement, which he owes to the manes of Jacobi.

XX.

JOHN GOTTLIEB FICHTE.

FICHTE TILL HIS APPOINTMENT AS PROFESSOR IN JENA.—THE FICHTEAN IDEALISM.—CHARGE OF ATHEISM.—FICHTE IN BERLIN.—RETURN TO THE RELIGIOUS STAND-POINT.—"DIRECTIONS FOR A BLESSED LIFE."—FICHTE'S LAST DAYS AND DEATH.

IN the village of Rammenau in Upper Lusatia, John Gottlieb Fichte was born, May 19th 1762. His father was a linen weaver, and himself gave the child his first instruction, when the loom was standing still and the garden work was accomplished, exercising him in reading, teaching him religious passages and hymns; very likely relating to him many things of his travels through Saxony and Franconia, and thus awaking aspirations for great things in the infant mind. As the boy became older it became his duty to read the daily morning and evening prayers in the family circle, and then already the father perhaps cherished the silent hope of one day hearing his son preach in the village pulpit. In the mean while the pastor of the place interested himself in the aspiring boy, being particularly pleased with the evidence of a good memory, given by the unhesitating repetition of a sermon which the child had heard. This talent brought him into favour with a noble lord also, in whose presence he was at one time called on to repeat a sermon, and who was so pleased with the performance that he promised to attend to his education from that period, and committed the boy to the charge of a country clergyman near Meissen. Here Fichte laid the foundation for the ancient languages. In his twelfth year he entered the city school of Meissen, and a little later the school Pforta by Naumburg, in which Klopstock was educated and which has sent forth so many great Germans. The monastic seclusion, which had already roused many a young heart in that school to resistance, became to him exceedingly oppressive and at last awakened in him the thought of secret flight. He actually fled with the intention of becoming a second Robinson Crusoe, but on an open hill, not far from the school, in the midst of a prayer which he offered to

God for his deliverance, he was struck with sorrow for his undertaking; an inner voice bade him retrace his step and he voluntarily returned. His sincere repentance not only procured him pardon but also milder treatment.

From the youth of Hamann and others we learn that the one-sided instruction, which at that time prevailed in most of the German schools, confining education almost entirely to the study of the ancient languages, was especially the system of the celebrated school Pforta. The so-called real sciences were not studied, nor polite literature; the German poets were read only by stealth, the solid Haller alone was used. In this clandestine manner Fichte, among other works, became acquainted with Lessing's polemic treatise against Gœtze; and now perhaps that polemic dart was sharpened which he afterwards, in the spirit of Lessing, hurled against his enemies. About Michaelmas 1780, Fichte entered the university of Jena, for the purpose of studying theology, but, although he preached at various places with success, eloquence was not natural to him; he was therefore soon absorbed in philosophical studies.

Being deprived of all help from others, he was obliged to provide for his future course himself, and then his good star led him to us in Switzerland by means of a tutor's situation which was offered him by the landlord of the "Sword" in Zurich, who desired to give his children more than a common education. Here Fichte sometimes preached in the city, as well as in the neighbouring country; here he made the acquaintance of Lavater; here, too, originated a love affair with the lady whom he afterwards married. She was the daughter of Rahn, the Keeper of the Public Scales, and the niece of Klopstock. In the meanwhile, however, Fichte felt himself obliged to seek his support in some other place, and being supplied with letters from Lavater and others, he returned to Germany. In this unsettled pecuniary condition, which drove him as far as Poland, he was continually studying more and more thoroughly the Kantian philosophy, whose devoted follower he had become. He did not rest till he became personally acquainted with Kant. He went to Könisberg, visited the Philosopher at his house and attended his lectures as a transient auditor. But he found himself satisfied neither at the one place nor the other. The reception at the house was cold, the discourse in the lecture room was drowsy. Still Fichte remained an enthusiastic disciple of the critical philosopher, and soon, as an author, became the representative of the Kantian system. "The attempt at a critique of all Revelation," ("Versuch einer Kritik aller Offenbarung,") appeared, a work in which the Kantian principles, in reference to the possibility of an extraordinary Revelation, are applied with masterly skill. It excited great attention. In public criticisms Kant himself was mentioned and praised as the author. Even to the minute parts of the work, it was thought that traces of Kant's style were discernible, until finally Kant declared that he was not the author, but a certain candidate of theology, Fichte, who was at that time tutor in the family of the Count of Krakow in West Prussia. This was the first thing that made Fichte's name renowned in Germany, but with the renown rose also a number of opponents and enemies, and the aspiring intellect was drawn into those confused literary contests, out of which even the matured mind never comes fully. In the midst of these contests Fichte travelled back to Zurich and consummated his marriage there in the fall of 1793.

"Half of my soul," so he writes to the lady while yet on the journey, "we will make the indissoluble covenant of virtue as soon as we shall see each other again; we will be to each other the staff and support in the path of virtue; we will remind and admonish each other when either becomes forgetful; for . . . . . I have resolutely determined to be an *upright man in the full sense of the term*, and for this I shall often have need of your assistance." The marriage took place in Baden, Argovie; and Lavater who was at first expected to perform the ceremony, but who resigned it to J. G. Schulthess, made the bridal couple rejoice with congratulatory verses.

About this time Fichte made the acquaintance of the author of "Lienhard and Gertrude," who, still living in retirement at Richterswyl was reflecting on his first essays on popular education. Pestalozzi and Fichte were pleased with each other and continued during life to be friends. In later years, Fichte said with enthusiasm that in Pestalozzi's system of education was to be found the true remedy for sick humanity.[1] Fichte, at first lived in Zurich in the house of his father-in-law, in the happiest relations. Here he was occupied from without with the great commotions, produced by the revolution, and from within with the further development and completion of his system. At the solicitation of Lavater he delivered philosophical lectures before the public of Zurich, and Lavater himself, however little he might be able to reconcile his own mind to the philosophical train of Fichte's thoughts, was one of his first and most enthusiastic auditors. A proof this is of the freshness of Lavater's mind, and of that high true liberality which at that time brought into close relation men of the most different modes of thinking, because the presentiment of something better, which was aimed at by all parties, and the pleasure in seeking was greater than the dissatisfaction experienced from transient contradictions. Later than this, when Fichte was already persecuted on account of atheism, Lavater wrote to him out of the spirit of Fichte's Philosophy the following lines :

> "Unerreichbarer Denker! Dein Dasein beweist mir das Dasein
> Eines ewigen Geistes, dem hohe Geister entstrahlen!
> Könntest je du zweifeln, ich stellte dich selbst vor dich selbst nur,
> Zeigte dir in dir selbst den Strahl des ewigen Geistes."[2]

Fichte was taken from the friendly relations of Zurich society by a call to a philosophical Professorship at Jena. His wife remained at Zurich for some time. With his appearance at Jena commences Fichte's public activity as teacher in the higher sense. Jena was at that time the centre of modern erudition. Here lived and taught Schiller, whose acquaintance Fichte had made previously, and who shared with him the admiration for the celebrated Kant, and from this place he entered into a relation with the Weimarians, Wieland, Gœthe, Herder; and made acquaintance also with Jacobi, Humboldt, the brothers Schlegel, and others. Youth flocked to Jena from all regions.

[1] In his "Reden an die deutsche Nation."

[2] Unattainable Thinker! Thy existence proves to me the existence of an Eternal Spirit from whom radiate noble spirits! Couldst thou ever doubt, I would only place thee before thyself, show thee in thyself the ray of the Eternal Spirit.

Swiss, Danes, Courlanders, Livonians, Poles, Hungarians, and Transylvanians, also several Frenchmen sat at the feet of the German teacher, to receive as it were the inmost spirit and kernel of science, with the *Wissenschaftslehre,* as Fichte called his Philosophy. Fichte fully felt the greatness and importance of his position as Academical teacher. He is perhaps the first since the days of the Reformation who has properly comprehended the duties of such a teacher. His influence upon the students was not intended to be merely scientific, in the common-sense of the word, not merely learned, not merely literal performance, which in case of necessity might be accomplished by letter. He was no dictating machine, he knew the power of the living word, and of personal intercourse. He desired to influence the Academical youth in a manner morally ennobling and intellectually inciting; to teach them to comprehend the calling and end of the learned from the highest and noblest point of view; to elevate them above common and every-day affairs and lead them to the ideal. He desired less to lead back into the antiquity of the past than to prepare, with poetical inspiration, a more beautiful, more powerful future. In this striving Fichte had much in common with Schiller. In Fichte's Lectures on the "Bestimmung des Gelehrten" and similar writings, as well as in his letters, we find the same morally impelling and purifying power, which we have recognized in Schiller's poems. But with this moral ideality was connected a bold transcending of what had been handed down from other ages and of the positive, a certain defiance which the youth were apt to regard as an expression of the feeling of moral strength, which was, however, viewed with suspicion by reflecting men and by those in authority. A cotèmporary and admirer of Fichte (Forberg) says :—"The spirit of the Fichtean philosophy is a proud and daring spirit, for which the sphere of human knowledge is too small; it strikes out a new course every step it takes, struggles with language in order to wrestle from it words to express the fulness of its thoughts; it does not lead, but seizes and forces us along, and touches no object without crushing it. . . . The distinguishing mark of Fichte's character is the highest integrity. Such a character generally knows least about delicacy and gentility. . . . His discourse therefore roars like a thunderstorm, which discharges its fire in separate strokes. His imagination is not vivid, but energetic and powerful. He penetrates the lowest depths of his subject, and moves about in the realm of ideas with a freedom which shows that he not only lives, but actually reigns in this invisible realm."

In reference to the effect which Fichte's Lectures produced upon the students, the same observer remarks:—"Fichte is believed in, as his predecessor Reinhold[1] had never been. He is, of course, understood much less, but on this very account is believed more obstinately. I and not=I, Ich und Nicht =Ich (the characteristic words of the Fichtean philosophy) are now the symbol of the philosophers of yesterday, as in the time of Kant and Reinhold, matter and form were. . . . Fichte intends to affect the world by means of his philosophy. *The inclination to restless activity, which dwells in the bosom of every noble youth, is carefully cherished and nourished by him,* that it may produce fruit at the proper time. He is continually inculcating that action! action![2] is the object of man, from which it is to be feared, that the majority of the youth, who take this to heart, will regard the summons to action as nothing else than a summons to destroy. Besides this the sentence is false. Man is not created to act; if he cannot act without doing wrong, he ought to remain inactive. Thus far this observer. Let us add to this what Fichte says of himself:—"The principal object of my life," he writes to Miss Rahn, "is to avail myself of every kind of improvement (not scientific, for I find much vanity in that), of character which my condition will possibly permit. I study the course of Providence in my life, and find that this may also perhaps be the plan of Providence in reference to myself, and I have,

[1] Reinhold forms the transition from Kant to Fichte in the History of Modern Philosophy. It is a remarkable fact for an historical purpose, that Reinhold proceeded from the Catholic Church, but by means of philosophy found his way into the Protestant Church; and indeed, the development of modern philosophy generally, till Schelling, belongs to Protestantism, and first since then a Catholic speculation has planted itself beside the Protestant.

[2] Schelling in one of his lectures says:—"Action! action! is the cry which resounds from all sides; it is mostly, however, raised by those who cannot get along with knowledge."—Tr.

in general, found that all the occurrences of my life have made my character more decided . . . . I have too little talent to insinuate myself into any one's favour, and to deal with persons whom I do not like; I can only get along with good, honest people, am too frank and unfit for court. . . I am as little fit to be a learned man by profession, as it is possible to be. I want not only to *think*, I want to *act*; I like least of all to think about trifles. . . . . I do not seek happiness; I know that I shall never find it. I have only one passion, only one want, only one full feeling of self, to effect that which lies without me. The more I act the happier I feel."

We thus find, from the testimony of others, and of Fichte himself, that he was not so much in pursuit of thought as of action, and we might therefore expect a philosophy, which impels directly to action. But we would deceive ourselves greatly, if we expected a practical philosophy, *i. e.*, a philosophy of life intelligible to all. There was no lack, at that time, of such practical philosophies; but that of Fichte was the farthest removed from these. What Fichte terms "action," is not action after the manner of a camp, an industrious activity; nor the quiet action of philanthropy for the public good; it is action which is intended to affect others definitely, to give the world a new tendency, a new impulse; transforming, reformatory, perhaps even revolutionary action; not, however, in a blind, hap-hazard manner: it is not to be mere agitation, but rather action, resulting from our deepest convictions and from the consciousness of the highest personal freedom. And *this* consciousness again was connected in the most intimate manner with Fichte's philosophy. This philosophy was not the fruit of merely thinking; it forced itself on him as he struggled for the truth. However abstract and unpopular, therefore, it may appear to those who are not accustomed to the technical language of speculation, with Fichte it was the fruit of the noblest and greatest moral struggle; it was deeply rooted in his heroic, I might say Titanic, character. This was the very thing which made it so accessible to the young men, even where they understood but half, had but a faint presentiment of the truth and were amazed. This was also felt by the opponents. They knew very well how to discover the revolutionary, which was contained in Fichte's mode of thinking, and was thrown like an electric spark in the minds of the youth; and it was probably quite a right conjecture of Fichte, when he supposed, that it was not so much his atheism which frightened the people, as his democracy, which, at this time of political excitement in the neighbouring country, appeared doubly dangerous. Since, however, the theoretical and practical were most intimately connected in him; since his unusual thoughts aimed at unusual actions, it was natural that the one should be watched in and with the other. Before we see why and how the grievous charge of atheism was made against him, we shall have to give a picture of his philosophy, as far as the nature of these lectures allows.

I shall, however, here first give some extracts from Fichte's letters to his wife, which show how he was regarded by the students, how highly he estimated himself, how boldly he spoke about matters and things, and how firm he thought he stood with the government, in spite of his opponents, while soon after it was quite different. "Last Friday," he writes, May 26th, 1794, "I delivered my first lecture. The largest lecture-room in Jena was too small, the entire entrance-hall, the yard was full, on desks and benches they stood over one another.[1] . . . . It is true that the students had a general prejudice in my favour, which I certainly did not destroy by my presence. My lecture, so far as I have heard, has been received with universal approbation. When I deal with them personally, I am very friendly and courteous, place myself on an equal footing with them, and thus win their confidence. . . . My relations to my colleagues are also very pleasant. I can now say more confidently that all have received me with open arms, and that many worthy men are seeking my special company. . . . I keep myself in a certain state of candour, am kind, open, and friendly to all."

Further on he writes: "The course has opened favourably. Respect among the students and a certain decorum also create respect among the professors, ministers, etc. The duke conversed with me a long time. Gœthe continually shows him-

[1] So it was, at one time, also with Melancthon at Wittenberg.

self a warm friend of mine. And I have reason to believe that the duke himself would rejoice in being able to do something for me."

Then again: "Be careful not to believe it, if some of these days it should be written to Zurich, that I have been called to an account in Weimar for my teachings, that I have been prohibited from writing this or that. . . . . In all Germany I am now the subject of general sarcasm, and everywhere strange reports are spread about me. This, however, is very fine; it shows that I am not altogether disregarded. The truth of my relations to our government is this; unlimited confidence is placed in my integrity and prudence, and plain hints have been given me to teach entirely according to my convictions, and that I shall be defended powerfully against all injury."

And in another letter of July 21st: "You look at the German sovereigns very strangely through your Zurich spectacles. What your aristocrats would do, *if* they had the power, that you expect from ours, because they *have* the power. The only difference is, that ours are not quite so stupid as yours. You are like the cow-herd boy, who desired to be king, so that he might be able to besmear his bread with as much syrup as he wanted; just so your aristocrats judge, and the rest of you look through their spectacles. . . . No one shall injure me, of this I assure you in few words. I offer no weak side, *and I have heart and courage.*"

In order to estimate the Fichtean philosophy and its influence on the Protestant Church and theology, which indeed was only transient, so far as it agrees with the object of these lectures, we must commence with Kant, whom Fichte at first joined with the greatest enthusiasm, till, going beyond his master, he announced his system, which in its essential principles contradicted that of Kant and produced a rupture in the philosophical school, which, to this hour, is not healed. I must, however, here remark, that it cannot be my purpose to give a scientific representation of Fichte's system, just as I have not given such of Kant. This must be left for the history of philosophy, from which we only take what is necessary for our purpose. For this reason we must refrain from passing a judgment on the Fichtean philosophy itself; for we would only be entitled to do this if we were able to examine the connection of the system with Fichte's personality, and the internal organic connection of the system itself. We only speak of the *impression* which the system has left in the consciousness of the Church and of the commotions it has occasioned; and therefore only form that conception of it which is necessary to comprehend to some degree that impression and those commotions.

Kant started from this, that the knowledge of man is limited by space and time, and that he can know nothing of God and divine things by means of the *pure* reason, whilst as amends for this he denoted God and immortality as requirements of the *practical* reason; above all, however, he represented *morality*, demanded by the categorical imperative as the essence of all religion. So Fichte, too, first of all, placed himself on this subjective stand-point of restrained and limited human knowledge. According to him, too, we do not know the essence of things, but only as they *appear* to us in our present condition. But whilst Kant accepted a real world objective to man, and only made the conception and contemplation of the same dependent on the arrangement of our knowledge, Fichte went farther, in the course of time, in this, namely, that he regarded the entire objective world itself a product of the human mind, as a reflection of the creations of the mind, which originate and move in us, either unconsciously or consciously. Nothing had reality for him, except the *Ego* (Ich), or the *consciousness* which, however, he did not think as something resting, idle, but as a continual act, as a creative power. In opposition to the plain, common sense of man, which simply insists that there is a world and in it a multitude of things perceived by our own senses, and of which we afterwards make representations (images) in our minds he asserted that there are representations, images in us, which we first attain unconsciously, and then through continued thinking. Man first *creates* the things in thinking, represents them to himself, places them before him by thinking, and in so far they exist for him. First of all the consciousness forms itself in man, or, in Fichte's words, the Ego sets (fixes) itself," (das Ich setzt sich selbst). This is the first act of our consciousness (or the first act of which we are conscious). With this connects itself the second act of our consciousness, namely that the Ego (I) can also think that which differs from it, which is not Ego, Nicht—Ich. "The Ego sets a non-Ego" (das Ich setzt ein Nicht Ich). Of this non-Ego (not I) man, however, knows only that it is the contrary of Ego. It is nothing which has a real, independent existence (out of our minds), nothing material, substantial, having extension in space. That which appears to us, as matter or as substance, is rather only a momentary checking of our thinking (just as the momentary congealing of a stream). That, too, which we call spirit, is not a substance, something conceivable out of us; therefore Fichte avoided the expressions of spirit and soul, because by these we are apt to understand something itself spiritless, something dead, unsubstantial, or ghost-like. He withdrew himself simply to the Ego, which, however, as already remarked, must not be thought as a resting, existing Ego, as one receiving its impressions from without, but as a productive power, a continually active and creative Ego. According to the above, it was quite consistent if this Idealism, this philosophy of the Ego, sought to remove from our notion of God, all that might remind us of anything material or substantial. Even the Scriptural expression, "God is a Spirit," was not fine and spiritual enough for our philosopher, since by spirit might easily be understood a personally restrained, hence a limited, being. Therefore Fichte says: "God is not *Existence,* but pure *Action,* just as I too am not existence, but pure action. God ceases to be infinite as soon as He is made an object of an idea, as soon as He is to be represented definitely to our minds, is to be comprehended. Every conception of God is an idol. If we abstract all that limits God, all that makes Him comprehensible to us, there remains for us a Being quite incomprehensible, pure Consciousness, Intelligence, spiritual Life (without any farther definition)." Thus Fichte finally found no other expression for denoting God than the Ego, in so far, of course, as it is not conceived as limited, personal, individual, but as an *absolute* Ego, transcending all finiteness and limitation.

He also called it the *moral order of the world.* It would certainly be doing Fichte injustice to interpret his system to mean that he wanted to make himself, J. G. Fichte, God. Against this he protested most solemnly, and it always requires little art, but on that account a more hateful disposition, to draw such conclusions from premises which are not understood in their connection with the entire system. We might say with more propriety that Fichte, like Spinoza, rather denied the existence of the world than of God; that he *apparently* denied the existence of God, in order to conceive Him very spiritually; for he did not want anything which is created to be attached to the Creator, lest He should be dragged down into the sphere of the finite. This attempt to spiritualize may even have a deep religious ground; it arouses from indolence the thinking mind, which is too apt to think of God in an anthropomorphitic manner, or which properly thinks nothing, but simply repeats thoughtless words and formulas, of which it can give no explanation. Fichte was not the first who attempted this intellectual soaring. Former thinkers, and indeed very Christian men among them,[1] had to submit to the degradation by the masses of what they gave as the expression of a mind struggling for proper ideas of God, to common-place reflections and wilful misrepresentations or ignorant distortions. It was said of many that they did not believe in God, because they did not conceive Him as materially and plainly as the masses. At the same time there is something dangerous in this striving, even if it may proceed from a noble disposition; for it may finally happen that by means of this diluting and spiritualizing process, everything will really vanish in mist, and that from the pure beholding of the sun the eye will more and more envelope itself in darkness. We ought certainly to be conscious of the fact that we, as men, can only know God in a human manner, that all our expressions in reference to Him are figurative and do not correspond to His nature; but since we are men, limited beings, we ought in humility to use the language adapted to our wants, and of which God himself was not ashamed, when He condescended to reveal Himself to us.

[1] We need but think of Origen and his opponents, or of J. Scotus Erigena and the later sects of the Middle Ages.

Let those philosophers, therefore, who attempt to lead man beyond himself into a region in which even our inner senses disappear and where we can no longer have a footing, be accountable, if, without regard to the impression which it makes upon other minds, they speak a language, necessarily subjected to misunderstanding on account of its remoteness from other human language; and they must also submit to the opposition which their bold speech occasions. Fichte was a teacher of Academic youths. At his feet sat many who were destined to proclaim to Christian congregations the God of the Gospel; a God, who is only Creator, if there are creatures of His creation, who has called a world into being, not as a visionary but as an actual, a real world; a world in which sin, misery, and affliction appear but too real, from which the mere *imagination* that they do not exist cannot save us, but which can only be removed by a higher reality, a divine fact, by God's act of love, as it appears historically in the redemption through Christ. If now the ground were taken from under the feet of those destined to proclaim such a doctrine, if nothing religious remained for them but their miserable Ego, of which they were not even as fully and energetically conscious as Fichte of his, must not many just scruples have arisen in the minds of those too who were not accustomed to restrain the freedom of investigation hastily? A difficult question now arose, which since then has frequently been asked, and which is, indeed, founded in the twofold nature of Protestantism, whether for the sake of learning free course shall be given to free investigation and a free publication of the results of the investigation, or whether restrictions shall be made for the interest of the Church, to which also belong the weak and the young. We call it a difficult question, because we do not like to give our unconditional approval to one side or the other. What would claim approval in one case might deserve blame in another. Where the acts are not finished, it is easy to do injustice to one or the other party. From a predilection in favour of learning, faith may be wronged, and from a zeal for the faith investigation may be improperly opposed; and if this difficulty is great even to an honest mind, it must be doubly so, when passions are excited on both sides. It may also be conjectured that it was so in the process against Fichte, which threw him out of the midst of his very brilliant career. Fichte was charged with no less an error than *atheism,* and to this day the learned are not agreed, whether this oft-abused term may be applied to Fichte's system as represented in his Wissenschaftslehre. To this must be added, as Fichte himself remarks, that his democracy was as much a thorn in the eyes of his opponents as his atheism. The fact that he disregarded all established customs offended many. He chose Sunday for the purpose of delivering moral lectures to the students. In this the consistory of Weimar, of which at that time Herder was a member, thought they recognized the secret intention of gradually undermining public worship, although Fichte protested solemnly against this, and appealed to the example of Gellert, whose moral lectures had also been delivered on Sunday, and to the fact, that the theatre in Weimar was opened on Sunday, and why not then the philosophical lecture room?

This dispute about reading lectures on Sunday was, however, only the prelude to a fiercer contest. Fichte published a work, "On the grounds of our Faith in the Divine Government of the World," in which the moral order of the world was denoted as God, and the assertion was made that we need and can conceive of no other God. "The existence of *this* God cannot be doubted; it is the most certain of all things, and the ground of all other certainty; but the idea of God as a particular substance is impossible and contradictory. It is proper to say this candidly to strike down the prating of the schools, so that the true religion of doing right cheerfully may be elevated." Many pious minds, of course, took offence at these expressions. Although Fichte might be satisfied with this moral order of the world, *the Christian's faith in God,* a faith too in "doing right cheerfully," but at the same time in a real God, could by no means be content with this philosophical theory. This faith would not, however, have been destroyed by this theory, even if no interdiction had been issued against it. Such an interdiction appeared. The book in which Fichte advocated the theory of the divine order of the world was attacked in the Electorate of Saxony, and from this place the attention of the court of Weimar was called to the dangers of Fichte's doctrine, "as one not only openly hostile to the Christian, but even to natural religion." In the written requisition of Dec. 18, 1798, it is said; "Since experience teaches sufficiently what mournful consequences for the general welfare, and especially for the safety of the States,[1] result from the tolerance of these unholy efforts to increase the inclination (already too prevalent to infidelity, and to banish the ideas[2] of God and religion from the hearts of man; therefore we cannot be indifferent in reference to our land, when teachers in neighbouring countries openly and fearlessly avow such dangerous principles." The government of Weimar was therefore called upon by its Saxon neighbour, "to punish the author of the essay, according to his desert, and in general to make such strict arrangements, that similar mischief may be checked powerfully in the University of Jena and also in the Gymnasia and other schools;" to which was added the threat, that if this was not acquiesced in, the Electorate of Saxony would forbid its children the privilege of visiting the University of Jena. Similar summonses, to prohibit the circulation of the accused writings, were sent to the other Protestant courts. Hanover complied with the request, whilst Prussia, which ten years previous had issued the strict religious edict,[3] refused to acquiesce. Yes, it was Prussia which kindled the first ray of hope in Fichte, that if he was driven from Saxony, he would find a retreat in its States. And this actually occurred. Fichte, however, having made an appeal to the public, anticipated a formal dismission, by handing in his resignation, which was accepted.

Encouraged by the Prussian minister Dohm, Fichte went

[1] Hinc illae lacrimae!

[2] What confusion in speaking of *ideas* which are to be banished from the *heart!* Ideas are only banished from the head, but therefore religion does not depend on ideas. *She* would first have to be banished from the *heart*, which no human philosophy can ever accomplish. The heart indeed may become corrupt, when the head is giddy or confused; but then the remedy does not consist in ideas, the renovation must commence with the depths of the heart, and this is only done by the Spirit of God.

[3] July 1788, by Fred. Will. II., against the errors of Socinians, Deists, Naturalists and others, which were spread under the name of "Enlightenment."—TR.

to Berlin, where he arrived on the first of July 1799; and when the king (Frederic William III.) was informed of the fact, he replied: "If Fichte is so quiet a citizen, so far from all dangerous alliances, as I understand him to be, I willingly grant him a retreat in my States. It is not the business of the State to give a decision in reference to his religious principles." According to Fichte's own letter to his wife, it seems as if the king had said: "If it is true that he is at enmity with God, then God may decide the matter with him, it is nothing to me;" a mode of expression which brings to memory Frederick the Great. Enough! Fichte, relying on the word of the king, spent the summer and autumn alone in Berlin, and then also brought his family thither from Jena. The letters which he wrote to his wife from Berlin, plainly bear the marks of mental disquietude, arising from inflicted injustice. The following expression is valuable to give us an idea of the state of his mind at that time: "*Since I have no humility,* I suppose I shall have to be *proud,* so as to have something to bring me through the world." The impression which Fichte's appeal to the public made on his friends was various. Whilst some placed him by the side of Luther, whose lot they thought he shared, and pointed to the legions who would assist him in the cause of enlightenment; others used the occasion to turn Fichte's thoughts to himself, and to remind him that his fate was not altogether uncalled for, but that it was rather the *philosophical* intolerance which had called forth the political as a counteraction. To these sincere and well-meaning friends Lavater belongs. In this matter, as in general, he despised the interference of rough physical force with the contests of the intellectual powers. "Where there is light (so he wrote to Fichte on the 12th of Sept. 1795), there is also opposition from without; where there is life, there the more lifeless revolts, by means of number and coalition. This we all experience! Every day I see more clearly that internal power excites external force against it, that positive force is eternally warring against its natural, real, inherent power. As the flesh opposes the spirit, so the world (the force of number) opposes those minds which disregard this force. Your condition and your philosophy, what a contrast! O, my dear friend! through what morasses and contrasts we must work our way." We have already seen how he turned off the charge of atheism, which was made against Fichte in a poem, by pointing to Fichte's personality. Now, however, after Fichte's appeal to the public had appeared, Lavater wrote him on the 7th of Feb. 1799, the following: "Your heart loves the truth, even if your understanding must look with a kind of pity down upon mine, which cannot touch the lowest part of yours.[1] My first feeling was that of compassion because you were attacked with such a dictatorial spirit, that no questions were first asked of you personally in reference to your opinions, and that the course of a worthy humanity was not taken. But, permit me to say it with the same openness, I was somewhat displeased to read so many sharp and trifling remarks against your opponents. Do you not think, my dear Sir, that it would have been better for your person and the cause of good, if you had treated them somewhat more gently and had done more justice to their intentions? . . *It is evidently the prevailing philosophy, by which the Church is oppressed.* In what does the prevailing philosophical Church distinguish itself from every common orthodox or hierarchical Church? Certainly not in tolerance and indulgence, certainly not in mildness and forbearance against its opponents, who scarcely dare open their mouths any more! What volumes of inhuman judgments, prostitutions, low insults, and cruelties might be gathered for publication! How often has this been represented to the critical philosophers, and what good has it done? And let me say it freely, your very appeal is very far from being free from this harshness and intolerance." And now Lavater declares with all frankness that his (Fichte's) God was not the God of Christianity, not the God whom humanity needs or is prepared for. . . . . "There is (he writes) among a million men scarcely one who can jump beyond himself so far as to think or even feel the least, at the contemplation of such a God as yours, and a God in the contemplation of whom we can neither think nor feel the least, is not only no God, but for those who thereby think and feel nothing, an absolute non-entity."

[1] Literally, which does not reach to the heels of your understanding.—Tr.

Fichte did not receive this letter of Lavater's very favourably. He thus expresses himself in reference to it to the philosopher Reinhold: "Lavater has also written me. Besides the common misapprehension of the true meaning of philosophy, he has also still a faith founded on authority, in Christ, Paul, etc., or to speak more properly in his *Zurich Interpretation of the Bible,* which makes it impossible for me to correct his ideas. I answered him briefly that he did not understand me, and promised him a more detailed answer which, on account of my disgust of the entire affair, I shall likely have to owe him forever."

This unfriendly position, which the so-called scientific stand-point assumed in reference to that of faith, continually became more hostile to Protestant Christianity, and we suffer from it to this day. It seems as if men did not want to understand each other, but desired to made the variance and chasm continually greater, instead of healing the difficulty; and yet it is remarkable in the case of Fichte, that after he had removed himself farthest from the common Christian feeling, he was led nearer and nearer it again. It was the very settlement in Berlin, too, which prepared a crisis for Fichte's inner life. The younger Fichte says of his father; "The deeper reflection of the spirit on itself, the proper completion and last maturity in his system and views of life begin with the epoch when he, free from all the pressing of prevailing and opposing opinions, unconcerned about the approbation or rejection of others, occupied himself only with self-cultivation. . . . . A *religious* manner of contemplating the world afterwards manifested itself in him, rendering him milder and solving many difficulties; and this manner of contemplation he embraced with no little confidence and power." Fichte himself, in the course of time, did not wish that the conflict had not occurred, for it had become the occasion to him of penetrating to the living fountain of inner invigoration. A conversion in its common acceptation, *i. e.,* a complete return to the orthodox doctrines of the Church, or a surrendering of his speculative stand-point, and a withdrawal to the purely devotional and practical can not be expected from a mind like Fichte's, much less a jumping from one extreme to the other or a sudden change of his language. Nor would much have been gained by this, either for Fichte or the cause of truth in general; for, however much danger for practical Christianity accompanied the increasing speculative tendency in Germany, still we will not deny that in it was manifested a freshness and quickness of spirit, which pointed to a revivification of the religious ideas, to an approaching spiritual regeneration of all religious thinking. "The thought of a living God," says the younger Fichte, "delivering man from the servitude of imperfection, and the will from the Tantalus labour of an endless struggling by means of the knowledge of the truth, that by Him the *good will, humility, and love* are taken for the deed, this simple thought, which had formerly been active in faith and experience, was far removed from the education of that age. For the recovery of this thought, the sanction of science and high mental improvement was necessary, both of which had torn themselves from faith. It is thus a remarkable fact that the very idealism of Fichte, which led him to the abyss of atheism, had to serve the purpose of leading to the deeper fundamental ideas of Christianity, to the idea of an entire yielding of the soul to God and of the blessing which lies in the communion with God in this life already, in opposition to the dry intellectual view of God, and of opposing to the one-sided *moral* stand-point, which had been adopted since Kant—one truly *religious*, in the deeper sense of the word.

After Fichte had again called attention to the deep importance of faith, in the book "Die Bestimmung des Menschen," which was published in Berlin at the close of the last century; after he had pointed out the importance of Christianity, "as the only true religion" in history, and the great importance of the Christian state in the "Grundzüge des gegenwärtigen Zeitalters," he attempted, especially in his "Anweisungen zum seligen Leben oder Religionslehre," a course of popular lectures, delivered in Berlin, 1806, to prove the agreement of his philosophy of that time with the principles of Christianity, which he regarded in a light entirely different from Kant. Kant and the Rationalists placed the essence of Christianity chiefly in morality and the fulfilment of the moral law, and, in accordance with this, esteemed and used with a special predilection those passages of Scripture, in which the various moral precepts are drawn in distinct outlines, as for instance, the Sermon on the Mount, and several Parables of Jesus in the first three Gospels (whilst they had no taste for John, who appeared to them a mystic); Fichte, on the other hand, threw himself on the Fourth Gospel, and regarded it as the only true source of the genuine doctrine of Christ; he of course did this in a one-sided manner, and with a denial of the other truths of Scripture, which belong fully as much to the totality of Christian doctrine and history as the Gospel of John.

"Only with John," says Fichte, "can the philosopher agree, for he alone has regard for reason, and appeals to the proof, which the philosopher recognises—the *inner* proof. 'If any man will do the will of Him that sent me, he shall know of the doctrine, whether it be of God.' . . . . The other announcers of Christianity build upon the external demonstration through miracles which, to us at least, proves nothing. Besides this, of all the Gospels, John contains what we seek and need, religious doctrines, whilst the best that the others give, is, without making up the deficiencies and interpreting by John, nothing more than *morality, which has a very subordinate value with us.*" With these last words, Fichte renounced most decidedly Kant and the Kantian Rationalism, and turned towards Mysticism, which values the inner abiding relation to God infinitely more than the accidental and transient manifestation of the disposition in the external relations of life. Whilst, however, he again brought the Gospel of John to honour, he could, as little as the Rationalists, or perhaps still less, agree with the Christianity of Paul; he denotes it in the most incomprehensible manner a *degeneration* of all Christianity, and why? Because Fichte, with all his approach towards that which is Christian, ignored entirely the nature of sin and the contrast between sin and redemption, which Paul holds up so prominently, and expected salvation only from a direct union with God, a union boldly jumping over the contrast by an ideal leap. "Christianity (he says, in contradiction to Paul) is not a means of reconciliation or of expiation; man can never separate himself from God, and in so far as he *imagines* himself separated from Him, he is a nothing, and therefore cannot sin, but around his brow the oppressive illusion of sin only places itself, to lead him to the true God." Here of course he might have learned from John, if he did not want to hear Paul: "If we say that we have no sin, we deceive ourselves, and the truth is not in us." (1 John i. 8.)

The immediateness of the relation between Christ and the Father, as it is especially represented in the Gospel of John, was taken by him as the expression of the relation that should exist between God and man generally. And this was right. He, however, took that which *ought* to be, and to which man can only come by purification after much struggle, and through connection with the Redeemer (for it has not yet appeared what we shall be) as already present, and in this again shows himself an Idealist, *i. e.*, unpractical and unhistorical. Nevertheless, it may produce a peculiar interest to follow a thinker like Fichte, in a time which had turned away to a great degree from the fundamental truths of Christianity, and to see how he arrayed Christianity so as to suit himself; how he again returned with his language to the Christian mode of expression; how he, without being compelled by any despotic command from without, through which he would never have suffered himself to be forced, was constrained to give the honour to eternal truth; and although much of that which Fichte proclaimed as Christianity was still controlled by the ideas, and expressed in the language of the school, we shall nevertheless feel a milder air blowing around us, than that which blew against us so sharp and cutting from the Wissenschaftslehre. The only real entity (Sein), these are the principal thoughts in his Religionslehre, is the Absolute or God. This absolute entity (Sein), however, is not only, does not remain hid in itself; it has also an *existence* (Dasein), that is, a revelation, a manifestation of itself. God reveals Himself in us, in our consciousness, and it is only the multifarious, much divided world, which draws us from God; we ought, however, to compress the eternal One (das ewige Eine) into a great focus of our spiritual life. This we can do religiously by faith, scientifically through the idea. Our finite Ego must take up in itself the absolute Ego by faith and by thought, and in this intimate union consist salvation and eternal life. Fichte expresses himself in a simple and comprehensible manner, in reference to this matter, thus: "Do you want to see God face to face, as He is in Himself? Do not seek Him beyond the clouds; thou canst find Him, wherever thou art. View the life of those who are devoted to Him, and thou beholdest Him; yield thyself to Him, and thou findest Him in thy breast."

If we remarked before, that Fichte regarded morality as something subordinate, he meant that morality, which estimates the value of actions more according to their external signification, their use in the world, &c. He very properly opposed this morality of expediency and the Pharisaism of work-holiness, and showed, from the true Protestant standpoint, how all depends on the *inner* disposition with which we act and on the *faith* whence these works proceed. In this respect he was not so far from St. Paul, as he generally appears to separate from him. "Religion," he says,[1] "is not mere devotional dreaming, it is not a business which can be followed on certain days or at certain hours, independent of other business; but it is the inner Spirit which penetrates all our . . . . thought and action, and immerses them in itself. . . . . It does not depend on the sphere, in which one acts. . . . To him who has only a humble vocation, this humble vocation itself is sanctified by religion, and through it receives, if not the material, still the form of the higher morality, for which nothing more is necessary, than that we recognise and love the will of God on and in us. He who tills the ground in this faith or performs the most unpretending manual labour with fidelity, is higher and happier than he who, without this faith (if this were possible), would bless humanity for a thousand years." Luther had said something quite similar, that the servant who sweeps the house, can do it in faith; consequently in a manner pleasing to God. This is the morality of subjectiveness, as Christianity (in direct opposition to ancient heathenism) and as especially Protestantism requires it, and here we find Fichte on the right foundation. Let us add to this a few more of his expressions, which agree perfectly with

[1] His expressions, too, in reference to the free will, in his addresses to the German nation, are entirely Pauline.

the very essence of the Gospel: "Love is higher than all reason, is itself the source of reason and the root of reality, the only creatress of life and of time; . . . . she is, as in general, the source of truth and certainty, so also the source of *perfected* truth in the true man and in his life." "The living life is love, and, as love, it owns and possesses what is beloved, is embraced and penetrated by it, blended and mingled with it, and is eternally one and the same love. . . . . In so far as man is love, and this he is in the root of his life always, he remains ever and eternally the one, the true, the eternal, just as God himself, ... and it is not a bold metaphor, but literal truth, what John says: 'He that dwelleth (remains) in love dwelleth (remains) in God, and God in him.'" "Salvation itself consists in love, and the eternal peace produced by love, and is unaccessible to reflection; conception can only express it negatively (can only say what it is not). It cannot be described positively, but can only be felt immediately. Doubt makes us miserable, drives us hither and thither, and spreads out before us an impenetrable night, in which our feet can find no safe path. The religious man is eternally freed from the possibility of doubt and uncertainty. He knows definitely every moment, what he *wills* and *ought* to will. Since for him the inmost root of his life, his will, comes undeniably always from Divinity, whose nod is infallible, and for that which the nod indicates he has an unerring eye, he knows certainly every moment what he shall know through all eternity, what he wills and ought to will, that through all eternity the fountain of divine love, which has been opened in him, will not become dry, but will preserve him and lead him eternally. This fountain is the root of his existence; he has beheld it clearly and his eye is fixed on it with deep love; how could the former ever dry up, how the latter ever turn in another direction? Nothing occurring around him surprises him. Whether he comprehends it or not, of one thing he is certain, that it is in God's world, and that in this there can be nothing which does not tend to good. He has no fear in reference to the future, for the absolutely Blessed is ever leading him towards it."

If now we ask, how did Fichte consider all this as brought about by Christianity, we shall find that the person of Jesus had with him a signification entirely different from that of the Rationalists. He does not behold in Him the teacher of morality, nor simply the moral example. No, exactly that oneness with God, as Christ expresses it in the Gospel of John, exactly that *real unity with the Father*, which the Rationalists desired to remove as a metaphysical formula of no use to morality, was to him the heart and the star of the Gospel. On this account he held himself so closely to John and his doctrine of the Logos having become flesh, in which he beheld the fulness of all religious knowledge. We would, however, make a great mistake, if from this we concluded that Fichte agreed with the old orthodox doctrine in reference to Christ. What this doctrine regarded as an historical fact, which had occurred once, that Fichte regarded as a fact eternally repeating itself, as occurring in every religious man. Christ was not the *Saviour* to him in the old sense; He was only the representative of that which is continually occurring still. "The eternal Word becomes flesh at all times, in every one, without exception, who understands, in a living manner, his oneness with God, and who really yields his entire individual life to the divine life in him, . . quite in the same manner as in Christ Jesus." It is true Fichte acknowledges that the insight into this absolute unity of human existence with the divine did not occur *before* Jesus; but this is a matter of indifference to him, a mere *historical* observation on which but little depends. "Is any one united with God," he says, "then it is all the same in what way he became so; and it were a very useless and wrong occupation continually to repeat the remembrance of the way instead of living in the matter." We think, however, that it is of great value to know this way, and Fichte himself acknowledges that all those, who, since the time of Jesus, have come to a union with God, have only done so through and by means of him; yes, "till the end of time (this is Fichte's honest and open confession) all the sensible will bow low before this Jesus of Nazareth, and all will humbly acknowledge the exceeding glory of this great 'phenomenon.'" He, however, thinks that Christ Himself does not lay the same stress in this recognition as the Church. He thought, like Herder, that in case Jesus (as human individual), would return to the world, He would be perfectly satisfied if He only found Christianity prevailing in the souls of men, whether His merits were praised in connection with this or were disregarded; "for this is in fact the least," he says, "that could be expected of such a man who already when He lived on earth sought not His own honour, but the honour of Him that sent Him." Fichte is quite right in saying that Christ did not seek this honour for His own sake; and we, too, believe that a *living* Christianity, even with many dogmatical errors in reference to the person of Jesus, yes, even with a partial denial of this personality, is better than that orthodox repetition of "Lord! Lord!" without the proper spirit and proper disposition. But Christ and Christianity, person and matter, the historical and metaphysical, can not be separated[1] as arbitrarily, as Fichte seems to suppose; hence love, which Fichte himself has so beautifully and enthusiastically given the pre-eminence as the essence of all religion, the more it obtains the predominance over the prejudices of the understanding, will involuntarily turn again to the person from whom it proceeds, and because it is *personal* love, love to *Christ*, it will become deeper and more fruitful.

At all events, Fichte has the merit of having directed the attention to the soul of religion, and of having freed it from the servitude of mere morality. Although so many, and even orthodox Christians, had conceived eternal life only as future, as in another world, and though Kant had founded the faith in God and immortality chiefly on the necessity of a retribution in another world, Fichte placed eternal life (quite in accordance with Scripture) in this, that we know God *here*, love Him, and feel ourselves united to Him in blessed communion; and this living in God was to Him, even in the earlier period of his life, before speculation had grown too strong for him, the sure guarantee for the future, just as it again became the same in his later years. Already in 1790 he had written from Leipzig to Miss Rahn: "Our understanding is too small to be a dwelling for Divinity, for this our heart only is a worthy house. The safest means of assuring ourselves of a life after death, is this—to lead such a life here that we can desire a future one. Whoever feels that, if there

[1] This arbitrary separation still belongs entirely to the stand-point of the Kantian Rationalism.

is a God, He must look down upon him graciously, is not moved by any arguments against His existence, and needs none for it. He who has sacrificed so much for virtue, that he can expect amends in a future life,[1] does not prove and believe the existence of such a life; he *feels* it. United, my dear helpmate, for this span of life and for eternity, we will strengthen this conviction, not by proofs, but by actions." Thus, too, he despises, in his "Anweisungen zum seligen Leben," the prospect of a refined, sensible prosperity in another life; because it rests on egoism, on personal self-love. The love of God, however, is to exterminate self-love; it is alone to fill the heart, and where it fills the heart it is already in this world the source of salvation. It does not depend upon the circumstances in which we live, here or there; God, who is to-day what he will be in all eternity, wants to make us happy through Himself, and thus there is no eternal life without Him, either in or beyond this world, except in Him. Fichte, as well as Schleiermacher after him, showed that there may be such a thing as an immoral and irreligious faith in immortality, such a one, as seeks only itself in the other world, not God. "This mode of thinking, expressed in the form of a prayer," says Fichte, "would run thus: 'Lord, my will only be done, and that, indeed, during all, and on that account blessed eternity, and for this Thou shalt have Thy will in this short and miserable temporal life;' whilst the truly pious pray thus: 'Lord, Thy will only be done, and by this means mine is done, for I have no other will than this, that Thy will be done.'" We shall afterwards see how this disposition could degenerate to a resignation of pride, which is very different from Christian submission, and how the sentence, true in itself, that eternal life is to commence here, was perverted into this, that it is *only* to be had here. It was very important that in opposition to the torpidity of the moral religious disposition, into which a great part of the cotemporaries had sunk, the attention was directed to the great importance of this life especially when so powerful a personality as Fichte's assisted in making the impression deep. And now we will turn our attention again for a moment to this personality.

[1] Here, of course, the Kantian philosophy made its appearance, but modified by adopting immediate feeling.

With all the ruggedness and angularity, which we encounter in Fichte's conduct, his high nobility of mind cannot be denied. Fichte's character proves itself Protestant,[1] reformatory, not only in the sphere of thought, but especially in that of life and morality. Just as he knew how to check the rudeness of student life, and was anxious to prevent duels by instituting courts of honour, so too, in times of political distress, he was one of the first who attempted to raise the sunken national feeling again, and "to inspire the disconsolate with courage and hope." He aimed at this in his fine "addresses to the German nation," which he delivered in the University of Berlin in the winter of 1808-1809, whilst his voice was often drowned by French drums passing through the streets, and when well-known spies were present in the lecture-room. Several times even the report was spread through the city that he had been seized and led away by the enemy. It is not the place here to enter more closely into an examination of the contents of these speeches, or to follow the active part which Fichte in his last days took in the German war for freedom. We will only refer to it so as to render the picture of the man complete.

Fichte expected the greatest blessings from a better education, one which not merely brings the command to be virtuous from without, but strengthens the will by love. "The rosy morn of the new world," he exclaims among other things, "has already appeared and gilds the mountain tops, and prefigures the day that is to come." Fichte did not live to see the longed-for day of freedom. In the newly-founded University of Berlin, he could act but a short time longer as teacher. In the spring of 1808, as he was about to commence his philosophical lectures, he was attacked with a dangerous sickness, from which he, however, recovered. Afterwards there were many interruptions by the preparations for war; in the meantime he had begun his lectures in the winter of 1813, when in 1814 his wife was attacked with a

[1] His philosophy was called by Fr. Schlegel, Protestantism carried to its farthest results. And that Fichte himself believed in a further progress of Protestantism, in which progress he felt himself a powerful agent, see "Grundzüge des gegenwärtigen Zeitalters," p. 412: "The Drama of the Church-reformation is by no means finished."

contagious disease. She had incurred the disease through the Christian faithfulness with which this excellent woman, principally urged to it by her husband, tended the sick soldiers in the lazaretto. With the greatest sacrifice and care Fichte now devoted himself to tend and nurse her. One evening he had already bid the unconscious sick wife farewell in order to lecture at the university, had lectured two hours in succession on the most abstract subjects with the greatest self-control, and had returned home with the thought that perhaps he would find her dead, just as a favourable crisis appeared and the physicians began to hope for the first time. The wife was saved, but it cost the life of the husband. The next day Fichte felt quite unwell, and soon the true nature of the disease became evident. He still received the account of Blücher's crossing the Rhine, and the rapid advance of the allies into France. This inspired his spirit once more with bold hopes, and the joy occasioned by the news so mingled with his feverish fancies, that he imagined himself taking part in the battle—his whole life, what had it been but a warfare, with the sword of the mind in his hand? When shortly before his death his son approached him with medicine, he gave him the significant answer, "Never mind that, I need no more medicine, I feel that I have recovered." In the night of Jan. 27th, 1814, Fichte died, not quite fifty-two years old, but in unimpaired strength of body and mind. His wife survived him five years, and was buried, as she had requested, at the feet of her husband in the cemetery before the Oranienburger Gate, Berlin. A high obelisk marks the place, with an inscription from Daniel xii. 3: "The teachers shall shine as the brightness of the firmament, and they that turn many to righteousness as the stars for ever and ever." How far these words of the prophet are applicable to Fichte as a philosophical teacher, of course depends on the judgment formed of the moral and religious contents of his system. This had, as we have seen, several grades; first, it only appeared as a consistent continuation of Kant; then it manifested itself as perfected Idealism, dismal and ghostly, and rendered more gloomy by the suspicion of atheism; finally, however, the setting star turned itself with greater brilliance towards Christianity, and although not in the form of a full, unreserved evangelical confession, as had been the case with some other Christian philosophers, still in a mode of philosophical thinking belonging to the Christian sphere. And this Christian knowledge might become to some the means of passing over to a simpler faith, to that righteousness of which the prophet in the above passage refers. If, however, as we have already observed, Fichte is to be estimated, not merely as a philosophical author and as a man of the school, but also as a man of common life, then this cheering trait may yet be mentioned from his life in the home-circle, that in the house of the distinguished philosopher each day, without exception, was closed with proper and solemn evening devotions, in which the domestics were also accustomed to take a part. After several verses had been sung from a choral-book, accompanied with the clavichord, the father of the family would make some remarks on some passage of the New Testament, most frequently on his favourite gospel of John. In these discourses he was less concerned about moral applications and rules of life than about freeing the mind from the distraction and vanity of the common affairs of life, and elevating the spirit to the eternal. That this produced beneficial effects on the members of the family and also on those less closely related the son of Fichte testifies to from his own experience; to whom we are also indebted for most of the knowledge of the life of his father.

XXI.

RICHTER, GOETHE, AND NOVALIS.

TENDENCIES ON POLITE LITERATURE CORRESPONDING TO THOSE OF SCHELLING AND JACOBI—JEAN PAUL RICHTER—GOETHE'S CONNECTION WITH SCHELLING'S SYSTEM—COMPARISON BETWEEN SCHILLER AND GOETHE IN REFERENCE TO THEIR RELATION TO CHRISTIANITY—GOETHE'S INFLUENCE—HIS POSITION IN REFERENCE TO PROTESTANTISM—NOVALIS.

As the Kantian philosophy found its poetical expression in Schiller, we find that the philosophy of Schelling has its representatives in modern literature, and these are the more numerous, because this philosophy is in its nature half poetry, and rises on the wings of fancy above the sphere of the common understanding. The Kantian philosophy was thoroughly prosaic, and Schiller's poetry had only planted itself by its side as its external complement. From the very beginning it entered into the most intimate relation with poetry. It awakened the slumbering poetical sympathy in many youthful hearts; it became the source of a new school of poets, who drew from it their power and nourishment. That poetical view of the world, which must lie at the basis of all action, if a true work of art is to be produced, was introduced by this philosophy; by it art has been entirely freed from the stiff rules to which the imitation of foreign productions had subjected it, and Goethe stands before us most prominently as the master of a new school of poetry.

Before, however, we follow the connection of Schelling's philosophy with Goethe on the one hand, and with the novelists on the other, we must ask the question, whether the philosophy of Jacobi, which we have found to be the antipode of Schelling's, has no poetical side. We can answer this question in the affirmative.

Jean Paul Richter was not only personally acquainted with the philosopher Jacobi and with Herder, but also publicly professed to accept the Christianity represented by these men, which, in distinction from all mystic obscurity and puritanic severity, he called a cheerful Christianity. In the "Greenland Processes" he gives the common orthodoxy a strong dose of satire. But he advocated an enlightenment better than that commonly advocated, he wanted a pious enlightenment and an enlightened piety, and both of these he finds in Jacobi. He agrees with his positive as well as negative principles, with what he affirms as well as with what he denies. With Jacobi he clings to the faith in a personal God and immortality, and expressed his hopes in the latter in a peculiar manner in his "Campanerthal;" but with him he also rejects what he calls the "narrowness of theological views and expectations," which attempt to confine the inner life within a Jewish-Christian system of doctrine. Jean Paul also wants a revelation, but not one historically finished, closed for ever, but a continued revelation of God to our hearts. He, as well as Jacobi, always speaks with the deepest reverence of Christ, "the purest of the mighty, the mightiest of the pure, who, with His pierced hands, lifted a world;" but he can as little adopt the Church view of Christ as the philosopher of Pempelfort. He, too, would rather raise himself to God with Christ than to come to Him through Christ. The orthodox doctrine of redemption is repulsive to him, but Herder's notion of the Son of Man, in which the purely human is represented in its highest transformation, has the most attraction for him.

Jean Paul never scoffed at religion in his writings, his feelings shrunk back from such low service; but he has occasionally given a humorous turn to religious definitions, in order to bring prominently before the mind the fact that in religion all definitions are incomplete. His faith, as he himself says, does not rest on separate proofs, as if on feet, which have but to be broken to overthrow it; but it is rooted with a thousand invisible fibres in the deep soil of feeling. Therefore, he thinks, a man "may be refuted till brought to silence, without convincing him; feeling survives judgment, just as pain survives the grounds of comfort."

Whilst he regarded orthodox dogmatics irreconcilable with modern learning, he on the other hand lamented, like Jacobi, the decay of religion, saw in it indications of sad omens for the future, and discerned no other means of avoiding them than by thorough cultivation. He does not think that the civil or ecclesiastical power, the state or the church, are called to reinstate religion again, but that this is the task of science and poetry. "The Muses only can become the persuaders of the great," and he regards the writings of the ancients "an eternal Bible." Jean Paul never penetrated to the heart of Christianity, without which no one can comprehend it fully; but he appropriated its blessings with his feelings, and gave man's inner life a truer place than many others. If Christianity had not existed his poetry would have been as impossible as the philosophy of Jacobi.

Though we have already hinted that Goethe sustained a similar relation to Schelling that Schiller did to Kant, Goethe was by no means dependent on Schelling's system, as Schiller was, for a time, on that of Kant. Goethe was too great, too independent, too original, ever to have become the mere echo of a system. He seemed at first inclined to agree with the philosophy of Jacobi; and the latter hoped to form a permanent friendship with him, but these friendly relations were severed. Jacobi dedicated his "Woldemar" to Goethe, with the deepest and warmest assurances of friendship, while the latter had already grown cold; and the most essential characteristic of Jacobi, the contemplation of his mind and heart, was offensive to Goethe. It appeared to him that it was a kind of sickness to attempt to watch the operations of one's own mind; he praised his own wisdom in not having reflected on his thoughts; to think for the sake of thinking appeared to him a waste of mind, a result of *ennui* and dull company. He disliked all that was not connected with the green tree of life, and he frequently acknowledged with pleasure that he had no special adaptation for philosophy. "I have always kept myself free from philosophy; my standpoint was always that of common sense. While he earnestly admonished persons to attain a knowledge of man, he nevertheless warned them against knowledge of self. He thought the sentence "know thyself" contained a contradiction in itself: he that looks into his heart, he thought, "is in as bad a condition as he who watches his own brain." He had, however, not only an aversion to philosophy founded on a knowledge of self, as advocated by Jacobi; but also to that which makes the world the object of its contemplation instead of self. "He detested all who made a world from their own errors, and wilfully vexed themselves with speculation. But though Goethe from his good taste sought to avoid the quaint, unnatural form which reminded one of the old scholasticism, still his view of life was most intimately connected with that manifested in Schelling's system. He himself acknowledges that he belongs to the school of "identity," and was born to it. He too looked upon life in its various forms as one, mind and sense, God and nature, the internal and the external, form and substance were one and the same to him. His studies of nature and his moral view of the world, were governed by this idea.

"Was waer ein Gott, der nur von aussen stiesse,
Im Kreis das All am Finger laufen liesse,

Ihm ziemt's die Welt im Innern zu bewegen,
Natur in sich, sich in Natur zu hegen,
So dass was in ihm lebt und weht und ist,
Nie seine Kraft, nie seinen Geist vermisst.[1]

He considers the moral world as an active play of the most diverse powers, that all struggle with sin is but necessary development. Schiller seeks to attain an exalted ideal of virtue, when he designates only that "which never happened anywhere," as able to satisfy the human mind for ever, when he longs for other circumstances than those which surround him, sometimes wishing himself back in the world of the Greeks, sometimes forward to a better period in the future. Goethe feels very well satisfied with the present, the agreeable of which he can speak and write so pleasantly, is natural to him; he is disturbed by nothing, neither by political nor religious life, nor the contest of different schools, he is raised above all contests, enjoying the calm peace of the gods; hence that much praised objectivity, that clearness and finish, that inner harmony and external completeness of his works, which all bear the stamp of the highest naturalness, not an imitated, affected naturalness, but one new-created, a nature born from the spirit; so that if worship of genius were admissible, one might be tempted to worship in Goethe the creative principle personified. The present world finds an advocate in Goethe. "We will not console each other with the hope of eternal life," he wrote to the Countess Juliana von Stolberg in 1775, "we must be happy yet in this life!"[2]

While previous ages since the reformation had placed the consciousness of God and the view of another world above all other considerations, and had connected all that was undertaken in this world with heaven; while this predominance of divine contemplation was carried to that extent, that this world was regarded as a vale of tears, and more taste was manifested for abstract controversies than for that which

[1] What were a God who would only impel from without, who would let the universe revolve at the end of His finger; it becomes Him to move the world from within, to cherish nature in Himself, Himself in nature, so that whatever lives and moves and has its being in Him, may never fail to have His power and spirit.

[2] The very opposite is however expressed in various places.

could make a worthy existence on earth possible ; the modern times are distinguished for a mode of contemplation, the very opposite of this in which the consciousness of the world is the prevailing one, and all the energies are exerted to make this life so beautiful and comfortable that even heaven is forgotten. And we know of no poet who expresses this disposition more fully than Goethe. Full of this worldly feeling he sings:

> " Wirklich ist es allerliebst
> Auf der lieben Erde,
> Darum schwer' ich feierlich
> Und ohn' alle Faehrde,
> Dass ich mich nicht freventlich
> Wegbegeben werde."[1]

This and similar carelessly written poems of Goethe would be misunderstood if regarded as the pure expression of gross and common worldliness, bent only on sensuality. Every one who knows what pleasantry is, will discover the meaning hidden in such verses. They express the triumph of genius over all gloom and difficulty, the easy and free elevation of an unfettered mind above the oppression and narrow limits of the external world, and with all their apparent triviality, they contain something highly poetical. Goethe's poetical talent is manifested especially in this, that he can find the whole and the general in the particular and the individual, the most important in that which is apparently most insignificant, and can change all that he touches with his magic wand, into a poetical being. There is more true poetry in perceiving in the motion of a wave, in the flight of a bird, an emblem of the eternal, a wonderful reference of natural life to our intellectual, than if Jacob's ladder must first be raised, to climb from star to star, to obtain a divine idea. In this respect Schiller differs from Goethe. The former strives, panting and breathless, to pursue the heavenly goddess, who eternally evades him, while the latter moves naturally, and every breath is a complete poem. But with all its high poetical worth, Goethe's view of the world has something delusive in it, if one attempts to make it the basis of morals

[1] It is really most lovely on this lovely earth, hence I swear solemnly and with out any deception, that I shall not wantonly depart from it.

and religion, if one seeks the real abiding reconciliation of heaven and earth in the "worldly gospel of poetry," and hopes with Goethe "that inner serenity and external comfort will free us from the troubles of this world." This view of the world may have something very comforting to cheerful natures, such as Goethe's was, but the unhappy, as well as those who feel keenly the unhappiness and misery of others, cannot be satisfied by it. The divine marble image of poetry may give us infinite delight while viewing it from an artistic stand-point, but how its insupportable coldness repels us when we attempt to embrace it, thinking that a sympathizing heart beats in its bosom!

No one can confirm us better in this opinion than Goethe himself, when he sings:—

Ein Gott hat
Jedem seine Bahn
Vorgezeichnet,
Die der Glueckliche
Rasch zum freudigen.
Ziele rennt;

Wem aber Unglueck
Das Herz zusammenzog,
Er straeubt vergebens
Sich gegen die Schranken
Des ehernen Fadens,
Den die doch bittere Scheere
Nur einmal loest.

Leicht ist's folgen den Wagen,
Den Fortuna fuehrt,
Wie der gemaechliche Trost
Auf gebesserten Wegen
Hinter des Fuersten Einzug.

Aber wer heilet die Schmerzen
Dess, dem Balsam zu Gift-ward?
Der sich Menschenhass
Aus der Fuelle der Liebe trank?
Erst *verachtet*, nun ein *veraechter*,
Zehrt er heimleich auf
Seinen eignen Werth
In ungenuegender Selbstsucht.[1]

[1] A God has marked out a course for every one, over which the fortunate man speedily runs to a joyful goal; but he, whose heart has been oppressed by mis-

We must leave it to others to draw a more extended parallel between Schiller and Goethe from a political point of view.[1] But a comparison between the two heroes of German literature, so far as their relation to Christianity is concerned, is necessary. In this matter the opinions are very different. While there are some who reject both poets as unchristian without any further investigation, it is remarkable that Goethe has generally found more favour than Schiller in the eyes of those whose views of Christianity are strict, while the reverse has seldom been the case. It depends on what is made the measure of the Christian in man, whether knowledge, the will, or the disposition. Goethe undoubtedly stands higher than Schiller in Christian knowledge, as he in general displays a mind of more enlarged views and less enveloped in the prejudices of a system. He could, for instance, judge the Scriptural history and Christian dogmas far more impartially than Schiller who was often passionately excited. How could it be otherwise than that the man in whose hands all received a living form, should also have received the phenomenon of Christianity of world-wide importance into this forming process, and should have worked it into his great picture of the world? What a richness of Christian views we find in "Faust!" what a taste for the finest shadings of Christian life in the "Confessions of a beautiful soul." Even the Moravian view of Christianity, he considers proper in its place, as his intercourse with the ingenious Miss von Klettenberg proves. What sound just judgments of the high value of the Bible and its educational importance we find in his Autobiography, and to some extent also in the notes to his Chromatics, and above all in his conversations with Eckermann! To give but one example, can anything stronger be

fortune, struggles in vain against the limits of the brazen thread, which the bitter scissors cut but once.

It is easy to follow the waggon driven by Fortuna, just as pleasure and comfort easily follow, on improved roads, the entrance of the prince.

But who heals the wounds of him to whom balsam became poison? who drank misanthrophy from the fulness of love? First *despised* now a *despiser*, he secretly feeds on his own dignity in unsatisfying selfishness.

[1] It is well known that they were at first repelled by each other, while afterwards they were bound together by the warmest friendship. Goethe appears noble in his relation to Schiller. Schiller had to be handled by him as an egg without a shell.

said to the despisers of the Bible, than that which is said by Goethe :—"The farther the ages advance in cultivation, the more can the Bible be used, partly as the foundation, partly as the means of education, not of course by superficial, but by really wise men." There are also other similar expressions. One thing is certain, that modern Christian apologists could draw many more proofs from Goethe's writings than from Schiller's, through which heresy appears almost everywhere.

In the practical sphere Goethe showed himself practical, too, whenever an insight into existing relations came under consideration; while Schiller was not at all practical. While Schiller, for instance, dreamed of improving the world by means of the theatre, and recommended the stage as a moral institution, a second church, as it were; so that many ministers of Schiller's age, following these hints, actually introduced poetical phrases and theatrical declamation from the stage into the pulpit; Goethe censured this mischief in a most masterly manner in his Faust. As Wagner says to Faust,[1] "I have often heard say, a player might instruct a priest." Faust replies, "Yes, when the priest is a player, as may likely enough come to pass occasionally;" and then continues, "If you do not feel it, you will not get it by hunting for it,—if it does not come from the soul, and subdue the hearts of all hearers with original delight, sit at it for ever—glue together, cook up a hash from the feast of others, and blow the paltry flames out of your own little heap of ashes. You may gain the admiration of children and apes, if you have a taste for it; but you will never touch the hearts of others if it does not flow fresh from your own."

Wagner then says, "But it is elocution that makes the orator's success. I feel well that I am still behind hand."

Faust replies, "Try what can be got by honest means. Be no tinkling fool! Reason and good sense express themselves with little art. And when you are seriously intent on saying something, is it necessary to hunt for words? Your speeches, I say, which are so highly polished, in which ye crisp the shreds of humanity, are unrefreshing as the mist-wind which whistles through the withered leaves of autumn."

In these few words Goethe has compressed more wisdom

[1] Hayward's Translation.

than can be found in many detailed theories of pulpit eloquence. In a like manner he displays his tact in things referring to divine worship. He felt that of all his numerous poems not one was fit to stand in a Lutheran hymn-book. All mingling of the sacred and profane was averse to his good taste. "Music," he says in W. Meister's "Wanderjahren," which mixes the sacred and profane character, "is wicked, and that which expresses weak, pitiful, miserable emotions is insipid; for it is not solemn enough to be sacred, and it lacks the chief characteristic of the opposite cheerfulness." How tender and beautiful in harmony with the Christian view of life is the remark in the "Wahlverwandschaften," that the celebration of a wedding should always be solemn, and that therefore stillness is much more appropriate for such an occasion than noisy ostentation.[1] We therefore repeat it, that as far as an insight into Christian matters is concerned, we everywhere find mental views in Goethe, such as we look for in vain in so definite a form in Schiller. But if insight is not the only measure of the Christian character, but rather the agreement and inclination of the heart, we could almost believe—without doing Goethe any injustice—that Schiller at times experienced deeper Christian emotions than Goethe. You remember those morning reflections of Schiller, that wrestling for truth, for certainty in religious matters. We do not find such struggles in Goethe's life. It is true he also doubted, when a boy, many things in the Bible, and desired an explanation of them from his religious instructor; but, as he himself says, he was more intent on advancing his doubts than on their solution, and the religious instructor knew no other way to relieve himself of the difficulty of answering the proposed questions than by exclaiming repeatedly, while shaking with laughter: "The foolish fellow! the foolish boy!" Later in his youth, he experienced many inner commotions, and it cost him a powerful struggle, before he could place himself in that quiet, ruling relation to the world, which he enjoyed in after life; but the struggle was not of a religious character, it was that of genius violently pressing onward against the established relations of the natural

[1] Schiller, on the other hand, speaks in a very frivolous manner of his own wedding; he calls it "a very merry scene."

and moral world, which may be compared to the Titan-storm, gaining heaven by its own divine power. But after the "nocturnal storm," Goethe soon reached the shore again.

Neither Schiller's nor Goethe's life is free from immoralities; but Goethe did not mind this so much, and Schiller's moral struggles were undoubtedly more earnest than those of Goethe. Goethe did not want to be a saint, nor a wicked ungodly man. According to his own words, he did not regard piety as the object of life, but rather as a means for attaining the highest cultivation through the purest peace of mind. It was Goethe's first principle to be temperate in all things, in art as well as in morality and religion. Thus the position may be explained which he took against boundless enlightenment, "Aufklaerung," as well as against what appeared to him to be boundless piety, religious extravagance. It is significant, that in his youth Goethe was the friend of Stelling and Lavater, and advocated their cause against the "Aufklaerer." No one has derided the insipidity of the so-called "Aufklaerer" more than Goethe. But it was rather the dullness of these men that Goethe attacked than their ungodliness, and he did not like to enter into a deep discussion of religious subjects. In the company of his pious friends he was always sprightly and full of life, and when Lavater and Basedow had quarrelled, till quite weary, about theological matters, Goethe would sing in his own peculiar manner,—

> "Prophets right, and prophets left,
> The worldling in the middle."

Nothing could better indicate the position he occupied among the theological disputants than these lines. We must not, therefore, be surprised that the same Goethe who attacked the "Aufklaerer" also opposed Lavater's Christianity; for in the course of time the difference between him and Lavater in reference to religion, and the impossibility of uniting their different standpoints, became more and more evident. "There are many recipes at my father's apothecary," Goethe writes to Lavater in 1782, "my plaster will not stick to you, nor your's to me;" and three years previous to this he had proposed to his friend that "they would no longer torment each other about their individual religions." In the same letter he professes to believe in the truth of the five senses, and in another place pities Lavater on account of his eternal struggling and wrestling. "I have pitied your thirst for Christ," he says, "you are in a worse condition than we heathen are, for in times of trouble our gods appear to us."

In another letter he says openly that he is not indeed an infidel, nor an antichristian, but that he is certainly not a Christian, and thus he has denoted his position in reference to Christianity better than we can.[1] He regarded the fanatical attacks of Voltaire foolish, because his insight into history was deeper than that of Voltaire, as well as for other reasons; but he regarded that view contracted which confined itself exclusively to Christianity, and expected to find all in it. He had no objection to the Christian character in others who appeared adapted to it, even regarded it with interest, so long as it was merely an object of contemplation to him, just as a portrait painter studies the original which he desires to represent on canvass; but he desired to occupy only the position of an observer. Already, when he wrote Werther, he put the following words in his mouth: "I honour religion. I feel that it is refreshment to many weary and hungry souls. But can it, must it be this to all? When you look on the world, you find that there are thousands to whom it was not all, and thousands to whom it will not be . . . . and must it be this then to me? Does not the Son of God say that they shall be around Him, whom the Father has given Him? How, then, if I have not been given to Him? How if the Father has retained me for Himself, as my heart tells me?" To Lavater he writes: "It elevates the soul, and occasions the most beautiful reflections, to see you seize the splendid, sparkling goblet with the greatest ardour, fill it brimful with your red, foaming beverage, and then quaff with joy the frothing draught. I do not envy you this good fortune of enjoying all in one individual; and since it is impossible for one individual to satisfy you per-

[1] In 1813 Goethe used the following expression to Fr. Jacobi: As poet and artist I am a polytheist, pantheist as a natural philosopher, and the one as decidedly as the other. And if I need a God for myself as a moral being, I am also provided for. The heavenly and divine things form so large a realm, that it requires the organs of all beings to perceive it.

fectly, it is fine that a picture of antiquity has come down to us, in which you can embody all things, in which you can mirror and worship yourself. But I must consider it wrong and robbery in you to pluck all the beautiful feathers of the various birds under heaven, as though they were usurped, and to adorn your bird of paradise exclusively with them; this must necessarily displease and grieve us who yield ourselves as disciples to the wisdom revealed through man to man, and as sons of God worship Him in ourselves as well as in all His children." With these words Goethe expressed the same idea which Strauss afterwards expressed thus, that nature does not generally give all its fulness to one individual. He, therefore, most likely regarded Christ as a welcome picture of antiquity, with which every one might connect his own ideal of man, in which all might see the better part of their own nature; but he did not regard Him as the only being in whom the Spirit dwells without measure.[1] In this point also we, therefore, find that Goethe's views and modern speculative philosophy meet, for we have learned that the same views were held by Fichte and Schelling.

Goethe's life has been divided into different periods, youth, manhood, and old age, and the first and last have been regarded as those in which the poet's heart was more open to religious impressions than in the middle period, and hence we must not be surprised to meet many contradictions in Goethe's writings; however, I believe that even in each period enough will be found that is contradictory. He himself says, "The world is full of contradictions, should not a book then contradict itself?" We will not attempt to point out or to reconcile these contradictions; the thing that interests us most is the impression that Goethe made on his age. It is a remarkable fact that, though Goethe was older than Schiller, still his dominion over the minds of men was later, and that the reign

[1] "You regard the Gospel as the most divine truth," Goethe says in one of his letters. "A voice from heaven would not convince me that water burns and that fire quenches, that a woman gives birth without knowing man, and that a dead man rises from the grave. I rather regard this as blasphemy against the great God and His revelation in nature. . . . You can find nothing more beautiful than the Gospel; I find a thousand pages of ancient and modern times written by men favoured of God, just as beautiful, and as useful, and indispensable to man."

of Goethe in the realm of mind had first to be preceded by that of Schiller, as the critical philosophy preceded Schelling's "Naturphilosophie," as rationalism preceded pantheism. By observing the course of German literature it may easily be seen that the enthusiasm for Schiller, which prevailed thirty or forty years ago in youthful minds, and received a new impulse from Theodore Koerner, gradually moderated, and its place was taken by Goethe's more imposing, life-like mode of thinking. This is the course which the so-called "worship of genius" has taken, first exaggeration, then relaxation, and finally the great dissatisfaction with the world of which every boy on the street can sing now. As every partial veneration of human greatness bears the seed of self-destruction in it, unless regulated and sustained by the worship of the only true God, so it was in this case. A longing for an imagined ideal, or the conceit of having found what has not yet been attained, are both equally dangerous; but one must be careful lest the last deception be greater than the first. Where there is longing and struggling, there is at least always a starting-point for the message of salvation, and a Saul, zealous for an ideal, may become a Paul. But if one says, "I am rich and have need of nothing," that spiritual condition of lukewarmness follows, of which it is said, "I would thou wert cold or hot." This state of lukewarmness in religious matters, this indifference about salvation, of which many boast, has been spread among a large class of men, through Goethe's view of the world, not that Goethe is to blame for this, but his blind admirers. The thoughtful man, who has an interest for God and heavenly things awakened in his childhood, must find many things in Goethe's works well adapted to develop and complete the inner man, many pearls well fitted to adorn the Christian, provided he possesses a high degree of cultivation. But if one has no definite aim in life, he will scarcely get one from Goethe. Goethe bears the same relation to the individual man as nature or a work of art. Both may be used for the glory of God, or may lead to idolatry. In reference to morality nature and art are silent, and so is Goethe. His motto is, "Do what is right in your own affairs. All else will take care of itself." But it does not take care of itself. Just as Goethe did not want to enter his own soul, so, too, he does not lead man to study himself; he teaches him how to get clear views of worldly matters, and in this respect all can learn of him; but he does not touch the conscience, he does not want to touch it, he lets every man alone. While the preceding period exalted morality to a false position, so that it even wanted to make art a servant of morality, Goethe and modern writers have treated art as a power independent of moral and political designs. But as it is very easy to pass from one error to another, men began to view the moral only with artistic eyes, and to value only its capacity for dramatic effect. The love of quiet, modest virtue, of what was contemptuously termed "common morality," continually diminished, and even the integrity, chastity, and honesty of simple Christians were lightly esteemed; while it was claimed that genius should not be judged by common rules of morality. It is of course becoming in judging of great men to be modest, and to confess that though we may be free from many of their faults, we are also behind them in the noblest virtues, and that frequently it is only our mediocrity which keeps us on the accustomed path of duty, while they are easily drawn aside by the mighty pressure of their genius; we should consider that perhaps one great thought and one great deed of such a man outweighs a thousand of our good-natured common thoughts and unimportant performances of duty; and it becomes us to ask whether the measure we apply is the right one, whether we understand the men whom we judge and the circumstances that surround them. This mistrust of our knowledge, this aversion to a censuring spirit is worthy of honour, and far removed from the idolatrous worship of genius. Christianity itself requires this fairness. But to say that great minds are not at all subject to the general moral law, that they are favourites of the gods, that they carry the standard by which they are to be judged entirely in themselves; in a word, that they are not subject to the divine law, —this is idolizing men, and I call special attention to the fact, *that this passion for idolizing men is to be found where pantheism has destroyed the faith in a living personal God.* If man wants to worship and adore, he cannot be satisfied with an empty general notion; he will and must worship something personal, and if he has lost sight of the personality of the Creator, he will transfer the worship to the creature. One has lived among men in whom the fulness of the Godhead dwelt, and of Him it is said, that He was made subject to the law, obeyed it, and fulfilled all righteousness, and therefore God has exalted Him, and given Him a name above all other names, that only through Him the highest names can have any place in the kingdom of God. The greatness of a name is not lost by this means, it continues to shine serenely as a star in the great constellation, undimmed as an emerald in the throne of God. Let us keep this in mind, too, in reference to Goethe. The most beautiful, the noblest of Goethe has already been received into this connection, and when the apostle says, "All is yours," Christianity, fully conscious of this right, has made use of Goethe, and truly those thoughtfully reverencing him, have acted more like the great poet than his idolatrous admirers. How high the master stood above the host of idolizing disciples, we may learn from one of his later conversations with Eckermann.[1] Here Goethe says, "All productiveness of the highest kind, every discovery, every great thought producing fruit, is in no man's power, and is elevated above all temporal might. These man is to regard as unexpected gifts from above, as pure children of God, which he is to receive and honour with joyful gratitude." Here and there we meet with such expressions in the life of this extraordinary man, and an unexpected flame of deepest religious feeling often bursts from his cold, apparently marble breast, and though we should not like to say with a certain Christian philosopher, that Goethe proclaimed the Gospel in his own language, still he was nearer the belief of the Gospel, the prevalence of an unmerited divine grace, than many with their formal Christianity. Though we can apply no moral standard to Goethe different from that applied to other men, still we gladly acknowledge that the way through which God leads such men is often hid from our eyes. The intimation

[1] In a former conversation he speaks unfavourably of the critique as used now, and also speaks of immortality. Though he speaks decidedly against those who only speculate idly about a future world (in a sentimental manner which was customary at the time of Tiedge's Urania), still he says as decidedly that all are dead for this life, who hope for no other. He also says that the Christian religion is a great power, highly elevated above all philosophy, and needing no support from it.

in this respect given by Goethe to Lavater is remarkable: "My God to whom I have been true, has secretly blessed me, for my condition is entirely hid from men; they see and hear nothing of it, but whatever can be revealed of it, I will joyfully communicate to you."

We will here give a quotation from his last conversations with Eckermann: "Let spiritual improvement continually increase, let natural science ever grow in extent and depth, and let the human mind be expanded as much as it please: it will never transcend the height and morality of Christianity, as it glows and shines in the Gospel."

Goethe's relation to Christianity is a subject which could be treated much more extensively than we have done in the few preceding remarks. So much may be said for and against Goethe; owing to his twofold nature, his deep knowledge, and his light, often frivolous manners, the matter may be contemplated from so many different points of view, that at one time we are as much surprised at the agreement of the essential views of Goethe with those of Christianity, as at another we must feel ourselves suddenly repulsed by the coldness and frivolity with which he treats the most sacred subjects. It could not be our object to form a complete judgment of Goethe, as we have not done this with Schiller, Pestalozzi, Fichte, Schelling, and others. It was our design merely to speak of what Goethe was for his age, how his age understood and received him, and how the Goethean culture influenced the former, and more especially our own age. It is certain that next to the modern speculative philosophy, which appeared at the close of the eighteenth and the beginning of the nineteenth century, it is Goethe who swayed and still sways the educated minds, who was the organ of the spirit of the age.

We have not, however, accomplished our object until we have more closely examined Goethe's position in reference to Protestantism. Goethe was not only a reformatory spirit, he was, to use his own language in his own sense, a productive spirit; he created a new period, especially in art; and though this at first appears to have no connection with the reformation of the Church, still we cannot regard it as a mere accident, that the very men who were called to give a new impulse to the literature of the eighteenth and nineteenth centuries, Lessing, Klopstock, Herder, Goethe, all proceeded from the Protestant Church, as well as Leibnitz, Wolf, Kant, Fichte, Schelling, and Hegel in the department of philosophy. All branches of the same trunk! Goethe himself must have recognized this connection, as appears from his opinion of Luther. In his conversations with Eckermann, Goethe says: "Luther was a spirit of a very important kind; he has already exerted an influence for many days, and the number of days which must pass before he will cease to be productive cannot be calculated." In this respect Goethe's modesty is really great and affecting in comparison to the dwarfish race of young reformers, who think they are already far above Luther. Goethe himself has cast the horoscope of such persons when, in 1816, he writes to Zelter: "The incredible conceit into which young men now grow, will in few years manifest itself in the greatest nonsense." And this has really been verified.[1]

In my opinion Goethe may be placed with Luther in one respect, that they both introduced a new period into the history of the German language. What Luther became to the Church by his pithy scriptural and ecclesiastical language, Goethe has become to the world and society by his plastic representation and clear conversational language. Both may boldly be placed side by side as unsurpassed classic models; of course, each in his own sphere. Otherwise, as far as the course and tendency of life is concerned, Luther and Goethe have few points of similarity, and the miner's son and Augustine monk forms a wonderful contrast to the son of the Frankfort senator, who sits in the lap of fortune, and developes, as if spontaneously, in the midst of cheerful pictures of art—just as the time of Wittenberg forms a contrast to that of Weimar! We might much sooner speak of Schiller, Herder, Fichte, and similar minds, if the object were to mention those who, like Luther, fought their way through a

[1] Goethe speaks in quite a Protestant manner of so-called "Liberalism." "The truly liberal man attempts to accomplish as much good as possible with the means within his reach; but he is careful not to attempt to destroy the imperfections, frequently unavoidable, with fire and sword. He is careful to remove open crimes gradually by wise proceedings, without at the same time destroying just as much good by a forcible mode of action."

youth of difficulties, and for one idea staked their lives, and who on the proper occasion would also have defied a world of devils in order to spread truth and to promote the right.

Goethe has been blamed for taking no active part in the political struggle of Germany against its oppressors. In this respect he has been compared with the much praised and highly esteemed Erasmus, with his reserve, his wit, his fine court-manners and court-favour. Still it appears to us that Goethe is lowered too much by this comparison. Each was, indeed, the most distinguished literary man of his age; but in Goethe there is evidently something fresher, more solid, more healthy. There is one point especially in Goethe's life, in which the inheritance from Luther was powerfully active in him, the time in which he wrote "Goetz von Berlichingen," in which even the strength of the age is painted in bold outline. "To risk life for the general good," it is said in Goetz, "this were a life indeed!" Goethe did not think so afterwards. But in his more advanced age he also manifested a deep insight into the nature of Protestantism, into its great historical significance. It cannot appear strange to any one that, with his broad comprehension, he also understood the historical position of Catholicism, that, as artist and poet, he also knew how to use the Catholic forms, and even manifested a preference for the number *seven* in the sacraments, because he thought the Protestant service had too little fulness and consistency to keep minds united. Yet Goethe certainly remained a Protestant fully and heartily, and more than once ridiculed the new Catholic poets of the romantic school.[1] He was tolerant in reference to differences of con-

[1] How little his taste was pleased with the Catholic worship, is evident from his own confession, namely, from the description of All-soul's-day. "I was seized with a wonderful longing that the head of the church would open his golden mouth, and, speaking with rapture of the unspeakable joy of the blessed, that he would fill our souls with rapture. When, however, I saw him simply moving to and fro before the altar, now turning to this side now to that, acting and mumbling like a common priest, the Protestant original sin began to stir in me, and the usual sacrifice of the mass did not at all please me." In another place he speaks of "deformed, quaint heathenism." His opinion of Rome's politics was not more favourable. "The Catholics are not to be trusted, they do not agree among themselves, but always adhere to each other when a Protestant is to be attacked."

fessions, and would even express this tolerance in a manner which appeared like indifference. But when he spoke seriously, he treated of Protestantism and its essential principles as well and distinctly as of Christianity in general. Thus, on the occasion of the approaching festival of the Reformation in Germany (1816), he pronounced the chief idea of Lutheranism well founded, since it rested on the decided contrast between the law and the gospel, and that therefore Lutheranism could never be united with Catholicism. On another occasion he says: "Protestantism is spread too far to disappear again, however much it may be modified by individualities."

We can distinguish three classes of novelists, those that really turned Catholic, those that externally remained Protestants, but did not deny their Catholic sympathies, and finally, those who, after vacillating for some time, gained a firm Protestant footing, and who then assisted to adorn Lutheranism with their romances. . . . As representative of the second class, I have chosen a man well known in the literary world. He is a poet beloved and esteemed, since a deep current of Christianity breathes in his poems, such as we have not found in the so-called classic poets, Schiller and Goethe; indeed such a depth of Christianity as we have scarcely found in Herder—I mean Hardenberg, or, as he styles himself as author, Novalis.

The tender ardour of romance has certainly nowhere been expressed more beautifully than in the spiritual songs of Novalis, which form a favourable contrast to the insipid moralizing rhymes of the period of the Illuminati; and though they do not bear the stamp of church hymns, still they are well adapted to be sung in quiet solitude, even within the heart.

We shall find in his prose writings some expressions which favour an indefinite pantheism, and others which plainly enough incline to Catholicism. The mingling of a romantic, sensual love with the religious led to the poetic adoration of the mother of the Saviour, which formed the bridge for such minds to pass over to Catholicism. This adoration of the Virgin is evidently manifested by Novalis. Several of his poems are addressed not merely as poetic fictions to the queen of heaven, but in the same manner as, in other cases, he addresses Christ as the Lord. He asserts that the power and glory of the heavenly virgin far surpasses all description, and that the source of salvation is in her.

Not only the adoration of the Virgin, but the entire structure of the Catholicism of the middle ages found much sympathy in the heart of Novalis, and he was its eloquent defender.

In a fragment of 1798 entitled, "Christendom of Europe," Novalis praises the "beautiful, brilliant" periods of the middle ages, in which *one* Christianity prevailed over our part of the globe, when one great common interest united the most remote provinces, when one head united the political powers, when ministers preached nothing but *love to the holy charming virgin of Christendom*, who, furnished with divine powers, was ready to deliver every believer from the most fearful dangers. He, however, does more than merely praise the poetical part of the worship, which we might pardon in the poet, he approves the opposition of the head of the church to the bold improvements of human faculties, and dangerous discoveries in the department of learning, as soon as these appeared to be at the expense of a holy opinion. He finds it quite proper that the pope should desire that men should not regard this earth as an insignificant planet, since with the loss of esteem for this our earthly habitation, that for our heavenly home is also lost; he praises the wisdom of the popes in assembling the educated around their courts, while they left the people in ignorance; hence he does not consider the restoration of science, and the Reformation following it, as other Protestants do, a blessing for humanity, but a misfortune, at least a temporary one. "Luther," he says, "treated Christianity in an arbitrary manner, *mistook its spirit*, and introduced another letter, another religion, the holy supremacy of the Bible, and by this means philosophy was unfortunately mingled with religious matters." To say, "Luther mistook the spirit of Christianity," is at least mistaking the spirit of Luther. And why has Luther mistaken the spirit of Christianity? Novalis says, "*because he introduced the holy supremacy of the Bible.*" Is not this again mistaking the spirit of the Reformation, the spirit of Protestantism? We certainly do not advocate that faith in Scripture which, by adhering so closely to the written letter of the Bible, loses sight of the richness of the life of the Church, as it has developed itself from century to century, or which does not permit the spirit to appear on account of this slavish adherence to the written letter. We have already denoted this a Protestant deficiency; but on this account shall the great deed of Luther in restoring the Bible to the Christian public, and placing it as a candlestick on the altar, instead of dumb images and symbols, be called an error? If again, Novalis further charges Protestants that "Luther was elevated by some to the rank of an Evangelist, and that his translation of the Bible was canonized," this is absolutely false. Luther's translation was never canonized, never declared the only valid one by a decree of any council; it has made its own way by its superior excellence, and by its side other translations have always been received. This fact was well known to Novalis, but he was prejudiced against the Reformation, because he unjustly blamed it for the degeneracy of Protestantism. It is thus quite natural that the entire history of Protestantism no longer appeared as a great supernatural phenomenon to a mind thus prejudiced, and which everywhere finds an oppressed, contracted sickly life. "*With the Reformation*," says Novalis, "*Christendom was at an end*, from that time it existed no longer, for all things stood in opposition to each other in sectarian divisions."

After this nothing could be expected but that Novalis himself should join the church which had been preserved from the curse of the Reformation. But he did not wish to do this, nor did he want the old Romanism to prevail again, he rather hoped that the crisis of unbelief with which he also felt himself influenced, would bring about a transformation in the church, and would restore true Catholicism, in which the separated would again be united, and for the accomplishment of this he placed great hopes in romance.

The political revolutions are an indication to him that there will be a change, and that the reconciliation of nations cannot proceed from cabinets, but must find its origin in religion. "War will never cease, unless the olive branch is seized which a scriptural power can give. Blood will flow through Europe till the nations become conscious of their terrible madness, and unite around their former altars in peace. Christendom must again become alive and active, and form a visible Church without distinction of countries, which receives all into its bosom. From an honourable European council Christendom will arise, and a religious awakening will flourish according to an all-embracing divine plan. Then no one will protest any more against Christian and worldly compulsion, for the very nature of the church will be true freedom, and all reforms will be carried on peacefully under the guidance of the church. When, and how soon? This is not the question. Only have patience, the holy time of eternal peace will and must come, when the new Jerusalem will be the capital of the world, and till then, partners of my faith, be cheerful and courageous amid the dangers of the age. Proclaim the divine Gospel by word and deed, and be faithful till death to the true eternal faith."

Thus Novalis spoke and hoped. If we once more review the short life of Novalis with all his manifold errors, a noble spirit will still address us, which struggled for light and purified itself in the fire. Had Novalis reached the age of manhood he would have judged differently of many things.

We cannot be angry with his youth, but much less can we choose him as our guide over the most giddy heights. Novalis died in the house of his parents in Weissenfels, the 25th of March, 1801, in his 29th year; young, indeed, but rich in sweet and bitter experiences. He had been sickly while yet a child. He was unfortunate in his first love, through the death of the lady; from the ruins he had built a family altar in marrying another lady. Of his friends Fr. Schlegel and Fichte had exerted a great influence over him. His love for the Redeemer, which, with all his inclination to Catholicism, still continued to be the key-note of his religious life, sustained him in his afflictions. The Bible which, with all his unjust opinions in reference to its spread, he still regarded highly as God's word, and higher than any other book, and also the writings of Lavater and Zinzendorf were the companions of his sick-bed. He died gently, amid the music of the piano which he had asked his brother to play. He had constantly sought for a symbol of the deepest spiritual relations between music and nature, to the study of which he devoted himself. "The expression of his face," says Tieck, "was very much like that of John the Evangelist, as given on the glorious plate by Albert Durer. . . . His friendliness, his geniality, made him universally beloved. . . He could be as happy as a child, he jested with cheerfulness, and permitted himself to become the object of jests for the company. Free from all vanity and pride of learning, a stranger to all affectation and hypocrisy, he was a genuine true man, the purest and most lovely embodiment of a noble immortal spirit."

XXII.

SCHLEIERMACHER.

NEW IMPULSE GIVEN TO PROTESTANTISM BY SCHLEIERMACHER—"MONOLOGUES" AND "ADDRESSES ON RELIGION."—MODERN PROTESTANT THEOLOGY.—SCHLEIERMACHER, DE WETTE, ETC.—SCHLEIERMACHER'S "SYSTEM OF FAITH (GLAUBENSLEHRE)."—PARALLEL BETWEEN HERDER AND SCHLEIERMACHER.

MODERN history points to Schleiermacher as the man from whom a new epoch in Protestant theology dates, with whom a new and energetic theological and religious tendency commenced.

The opinion that the Moravians founded by Zinzendorf form a communion calculated to gather and keep members in the fold of Christ, is confirmed by the fact that several men who exerted a great influence in their age proceeded from this body, and in it received their first spiritual impulse. This was the case with Schleiermacher. He was born in Breslau, Nov. 21, 1768. He pursued his collegiate and a part of his theological studies in the Moravian institutions in Niesky and Barby. Afterwards he withdrew from the Moravian community, and continued his studies in Halle; still, to the end of his life, he acknowledged the beneficial influences his early education in it had exerted on him. "Piety," he says, "was the womb in whose holy darkness my young life was nourished and prepared for the world still unknown to me; in it my spirit breathed before it found its peculiar sphere in science and life."

When preacher of the hospital in Bèrlin (from 1796-1802), Schleiermacher entered into a more intimate relation with the brothers Schlegel and the other minds of the romantic school. To this period also belong his studies of Plato, and during it he published the two works of his youth, the "Addresses on Religion," and the "Monologues." We begin with the last (1800), because they give us a better view of the inner life of the man as it reveals itself to his own consciousness, and to his fellow men, than a mere biographical sketch can possibly give.

While Goethe declares the investigation and contemplation of self a weakness, Schleiermacher asserts the very opposite; and it seems as if it is spoken against Goethe himself when he says:—"Whoever only sees and knows the external phenomena of the mind, without understanding the activity in the depths of his soul; whoever has only an idea of his outward life and its changes, without viewing that which is within, continues to be *the slave of time and necessity* and all his thoughts and reflections bear their impress." A spirit similar to that of Fichte breathes in these Monologues. To conquer self, to have eternal life in us even in this world, to be conscious of the Ego as something indestructible, this is the fitting end to be sought. "Begin thy eternal life *now,*" he says, "in the continual contemplation of self; be not anxious about that which is to come, weep not for that which perishes; but be careful not to lose thyself, and weep if thou art carried along with the stream of time without having heaven within thee." "It requires but one free resolution to be a man; whoever has formed this resolution will always be one; he who ceases to be a man has never been one." With a joyful pride the speaker remembers the time when he came to a consciousness of man, not through a system of philosophy, but through the inner revelation of a bright moment, through an act of his own; and he assures us *that since then he never lost sight of himself.* In direct opposition to the abstract generalizing system of morals which regards men merely as mathematical quantities, as parts of one and the same mass, Schleiermacher says in his Monologues *that each man ought to represent humanity in a peculiar manner.* He readily acknowledged that it was not his calling to become an artist, who makes beautiful images of the external world, and delights in the perfection of forms; and here again we find that he forms a decided contrast to Goethe. He believed it to be his calling, his task, to work upon himself, not to produce a work outside of himself. And this task, he thought, could only be performed in communion with others. He, however, regarded that as the true communion in which each one permits the other to act out his own peculiarities: but each is also the supplement of the other, so that all together form a true picture of humanity.

A powerful, and at the same time noble, self-confidence is expressed in the Monologues—a self-confidence which even rises to a prediction of his own future—in these much admired words:—"I will bring my mind to old age unimpaired, the youthful spirit shall never forsake me; what delights me now shall always delight me; my will shall remain strong, my fancy lively; nothing shall tear from me the magic key which opens the mysterious gate of the higher world, and never shall the fire of love be quenched. I will not see the dreaded weakness of old age: I promise to scorn every vexation that interferes with the object of my existence, and vow to myself an eternal youth. . . . The spirit that impels humanity onward shall never forsake me, nor the longing which is never satisfied with what was, but ever goes to meet what is to come. Let this be the glory I seek to know, that my race is infinite, but that I am never to stand still in the course. . . . I shall never think myself old till I have finished; but I shall never finish while I know and will what I ought. . . . Till my end I will become stronger and livelier by every act, and more lovely by every improvement of self. I will marry youth to old age, so that the latter may have the fulness of the former, and may be penetrated by its animating warmth. By the contemplation of self man gains the ascendency over despondency and weakness, so that they cannot even approach him; for eternal youth and joy spring from the inner consciousness and actions of freedom. I have apprehended this, and will never let it go. And thus with smiles I see the light of the eyes vanish, and the grey hair appearing among the light-coloured locks. Nothing that may occur can grieve my heart; the pulse of the inner life continues vigorous till death."

Schleiermacher kept his word. All who knew him in his old age must remember the impression the youthful grey-haired man made on them. Whoever compares these Monologues with his later Christian writings, must see that in the former the moral courage and confidence in his own powers, even a daring, moral defiance, are much more prominent than that humility and "*feeling of dependence*" which afterwards became the foundation of Schleiermacher's theology. He was conscious of this fact himself in his more advanced age, and in a new edition of the Monologues declared that in them he had only expressed the ideal he then strived to attain, and that the contemplation of self was held purely from the ethical standpoint. He wanted to remove the one-sided impression which the Monologues gave of his character, by publishing a series of religious soliloquies, as a supplement to the book. Though he never did this, we may regard the "Addresses on Religion," which were published a year before the Monologues (in 1799), as such a supplement. These "Addresses on Religion to the educated among its despisers," produced a wonderful effect on their age. Not only men like Werner, but many young men, to whom all that is called religion appeared like a riddle, were ennobled and edified by these Addresses. In order to realise this, we must transfer ourselves to the age in which they were written (and the same must be done in judging of the Monologues), and Schleiermacher himself, in the third edition (1821), calls attention to the fact that the times had changed remarkably, and that it appeared that the persons for whom the Addresses were originally intended, no longer existed.[1]

[1] "In looking about among the educated (he continues) one might find it more necessary to write addresses to those affecting piety and to slaves of the letter, to the ignorant and harshly censuring, superstitious and hyperorthodox." This Schleiermacher wrote in 1821, twenty-two years after the publication of the first edition of the Addresses. It is now (1844) just twenty-two years since then. And what is the aspect of things now? We have slaves of the letter and scoffers, and of what kind!

We must, therefore, call to mind the fact, that through the Kantian philosophy, which still had its followers among the educated, religion had been changed to mere morality, and that all that refers to the public exercises of religion was regarded as merely for that class of individuals who could not attain pure morality. The attendance of divine worship was frequently justified by the educated on the ground that it was not for their own sake, but to set a good example. This despising of religion, through an entire misapprehension of its true nature, Schleiermacher opposed in his Addresses in the most decided manner. In opposition both to the view that religion exists only for the sake of learning (whether as dead matter of transmitted dogmas, or as an interesting subject for philosophical discussion), and to that also which degrades it to a mere moral corrective, a mass of mere commandments and prohibitions, he attempted to restore it to its proper sphere and original rights, by making the feeling its seat. By feeling he did not mean the agitation of transient emotions, which ceased as rapidly as they were excited, and become the deceitful play of the frame of mind at the moment, not that irritability which he attacked earnestly; but the inmost part of man, the central point, the focus of his spiritual life, the source and root of all our thinking, striving, and acting. Religion cannot be learned from anything external; it cannot be imparted by dogmas and precepts; it must originate in the heart of the pious as something felt and experienced, and must announce itself as a power controlling all, appropriating all. The religious man is given to reflection, to the contemplation of the depths of his soul, and all else, whether it appears as definite knowledge and reality, is regarded as secondary and derivative.

In these fundamental principles of the nature of religion Schleiermacher agrees with F. H. Jacobi, who, as we have seen, also tried to free divine things from the slavery of dead notions, whether of theology or philosophy, and to place them in the depths of the soul, not to lie there buried as hidden treasures in holy darkness, but that they might arise from this depth to the light, like pure solid gold, as the inalienable possession of our nature dependent on no change of systems. But while Jacobi had viewed religion more in its generality, and had failed to show it in its historical definiteness as essentially Christian, Schleiermacher showed that the so-called *natural* religion, to which the educated of the age were mostly inclined, is a chimera, a mere abstraction of the understanding, and that religion only exerts an influence, when it appears as a definite, positive power. He gave special prominence to the element of society in religion, which Jacobi had entirely neglected, and showed, that in all ages, those individuals who were peculiarly affected by the religious life, also affected society in general, and as founders of religion gathered a communion around them. Without mentioning Christ except in connection with the other founders of religions, without denoting the *Christian* religion as that one which is alone destined to be the real religion of the human race, still in these Addresses he pointed his age to the way which led out of these generalities, to that which is definitely Christian. "These Addresses," as a modern theologian very justly remarks, "are rather apologies for religion in general than for Christianity in particular; they have been delivered, as it were, in the forecourt of theology, in the court of the heathen;" and yet they evidently contain the foundation of what Schleiermacher afterwards developed in his "Glaubenslehre" (Doctrine of faith).

The grievous charge of Pantheism was raised against these Addresses—a charge that is little expected after we have seen the relation in which Schleiermacher stood to Jacobi. It is indeed true that the Addresses bear the impress of Pantheism in their entire tone and mode of expression. Neither a *personal* God nor *personal* immortality, as held by Rationalism, found a place in them. On the contrary, there are passages enough which call to mind the very opposite of Jacobi's view, the philosophy of Schelling; passages in which the all, the universe, the absolute, take the place of a Being known and called by the name of God, and in which it seems to be the highest aim of our desires to be absorbed in this One and All. But here too, we must think of the time when these Addresses were written, and of the people to whom they were addressed. There was a faith in a personal God which reverenced in God a Being supernatural and distinct from the world, who, however, enters into no near relation to humanity, but lives a life of self-complacency, unconcerned about the world and its inhabitants, and who at best, as He has created the world, will also at one time return to judge it. In opposition to this cold deistic faith, at that time haunting many who called themselves the educated, and which still haunts many minds and hearts, Schleiermacher placed the living spiritual view of a God dwelling in the world, always present with us, uniting Himself with our nature and becoming our friend, and making us happy by making His habitation within us. It cannot be denied that in doing this he not only bordered on Pantheistic modes of expression, but actually adopted them more than was necessary to the attainment of his end; but it cannot be asserted that in after life Schleiermacher never attained a mode of thinking different from the Pantheistic. This idea is not only contradicted by his own explicit expressions, but also his entire Christian development. It was in direct opposition to the common sort of "Alleinheitter," as he called those who only hid their unbelief of the supernatural behind Pantheism, and also in opposition to the romantic poetasters who made sport of religion in their insipid poetry, that he had already in his Addresses said that only when philosophers would become religious and seek God, like Spinoza, and the artists become pious and love Christ, like Novalis, the time of resurrection would come for both worlds—the worlds of philosophy and of art.

In reference to immortality Schleiermacher declares that the common manner of thinking of it neither agrees with piety nor proceeds from it; that with many the belief in immortality is even *irreligious*, because their desire to be immortal has no other ground than their aversion to the real object of religion; because they are more anxious to find the sharply defined outlines of their own personality again, than to find God and the divine life. To such he thinks the word of the Lord applicable, "he that loseth his life for my sake shall find it," and vice versa. The more they long for an immortality of which they can form no conception, the more they lose of that immortality which they might enjoy already in this world. He who has learned to be more than himself, knows that he loses but little when he loses himself. And only he who is united with God, in whose soul a great and holy longing has originated, has a right to immortality; and only with such a man can we speak of the hope which death gives, and of the eternity to which we infallibly rise after death.

Schleiermacher's mind was still more decidedly directed to theological science, by being called to a professorship of philosophy and theology in Halle in 1802, and by an appointment in the newly founded University of Berlin in 1810;[1] and henceforth we shall see him moving in the more definite sphere of theological activity.

In mentioning Schleiermacher as the man from whom a new period in Protestant theology dates, we of course did not mean that it was in the power of a single man, however talented he might be, to give a new tendency to the age, and to give it the impress of his spirit exclusively; nor that only one man is to be taken into the account in this matter. Schleiermacher, who himself acknowledged that it was only in connection with others that he could accomplish any thing great, would have been the first to object to assigning himself such a place in history. In this period we find a general striving to reconcile the difficulties between Rationalism and Supernaturalism in an intellectual manner. Thus some by speculative philosophy, as the venerable Daubin[1] in Heidelberg, attempted to introduce a profound mode of theological thinking, which was to penetrate the lowest depths of the dogmas; while others sought on the psychological way, which Kant and Fichte had before tried, to separate what belongs to knowledge in religious matters, from that which belongs to faith and anticipation, two powers of the mind not sufficiently regarded by Kant, but which are as real as the

[1] The positions occupied by Schleiermacher are the following:—1794, assistant curate at Landswerth on the Warthe; 1796-1802, preacher of the Hospital in Berlin; 1802, court preacher in Stolpe, and the same year university preacher and professor at Halle. In 1807 he returned to Berlin, and, like Fichte, delivered lectures to a mixed audience. In 1809 he became preacher of the Trinity Church, Berlin; 1810, professor there; and 1811 member of the academy. It is very significant that he was at the same time preacher and professor, and that his professorship was divided between theology and philosophy.

[2] Born in Cassel 1765, formerly professor in Hannau.

faculty of knowing. They attempted to prevent the rough treatment of the mysteries of faith by directing attention to the insufficiency of human language, and to lead the religious thinker to anticipate something higher, behind the symbolical expressions, something eluding both our language and the representations of our senses. In the place of a merely intellectual and cold, calculating mode of contemplation, they wanted one distinctly conscious of its activity, piously animated, one akin to that with which we regard a beautiful work of art, and which, on this account, has been called the esthetic. And here is the place to mention the man who first introduced this mode of contemplation into theology, and thus with Schleiermacher exerted on it an impelling and renovating influence.

But if I have determined to mention the living as little as possible, a still more tender regard comes into consideration here, which prevents me from unfolding to you the system of a teacher who is entitled, both by his local and personal relations to us all, to give an account of himself in his own way; and it may suffice that I have merely referred to his efforts, and those of others, which we regard as a supplement to those of Schleiermacher.[1]

[1] To what I have said by word of mouth the following may be added. The tendency of De Wette, like that of Protestantism in general, is double, critically negative, and dogmatically positive. Many who know only the former side of De Wette's labours, his free criticism, namely, in reference to the sacred canon and mythical treatment of the Old Testament history, do him injustice in placing him, on that account, in the same category with the destructive minds. Whoever is acquainted with the history of theological science, knows that De Wette opposed Rationalism, and advocated, of course conditionally, and from the stand-point of his philosophical mode of thinking, Old-Lutheran orthodoxy. He published the statement that "the person of Jesus, His life and death, and faith in him form the centre of Christianity," (see his work, "Religion and Theology," p. 444), on which account he was regarded as a mystic by the real Rationalists, see his Dogmatics, and especially his easily understood work on "Das Wesen des christlichen Glaubens vom Standpunkte des Glaubens dargestellt," (Basle, 1846.) De Wette and Schleiermacher were charged with being vacillating and undecided in their judgment; but it is a question whether real science is more promoted by rendering a verdict from orthodox or speculative premises, and then being done with the matter, or by modestly saying non-liquet in things which are hypothetical in their nature. In reference to his essential convictions, De Wette always sustained himself. To test these convictions themselves is the business of science. Historical fidelity required this brief explanation.

[Hagenbach now follows the political history of Germany for some time, refers to the three hundredth aniversary of the Reformation, etc., only now and then mentioning Schleiermacher. He refers to the fact that Schleiermacher considered the ninety-five theses of Claus Harms against rationalism an arrogant undertaking, though he esteemed Harms himself as a well-meaning, ingenious, and truly Christian man, and was far from being a friend to rationalism. Speaking of the attempt in Prussia to unite the Lutheran and Reformed Churches, Hagenbach says: "The same persons who were called on to assist in affecting a union, as Schleiermacher for instance, spoke of the differences of the two confessions. Among the Reformed theologians Schleiermacher was the first, after a long while, who again defended the doctrine of election in an acute manner." The union of the two churches was actually accomplished in 1821. In order to meet the wants of the times the king had a liturgy formed, which was introduced into the court and garrison churches, and was recommended to all the other congregations of the land. But it was impossible to please all. To the strict Lutherans the liturgy appeared too indefinite and yielding too much to the Reformed. To the Reformed, on the other hand, "the lighting of candles by day-light, the kneeling, the singing of the minister before the altar, etc., appeared quite Catholic." The Rationalists found the liturgy too orthodox. "There were some also who carried their dissatisfaction with political matters into this department, and charged the king with the intention of acquiring dominion over the conscience in order to enable him to accomplish other measures more easily. The dispute soon became a legal one, and the question, how far has the king, as ruler of the land, a right to prescribe forms for the use of public worship, and to force a certain mode of divine worship in the churches, was answered differently by jurists and theologians. In this dispute Schleiermacher advocated the freedom of conscience." (The liturgic right of an Evangelical ruler, by Pacificus Sincerus, 1824). Hagenbach then, after giving a short account of Steffen's activity in defending Lutheranism, returns to Schleiermacher.—Tr.]

To return to Schleiermacher, as we have seen him taking an active part in all the great movements of the church, so we find him in his two-fold relation as learned theologian and preacher, affecting the religious convictions in an instructive, positive and corrective manner. His "Glaubenslehre" (system of faith), the first edition of which was published in 1821, was intended to be a system of faith of the Evangelical, that is, united church, and to satisfy both the scientific and religious wants of the age. We cannot give a detailed analysis and criticism of the work, but will only give its outlines. His system of faith differs chiefly from all those preceding, in that it was really to be a *system of faith*, a statement of what was *believed*, and not the product of a philosophical school. Schleiermacher, who possessed the very highest philosophical culture, and was distinguished as an author in the department of philosophy, opposed all mingling of philosophy and theology.[1] He does not think that theology stands or falls with any philosophical system, but with religion and the church. Where there is no religion there is no theology, and where there is no experience of divine things there is no understanding of them, however rich and extensive philosophical knowledge may be. Nor is religion an affair of knowledge chiefly, but of the inmost self-consciousness and feeling, and indeed Schleiermacher based his whole theology on this feeling of dependence on God. He does not consider it the business of dogmatics to answer the question how God is in Himself, but how He is related to our pious feeling. As, however, the pious feeling developes in the community, a Christian system of faith must also represent the Christian feeling of a community as it lives in the church. But Schleiermacher does not regard the Christian society as a rough mass of people of all kinds of opinions, but as a religious organism, the body of which Christ is the head. He regarded Christ the Redeemer, not as an ideal creation of the mind, but the real historical Christ, as He lived in history, and still lives in the Church, as the centre of Christian theology. He will have nothing to do with a doctrine of Christ which can be comprehended and represented as nothing but doctrine, and entirely distinct from his person; but first, when we

[1] "Speculation and faith are often regarded as standing opposite each other in a hostile manner; but it was peculiar in this man that he united both most intimately, without doing injustice to the freedom and depth of the one, or to the simplicity of the other."—*W. von Humboldt.*

enter into a living relation to the "Redeemer," do we become partakers of Christianity according to its true nature? He continually proclaimed in his sermons, as well as theological writings, that with Christ something entirely new begins in the history of the world as well as in that of an individual; that with him, the Sinless-One, the mere dominion of nature, the dominion of sin, ceases, and the reign of grace, the unlimited dominion of divine Spirit, commences and spreads, hence, that without Christ no salvation can be found; and by this means Schleiermacher brought theology back to faith. But in doing this he thought the principal thing was accomplished. While, therefore, on the one hand with his decided faith in Christ, from which he would not let an iota be taken away, he might appear as a mystic or a philosophical Moravian who made even the absurd plausible with his dialectics, he gave offence on the other by the freethinking manner in which he expressed himself in reference to some parts of dogmatics, and some books of Scripture, and their relation to the entire canon,[1] for he did not regard these as the essence of Christianity, but thought this consisted in the free grace of God in Christ.

Schleiermacher can be compared with Herder in this respect, that both were blamed by some for orthodoxy, by others for heterodoxy, and neither belonged to any leagued fraternity of philosophers or school of theology. Both gave a great impulse to young men, Herder by means of his letters on the study of theology, and Schleiermacher by means of his outline of the study of theology (Berlin 1830.)[2] Both had this in common, too, that they were not mere theologians, but with their general knowledge were also active as authors in other departments, and thus acquired a reputation in circles not theological. But while Herder was more brilliant as a poet, Schleiermacher surpassed him in philosophical culture. Herder made the dark bright by his quick flashes of thought. Schleiermacher took the fine thread, on which the most difficult inquiries were hanging, through the labyrinth of conflicting contrasts. In the latter fancy steps behind dialectics, behind an understanding supported by feeling. While

[1] See his Kritisches Sendschreiben on the first epistle of Timothy (Berlin, 1807), and his work on Luke, 1817.

[2] Translated into English. (Edin. 1850.)

Herder connected a deep insight into oriental life, with his taste for the ancient spirit of the Greeks, Schleiermacher's education continued to be entirely occidental. It has, therefore, been charged against the latter, that he regarded the great significance of the Old Testament too little, while Herder was quite at home here, and might rather be said to have valued the New Testament too lightly.

We may therefore say that both form supplements to each other in a certain sense, and it is not without significance that Herder stands at the commencement of the critical period, and Schleiermacher at its end. And as we began the historical representation of this critical period with Herder, we may close it with Schleiermacher, since what remains to be said belongs too much to the present to be ripe for history. Only let the following be mentioned—Schleiermacher was rejoiced with numerous intellectual descendants: for we not only count those among his followers who repeated his system in his own words, but we value the impulse which he gave to the study of theology in general, and the blessing he brought indirectly through others. Many started from him who afterwards took another course, most of them are more positive than he. Yet it was frequently alleged that he led persons to pietism. Others took a different course. But we may confidently say that no theologian of any importance, whatever might be his tendency, has appeared in the last decennaries who did not, for a while at least, sit at the feet of Schleiermacher, exercise his mind on his powerful thoughts, and gain great and enlarged views from the study of his works. Of course there was a counteraction manifested from various sides. The older rationalism felt itself uncomfortably influenced by the new life which now began to be unfolded in the church, accused Schleiermacher of ambiguity, and especially of pantheism, which they said he enveloped skilfully in Christian expressions;[1] but while we have seen that this charge was just when applied to those who arbitrarily deviate from the historical basis of Christianity, and resolve all in the mist of their speculation, yet when applied to Schleiermacher it could only be founded on an error. Nor

[1] Even the name Schleiermacher (maker of veils), was used for many witticisms.

was the theology of Schleiermacher acceptable to the strictly orthodox party (Harms, for instance); they avoided, even detested, the sharpness of his criticism, and demanded an unconditional return to the old system. Their number increased visibly; they gradually gathered around names that were becoming prominent, and created their organs. Soon all was changed on the theological horizon. While ten or twenty years previous not enough of the old could be thrown aside, now among the younger race a real rivalry was manifested to surpass the fathers and grandfathers in pure orthodoxy. Remarkable! The young longed for the old again, and the old were unwilling to leave that which had once been fresh and new to them. As now, a new philosophy appeared which overthrew entirely the authority of Kant and his school, and promised orthodoxy a firm support, while it threatened rationalism with destruction—the triumph was apparently complete. Only one question remained, whether this philosophy could be permanently trusted, or whether behind it an enemy might not be lurking who was more dangerous than the former? This new philosophy is the system of Hegel, of which much has already been said, and of which we will speak in the next place.

XXIII.

HEGEL AND HIS SUCCESSORS.

HEGEL: HIS PHILOSOPHY AND OTHER TENDENCIES OF OUR DAY.—RIGHT AND LEFT SIDE OF HIS PHILOSOPHY.—STRAUSS.—FEUERBACH AND BRUNO BAUR.—OTHER PHILOSOPHICAL TENDENCIES.—MODERN SCIENCE AND THE PRESENT THEOLOGY.—PRACTICAL CHRISTIANITY OF OUR DAY.—MODERN PIETISM

WITH the Hegelian philosophy we come to the last stadium in the history of the development of Protestantism on the part of science; with it we enter the present, and step upon the unsafe border of what cannot yet be embraced in history. Hegel himself is no longer among the living, and hence it might be thought that his system is concluded, and belongs to the past, if the effects of the Hegelian philosophy had not first become evident after his death, and that too, in different tendencies; so that, with the material itself so hard, it becomes doubly difficult to determine what Hegel himself desired in reference to religion and the church. If, in treating of former philosophers, Kant, Fichte, and Schelling, we had to deny ourselves the pleasure of obtaining a satisfactory insight into the internal connection of each system, we must be still more modest in our wishes here, for only a perfect knowledge of the former systems can enable us to understand this. Besides, no other philosophy is so purely and exclusively speculative as this; none offers less popular points, none is so difficult to be transposed into other words and conceptions, without disturbing its own nature, because Hegel himself with certain words connects only certain ideas, and expects us to study ourselves into a language entirely new. A Hegelian lexicon, and a Hegelian grammar are, however, not so easily formed. We shall therefore, as far as the system is concerned, have to be satisfied with little, and can only bring to view that which stands in the nearest relation to the religious and Christian view of life. Here the following main points may suffice.

Schleiermacher as well as Jacobi, placed the essence of religion chiefly in feeling, and regarded knowledge as secondary, while Hegel on the other hand insisted on *knowledge* above all other things. Feeling he regards as merely a subordinate form of religion, even the worst of all forms, because it is only subjective, that is, concerns only one individual. Consequently that feeling of dependence in which Schleiermacher places religion, is no better in his eyes than the instinctive feeling of dependence that attaches the dog to his master. But in the department of knowledge too, Hegel makes a distinction between the religious conception as it proceeds from feeling, or from the idea in the mind. The lower classes of people may be satisfied with religious conceptions (as of heaven, hell, etc.,) but not the real thinker. He rather discovers a contradiction between that which the conception is intended to express, and what it really does express; this contradiction must be solved, it must, as Hegel says, be raised, that is, must be changed to something higher, something standing above the contradiction. The gradation of religious knowledge in individuals as well as nations is this; a man receives the religious matter offered him as something external, something heterogeneous and objective to him, without being thoroughly penetrated by it. The next requirement therefore is, that he inquire into the matter, penetrate it, appropriate it to himself, in doing this, however, it easily happens that he subjects what is given, to his own arbitrary choice, and makes the things what he desires them to be, instead of taking them as they are. The ancient times took the former course in reference to religion; positive orthodoxy took the material handed down to it, just as it was offered, as a brittle tough-mass, reason subjected its opinions and inclinations to what the church determined. The modern time, however, is distinguished by the attempt to arrange and appropriate what is transmitted. In the former, therefore, objective torpidity appeared; in the latter subjective arbitrariness. The new philosophy attempts to elevate the thinking mind above both stand-points, since it neither permits the material offered to remain objective to us, nor allows it to be drawn to ourselves, while the thinking is subject to our own arbitrary choice. The enmity between the "thing in itself," or the thing per se, and the thinking Ego is to be solved in this way, that the individual does not place himself, thinking, guessing, and supposing, in opposition to things, and form a casual conception of them according to his own pleasure; but that with self-denial (yet with freedom) he examine them, permit the spirit prevailing in them to influence him, and thus consciously make himself master of the conception. Thus far we can but recognize a beneficial progress of knowledge in Hegel's principles of thought. What Schelling had asserted of nature and our relations to it, that we must watch for its secrets, must enter its quiet dreams, its fancies and its thoughts, if we desire to attain a living view of it; this Hegel required, with less poetry indeed, but with the sterner demand of thought, of those things which belong to history and morality, of the works of art, of law and of religion. He wanted to furnish a false realism, with an ideal view of things, as much as to lead a partial idealism back to reality; he wanted the material, the solid, to be spiritualized, but the airy and the spiritual which had been separated from its body to be embodied again. He wanted the period of negation to be followed by one of affirmation, the period of doubt by one of certainty. The spirit was to apprehend and comprehend itself, even its lowest depths, and was no longer to wander about as a dreamer among the dreaming.

In direct opposition to Kant, who had denied reason the right to philosophize about divine things, Hegel demanded the right of searching after God. But he did not want to do this in the old way, as if the finite could of itself comprehend the infinite. The manner is rather inverted; God comprehends himself in man, comes to consciousness in him; for as God, (according to the Bible), once became man in Christ, so He (according to Hegel) is still continually becoming man in us. Reason and Revelation, according to Hegel, do not contradict each other; the latter, however, places that as general truth for the conception, which the former brings to the perception more in images. If now, according to Hegel, the essence of real philosophy consists in not merely knowing the human, but in knowing God as He is, then this is a prerogative which philosophy has in common with the Christian Revelation, though in a different manner; for the essence of the Christian Revelation cannot consist in this, that it dismisses us with a few moral common-place instructions, but that it reveals to us the depths of the Godhead. Hegel asks, with Lessing, "What were a Revelation which reveals nothing?" Hegel thinks the essence of revelation consists in revealing God as the Triune One. Thus he calls God in His abstract generality the Father; in so far, however, as He, the Known, is distinguished from the Knowing, with whom He is, however, one and the same, He is called the Son, while it is the Spirit who brings the Father and Son in the essence of God to a unity of consciousness. Here the plain Christian may very properly ask, whether these depths, to which the Hegelian speculation requires us to descend, are the same depths to which the Christian doctrine of Redemption leads those longing for salvation. And, after a little reflection, he will find, unless he is beguiled by forms, that the knowledge to which the Bible leads us, is not a knowledge for the sake of knowing and comprehending merely, but that it serves for the confirmation of our salvation, and that the doctrine of the Father, Son, and Spirit, has significance for us only, as we love the Father, like children, yield ourselves to Christ for salvation, and to the Spirit for reproof and sanctification ; for "if I understand all mysteries," says the apostle, "and have not charity, piety, I am nothing." This *practical* significance of religious knowledge, which aims at our salvation, which Pietism frequently regarded too gloomily, and Rationalism sometimes too insipidly, was too much neglected by Hegel. We allow his speculative tendency its perfect right in its proper place ; but it must not push aside religion, or attempt to elevate itself above it. And here Hegel and Schleiermacher differ most widely, for while the former permits religion and theology to be absorbed by philosophy, the latter keeps them distinct, and grants the life of religious emotions and pious communion ; in a word, the life of faith, a free, vigorous, prosperity on its own root, even independent of the course of development of philosophical systems, without, however, by this means closing it against the influences of speculation. And till the present day it is a question whether those who think the stand-point of believers does not reach that of philosophers, may not be answered that their thinking does not reach the stand-point of true faith. As little, however, as sound can be smelled, or colour tasted, can the two departments be mingled in the mind. Here is another very important difference between Hegel and Schleiermacher. Since Schleiermacher does not make religion dependent on philosophical thinking, but regards it as something experienced by the pious, the definite historical appearance of the Saviour in the world, the *historical Christ,* and the institution of the Church founded by Him, have far more significance in Schleiermacher's system of theology than in Hegel's, in whose writings it is often uncertain how far the expressions about the God-man refer to Christ who really appeared, or only to the ideal speculative Christ, to whom the historical Christ is related very nearly as a single specimen to the genius which it represents. We shall return to this point in speaking of Strauss.

If in the meantime we ask what influence Hegel exerted on his age, we see him taking a stand in decided opposition to the then prevailing Rationalism. What they called reason he attacked as a mischievous confusion of prejudices, flat nonsense, and dead formalism. In opposition to the insipid reasoning "enlightenment" of the understanding, he advocated the profound orthodoxy, and again brought into honour the despised scholastics. He denied that the Rationalists had a theology, since to them God was an unknown something, of whom they could say nothing. The exact grammatical-historical interpretation of the Bible, for which many of the rationalistic school became famous, seemed to him spiritless, and a stooping to the letter, in which opinion, of course, his followers too willingly agreed with him. But Hegel also opposed decidedly the political liberalism then foaming and fermenting among the students. In the strictest opposition to the ideal improvers of the world, who were dissatisfied with the present, and dreamed of new forms of government, and new state organizations, he advanced the proposition, so often misapplied afterwards, because misunderstood, that whatever *really* exists, is also *right* and *reasonable*. This statement, properly understood, became a great law for the study of history. How very different appeared now the middle ages, for instance, and all that had been formed and fashioned since then! While formerly each one had placed himself above history, now each one learned to subject himself to it, and gained a respect for that which had become historical. Thus, this philosophy at its first appearance was favourably received by those who feared the political enthusiasm of an excited youth. The *historical* school, too, appeared to receive as firm a support from Hegel in the departments of law, of art, and politics, and the orthodoxy of the Church. And yet how soon matters changed. Scarcely had Hegel closed his eyes in death, when, in close connection with what the July revolution in France (1830) had accomplished, the disciples of this very philosophy, under the name of *Young Germany*, proclaimed a doctrine which men of order had much more right to fear, than the political youthful dreams of the so-called Teutomanes (Deutschthuemler). With the same logical skill with which the master appeared to build up they pulled down. And this they did (apparently, at least), without being false to the system; for if revolutionizing had once become the order of the day, consequently something within the sphere of reality, it could appear justifiable from the proposition that the real is the right. If the political horizon changed, the theories adapted to the times also changed. France, which had taken the lead, now appeared as the model-state, and the hero of the former age. Napoleon, with whom Hegel had already shown much sympathy, became the hero of Young Germany. The old Wartburg stories, German coats, &c., were laughed at, and cosmopolitism, as it was reflected in France, was made a political dogma. If this had happened only in politics it would concern us no further; but the same thing was experienced in the department of theology; Hegel had restored the positive in theology to authority; in his system, orthodoxy appeared to receive a new and firm, because scientific support, though it was evident to those who did not permit themselves to be deceived by forms that Hegel's orthodoxy was not very serious, or at least not so much so as the admirers of the master desired it to be considered. The Hegelian trinity was neither that of Athanasius and the symbolical books, nor that of the Bible and Bible-Christians, and Hegel could less repel the suspicion of pantheism, than Schleiermacher, whose speculative views found their supplement in those of faith. The indefinite, the ambiguous, and the oracular, which with all his logical acuteness and strictness of method, were not wanting in Hegel's works, could of themselves make it possible that the disciples, soon after his death, should dispute about the master's words, and should separate into two parties, who, with a somewhat distorted reference to the political parties in parliament,[1] were called the right and left side. The right side, represented by honourable, learned, and clever men, by those who had received their first impulse from Schleiermacher, attempted to prove that Hegel was quite serious in reference to Christianity, and that only by pursuing this course a real mediation could be found between Rationalism and Supernaturalism. The charge

[1] In both houses in Prussia those who sided with the king formerly sat on the right side. The term was first applied to the Hegelians by Bauer.—Tr.

that the new speculation changes the doctrines of the church by misinterpretation, is refuted by it in replying that it made them profounder and gave them life, while they had formerly been petrified by some, and rendered shallow by others; Pantheism (they taught, moreover), is a bugbear to those only who cannot reconcile themselves to a God dwelling in the world, and who need a personal God for their selfish and personal aims. The left side, as is well known, found its most decided and ready advocate in Strauss, who openly declared in his "Life of Jesus," that what the church and the believing world has hitherto regarded as history is but a myth. The term myth was nothing new. Neither did it originate in the Hegelian school. The theologians of a mediating tendency had long cherished the thought that not every story in the Bible is to be received as real history, still less to be so interpreted as to appear natural, as the Rationalists had attempted to do; but that events of the higher spiritual life, as they occur at all times in the department of faith, meet us in the form of histories, whose eternal contents are to be separated from the surrounding form. Already had Origen tended to this with his allegorical interpretations, and the mystics had attempted something similar. Clearly conscious of what it was doing, the new theology attempted to separate the historical, and the symbolical wrapped in a historical dress. With this new (modern) aim as his starting point, De Wette referred a large part of the Old Testament histories to the mythical, and Schleiermacher, too, had not hesitated to receive those accounts of the Gospel which relate to the first childhood of Jesus and his ascension as the poetical expression of the truth, that the beginning and end of this wonderful life are to be measured as little by the laws of common experience as the life itself. It was thought that by this means such accounts would be taken out of the hands of unbelievers, since they were taken into a region which the common prosaic understanding could not enter.

But what was thus kept within bounds, Strauss carried beyond all limits, since he did not only regard the dress as containing mythical elements, but the kernel itself of the life of Jesus as the product of a pious poetical fancy, such as had been possessed by the first Christian congregations. He did not permit the waves of poetical genius to sport on the surface of the Gospel accounts, but from the depths of the whole the new interpreter conjured a giant-spirit, hitherto unknown, which succeeded in moving the earth out of its course and in calling into existence a religion, like the Christian, by means of pious poetry. Strauss suddenly inverted the relation that had been received till then, Christ had not founded the Church, but the Church had invented Christ, had formed him out of the predictions of the Old Testament and the hopes and expectations of the age founded on them. A rich layer of miracle-stories had formed itself around this small kernel, so that it would be very difficult to find in it any thing purely historical according to this presupposition.[1] Independent of the improbable and arbitrary grounds on which Strauss attempted to establish the particulars of this view, it always appeared very remarkable to the more thoughtful, who were not led astray by the illusive appearance of the argument, that such a Christian association could think and live itself into such an ideal, if it did not bring with it the remembrance of something, that had really been experienced, that had really been seen. The *personal* support is wanting here in history, as it is universally in the pantheistic systems. Strauss, however, would have given a powerful proof of the power of the religious idea, if this idea had really succeeded in inventing a Christ. One would then think of the words of Herder: "If the fishermen of Galilee have invented such a history, God be praised that they invented it," or of those of Claudius, that one might even die for such an idea. Strauss himself asserted, that according to his notion the historical Christ indeed is lost, but that his ideal divine-human Christ did more for religious elevation, than the Jesus of the Rationalists, who was indeed historical, but only human and robbed of all identity. How little support an ideal Christianity had, the historical foundation being taken from it, soon became evident, and but a few years passed after the appearance of the "Life of Jesus" before the entire Christian doctrine, with which Strauss had comforted his readers in his appendix, was torn to pieces

[1] Strauss boasted, that he was free from all presuppositions, whilst he overlooked those, from which he started, and which others proved on him.

and scattered to the winds. Those who had hoped Strauss would build up dogmatically what he had torn down historically, found themselves grievously disappointed at the appearance of his Dogmatics (Glaubenslehre) 1840. Now it was asserted, that modern science and the faith of Christians could never agree, and that a reconciliation was impossible. And in this others soon agreed with Strauss. There were those who went even farther than Strauss, who called that which he had considered pious poetry the sum of religious enthusiasm, and the designed invention of an individual (as Bruno Bauer), and who not only regarded all positive (revealed) religion as false, but (with Feuerbach) the religion of man in general as self-deception. What else could follow from these presuppositions, but the conclusion so welcome to many, that the gloomy religion which constrained men would cease and make place for a cheerful philosophy? If now to this philosophy a new poetical school is united, corresponding with it, which orders the cross to be torn from the earth and which promises to conjure up, not the ancient gods of Greece (in the sense of Schiller), but gross heathenism, then, of course, the history of Protestantism is ended, if the edge of a bottomless abyss is really the object which Protestantism has to gain.

It would indeed make me sad, if now, after leading you through so many windings and turnings of the way, through dry deserts and steppes, and also through many cultivated regions, through many luxuriant groves, I should have to lay down the guide's staff and say: we have come to our journey's end. But, God be praised! we have only followed one side to its termination, where endless negation ends in annihilation; but in doing this we have fulfilled the sad duty of shewing whither a philosophy, torn loose from the heart of God, must lead. There is something quite peculiar about the Hegelian philosophy. No one protested more than Hegel against a mode of thinking which, without viewing the things as they are, philosophizes merely from certain presuppositions, he has well designated this mode of thinking the *abstract* and opposed to it the *concrete*. He very properly demanded, that thought should master the world and its phenomena even to their deepest roots, that it should sound things to their utmost depths, and should comprehend life in its freshness and vigour. By doing this he has given the human mind a great task to perform, and spared philosophers a number of erroneous paths. And on this account we will recognize in all its greatness and importance this merit of the Hegelian philosophy, that it called the mind, from its ideal dreams, back to reality. But it must appear stranger on this very account, that the great mass of Hegelians fell into the very error which the master wanted to avoid; for it is not easy for philosophy to appear more abstract and arbitrary, than in the mouths of the haughty admirers of this system. No other has been more riveted and spellbound in a spiritless mechanism, than this which is continually speaking of spirit; none has more fully denied life as it is, and none is more guilty of making just what it pleases of things, than *this* philosophy in *these* hands; none can play more deceitfully with words, none wipes away more fully the fragrance and lustre of reality, none so volatilizes the personal, actual, individual life, which it regards merely as a fleeting shadow, as a subsiding wave, as the "vanishing property" of things: hence, before it vanishes also human personality in history, as the personality of God in the Universe.

We do not want any one to take this as a judgment in reference to Hegel's philosophy, as the founder himself viewed it. We speak of those who have unfortunately applied its real or supposed results to a destructive theology. Even, then, if Hegelianism may be regarded as a giant's sword, which in the hands of a hero can cause many wounds, and may also sustain many valiant attacks with honour; still in the hands of the children of our times, it is a sword with which much evil will be effected.

We will not attempt to decide whether the worthy men of the so-called right side will succeed in wresting the sword from those of the left, and then wield it so as to gain for its master and itself the victorious wreath. Nor is it clear to us what Schelling will put in place of his old system, which at one time opened the way for Hegel. In the mean time, it is our comfort that the destiny of religion, of the Church, of theology, yea, the destiny of Christianity and Protestantism, is not dependent on the course of this or that school of philosophy, not on the victory of one or the other system; but that living powers are concerned in the matter, of which our philosophy, even the latest, does not dream,—powers which God himself placed in the religious nature of man, which He awakened and called out by the Spirit of Christ, which He has preserved in His Church, and which He has renewed and increased in extraordinary times, as in the Reformation. These vital powers philosophy may try to comprehend; but it can never produce. By inquiring we shall discover that Protestantism is not in so bad a condition as a glance at the results of the latest philosophy and criticism has indicated. If, before we turn our attention to practical life, we remain in the scientific, yea, philosophical department a few moments, we must say, if we do not listen to one party only, that there is still *faith,* and an energetic faith, indeed, to which the acquisition of knowledge is a matter of earnest endeavour. By the side of the Hegelian philosophy another has always sustained itself, which we may call the philosophy of the personal God, and which will not lack followers, whether it places itself in the line of the great historical development, and leads Hegel beyond himself (from pantheism to theism), or turning away from Hegel, pursues its own course. One thing is certain, that the speculative tendency of modern times has, with all its degeneracy, the merit that it necessitates the mind to descend to the depths of knowledge. A superficial reasoning, as it was still possible under the name of philosophy thirty, forty years ago, has now become impossible. The essence of things is being more and more penetrated. Subjective opinion and liking, the following of whimsical notions from a prejudicial stand-point, can no more prevail against the enlarged views to which our age is accustomed. The stiff, awkward manner of former polemics has made room for quick dialectics, which instead of insisting on its proposition with obstinacy, studies the opinion of an opponent, and instead of striking it down from the outside, rather seeks to refute it from its own inner construction, after it has thoroughly examined and penetrated it. Even if the desolations which the so-called left side of the speculative school occasions in ecclesiastical, political, and moral life are greater and sink deeper than the negative effects of Rationalism, still the dull and shallow mode of thinking, which at one time claimed to be the only rational one, can no more prevail. Even those who boldly assert that religion and Christianity have been superseded by the cultivation of modern times, speak more favourably and more reasonably of former religious conditions than the "illuminati" of those times. They at least admit, that what they consider unsatisfactory for our time was much and all to another time, yea, that there it had its full historical right. They acknowledge the merits of the old theologians of the middle ages, of Luther and his time, of Mysticism and Pietism, even if they deny these appearances the right of lasting for ever. In our day nature and art, history and politics are also viewed from a more intellectual point of view, with eyes more alive than formerly.

Language itself has gained much, and with it the fulness of thought has increased. It must, it is true, also have aided in covering many weaknesses and in gilding over much which cannot stand the test of examination; and as Schiller once said that language makes poetry for us, so now it might be said, that it philosophizes for us. Now, no one wants it to be said of him, that he speaks of things he has not fathomed, that owing to contracted views he sees but one side; and even if there is much that is superficial and doubtful, still every one wants to save the appearance of depth, while formerly people boasted of ignorance as well as insolence. But there is more than an appearance of profoundness even among those who take the lead in the negative movement. In a word, education has become too general for individuals to distract the multitude with transient imaginations and dreams, and to check the course of investigation. Study and labour is now required of every one, be he friend or foe. Whoever desires to build up or tear down must give himself some trouble; he must command respect from his opponent by knowledge, and must prove his fitness, otherwise he is not permitted to enter the dispute. Every one acquainted with the course of modern theology will agree with me, that more is required of a young candidate in our day than twenty or thirty years ago. While the earlier of Rationalism[1] had de-

[1] The later Rationalism (after Kant) differs favourably from the earlier by positive learning. The later was, however, frequently dead and useless, which Hegel not unjustly charged it with.

creased the amount that was to be learned from the Bible, Church history, and dogmatics, because it regarded this apparatus as superficial, and thought that all might be deduced from reason, and at best a few passages from the Bible as starting points; and while an erring Pietism interpreted the words, "To love Christ is better than all knowledge," in favour of ignorance; the science of our day, whatever theological views it may favour, demands a solid, exegetical, historical, and philosophical education. The theologian is expected to know everything that pertains to his department, to trace it to its historical origin and to know how to resolve it into its constituent elements. While the former interpreters of Scripture of both parties made the mistake, that they only sought for their own opinions in the Bible, and shewed their skill in twisting a passage so as to suit their own system, modern theological science has freed itself from this objectionable use of Scripture, and aims at an explanation as independent as possible from personal opinions. Thus, for instance, the natural explanation of miracles has lost its ground for ever, and Strauss has done the most to represent it in its entire ridiculousness and absurdity, and to make its revivification impossible. The study of the Bible has not only increased in impartiality, but in activity and interest within the last ten years. How different the explanation of an epistle of Paul, how different the interpretation of the gospel of John in the universities now from what it was twenty-five years ago! Since that time there has been an activity in the investigation of the Scriptures and an emulation which, with all its mistakes, can only fill us with joy. The desire is no longer merely to explain meagrely the written letter, but to penetrate the inmost souls of the authors of the Bible, and to learn to understand them from these depths. The impulse which Herder had given more than half a century ago to this matter now first began to be generally felt, and with more effect, since the other means of interpretation had increased and been purified since that time.[1]

While at the time of the "illuminism" Church history

[1] The same was the case in languages and the studies of antiquity. Creuzer's "Symbolik" introduced quite another view of the mythological, to say nothing of the great reform brought into philology by F. A. Wolf.

was regarded as a history of human folly, as a collection of singular anecdotes for the amusement of enlightened minds, now the breathing and moving of the Christian spirit again began to be observed in various periods; persons, too, began to perceive a life behind these forms which had become strange to us—a life which ought not to be strange to us. At first persons were startled when Neander declared the task of the Church historian to be, "to represent the history of the Church of Christ as a speaking proof of the divine power of Christianity, as a school of Christian experience, a voice of edification resounding through all ages, of instruction, of warning for all who are willing to hear." Though this language was called pietistic, still the method of viewing the subject adopted by Neander and others similar to it, soon gained the ascendency. Men were tired of abstract generalities. In explaining history, the concrete was again desired, the living, the coloured, the fragrant. With a predilection beyond all precedent the attention was again turned to the particulars in historical studies; men loved to give the lives of distinguished men, of eminent lights of the Church, with unbiassed judgment, and their mode of thinking, their inclinations, and even their weaknesses were studied. Men placed themselves in the spirit of the age in which they lived; instead of a dry narration of facts came a life-like representation, in which light and shade were properly distributed, as in a good picture. An interest was again taken in the monuments of Christian art and manners; in church buildings more was to be seen again than a mere mass of stones; and as the taste for the symbolical again began to develop, a meaning began to be perceived behind the dogmas of the Church, where formerly nothing but nonsense had been discovered. Men began to turn their attention especially to the ancient hymns of the Church, and while in the last twenty years of the previous century men seemed to have nothing better to do than to put rhyming prose in the place of poetry, about the thirtieth year of this century a great dissatisfaction with what that period had produced manifested itself, and since then has continually increased. Whoever will compare the improvements in the hymn-books made in our time with those of the last twenty years of last century, will clearly perceive that a different spirit breathes in them. Preaching, too, was different. The stiff, logical conformity to rules, which was still esteemed above all other methods of sermonizing at the time of Reinhard, had to give place to a greater variety of forms, a freer effusion. The most different methods of preaching appeared side by side. While Schleiermacher unfolded, in a closely connected succession of thoughts, the deepest views of Christian life for the educated with a peculiar art of speech, Draeseke overpowered with his bold figures and flashes of thought, and others moved the masses turned aside from God, by sermons on repentance. . . . Harms' bold requirement, in opposition to the subjection to rules, was: "We must speak with tongues." With this striving after originality, much embellishment, much exaggeration and untruth may have been connected (as is the case with the highly gifted F. Krummacher, and many other preachers of late years), still it cannot be denied that the progress which the German language has made through its poets, had beneficial effects on pulpit eloquence.

With all the complaints of the neglect of the church and church-affairs in this age, the churches in the large cities, which were empty at the time of the revolution and of the French imperial reign, were filled at a later period, and with persons of the higher and educated classes. Thus we find in the last ten years a lively interest in ecclesiastical life, Divine worship, and the constitution of the Church, instead of the former neglect. Schleiermacher did his share in bringing about this result. While at the time of Rationalism the attendance at church was regarded merely as respect for the preacher, since all the rest, singing, prayer, and sacrament, were considered mere secondary matters, intended for the weak only, yea, while persons freely acknowledged that the educated attended church only for the sake of the example, and while even ministers dared to recommend the attendance only on this account: now persons found that man has other wants than merely to instruct or divert himself, that he needs edification for his soul, for the welfare of his own inner life, and that this finds its deep support and living expression only in the congregation of believers. Even Hegel himself called divine worship the highest art of the human spirit, which the disciples of the left side of course refer to the worship of their genius. In reference to the constitution of the Church and its external affairs, the interest was not only awakened among the ministry but also among the laity. While during the period of Rationalism the territorial system was the prevailing one, that system by which the affairs of the Church came under the authority of the State, just as the affairs of justice, of police and finance, because ministers were to a certain degree expected to be used as moral police officers, as civil officers of public morality: now again it was remembered, that Christ did not found His Church in consequence of a government order proceeding from the Emperor Augustus or King Herod, and that His apostles did not preach on account of the government, however much they taught obedience to it, but that till the time of Constantine the Church stood free, ordered its own affairs, and relied on no other power but that of the Holy Spirit, the original vital power of the Church. Persons looked to North America, where the Church developes itself freely, without being supported or hindered by the State. Others objected against this, and not unjustly, that the times had changed, that it belonged to Christianity, not to remain one sect or to be divided into many, as is the case in North America, but rather to penetrate with its living breath the life of the State and people, and that therefore a free activity of the Church in the State was certainly more advantageous to both than the forcible and unnatural separation of the two. Indeed, the Christian state (quite different from the State-Police-Church), was designated by the Hegelian philosophy as the only rational, only real state. Although opinions differ on this subject even in our day, still the fact that many reflected on the relation of Church and State, and thought the matter worthy of their consideration, is an important and cheering indication. But men did not stop with theories. In different parts of Germany a path was opened for ecclesiastical life, by the establishment and regulation of Synods. This was the case in the Rhine-provinces of Prussia and in Baden; and in other countries attempts at least were made to promote congregational life in the Church by means of Church-discipline and Church-officers. In this matter, too, Schleiermacher took the lead with his regulating mind.

But not only in the ecclesiastical department, so far as this is bounded by certain visible limits, but in the great department of Christian life and activity, in that which, in opposition to all human limitation, we call the kingdom of God, we notice in the last ten years a great activity and movement, a devotion to the cause of Christ, such as we find nowhere else in the entire history of Protestantism, from the Reformation till the present time. While formerly (with few exceptions) it seemed to be reserved for Pietism, Methodism, and Moravians to carry on missions among the heathens, to spread the Bible and Christian knowledge among the people, to erect Christian institutions of charity and those for the training of the young, and while then in opposition to these efforts philanthropy attempted something similar from its own standpoint, we find that now the truly Christian spirit, which is both divine and human, attempts continually to effect a practical union of hearts, where it was utterly impossible to do this on the basis of the written letter. Thus the Missionary and Bible Societies, which first became native to the European continent since the second decade of this century, have actually accomplished that union,[1] about which men had so long racked their brains; thus men of very different views and opinions have assisted each other in performing Christian works of love, uniting our evangelical basis. The Christian and philanthropic, who at first were hostile, approached each other. Let men, if they choose, say that this wide-spread and continually increasing activity is pietistic, and based on pietistic principles; yet it must at least be acknowledged, that Pietism in our day is still a power which makes itself felt, and which will not soon withdraw to give the field to liberalism, communism, &c.; it must be acknowledged, that the positive power of Protestantism still matches the negative, even if we cannot suppress the wish, that a still more decided and more general understanding might be accomplished between those who desire the

[1] This commendation, we are sorry to say, must again be limited at this time, in which blind indiscretion, adhering so tenaciously to its confession of faith, threatens to destroy the beautiful harmony.

advancement of both the good and the true of Protestantism, its light and its power. It will not do to give up hope or to fold the hands in discouragement, however gloomy the prospect may occasionally be. Very fortunately, too, that which excites attention among the learned and appears in a systematic form, is not always what holds and supports the Church ; it is the Spirit that bloweth how and where it listeth, who prepares his instruments in a thousand different ways, that Spirit, who often appears most powerful in those who appear weak in the eyes of the world. It will not do to forget that the power of faith, as it lived in a Luther, has often manifested itself in a quiet, humble sphere of activity, and has borne witness of the nature of the evangelical Spirit.

XXIV.

THE RISE OF THE PROTESTANT SPIRIT IN THE ROMAN CATHOLIC CHURCH DURING THE PAST AND THE PRESENT CENTURIES.

QUESNEL—THE APPELLANTS AND THE CONVULSIONISTS—THE JESUITS IN PARAGUAY—DISBANDING OF THE ORDER—GANGANELLI—THE ILLUMINATI—JOSEPH II. AND HIS REFORMS—THE FRENCH REVOLUTION—THE THEOPHILANTHROPISTS—BUONAPARTE AND THE PAPAL AGREEMENT—ST. MARTIN AND CHATEAUBRIAND—NAPOLEON'S TREATMENT OF PIUS VII.—NEW AGREEMENTS WITH THE POPE—THE RESTORATION OF THE BOURBONS—RE-ESTABLISHMENT OF THE JESUITS—LAMENNAIS—GERMAN CATHOLICISM AND ITS REPRESENTATIVES—RELATION OF CATHOLICISM TO PROTESTANTISM AT THE MOST RECENT PERIOD—GLANCES INTO THE FUTURE—CONCLUSION.

To make the picture complete which we have drawn of the rise and growth of Protestantism in the present and during the past century, we must touch in outline the changes in the Catholic Church, in order to show how tendencies towards a reform have been developing within it, and how Protestantism has exerted power even in that Church. Even before the last century, it was plain that since the great Reformation there have not been lacking in the Catholic Church efforts to correct the abuses which have crept into her, to set limits to the Papal authority, to reform the cloister life, to promote better education among the people, to make the services of public worship more conformable to the changed conditions of society, and through the introduction of a more rigid moral discipline, to recover that respect for the Church and its institutions which has been in great measure lost through the degeneracies of earlier days. With this tendency was united another, viz., to check the expansive power of Protestantism, to disallow the rise of free thought and the utterance of reformatory ideas within the Catholic Church, to put new props under a falling hierarchy, and, whenever possible, to enlarge the circle of true believers. But during the eighteenth century not only was the Papal dignity exposed to many and severe assaults, but the order of Jesuits, who had before been all-powerful, were also shorn of their old strength. Going back to the beginning of the eighteenth century, we find Jesuitism struggling fiercely with Jansenism, the adherents to the former leaning rather to the Pope, the adherents of the latter leaning rather to the reformers. This controversy acquired new vigour at the appearance of a devotional book much prized by the Jansenists. This was the New Testament with explanatory notes in a strongly evangelical view, and thoroughly favouring the doctrine of justification by faith instead of works. The author of this work, Paschasius Quesnel, was a Jansenist, driven out of France, and residing in the Netherlands. The Pope then ruling, Clement XI., put a hundred and one passages of this work under the ban, stigmatising them as heretical, dangerous, and offensive to pious ears; and yet among the condemned passages are some which were quoted literally not only from the Scriptures, but also from the Fathers, and particularly from Saint Augustine. This roused the French clergy, and the Bishop of Paris, Cardinal Noailles, opposed the acceptance of the Papal bull of condemnation. Those who sided with the Cardinal were styled Appellants. They had a long struggle with the court, which more from state policy than from religious principle stood by the Pope. When Louis XV. ascended the throne, the adoption of the Papal bull was earnestly contended against, yet it in the end gained the day. One of the Appellants, a Parisian deacon, who afterwards took the name of St. Francis of Paris, had defended himself even to death for the sake of Jansenism, and was buried in the churchyard of St. Medard. A crowd of people flocked to his grave, at which miracles began to occur, and many sick persons who lay down upon it were healed at once of severe diseases. It was all in vain that the Archbishop of Sens declared that the miracles were false: the people declared that they were true. Similar occurrences took place in the churches, until the king was obliged to close them, and then the manifestations were confined to the private houses of the Convulsionists, as they were called. After a while the affair died away; and as Voltaire said later, the grave of St. Francis of Paris became the grave also of Jansenism.

The Jesuits came off conquerors from this field, but unexpected difficulties lay in their path. Though they were victorious in the affairs of religious faith, yet their worldly power was soon to meet a determined adversary. On the shores of Paraguay and Uraguay in South America, a state had been openly founded, in which the Jesuits had uncontrolled sway. All the avenues of approach were through fortifications which the order had constructed. But when a treaty, concluded between Spain and Portugal in 1750, had given a part of Paraguay to the latter country, the savage natives in 1753 denied the Portuguese access to the country. The Jesuits were regarded as the cause of this act, and the Portuguese minister Carvalho, Marquis of Pombal, determined on their downfall. A murderous attack on the king of Portugal awakened the suspicion that this order was accessory to the deed. A formal charge of high treason was preferred against the Jesuits, and by a decree of the third of September, 1759, they were driven from Portugal, and their return forbidden under pain of death. The order had received a powerful blow which passed through its whole ranks like an electrical shock. In France their polity was subjected to a thorough investigation, and the body was disbanded in the spring of 1764. Notwithstanding a bull of Pope Clement XIII., declaring the sanctity of the Order of Jesus, the Jesuits were speedily driven from Spain and Naples and all the dominions of the Bourbons. Indeed, the monarchs of this family exerted so much influence over the successor of Clement XIII., the sceptical Ganganelli, Pope Clement XIV., as to induce him to issue in 1773 the famous bull, Dominus a redempter noster, and to dissolve the order. The advent of this Pope and his decisive action in disbanding the Jesuits are significant facts in the history of Catholic Protestantism. It is curious to observe how the upheaving of events and the general ferment of those times, from which not even the Catholic Church remained free, affected even the head of the hierarchy, and caused the name of a pope to appear on the list of reformers.

Antonio Ganganelli was the son of a physician: he had been educated as a Franciscan, and had awakened great expectations. Already under Benedict XIV. he had attained to much consideration, Clement XIII. gave him the cardinal's hat, and in 1769 he saw himself in the chair of St. Peter, after the opponents of the Jesuits had assured themselves of his co-operation. In the days of Gregory VII. it was the policy of the papal power to humiliate all worldly potentates, and give them a place at his feet, but Ganganelli understood the temper of his times, and saw that his first care must be to be on good terms with the kings: he therefore took all pains to re-establish peace where it was disturbed; and in order not to vex the Protestants, he omitted on Green Thursday that passage in the communion service condemning heretics. But he well knew the danger of breaking up the Order of Jesuits; in signing the bull for their disbanding, he signed his own death warrant, for soon after there followed a numbness of his limbs, which was ascribed to the poison of Jesuits. He died in 1774.

When we look with unprejudiced eyes at the efforts of the Portuguese minister and of the Bourbon courts, to overthrow the Jesuits, the issue may seem to us a great gain; but our joy would have been less alloyed, had those efforts been less tyrannical in their nature, and one kind of despotism not been exchanged for another. It is a striking proof of the variety in the ideas of tolerance prevalent in the eighteenth century, that Frederick the Great, who stood at the head of the great sceptical movement of the time, gave the Jesuits a home in Silesia when they had been driven from all Catholic countries; and that Catherine II. of Russia granted them entrance to Poland. Yet in Catholic countries, especially in Bavaria, the influence of the Order was perpetuated, mainly by those who had been compelled to openly abjure their faith, but who were secretly true to it, and all the more dangerous. But Germany became the centre of the struggle, and, as it had been for Protestantism, the arena of the strife.

In Germany also the Jesuits had exercised a wide influence: public instruction was almost completely in their hands, and German courts, like that of Vienna at the time of Maria Theresa, those of Bavaria, and of the Palatinate in special, were wholly in their control. But about the same time that the Jesuits were driven from South America, the day began to dawn in Germany, first in matters of science and then in ecclesiastical matters, more especially as to the relation of the German Catholic Church and its clergy to Rome. The voices which at the time of the great Reformation were raised in favour of an independence of Rome, now came from the clergy itself. A prelate of high rank, the Archbishop of Treves, had, as early as when Clement XIII. sat in the papal chair (1765), published a work under the assumed name of Justinus Febronius, in which he asserted the ancient rights of the bishop in contrast to those of the pope, and pleaded for a return of the independent German Catholic Church, as it existed before the Council of Trent; a work which the friends of the hierarchy and the Jesuits most of all, were specially bitter against, and whose author was at last compelled to retract, when the influence which it had exerted upon the whole Catholic world could not be recalled. And in the other departments of theological science there were constantly manifested the proofs of the influence of the sceptical literature of Protestant countries, great as was the demand for that literature, even among the Catholic clergy.

Some sought to influence the youth through better school books, some by a freer method of study; and some of the results of protestant criticism were carried from Göttingen to

Mayence; but efforts were made at once to correct all these unfavourable movements. The friends of scepticism did not dare to publicly proclaim themselves, and there was nothing left to them but to work just as much in the dark as their opponents, and to found an Order which, in its administration and economy, should have much in common with the Jesuits, while it should secretly be in entire antagonism with them. This was the noted Order of Illuminati, whose founder, Adam Weishaupt, a professor of law in Ingolstadt, had been a protegè of the Jesuits. Into the dark divisions of this Order, their relation to the Freemasons and their final fate, we do not need to enter. We only wish to call attention to the strange blending of scepticism and mysticism in those times, for in the same epoch when some were shattering the very foundations of the Catholic faith, others were testifying to miracles in their midst, and were even drawing Protestants into their circles.

Among the Catholics, as among the Protestants, the various grades of religionists are here in union, there in direct antagonism. Parallel with the tendency to more freedom of thought (not so marked indeed in the Romish Church as in its rival), there was also a tendency to a veiled mysticism, similar to that of Claudius, Stilling, Lavater, and other protestants: to a faith, in other words, which appeals to the pious feelings, and which, resting on the basis of an inward spirituality, set aside a dead orthodoxy with just as little compunction as a one-sided infidelity. As an example of this tendency we might cite the noble Michael Sailer, the friend of Lavater.

Before we trace these developments in Catholicism further, we ought to speak of a monarch, who was, in a certain sense, to the Catholic Church what Frederick the Great was to the Protestant Church. Joseph Second had been from 1765 regent with his mother Maria Theresa, but at 1780, as Emperor of Germany, we see him enter with eager interest into the great sceptical movements of his country. His plan, shared by his minister Kaunitz, was to render the German Catholic Church as independent of Rome as possible, and to establish an enlightened order of priesthood within this independent Church, which, removed from Jesuitical and monkish influence, should diffuse a reasonable religion among the people, and widen the culture of the youth. To accomplish this, he forbade the carrying out of any papal orders without his previous assent to them, broke up the intimacy between the monks and foreigners of influence, destroyed many cloisters, and gave their revenues to parishes, schools, and seminaries, which were established according to his ideas. He introduced many measures to simplify public worship, hymns were composed in German, and Bibles printed in the same tongue and without the Romish running commentary. In vain did the Archbishop of Vienna, first an opponent and then a friend of the Jesuits, strive to induce him to stop in his course. The pope, Pius Sixth, whom the altered times did not permit to summon defected princes to his threshold, was compelled, after all letters missive had failed, to take the extreme step of making a journey himself to Vienna. This was in 1782. Venerable and yet noble and commanding in aspect, eloquent, and with a sweet toned voice, he was complacent enough to suppose that he could make some impression on the emperor. But he gained nothing more than a very respectful treatment, and the certainty that although he had made an imposing effect upon the crowd to which he gave his blessing, he had not succeeded in saving a single one of the cloisters whose doom had been written. Still we must confess that the emperor did not succeed in imposing durability on his reforms. We have not the space to enter on a thorough inquiry into the system of reformation adopted by Joseph, although such a review would disclose ideas at the foundation not unlike that on which Luther builded. Yet we have gone far enough already to draw the lesson, that there was altogether too much reform attempted on a mere theory, without reference to the conditions and the demands of the times, and that zeal was most truly effective when joined with an appreciation of the proper moment to strike a blow.

The most important event in the German Catholic church during Joseph's reign was the conference of the electors and archbishops of Mayence, Treves, Cologne, and Salzburg, at Ems in the summer of 1786, having as its object the bidding defiance to the Romish nuncio at Munich, and the establishing of the German bishoprics on a basis independent of Rome. But the work which they began failed in consequence of the obstinacy of the bishops, who more willingly obeyed their distant authority than that so near them, and they clung the more tenaciously to the papal chair.

But had Joseph the Second sought in vain to impose a reform upon the Catholic Church in accordance with the idea of the eighteenth century, the French Revolution which now broke out, threatened to put an end not only to the priesthood and the hierarchy, but to the church in every form. The extreme depression of the Catholic Church, its property proclaimed as the property of the nation, its priests compelled to swear allegiance to the citizens' constitution, or to flee the land, and the breaking up of the papal power, are hardly to be spoken of in connection with those extreme revolutionary dogmas which came in vogue during the reign of terror. And there seems to be a visible chain of events in the course of history, in that the very nation which had poured out the blood of the Huguenots as water, ostensibly for the Saviour's sake, now sought to obliterate all traces of Christianity, even to the reckoning of time, and that priests who under other circumstances would have lent their hands to the murder of Protestants, now out of fear, forswore as imposture the very faith which they had professed. In the very cemeteries where they had professed to witness miracles, they recorded Death is an eternal sleep; and the very deification of reason became a theme for dramatic blasphemy. After the personality of God had been flippantly disowned, the National Convention, at the instigation of Robespierre, decreed a belief in a Supreme existence, and in the immortality of the soul, and the eighth of July was consecrated as a national festival, to celebrate the honours of this new God, and was kept as only Frenchmen can. The only trace of the old Catholic faith to be seen in this was that the modern religion was decreed by law, Robespierre taking the place of the Pope. Very soon in 1795, universal freedom of belief, and a tolerance of all beliefs was granted, and it was seen at once that neither Christianity nor Catholicism in its ancient form had been driven out of the hearts of the people. The masses pressed into the churches, and new anxieties arose among the civil authorities, lest with the revival of love of the old faith, there should be a revival of a desire to have a king again. Deism too began to seek uniformity in the expression of its convictions. Every element of Christian doctrine had been brought into discredit through deistical writings, and yet men could not rid themselves of a belief in the eternal. A new religion must be organised, and a service must be instituted for the edification of the educated classes. The foundation was laid in the year 1796 by five gentlemen, all heads of families, who designated themselves Theophilanthropists, and met every week for prayer and moral conversation, and singing songs to the glory of God. Soon their number was increased, and in 1798 Reveillere Lepaux became the leader of the organization. The Directory of Paris assigned ten churches to the new order, and the novel method of worship extended itself widely, as far even as the provinces. And what was the substance of the faith of the Theophilanthropists? Their doctrine was limited to a belief in the existence of God, as an exalted ruler of the earth, and in the immortality of the soul. These two lofty conceptions formed the staple of their hymns and their harangues, all else was confined to a dry and general morality, whose highest goal was to teach how to be useful to one's native land. A simple altar on which flowers and fruits were laid in their season as thankofferings, and a platform for the speaker, were the central features of the place of worship. The walls were decorated with inscriptions like the following:—Children obey your parents, and honour your elders—Fathers and mothers instruct your children—Husbands and wives be mutually devoted to each other. In the place of the traditional festivals of the Church new ones were ordained, conformed to the seasons of the year; in the place of the sacraments, arbitrary and sentimental ceremonies, and so, too, at the birth of children, at the taking in of new members, at the celebration of marriage, at the distribution of prizes to children, and at funerals. It was impossible to avoid absolutely the adoption of Christian rites, although they were first robbed of their old significance. But this, instead of giving new value to the novel service, imparted to it a kind of unnaturalness which made its barrenness the more apparent, and showed that it could no more satisfy the wants of men for any length of time than distilled water could take the place of wine in supplying the needs of an empty stomach. The real activity of the order ceased in five years, and in 1802 their places of meeting were taken away from them. With Bonaparte's Consulship a new order of things in French Catholicism supervened. Men were convinced again, as if awaking from a dream, of the need of certain established religious dogmas and forms for the people, and so, as a work of political necessity, a compact was entered into in the year 1801 between Napoleon and the Pope, through the instrumentality of the diplomatic Consalvi. And as times of the greatest anxiety and distress have always drawn some souls back to the depth of religious feeling, so even during the reign of terror in France, Catholic mysticism throve on the recollections of a glorious past, and in the person of Saint Martin rose from its ashes, baptized in a new glow of devotion. The writer who has had the skill to awaken the interest of the reading world in the life of Zinzendorf, Varnhagen von Ense, has preserved for us some remembrances of these modern mystics, as well as of his relation to the Duchess of Bourbon, aunt of Louis Philippe, and has well characterized this manifestation of religiousness as "a beneficent flame, which in humble and lowly places reveals the brightest gems." "It is," he says, "like all the purest spiritual life in the Catholic Church, really half Protestant, although not deserting its old form, and putting on a new one." Less deeply than St. Martin worked Chateaubriand, through his work entitled "The Genius of Christianity," an apology for the old romantic Catholicism, and by his "Attala," the "Martyrs," and other writings, in which the glowing style is more remarkable than the clearness and the thoroughness of his judgment. But, most singularly, the effort of Chateaubriand to commend Christianity on the esthetical side harmonizes strangely with the efforts of German Protestants of the romantic school.

The truce between the Pope and the Emperor did not last long. Napoleon did indeed go so far in order to sanction his newly assumed imperatorial dignity in the eyes of the people as to be crowned by the Pope in 1804; but he showed how much his heart was in the matter by issuing, on his own responsibility, a Catechism for the youth of the empire, in which he accepted the decisions of the Council of Trent indeed, but also inserted as a prime dogma of the true faith, unhesitating obedience to the Emperor. The demand of this unconditional obedience, plunging Pope and Emperor into old difficulties once more, brought around new developments. Political legislation continually clashed with the traditions of the Church, and not in one or two points merely, but continually, particularly in matters of divorce and marriage, and the magnates of the Church saw that the Emperor was continually hampering and narrowing their power. When Pius was on the point of lending his hand to the designs of France, or Austria and England, he saw himself anew treated as an enemy. French troops took possession of Rome in February 1808, disbanded the College of Cardinals and the Papal army, and deprived the Pope of his worldly authority. The latter protesting, and resorting to the old spiritual weapon, the ban, had to learn how time had blunted its edge. And the personal worth of the Pope stands out in all the more effective light, in that, when thousands had forsworn allegiance to him, he displayed such resignation as he lay in his prison at Savona, as to draw from his conqueror the confession that he was "a really excellent man, and an angel of goodness." Yet Napoleon sought in vain to establish a National Church independent of Rome, whose central point should be Paris, and to impose his own liberalism upon Spain. The fanaticism of the Spanish clergy rose like a wall against his designs, and the convocation of French, Italian, and German bishops, held in 1811, was without effect. Once more, and still unfortunately, Napoleon sought to make peace with the Pope: on the 23d of January, 1813, the Agreement of Fontainebleau was entered into, in which the right of appointing bishops was taken from the Pope, but nothing was said as to his temporal rule. This mutual agreement was issued on an edict of the Emperor; and full of dismay and forebodings Pius returned to Rome, yet he outlived the triumph of seeing its great adversary, attacked on every side, consent to the restoration of the States of the Church. Napoleon's downfall followed. The Catholic Church saw in that event as much hope of its own resurrection as the Protestant Church did of its. The Restoration (under Louis XVIII) re-established the papal power, and again made the Roman Catholic religion the national faith of France. Even the Jesuits were restored to power, and pressed back into the countries whence they had been banished. As in the Protestant Church of Germany, hand in hand with a newly awakened spiritual life appeared also a subtle hypocrisy, and a hard spirit of intolerance, not to say persecution, so in the Catholic Church there arose a priestly spirit which aimed rather at the acquisition of worldly power than of adding to God's glory. On the other hand the prevailing liberalism misunderstood and neglected the deeper needs of the soul and the true moral wants of the nation. And so France, which had been one of the cradles of the Reformation, became, after the bloody days of the Revolution, a kind of ferry-boat, playing between the shores of unbelief and superstition, and few wise enough to hold the rudder. Why should I dwell longer on the strife? The well-remembered July days of 1830 dashed anew to the ground the hopes of the hierarchy, and it needed a Lamennais to reconstruct, in the "Words of a Believer," a political system which should offer a truce even to speculative unbelief. Some striking religious phenomena, like the appearance of Lacordaire, the eminent preacher of the Atonement, and that of the elegant Abbè Chatel, drew the curiosity of Paris, as did more worldly things. St. Simonism could no better sustain itself than its older brother Theophilanthropism, although it strove to live again in its own child, Communism, and to introduce itself as a new Gospel, and to diffuse the choicest blessings among humanity.

Still nearer to the subject of our present thought lies the fate of German Catholicism in the latest times. Here again we reach solid ground, for a far more intimate action and reaction between Protestantism and Catholicism displays itself with the Germans than with the French. The general advanced state of learning with the former is an admirable preparative for an intelligent appreciation of doctrinal differences. Even opponents, and decisive opponents, have a common interest in science, and come to a mutual understanding in it by appealing to its general principles. I affirm with confidence that a learned German Catholic can sooner come to an appreciation of the points of religious belief of a German Protestant, and *vice versâ*, than a German Protestant can with a French or English brother of his own faith.

German Catholics and German Protestants have imbibed philosophy at the same breasts, while each has converted it into uses quite different from the other. The Catholic theology of Germany has run through the same course of development with the Protestant. Side by side in both, by a cold and negative rationalism has been a spiritual minded mysticism; in both the critical method, idealism and pantheism have had their adherents. The same terminology, the same speculative and dialectical studies, the same extent of research we find in those who are interpreting the decisions of the Council of Trent, which we find among Protestants in tracing the harmony of Scripture. Biblical criticism too, and the study of ancient manners and customs, first awakened at the great Reformation, were largely prosecuted among Catholic schools, and the Protestant received instruction from the lips of Hug and Jahn, of Möhler and Frantz Baader, while the Catholic learned of Schleiermacher, of Lücke and Neander. There was some crossing of swords, it is true, but it was not a mere affair of fencing, science was advanced, and although some passion entered of course, yet mutual regard was engendered, and the fire of the older polemics was quenched.

But when we institute a comparison of the relations which now exist between the leading spirits of both confessions, and those which existed in the era of good feeling, the age of Lavater and of Sailer, we have to meet and answer this question: Shall we regret this change or felicitate ourselves upon it? I think we must do both. A blind jealousy is always to be regretted, alike on Protestant and on Catholic soil; and equally pitiable is that dazzling illusion, which under the pretence of calling God the eternal judge, masks worldly desires and selfish aims with spiritual zeal or a specious liberality; and so far as we see these things, the change is to be regretted. But we must also congratulate ourselves upon the altered conditions of the relations between Catholics and Protestants, in consideration of the increased weight which fixed religious convictions have in the polity of states, as well as in the formation of individual character. The more complete the renunciation of religion by the popular mind, the more welcome will be every expression of pious feeling, provided only that it be sincere; yes, welcome will it be, even with those sharp and rough edges, which keep it from melting into effeminacy; and yet, much as it were to be wished that Catholics and Protestants could combine in all those efforts which look to the general good of men, we have to confess that such a combination is not to be easily effected. But even without such a combination much can be gained, if the Catholic Christian and the Protestant Christian, each from their own stand-point, unite in their opposition to Anti-Christ, even at the peril of being charged with forming an alliance between Jesuitism and Pietism, between ultramontane and methodistical severity. These names are not to be feared above all things, for they have covered all varieties of Christian attainment and experience. We do not deny that there may be extreme views in both parties, and these extreme views may come into hostile collison. But as we in the Protestant fold have to distinguish between what is merely a negative denying and a positive upholding of supposed truths, between a false and a real orthodoxy, between sincere piety and its caricature, so must we distinguish between the severity of ultramontanism, and the Catholicism of Sailer and Wiffenberg, between the theology of Möhler and Hirscher, and the theology of the cloisters and of the Jesuits. Only let Catholicism cease talking of its unity. For where is its boasted unity? We wish indeed that the Catholic church may be delivered still from the evil of perfect unity, for the mere semblance of unity is nothing. Just as soon as spiritual life manifests itself, it takes various forms to express itself, and that variety which we now detect in the Romish church is the very means of preserving it from stagnation and ruin. Whether Catholicism will ever be able to exist without a Pope, and direct dependence upon him, whether the marriage of its clergy and the celebrating mass in the vernacular can be united with the other dogmas and sacramental ceremonies of the church, without shattering the latter; whether we shall ever see a German Catholic Church, a Swiss Catholic Church, a French Catholic Church, are questions which we dare not try to answer. We do not even know the destinies of our Protestant Church. But we may venture upon the assertion that the Catholic Church must no more necessarily begin its reformation at the same point where we began in the sixteenth century, and traverse the same course which we have traversed than that we must necessarily be swallowed up by Catholicism, or willingly go back to it again. We do not forget that the Catholic Church, whether it confesses it or not, had a share in the great Reformation, and that Protestantism has largely helped to purify her ; nor do we deny nor refuse to acknowledge publicly that we have not gone to the end of our Protestantism, and have many fields yet to struggle through, where the experiences of our sister church will doubtless do us service. It would be a very mechanical view if we supposed that there were only two ways of coming to the goal, that the Catholic church must become Protestant, or the Protestant church Catholic, one absorbing the other. Far otherwise will it be. The issue will be much more simple than this. Two powers are given to us both, the Church and the Gospel. Through the Gospel the Church is founded, and through the Church shall the Gospel be preserved, spread abroad, and expand into new life. But history has taught us that under a Church of wide and encroaching power, the Gospel has been more and more tampered with and put out of sight, and subjected to Romish tyranny. The Reformation of the sixteenth century restored the Gospel in its simplicity, so far as was allowed of God; but one Church had no share in that Reformation, and yet there are many who ask, where is the true Evangelical Church? Where its established statutes and forms? Where its visible barriers? Where its constitution, its unity? It is true we cannot point to any completed church, scarcely to the outline of such a one. But shall we expect from without what we ought only to expect from within? We desire an *Evangelical* Church, and nothing can further our wish more than what flows from the spirit of the Gospel, and the joyful message of Jesus and the free grace of God. To all that is not born of the Gospel we remain unchangeably Protestant, however proudly it may lay claim to the Catholic name. But inasmuch as the Gospel is to be proclaimed to all creatures, we also belong to the Catholic church, that is, the fellowship of saints. If the church, which has thus far called itself exclusively the Catholic church, will let the word "Roman" drop, will ask no longer what does Rome teach, but will return to the Gospel ground and renew itself on *this* ground; it need not traverse in a long and painful circuit the waste places of our older protestant theology, in order to become a true *reformed* church. God will shorten the way for it, and then can we enter, if we wish, that thoroughly purified mansion, from which the popish leaven has been wholly cast out.

But if, on the other hand, our Protestant Church will hold fast to the one only ground which is laid down—will, with the needful care for the negative and critical elements, also cherish a positive faith, one which is not one-sided through mere knowledge, but which is strong in the formation of active Christian character, in its energetic working, and in the union of faith and love, then, out of these shapeless elements as they now are, God will create a body which shall correspond to the spirit which dwells in our Protestantism, and the invisible Church will then find more fit and noble expression than ever. In one word, the more evangelical the Catholic Church becomes, and the more church-like the Evangelical Church becomes, the nearer will both come, only in a change of paths, to the common goal of perfection. But how will this be done? Will and can the Catholic Church, so far as we can see, ever cease to be Roman Catholic? Will it ever give the Bible freely to the people? On the other hand, has the Protestant Church ground for an expectation of a speedy and happy formation anew, and including what is now beyond its pale? These are questions which we can ask but cannot answer. We will not absolutely affirm nor deny in these matters, least of all will we expect to compel the developments of the future to follow our bidding, or be controlled by our might. Who can conjecture, without plunging into millennarial dreams, whether a truly evangelical Catholic Church and a thoroughly organized Protestant Church will ever be united and form the world's great Church, and be indeed one fold and one shepherd? Sometimes it seems to be God's plan to allow both churches to mature side by side, not as if one were true wheat and the other nothing but weeds, but both guarding lest weeds spring up within it, whether they come up of themselves, or are transferred from the neighbouring garden. Only let false zeal be just as far removed as false liberality and indifference. Never was more need of keeping strict watch upon the movements of our opponents than now. But mere heat, the fierce polemics of older times, will not accomplish our end, still less the imitation of what we condemn in our adversaries. We will have no Protestant pope and no Protestant Jesuits, even if by means of these we could be freed of the Romish ones. Evangelical Protestants we will remain, fast grounded on the word which Jesus and His apostles have given to us as our everlasting and living basis, but free also from all human authority. So far as in us lies, we will maintain peace with all men, will seek no strife, but we will not go out of the way in which fealty to our Master leads us; and we will always hold ourselves ready to give an answer to every man for the faith that is within us. Far be it from us to say that the Spirit of God has wholly deserted the old church. We will on the other hand rejoice in the goodness which secretly ripens in it yet, and which, if not *through* Rome, *in spite of* Rome, finds expression. How far this has been done, *they* can better determine than we, who stand in external relations with that Church. But without wishing to deny to others the satisfaction in which they find their joy and pride, we must still thankfully confess that we have abundant reason to see the hand of God resting in blessing on our evangelical Church.

So we will not see any sadness in these times. Sad though they may seem to some, it was darker in the days of the thirty years' war in Germany, in the days of Charles First in England, far darker in the days of the French Revolution. Through all these troublous epochs Protestantism has lived, and has raised its head in triumph above the crumbling form of fallen superstition. So far from again imposing upon itself the yoke of Rome, it has given new life and impulse to Catholicism; and if a new papacy has striven to rise within its pale, it has been able to hold itself free from bondage. Though it sprang from a great Reformation, it has held itself aloof from all Revolution, has given to God what is God's, and to Cæsar what is Cæsar's; has cherished the state and the family as institutions divinely ordered, and has sought to find in both the central meaning, and to always hold it in view. It has kept itself free from despotism of all shades, from the tyranny alike of Jesuits and of demagogues. Wherever it has wandered from its true path, God has graciously led it back through the way of salutary discipline, and its history is faithfully recorded in order that we might be warned, and taught, and encouraged, and quickened according to our needs. And may God grant to it a yet grander and more prosperous destiny!

APPENDIX.

A.

As Hagenbach gives no account of Schelling's life, we append a short sketch of it here, for the material of which we are partly indebted to the history of German literature by Henry Kurtz, partly to Schwegler and other sources.

Frederic William Schelling was born at Leonberg, Wurtemberg, January 27, 1775. His mind having developed unusually early he entered the university of Tubingen in his fifteenth year, where he devoted himself to philology and mythology, especially to Kant's philosophy. He spent a short time in the university of Leipzig, and then entered the university of Jena. While student he was on friendly relations with Hoelderlin and Hegel. With the latter he afterwards carried on a friendly correspondence. The letters of Hegel to Schelling indicate that a warm attachment existed between them, and that they felt themselves united in the cause of truth. Schelling had at first devoted himself to the study of medicine, but being attracted by the charming lectures of Fichte in Jena, he turned to the study of philosophy and became a disciple and co-labourer of Fichte. As early as 1798 he became professor of philosophy, and in 1800 professor in ordinary, as successor of Fichte, who had removed from Jena. The idealism of Fichte could not, however, satisfy him long, and he soon struck out a new course. Hegel, who had been a warm friend of Schelling's, now became an enthusiastic admirer, adopted his system, and in connection with him published the "Critical Journal of Philosophy" at Jena. In 1803 Schelling accepted a call to Wurzberg, as professor of philosophy. In 1807 he went to Munich as member of the newly established academy of sciences. In 1808 he received the appointment of secretary-general in the academy of the plastic arts and was ennobled. A quarrel with the president occasioned his leaving Munich. He went to Erlangen, where he delivered lectures on philosophy. An effort being made to render the newly founded (1807) university of Munich distinguished by calling eminent men as professors, he was appointed professor of philosophy, with the title of privy aulic-counsellor; and soon he became privy counsellor, superior of the academy of sciences, and conservator of scientific collections. He went to Berlin in 1841, where he had been created member of the academy of sciences, and delivered lectures in the university, chiefly on "Philosophy and Mythology" and "Revelation." He died August 20, 1854, at Ragaz in the canton of St. Gall, Switzerland, to the bath of which place he had gone to recover his failing health.

He became an author when quite young, first in 1792 at the time of his promotion, when, in a dissertation on the third chapter of Genesis, he gave an interesting philosophical interpretation of the Mosaic account of the fall. He published no large works during the last ten years of his life, and the publication of his later works commenced after his death. They are not, however, all published yet.

Of the spirit manifested by Schelling towards his opponents, Kurtz says: "His system, which his friend Hegel adopted, met with much opposition. He was accused of irreligion and pantheism; he defended himself in the 'Critical Journal of Philosophy,' often in an unworthy, insulting manner, since he generally, instead of simply refuting the arguments of his opponents, with haughty presumption declared that they were not capable of following his speculations. After he had been silent for nearly twenty years, during which time Hegel had made a new system which placed all others in the background, Schelling, in a translation of Cousin's work on French and German philosophy, expressed himself, in his insolent way, with contempt, in reference to Hegel, whom he never dared attack openly during his life."

In the sketch given by Hagenbach, the later philosophy of Schelling is not at all taken into the account, and hence he does not pretend to give an opinion of the entire system of

Schelling in its relation to Christianity. To do this is a very difficult task, for this system contains such various elements—the abstract philosophical, the deep mystical, the romantic and poetical, the idealistic and natural. We can take no one fundamental principle of this philosophy by which to judge of its relation to Christianity—can find no thread which runs through the system to which all the parts are connected, and which followed will lead us directly to Christianity or away from it; but as Schwegler remarks: "This system is not a closed, complete one, to which his separate writings are related as fragments; but it is really like the Platonic philosophy, a history of development, a series of grades of culture through which the philosopher himself passed. Instead of elaborating the several sciences systematically from the standpoint of his principle, Schelling always commenced at the beginning, trying new foundations, new standpoints, mostly (like Plato) starting from other philosophies (*Fichte, Spinoza,* Neo-Platonism, *Leibnitz, Jacob Boehm,* Gnosticism), which he sought to weave into his system in their order." Owing to this fact Schelling's philosophy is divided into five periods by Schwegler. First period: Schelling proceeds from Fichte. Second period: Standpoint of distinguishing between the philosophy of nature and of mind. Third period: The period of Spinozism, or the indifference of the ideal and the real. Fourth period: Mystical turn of Schelling's philosophy, it connects itself with Neoplatonism. Fifth period: Attempts at a Theogony and Cosmogony, according to Jacob Boehm.

Of this last period Schwegler himself says, a judgment cannot be formed fully as yet—that must be left to the future, when all Schelling's works shall have been published, and when the world has had time to examine and criticise.

Of Schelling's "Positive Philosophy of Revelation" Henry Kurz says: "Nearly all opinions agreed that the new philosophy did not meet the great expectations that had been excited, and that this, like his former system, was in fact only a play of the fancy, that it lacked internal connection and arguments, and Schelling, instead of proving his propositions, advanced them with a certain arrogance as the words of a prophet, and demanded that they should be accepted unconditionally as true."

B

Hagenbach's account of Hegel is so brief that it will not be ill-timed to append the following abstract of his life from his biography by Rosenkranz:—

"George William Frederic Hegel was born in Stuttgart, August 27th, 1770. Having prepared himself well in the gymnasium of his native city, he entered the University of Tübingen in his eighteenth year, to study theology, with which he soon connected philosophy. He excited no particular attention while a student. He passed the candidate's examination in 1793, after which he became tutor in Berne, then in Frankfort-on-the-Maine, where he remained till 1800. During this time he continued his studies with restless zeal. His mind was at first occupied with theological investigations, later chiefly with history and politics, and during the last years of this period he turned his attention exclusively to the study of philosophy, to which he determined to devote his life. He now went to Jena to fit himself for the office of teaching, and adopted and defended the system of Schelling, with whom he had already formed an intimate acquaintance in Tübingen. From Schelling's standpoint he wrote his first small work on 'The difference between Fichte's and Schelling's System of Philosophy,' in 1801, and assisted Schelling in editing the 'Critical Journal of Philosophy,' 1802-3. He at first received but little encouragement as academic teacher, he was, however, made professor in 1805. But this position was only occupied a very short time, owing to the unsettled condition of political matters. 'Amid the thunder of the cannon at the battle of Jena,' Schwegler says, 'he completed the "Phaenomenologie des Geistes," his first large and independent masterpiece, the crown of his labours in Jena.' From Jena he went to Bamberg, in 1806, where he edited for two years the 'Franconian Mercury,' which he conducted in the spirit and for the interest of the government of Napoleon. He went to Nurnberg as rector of the Gymnasium in the autumn of 1808. He wrote his Logic 1812-16. In 1816 he became Professor of Philosophy in Heidelberg, and there published his 'Encyclopædia of the Philosophical Sciences' in 1817. He received a call to Berlin in 1818, to fill the place of Fichte, vacant since his death, with which period his great fame and extensive activity may properly be said to commence. For much of his influence he was indebted to the encouragement he received from the government, which thought it found a powerful support in his system. He preferred the society of simple, unpretending persons, and did not attempt to shine in social circles. He did not, like the philosophers of the seventeenth and eighteenth centuries—Bruno, Campanella, Des Cartes, Spinoza, Malebranche, Leibnitz, Wolf, Locke, Hume, and Kant—devote himself to celibacy, but rather followed the example of Fichte. He was married on the 16th of September 1811, to Mary von Tucher, 'of one of the oldest and best known families of Nurnberg, whose beauty, unusual intellectual attainments, and amiability,' gained the affections of Hegel. The verses he sent her about the time of their engagement are so tender, so affectionate, that you would scarcely suspect that their author was the profound philosopher at the age of forty. To give a nearer insight into the state of his mind at that time, I will quote part of a letter written shortly before his marriage to the lady (the letter is given by Rosenkranz): 'Marriage is essentially a religious bond; love has necessarily for its supplement a higher element than simply what it is in itself. What is called "satisfaction," and "being quite happy," can only be attained by religion and the feeling of duty.' Hegel was so happy in his marriage that he wrote to Niethammer: 'When a man has found an occupation and a wife he loves, then he is properly done with this life.' He had two sons, Charles and Immanuel. Being suddenly attacked by cholera, he died in Berlin, in the height of his fame, November 14th, 1831, at 5½ P. M."

That Hegel's views, even when only twenty-five, were not so very orthodox, may be seen from an extract from a letter to Schelling, written in 1795. Speaking of an essay of the latter he says: "I have found in it a confirmation of a suspicion long cherished, that, for us and humanity, it would perhaps have been more honourable if any one, be it which it may, of the heresies condemned by councils and decrees, had become the public system of faith, than that the orthodox system should have retained the supremacy."

However much Hegel himself may have been charged with Pantheism, and however much this may have been drawn from his philosophy, it is evident that he himself thought quite differently in reference to his system. That he actually believed his philosophy agreed with Christianity, may be seen from some of his own expressions, and is also advocated by some of his followers. In a review of some remarks of Dr. Tholuck, Hegel attempted to show that the former was not so very far removed from the advocates of *Enlightenment*, from the view he took of the doctrine of the Trinity: hence it was said that Hegel wanted to be more orthodox than Dr. Tholuck. The great value whieh Hegel placed in knowledge made it quite natural that he should oppose the theology of feeling, and especially that form of feeling which Schleiermacher advocated—the feeling of dependence,—but this argues nothing against his Christianity.

In 1829, "Aphorisms" appeared, by C. F. Goeschel, in which the author, after showing that Jacobi's philosophy did not agree with Christianity, as many supposed, attempted to prove that the speculative philosophy, even that which was decried as atheistical, really agreed with Christianity, in which Hegel's philosophy was included. Hegel, as his biographer says, showed in a lengthy notice of the work that he considered it quite an honour that his philosophy had thus been proved Christian. To many this appeared strange, thinking that Hegel's system was far removed from Christianity. "But to us," says the biographer, "who have learned to know Hegel's relation to theology from the beginning, there is nothing surprising in the fact that Hegel was convinced that in his speculation he was not only not in contradiction to the essence of the Christian faith, but rather in unison with it."

Speaking of Hegel's "proof of the existence of God," Rosenkranz says: "This work is very valuable in reference to Hegel's religious convictions, because through it can be decided most unequivocally that he accepted a personal God." And in another place he says: "He (Hegel) declared himself most decidedly and in very plain words for personality, freedom, and immortality. He acknowledged that Jacobi was quite right in regarding the Absolute as spirit, as personal. . . . . Hegel says: 'God is not a dead, but a living God.'"

Of the Christian character of this philosophy Rosenkranz says, in the introduction to the life of Hegel: "The Hegelian philosophy, as far as religion is concerned, is essentially *Protestant.* The philosophy itself was, however, always of the opinion that it was truly Christian, and that therefore it would have to war against much that is unchristian. It has confessed itself to be Protestant, and will continue to bear before Protestantism the oriflame of freedom, by means of the self-knowledge and self-willing of what is eternally true. It seemed for a while as if Schelling would, with greater success, take this mission from it. But this opinion soon vanished, because Schelling waved the moral element of Christianity too much, and was concerned exclusively about a system of dogmatics, whose doctrines of the Trinity, whose Christology and Satanology are heretical, and whose conception of the Church is negative in respect to all existing churches—a postulate of the future."

TURNBULL AND SPEARS, PRINTERS, EDINBURGH

Books for the Library of Clergymen and Educated Laymen.

CLARK'S FOREIGN THEOLOGICAL LIBRARY.

ANNUAL SUBSCRIPTION, ONE GUINEA (PAYABLE IN ADVANCE), FOR WHICH FOUR VOLUMES, DEMY 8vo, ARE DELIVERED.

EXTRACT FROM FRASER'S MAGAZINE.

'There is clearly an awakened interest in the New Testament throughout the country: our village Chrysostoms are beginning to read Clark's translations of Olshausen; our urban and suburban pastors are beginning to find out that there are fresher waters than Barnes can minister.' . . . 'Are you sincere and reflective? You have got the very Commentary you need in Olshausen,—the very exposition of a vital part of the Gospels which you are dimly craving for, in Rudolph Stier; both of which are at your hands in a readable English version. You will rise from the perusal of either a wiser and a better man.'

The following are the Contents of each of the Series. Each Work may be had separately at the price within parentheses.

*** A Selection of Twelve Volumes from First Series will be supplied at the Subscription Price of Three Guineas; or Twenty Volumes from First and Second Series at the Subscription Price of Five Guineas (or a larger number at same ratio).

FIRST SERIES.

Twenty-nine Vols. Subscription price, L.7, 12s. 6d.

Hengstenberg's Commentary on the Psalms. 3 Vols. (L.1, 13s.)
Hagenbach's Compendium of the History of Doctrines. 2 Vols. (L.1, 1s.)
Gieseler's Compendium of Ecclesiastical History. 5 Vols. (L.2, 12s. 6d.)
Neander's General Church History. 9 Vols. (L.2, 11s. 6d.)
Olshausen on the Gospels and Acts. 4 Vols. (L.2, 2s.)
Olshausen on the Romans. (10s. 6d.)
Olshausen on the Corinthians. (9s.)
Olshausen on the Galatians, Ephesians, Colossians, and Thessalonians. (10s. 6d.)
Olshausen on Philippians, Titus, and Timothy. (10s. 6d.)
Olshausen and Ebrard on the Hebrews. (10s. 6d.)
Havernick's General Introduction to the Old Testament. (10s. 6d.)

SECOND SERIES.

Twenty Vols. Subscription price, L.5, 5s.

Stier on the Words of the Lord Jesus. 8 Vols. (L.4, 4s.)
Hengstenberg's Christology of the Old Testament. 4 Vols. (L 2, 2s.)
Ullmann's Reformers before the Reformation. 2 Vols. (L.1, 1s.)
Keil on Joshua. 1 Vol. (10s. 6d.)
Keil on Kings and Chronicles. 2 Vols. (L.1, 1s.)
Baumgarten's Apostolic History. 3 Vols. (L.1, 7s.)

THIRD SERIES.

Twenty-four Vols. (1859–60–61–62–63–64). Subscription price, L.6, 6s.

N.B.—A single Year's Books (except in the case of the current Year) cannot be supplied separately. Non-subscribers, price 10s. 6d. each Vol., with exceptions marked.

*** *No Selection* allowed from this Series. The following is the order of Publication, but any Two Years or more can be had at Subscription price:—

1st Year (1859).

Kurtz on Old Covenant Dispensation, 3 Vols.
Stier on the Risen Saviour, etc., 1 Vol.

2d Year (1860).

Hengstenberg on Ecclesiastes, 1 Vol. (9s.)
Tholuck on St John, 1 Vol. (9s.)
Tholuck's Sermon on the Mount, 1 Vol.
Ebrard on Epistles of John, 1 Vol.

3d Year (1861).

Lange on St Matthew's Gospel, Vols. I. and II.
Dorner on Person of Christ. Div. I., Vol. I.; and Div. II., Vol. I.

4th Year (1862).

Dorner on Person of Christ, Div. I., Vol. II.
Dorner on Person of Christ, Div. II., Vol. II.
Lange on Matthew and Mark, Vol. III.
Oosterzee on St Luke. Edited by Dr Lange. Vol. I. (9s.)

5th Year (1863).

Oosterzee on St Luke. Edited by Dr Lange. Vol. II. (Completion.) (9s.)
Dorner on Person of Christ, Div. II., Vol. III.
Kurtz on the Old Testament Sacrifices.
Ebrard's Gospel History.

6th Year (1864).

Lange, Commentary on the Acts of the Apostles, 2 Vols.
Keil and Delitzsch, Commentary on the Pentateuch, Vols. I. and II.

Subscribers' Names received by all Booksellers.

For Lange's Life of Christ, *see separate Prospectus.*

EDINBURGH: T. AND T. CLARK.

London (for Non-subscribers only): Hamilton, Adams, and Co.

JOHN ALBERT BENGEL'S

GNOMON OF THE NEW TESTAMENT.

Now First Translated into English.

WITH ORIGINAL NOTES, EXPLANATORY AND ILLUSTRATIVE.

The Translation is comprised in Five Large Volumes, Demy 8vo, of (on an average) fully 550 pages each.

SUBSCRIPTION, 31s. 6d., *or free by Post* 35s.

The very large demand for Bengel's Gnomon enables the Publishers still to supply it at the Subscription Price.

The whole work is issued under the Editorship of the Rev. ANDREW R. FAUSSET, M.A., Rector of St Cuthbert's, York, late University and Queen's Scholar, and Senior Classical and Gold Medalist, T.C.D.

'There are few devout students of the Bible who have not long held Bengel in the highest estimation, nay, revered and loved him. It was not, however, without some apprehension for his reputation with English readers that we saw the announcement of a translation of his work. We feared that his sentences, terse and condensed as they are, would necessarily lose much of their pointedness and force by being clothed in another garb. But we confess, gladly, to a surprise at the success the translators have achieved in preserving so much of the spirit of the original. We are bound to say that it is executed in the most scholarlike and able manner. The translation has the merit of being faithful and perspicuous. Its publication will, we are confident, do much to bring back readers to the *devout* study of the Bible, and at the same time prove one of the most valuable of exegetical aids. The "getting up" of those volumes, combined with their marvellous cheapness, cannot fail, we should hope, to command for them a large sale.'—*Eclectic Review.*

CHEAP RE-ISSUE

OF THE WHOLE

WORKS OF DR JOHN OWEN.

Edited by Rev. W. H. GOOLD, D.D., Edinburgh,

WITH LIFE BY REV. ANDREW THOMSON, D.D.

In 24 Volumes, demy 8vo, handsomely bound in cloth, lettered.

With Two Portraits of Dr Owen.

Several years have now elapsed since the first publication of this Edition of the Works of the greatest of Puritan Divines. Time has tested its merits; and it is now admitted, on all hands, to be the only correct and complete edition.

At the time of publication it was considered—as it really was—a miracle of cheapness, having been issued, by Subscription, for Five Guineas.

In consequence of the abolition of the Paper Duty, the Publishers now Re-issue the Twenty-four Volumes for

FOUR GUINEAS.

As there are above Fourteen Thousand Pages in all, each Volume therefore averages *Five Hundred and Ninety Pages.*

'You will find that in John Owen the learning of Lightfoot, the strength of Charnock, the analysis of Howe, the savour of Leighton, the raciness of Heywood, the glow of Baxter, the copiousness of Barrow, the splendour of Bates, are all combined. We should quickly restore the race of great divines if our candidates were disciplined in such lore.' —*The late Dr Hamilton of Leeds.*

WORKS OF JOHN CALVIN,

IN 51 VOLUMES, DEMY 8vo.

MESSRS CLARK beg respectfully to announce that the whole STOCK and COPYRIGHTS of the WORKS OF CALVIN, published by the Calvin Translation Society, are now their property, and that this valuable Series will be issued by them on the following very favourable terms:—

1. Complete Sets in 51 Volumes, Nine Guineas. (Original Subscription price about L.13.) The 'LETTERS,' edited by Dr BONNET, 2 vols., 10s. 6d. additional.
2. Complete Sets of Commentaries, 45 vols., L.7, 17s. 6d.
3. A *Selection* of Six Volumes (or more at the same proportion), for 21s., with the exception of the Institutes, 3 vols.
4. Any Separate Volume (except INSTITUTES), 6s.

THE CONTENTS OF THE SERIES ARE AS FOLLOW:—

Institutes of the Christian Religion, 3 vols.; Tracts on the Reformation, 3 vols.; Commentary on Genesis, 2 vols.; Harmony of the last Four Books of the Pentateuch, 4 vols.; Commentary on Joshua, 1 vol.; the Psalms, 5 vols.; Isaiah, 4 vols.; Jeremiah and Lamentations, 5 vols.; Ezekiel, 2 vols.; Daniel, 2 vols.; Hosea, 1 vol.; Joel, Amos, and Obadiah, 1 vol.; Jonah, Micah, and Nahum, 1 vol.; Habakkuk, Zephaniah, and Haggai, 1 vol.; Zechariah and Malachi, 1 vol.; Harmony of the Synoptical Evangelists, 3 vols.; Commentary on John's Gospel, 2 vols.; Acts of the Apostles, 2 vols.; Romans, 1 vol.; Corinthians, 2 vols.; Galatians and Ephesians, 1 vol.; Philippians, Colossians, and Thessalonians, 1 vol.; Timothy, Titus, and Philemon, 1 vol.; Hebrews, 1 vol.; Peter, John, James, and Jude, 1 vol.

In two volumes, 8vo, price 14s. (1300 pages),

THE INSTITUTES OF THE CHRISTIAN RELIGION.

By JOHN CALVIN.

Translated by HENRY BEVERIDGE.

THIS translation of Calvin's Institutes was originally executed for the 'Calvin Translation Society,' and is universally acknowledged to be the best English version of the work. The Publishers have reprinted it in an elegant form, and have, at the same time, fixed a price so low as to bring it within the reach of all.

In one volume, 8vo, price 8s. 6d.,

CALVIN:

HIS LIFE, LABOURS, AND WRITINGS.

By FELIX BUNGENER,

AUTHOR OF THE 'HISTORY OF THE COUNCIL OF TRENT,' ETC., ETC.

'M. Bungener's French vivacity has admirably combined with critical care and with admiring reverence, to furnish what we venture to think the best portrait of Calvin hitherto drawn. He tells us all that we need to know, and, instead of overlaying his work with minute details and needless disquisitions, he simply presents the disencumbered features, and preserves the true proportions of the great Reformer's character. We heartily commend the work.'—*Patriot.*

'Few will sit down to this volume without resolving to read it to the close.'—*Clerical Journal.*

In demy 8vo, price 10s. 6d.,

THE EARLY SCOTTISH CHURCH:

THE ECCLESIASTICAL HISTORY OF SCOTLAND FROM THE FIRST TO THE MIDDLE OF THE TWELFTH CENTURY.

By the Rev. THOMAS M'LAUCHLAN, M.A., F.S.A.S., Edinburgh.

THE purpose of this work is to trace the Early Planting of Christianity in Scotland, carrying it down to the period of the final establishment of Diocesan Episcopacy by David I. Sketches are given of the contemporaneous Civil History of the Kingdom, and Biographical Notices of the more distinguished of the early Missionaries, in so far as materials for such a purpose exist. The organization and practice of the early Celtic Church is made the subject of full and, it is hoped, impartial discussion. The work is intended to fill a void which has hitherto existed in the early history of Scotland.

Chapter I. The Roman Power in Scotland; II. and III. The Native Inhabitants during the Roman Occupation; IV. Religion during the Roman Period; V. Christianity under the Roman Government; VI. The Period succeeding the Roman Occupation; VII. The Mission of Ninian; VIII. The Mission of Palladius to the Scots; IX. The Mission of St Patrick; X. Servanus, Ternan, and Kentigern; XI. The Civil History of Scotland during the Sixth Century; XII. The Mission of Columba; XIII. The Institution at Iona; XIV. The Doctrine and Discipline of Iona; XV. The Death of Columba—His Contemporaries; XVI. Events succeeding the Death of Columba; XVII. The Mission of Aidan, etc.; XVIII. The Controversy regarding Easter and the Tonsure; XIX. The Events of the Eighth Century; XX. The Events of the Ninth Century; XXI. The Events of the Tenth Century; XXII. The Events of the Eleventh Century; XXIII. The Events of the first half of the Twelfth Century—Dioceses of Orkney, Caithness, Ross, Moray, Aberdeen, and Brechin; XXIV. The first half of the Twelfth Century—the Diocese of St Andrews; XXV. The Closing History of the Early Church.

In two volumes, demy 8vo, price 21s.,

A HISTORY OF CHRISTIAN DOCTRINE.

By WILLIAM G. J. SHEDD, D.D.,

PROFESSOR OF THEOLOGY IN UNION COLLEGE, NEW YORK.

Book I. Influence of Philosophical Systems upon the Construction of Christian Doctrine; Book II. History of Apologies; Book III. History of Theology (Trinitarianism) and Christology; Book IV. History of Anthropology; Book V. History of Soteriology; Book VI. History of Eschatology; Book VII. History of Symbols.

In demy 8vo, price 9s.,

GERMAN RATIONALISM:

IN ITS RISE, PROGRESS, AND DECLINE. A CONTRIBUTION TO THE CHURCH HISTORY OF THE 18TH AND 19TH CENTURIES.

By Dr K. HAGENBACH.

I. Characteristics of the 18th Century; II. A Brief Survey of the Rise of Rationalism in Germany; III. Life and Manners in Germany, 1700–1750; IV. Pietism and its Opponents; V. The Pioneers of Rationalism; VI. Frederick the Great and his Age; VII. Theological Science, including Biblical Criticism, 1700–50; VIII. Lessing; IX. Infidelity carried to its furthest issue; X. Thoroughgoing Protests against Infidelity; XI. Half-way Rationalism; XII. Zinzendorf; XIII. Swedenborg, Stilling, Lavater, etc.; XIV. Herder; XV. Kant; XVI. Schiller; XVII. Salzmann, Campe, Pestalozzi, Hamann, and Claudius; XVIII. Schelling; XIX. Jacobi; XX. Fichte; XXI. Richter, Goethe, and Novalis; XXII. Schleiermacher; XXIII. Hegel and his Successors; XXIV. Rise of the Protestant Spirit in the Roman Catholic Church during the 18th and 19th Centuries.

WORKS BY THE LATE WILLIAM CUNNINGHAM, D.D.,

PRINCIPAL AND PROFESSOR OF CHURCH HISTORY, NEW COLLEGE, EDINBURGH.

In two vols. demy 8vo, price 21s., Second Edition,

HISTORICAL THEOLOGY:

A REVIEW OF THE PRINCIPAL DOCTRINAL DISCUSSIONS IN THE CHRISTIAN CHURCH SINCE THE APOSTOLIC AGE.

Chapter 1. The Church; 2. The Council of Jerusalem; 3. The Apostles' Creed; 4. The Apostolical Fathers; 5. Heresies of the Apostolical Age; 6. The Fathers of the Second and Third Centuries; 7. The Church of the Second and Third Centuries; 8. The Constitution of the Church; 9. The Doctrine of the Trinity; 10. The Person of Christ; 11. The Pelagian Controversy; 12. Worship of Saints and Images; 13. The Civil and Ecclesiastical Authorities; 14. The Scholastic Theology; 15. The Canon Law; 16. Witnesses for the Truth during Middle Ages; 17. The Church at the Reformation; 18. The Council of Trent; 19. The Doctrine of the Fall; 20. Doctrine of the Will; 21. Justification; 22. The Sacramental Principle; 23. The Socinian Controversy; 24. Doctrine of the Atonement; 25. The Arminian Controversy; 26. Church Government; 27. The Erastian Controversy.

In demy 8vo (624 pages), price 10s. 6d.,

THE REFORMERS AND THE THEOLOGY OF THE REFORMATION.

Chapter 1. Leaders of the Reformation; 2. Luther; 3. The Reformers and the Doctrine of Assurance; 4. Melancthon and the Theology of the Church of England; 5. Zwingle and the Doctrine of the Sacraments; 6. John Calvin; 7. Calvin and Beza; 8. Calvinism and Arminianism; 9. Calvinism and the Doctrine of Philosophical Necessity; 10. Calvinism and its Practical Application; 11. The Reformers and the Lessons from their History.

'This volume is a most magnificent vindication of the Reformation, in both its men and its doctrines, suited to the present time and to the present state of the controversy.' —*Witness.*

In one vol. demy 8vo, price 10s. 6d.,

DISCUSSIONS ON CHURCH PRINCIPLES:

POPISH, ERASTIAN, AND PRESBYTERIAN.

Chapter 1. The Errors of Romanism; 2. Romanist Theory of Development; 3. The Temporal Sovereignty of the Pope; 4. The Temporal Supremacy of the Pope; 5. The Liberties of the Gallican Church; 6. Royal Supremacy in Church of England; 7. Relation between Church and State; 8. The Westminster Confession on Relation between Church and State; 9. Church Power; 10. Principles of the Free Church; 11. The Rights of the Christian People; 12. The Principle of Non-Intrusion; 13. Patronage and Popular Election.

In the Press. In demy 8vo,

INSPIRATION:

THE INFALLIBLE TRUTH, AND DIVINE AUTHORITY OF SCRIPTURE.

By JAMES BANNERMAN, D.D.,

PROFESSOR OF THEOLOGY, NEW COLLEGE, EDINBURGH.

WORKS OF PATRICK FAIRBAIRN, D.D.,

PRINCIPAL AND PROFESSOR OF THEOLOGY IN THE FREE CHURCH COLLEGE, GLASGOW.

In two volumes, demy 8vo, price 21s., Fourth Edition,

THE TYPOLOGY OF SCRIPTURE,

VIEWED IN CONNECTION WITH THE WHOLE SERIES OF THE DIVINE DISPENSATIONS.

'I now say, no Biblical student should be without Professor Fairbairn's Typology.'—*Dr S. Lee, in his 'Events and Times of the Visions of Daniel.'*

'As the product of the labours of an original thinker, and of a sound theologian, who has at the same time scarcely left unexamined one previous writer on the subject, ancient or modern, this work will be a most valuable accession to the library of the theological student. As a whole, we believe it may, with the strictest truth, be pronounced the best work on the subject that has yet been published.'—*Record.*

'A work fresh and comprehensive, learned and sensible, and full of practical religious feeling.'—*British and Foreign Evangelical Review.*

In demy octavo, price 10s. 6d., Third Edition,

EZEKIEL, AND THE BOOK OF HIS PROPHECY.

AN EXPOSITION; WITH A NEW TRANSLATION.

In demy octavo, price 10s. 6d., Second Edition,

PROPHECY,

VIEWED IN ITS DISTINCTIVE NATURE; ITS SPECIAL FUNCTIONS AND PROPER INTERPRETATION.

'Its completeness, its clearness, its thorough investigation of the whole subject in a systematic way, will render it, I think, the standard work on prophecy from this time.'—*Rev. Dr Candlish.*

In demy octavo, price 10s. 6d.,

HERMENEUTICAL MANUAL;

OR, INTRODUCTION TO THE EXEGETICAL STUDY OF THE SCRIPTURES OF THE NEW TESTAMENT.

Part I. Discussion of Facts and Principles bearing on the Language and Interpretation of the New Testament.

Part II. Dissertations on particular subjects connected with the Exegesis of the New Testament.

Part III. On the Use made of Old Testament Scripture in the Writings of the New Testament.

'Dr Fairbairn has precisely the training which would enable him to give a fresh and suggestive book on Hermeneutics. Without going into any tedious detail, it presents the points that are important to a student. There is a breadth of view, a clearness and manliness of thought, and a ripeness of learning, which make the work one of peculiar freshness and interest. I consider it a very valuable addition to every student's library.' —*Rev. Dr Moore, Author of the able Commentary on 'The Prophets of the Restoration.'*

www.ingramcontent.com/pod-product-compliance
Lightning Source LLC
LaVergne TN
LVHW021143110826
845150LV00005B/1112